for
Allison & Annelise
sisters and friends

Vos magis quam libros diligo.

READING THE BIBLE WITH THE DEAD

Reading the Bible with the Dead

What You Can Learn from the History of Exegesis
That You Can't Learn from Exegesis Alone

John L. Thompson

WILLIAM B. EERDMANS PUBLISHING COMPANY
GRAND RAPIDS, MICHIGAN / CAMBRIDGE, U.K.

© 2007 John L. Thompson

Published 2007 by
Wm. B. Eerdmans Publishing Co.
2140 Oak Industrial Drive N.E., Grand Rapids, Michigan 49505 /
P.O. Box 163, Cambridge CB3 9PU U.K.

Printed in the United States of America

12 11 10 09 08 07   7 6 5 4 3 2 1

Library of Congress Cataloging-in-Publication Data

Thompson, John Lee.
Reading the Bible with the dead: what you can learn from the history of exegesis
that you can't learn from exegesis alone / John L. Thompson.
p.   cm.
Includes bibliographical references.
ISBN: 978-0-8028-0753-3 (pbk.: alk. paper)
1. Bible — Criticism, interpretation, etc. — History.   I. Title.

BS500.T56   2007
220.609 — dc22

2006039043

www.eerdmans.com

The appendix to this book and related resources are available at
http://purl.oclc.org/net/jlt/exegesis

Contents

CONTENTS

Preface

I am a church historian who specializes in the history of the interpretation of the Bible. I am also a Presbyterian minister, ordained to my calling as a seminary professor. This book represents my attempt to pull these two worlds of scholarship and church closer together by writing something *useful* to both — something to connect my love for the writers and writings of the Christian past with my love and concern for the practices and practitioners of Christianity today.

At the broadest level, I hope this book will deepen the insights of anyone who loves the Bible but who also wrestles with it, even as Jacob wrestled a blessing from the angel in Genesis 32. Within that circle of readers, however, my seminary students were particularly in view as I wrote, for their vocations will entail reading, interpreting, and engaging the Scriptures as daily, central, and arduous tasks. Naturally, because the pastoral office is also a calling to a discipline of study and reflection, I hope this book will prove equally useful to those who are already pastors and preachers. And because a book about how the church has read important but difficult parts of the Bible necessarily intersects heavily with two developing fields of study — the history of biblical exegesis and the theological interpretation of scripture — this is also a book for biblical and systematic theologians, whether lay or academic.

Of course, as an academic historian, I know very well that to assert anything about the "utility" of history risks the charge that one has sacrificed the objectivity of one's scholarship to the influences of some alien agenda — as if it were okay to be *interested* in the past, just so long as you don't go *learning* from it! As a matter of fact, I do find it risky to wade into the past with too confident an agenda or with an uncritical demand for easy lessons and pious blessings. But I find it just as worrisome to presume to find nothing in the past except error and benightedness. Perhaps I can parry at least some of these objections with a personal confession, by telling you that the history of the Christian church is not only something I teach and write about for a living, it's also something that *orients* me. This history tells me who I am as a Christian, and does so in ways that crucially supplement the story we call the gospel by showing how the gospel has been lived by the church. So when I say that history may be *useful*, what I mean to suggest is that an informed appreciation of the past ought to be an ingredient in any attempt not only to live and practice our faith, but to do so with the sort of reflectiveness and discernment that the Bible calls *wisdom*.

What readers will find here, then, is a series of studies of difficult texts and topics in the Bible. None of these studies is as exhaustive as I would have liked to make it, but — as I've said — I've tried to write something useful! Accordingly, I have kept these studies fairly short, in the hope that any given chapter might be perused in an hour or so, recognizing that the time of students and pastors is always at a premium. Each chapter concludes with my own reflections about what sorts of insights the history of exegesis has to offer that are unlikely to be found in modern-day lexicons and commentaries. I've also compiled a "finding guide" of patristic, medieval, and Reformation-era commentaries available in English, to help readers continue their journey into the past. And, at the urging of one of my former students, now a pastor, I've established a web-page where I have posted some sample sermons that try to model a fruitful interaction between proclamation, exegesis, and the history of interpretation.

As that last sentence suggests, I received help and advice along the way from many sources. While still in the planning stages, the project was commended by my friends and colleagues Ellen Davis, Elsie McKee, and Richard Muller. An initial burst of progress was made possible in 2003, when the Association of Theological Schools awarded me a Lilly Faculty Fellowship that extended a one-term sabbatical into a year of research. Further sabbatical leave from Fuller Theological Seminary enabled me to complete the work.

Significant momentum was added at later stages by some of my students, including Elizabeth Ball, Dan Oliva, Greg Parker, Edna Payne, Chris Tweitmann, and Emrys Tyler. Now in various positions of ministry, these friends offered me a fine mixture of inspiration, proofreading, anguished tales from classroom and parish, and wonderfully close readings of draft chapters from both student and pastoral perspectives. Helpful feedback was given also by David Vinson, by my colleagues Richard Mouw and Clay Schmidt, and by my father-in-law, Robert Meye. Parts of the manuscript were discussed (should I say dissected?) with my treasured colleagues in church history here at Fuller, including James Bradley, Grayson Carter, Nate Feldmeth, Mel Robeck, and Charlie Scalise. And I owe special thanks to my research assistants: Tim Howerzyl, who shouldered much of the burden of preparing the finding guide, and Melissa Ramos, who read proofs and labored with me on the index.

There are three more individuals for whom my gratitude comes easily. First, anyone who knows me well will probably hear echoes in this book also of the mind and heart of my wife, companion, and colleague, Marianne Meye Thompson. That is as it should be. If I bear any impress of her character in my life and writing, I count it gain.

Last but not least, my daughters, two graceful and witty young women who have shaped me more than they know. Over the course of the many rewrites of these chapters, I suppose it was inevitable that some of my pages should end up valued less for their profundity than as scratch paper for schoolwork. What could possibly be more satisfying, then, than to have a daughter wander into the study, poring over the wrong side of her scribbled algebra formulas, only to remark that this was some interesting stuff, Dad, and she'd like to read it when it was done. Skcczix, Gonzo — this one's for you.

La Cañada, California   J.L.T.
Three Kings Day, 2007

On Reading with the Dead

*Why Anyone Who Cares about the Bible
Should Also Care about the History of Its Interpretation*

S ome years ago, I was asked by the student body president at my school to give that year's baccalaureate sermon, on any text I thought appropriate. I'd spent my previous sabbatical researching the history of the interpretation of a handful of Old Testament stories, all of which dealt with women who had been abused, marginalized, or killed. These stories remained much on my mind, and as I pondered what to preach on for baccalaureate, there was a voice within my head that kept urging me to preach on Judges 11 — where Jephthah's daughter is sacrificed to fulfill her father's foolish vow.

I had over three months to decide on a text, and I must have made and unmade my decision half a dozen times. Sometimes I wondered if it would be in bad taste to recount such a depressing tale on such a happy occasion. At other moments, however, I was positively exhilarated at the prospect — largely on account of some of the amazing and encouraging things I had learned about the way commentators over the centuries have responded to this story. Nonetheless, whenever I have mentioned to other pastors and preachers that I actually chose to preach on the sacrifice of Jephthah's daughter, the response has routinely been a widening of the eyes in unbelief: "You're kidding! I would *never* preach on that!"

That's the response I would expect. Judges 11 is filled with foolishness and tragedy: an honorable daughter is needlessly slain by her soldier father. What's worse, her father's death-dealing act seems to be related, somehow, to his anointing with the spirit of God. So, was her death *divinely* arranged? Maybe, but the text is not very clear. And, adding further to the cruel ambiguity, there is virtually nothing in the text of Judges 11 that says whether Jephthah was right or wrong — much less whether we should go and do likewise.

The Bad Habits of Bible Readers

Every preacher knows, as do most serious readers of the Bible, that there are lots and lots of stories in the Bible that people would just as soon avoid. My own research has drawn me to scrutinize not only Jephthah's daughter, but many similar narratives, including Sarah and Abraham's stark expulsion of Hagar and Ishmael into the desert, Lot's willingness to surrender his daughters to the men of Sodom, and the gang-rape and dismemberment of the Levite's concubine in Judges 19. When was the last time you heard *any* sort of sermon on these stories, much less a "good" sermon? In all likelihood, never.

In general, we aren't in the habit of reading stories that upset us, and we certainly don't hear them preached. Sometimes such stories are avoided simply because they are so gruesome, or so violent, or because the "moral" of the story seems so elusive. But there are other forces at work that have the effect of editing or censoring the Bible. For example, the Revised Common Lectionary — the weekly directory of Scripture passages for Sunday worship that many churches use — bypasses with surgical precision not only even fragmentary imprecations in the Psalter, but also virtually every text that pertains to violence against women or that describes male-female relations in hierarchical terms.[1] A similar "sanitizing" impulse seems to have led over the past two centuries to the removal of most tales of sex and violence from children's Bibles, though it was not always so![2] Indeed, although Phyllis Trible's pioneering study of Old Testament women[3] appeared over twenty years ago as lectures carrying the subtitle, "Unpreached Stories of Faith," these texts remain today mostly as she found them: unpreached.

It is instructive to look at the array of texts that preachers and other readers unconsciously avoid. The problem is an old one. Long ago, in the third century, Origen of Alexandria gave voice to the view — by no means

2

original to him — that there were indeed unedifying texts in the inspired word of God. For Origen, such texts included not only instances where biblical heroes acted scandalously, but also narratives that depicted God in embarrassing or impossible ways, such as Genesis 2, which describes God as if the deity literally possessed a body and could go strolling in the garden. Origen argued that such a portrait had to be a figure of speech, not the literal truth.

Closer to our own day, guides to the "hard sayings" of Jesus or Paul regularly appear on publishers' backlists. And although Origen's selections don't exactly correspond to the passages that bother readers today, there is significant overlap and the rationale for identifying hard texts is often similar. Writing in *The Christian Century,* Barbara Brown Taylor recounted her attempt to teach a class on "preaching difficult texts."[4] Polling her students on the first day, she had little trouble generating a list of texts in this category. At the top of her students' lists were miracle stories. Second place went to narratives involving "God-sanctioned violence," followed closely by passages that seem to exclude women, homosexuals, "the Jews," and other religions. "Cryptic texts" finished fourth. Again, while the distance between modern sensibilities and those of Origen is easy to gauge, it seems that stories of divinely sanctioned violence, stories of abuse or marginalization, and just plain obscure texts are perennially troublesome to readers — and, consequently, widely avoided.

A Conspiracy of Silence?

Nonetheless, there is a significant category of readers — sometimes within the church and its congregations, sometimes alienated from the church — for whom such "neglected" texts are of great interest. One of the most important developments in the interpretation of the Bible in the last thirty years stems from the way Western culture has turned its attention to the margins of society. In history, this is sometimes called a shift to "history from below." In the field of theology, such changes have given rise to various *contextual theologies,* and much has been written about the Bible from the perspective of "contextual" interpreters. These scholars include liberation theologians, African American and feminist critics, and others — such as womanist and mujerista theologians[5] — whose perspectives and contexts are more focused still. Why are such writers interested in these hard texts?

The answer is not hard to find. In most cases, these scholars harbor an understandable concern (if not anger) toward Christianity and the Bible for having perpetuated such social sins as imperialism, slavery, patriarchy, and misogyny in the name of religion and, often, in the name of theology and exegesis. The Bible itself is often indicted as the product of patriarchy and as a perpetuator of patriarchy — at least if the Bible continues to be read and proclaimed by patriarchal interpreters. Accordingly, contextual interpreters typically bring to bear what has come to be called a "hermeneutic of suspicion." Such a hermeneutic assumes that every text and every interpretation is guided by the self-interest of its author. This means that all stories are told in a particular way, even in the Bible, so as to enhance the authority of the author and undercut competing claims. In simpler terms, such a hermeneutic looks to see which perspectives and characters the Bible valorizes or vilifies, yet reserves the right to dissent from the Bible's judgments. One of the tasks of such contextual interpretations is to recover perspectives and insights that have traditionally been neglected or suppressed. Not surprisingly, such perspectives often mirror contemporary social situations, so that feminist interpreters (for example) are especially adept at seeing and decrying injustices against women in the Bible, even to the point of defending biblical women against their mistreatment by the narrator — or even by the deity.

Although pastors and congregations are often widely divided over such interpretations, there are reasons to argue that the church risks great loss by neglecting such readers and their interests. First, the accusations of patriarchy and other sins that are leveled against the Bible and the church are not without substance. The church has often enough sided with oppressors and used the Bible to reinforce pat convictions. Sometimes it is alleged that the church's neglect of such conflicted stories in the Bible is proof that Christians would prefer to cover over the sins of the past rather than confront them. Indeed, the perception that the sufferings of women are greeted with silence by both the Bible and the church is one reason why many readers so readily agreed with Trible that such stories are truly "texts of terror." Hence, the critiques offered by contextual interpreters deserve a thoughtful hearing and an equally thoughtful response. Second, even when one is put off by such radical questioning of the Bible, there is every reason to suppose that similar questions and similarly painful experiences are already present in most congregations, just waiting to be exposed and — one may hope — addressed, not demeaned. In other words, these are

4

often the questions not just of academics but also of our real parishioners and neighbors. Finally, and most pertinent to this book, these contextual readings often do an excellent job of modeling a close reading of hard texts. They may make the problems in such texts even harder and more painful, but they don't turn a blind eye.

The Benefits of Hard Texts

If neglecting difficult stories risks surrendering the Bible to some of Christendom's most radical critics, attending to such texts offers, conversely, some potential benefits that are positive, not just polemical. Still, many of these *are* shocking stories. Why should we want to see them restored to the preaching rotation? One traditional argument begs the question by simply asserting that if these stories are in the Bible, they must be there for a reason and they therefore ought to be read and preached. Such an instinct may be valid, but it would be helpful to have some idea of what to expect beforehand.

Perhaps a better reason to return to these difficult texts — already mentioned above — lies in their *currency* for us. Violence in today's world is both domestic and international, and anyone who has been so harmed or abused does not have to look far to find "enemies" that look a lot like those of the psalmist. What might we learn, then, from the imprecations in the psalms? Similarly, feminist and liberation theology has made us aware of how dominant culture can also dominate and marginalize those whose voices are suppressed. By learning to attend to marginalized characters in Bible stories, we just might learn to see our neighbors with new and compassionate eyes. Is it not the case that members of our own churches bear many of the same scars and open wounds as the characters in the Bible's hardest tales? Confronting the abuse and victimization portrayed in the Bible may open the door to confrontations needed in cities and families.

To be sure, sermons on such stories have the potential for good or ill. After I preached on Jephthah's daughter, I was stunned at the reports that filtered back. Apparently, there were some in attendance who were at that moment struggling with the effects of past abuse, but who found encouragement and even some closure in my remarks. I know of other cases, however, where a sermon has verged on the destructive. You probably remember the multiple misdeeds of Abraham. When he sojourns into Egypt, he lies about his wife so that she is taken by Pharaoh and put in danger of adultery. The Bible does not say this is wrong. Later, Abraham commits polygamy with Hagar. The Bible does not say he is wrong. Likewise, when Abraham drives Hagar and Ishmael into the desert, the Bible never says he was wrong. How should we treat these silences in the Bible? A friend of mine once heard a pastor proclaim that wives ought to submit to their husbands no matter what their husbands ask them to do — *even if the woman's conscience were to object.* His proof-text for this argument was based on the lie that Abraham told to Pharaoh. If the Bible didn't condemn Abraham for exposing his wife to adultery, this must be a good example for Christian men to follow as well — right?

Finding Allies in Our Neglected Past

How I wish I had been present with my friend, above, to point out to that pastor how frightfully clever and original his argument was — so clever, so original, that no credible writer in the history of the church has ever seriously advanced it! The difficult and ambiguous texts of the Bible are not to be underestimated. They are not to be approached lightly — nor, I would argue, alone.

Back when I was a seminary student, I was deeply (and rightly) captivated by the Bible. I had a dozen binders for storing notes on the Bible, with a different color for each section of the Bible. I also had a color-coded scheme for marking the text of various gospels and epistles that I possessed — retyped, double-spaced, on punched paper. Problems of interpretation fascinated me, as did all the themes and theology of the Scriptures. As a budding minister, I thought the goal was to become a biblical scholar, and I looked forward to any course that would focus directly on the Bible. None of this enthusiasm, however, extended to courses in history. I was quite unexcited by the year's worth of church history I knew I would eventually have to take, and I kept postponing it. History was boring. Everyone knew that. Even the prospect of studying *church* history struck me as surely second best. Who would want to read the uninspired opinions of dead theologians when you could go straight to the inspired word of God and figure it out for yourself?

Perhaps the preacher's two greatest temptations are these: to plagiarize one's sermons (how the Internet has helped with this one!), or to imagine that the nobler path is to figure everything out for yourself. In her essay in *The Christian Century,* Barbara Brown Taylor suggests that one benefit of preaching difficult texts might be the freshness of the sermon that would have to result:

> When we engage these lesser-known stories, we are not protected from them by layers of interpretation. The commentaries do not say much about them, and it is often up to us to wrestle them on our own. . . . Preaching these texts, we have no choice but to sound fresh. The only voices we have heard addressing them out loud are our own.[6]

Taylor's suggestion is plausible, but ultimately worrisome. One might ask if ignorance of old commentaries is really the best way to escape these "layers of interpretation." Would not an informed knowledge of exegetical tradition be a better way to gain such freedom and freshness? Wouldn't it help to acquire a critical appreciation for what has gone before as well as a critical perspective on one's own originality? In any case, it is rarely true that "commentaries do not say much" about these lesser-known texts. At best, it is true only that *recent* commentaries and sermons may not do so. Somewhere in the distant past, other preachers and commentators — often those dismissed as "premodern" or "precritical" — have almost certainly faced these obscure, ambiguous, offensive, yet urgent Bible texts and problems. Isn't there some sort of help to be derived from traditional Christian exegesis?

I believe there is, but it's not easy to get. What that pastor who treated the consciences of Christian wives so lightly surely did not know (though he could not easily have availed himself of it) is the huge body of commentary on the Bible that has grown up over twenty centuries. Were one to consult, say, thirty or forty representative commentaries on Genesis, one would find that most of them worry over how Abraham exposed Sarah to adultery by his deceitful approach to Pharaoh. A few labor to excuse Abraham. None admires his action. And no one commends him as a model for Christian husbands today.[7] Why would anyone want to improve on such a remarkable degree of consensus over so many centuries?

It would be ideal if every sermon, every Bible study, every casual reading of Scripture could be informed by an awareness of the historic range of exegetical opinion, both consensus and dissent. To be sure, huge collections of sources in translation are now being published that could assist such an ideal — including InterVarsity's *Ancient Christian Commentary on Scripture* and a similar project from Eerdmans, *The Church's Bible* — but pastors who already have too much to read will find it hard to troll through so many volumes and excerpts, much less assimilate it all for a sermon. My own goal in writing this book is to offer something easier to use: a digest of the history of the interpretation of some passages and issues that ought to be of great interest to readers and hearers today, and for which the history of interpretation can offer not merely novel perspectives, but also insights and arguments likely to encourage and to surprise.

What Sort of Surprises?

As a historian, I honestly don't think I would ever have imagined becoming an advocate for these neglected stories in Scripture if I hadn't first found myself reading this other body of widely neglected literature: the biblical commentaries of the early church, the Middle Ages, and the Reformation era. Reading these old books, I found other reasons — and other resources — for paying renewed attention to some of the Bible's more difficult texts.

Twenty years ago, when I was working on my doctoral dissertation, I spent more than a few years reading dozens of biblical commentators, looking to establish a context for some of the curiouser remarks of John Calvin about the role of women in Scripture and (more to the point for him) in his own sixteenth-century church. As is often the case in doctoral research, I learned a lot on many occasions when I was actually on my way to looking up something else. I learned, for instance, that these "precritical" commentators often displayed a strikingly "modern" concern over how it was possible for a male-oriented rite like circumcision to be the sign of a covenant that clearly included also women. I learned that there were some amazing lines of moral argument that commentators were willing to invoke in order to explain, if not excuse, the misdeeds of the patriarchs. And I learned that although many may assume that they know where these venerable male commentators were likely to come down on issues still contested today — such as whether women must wear veils, whether they may speak, teach, or lead in church — there was considerable dissent and diversity of opinion behind the scenes.

Since then, I have continued to read and write about the history of biblical interpretation, with a special interest in how traditional commentators apply the Bible's precepts about gender to diverse historical and cultural settings. Reading these precritical commentaries[8] alongside the works of feminist and other contemporary Bible scholars, I gradually awoke to an obvious question. On the one hand, I personally found much to appreciate in precritical exegesis, especially its attention to detail and its concern for "applying" the text. On the other hand, I constantly saw how precritical exegesis is dismissed not only by all sorts of modern historical critics, but also by feminists, for whom these older commentators simply represent more patriarchal opinions. Consequently, this question arose: feminist interpreters often decry the neglect of biblical women both by Scripture and by Scripture's interpreters, but (I asked) has this always been so? It's easy to *assume* that ancient and medieval male commentators would neglect the women of Scripture, as has often been the case in recent generations. But if no one ever reads these old commentators, how can we be sure of what they thought or did? So I began a project of reading precritical commentary on those texts that often interest or distress feminist readers, all the while bearing in mind the kinds of questions and concerns that feminist and other modern readers have.

My more recent findings continue to add surprises. One moving discovery was finding a number of poignant laments raised on behalf of biblical women such as Hagar and Jephthah's daughter. Coming from the pens of church fathers, medieval monks, and Protestant Reformers, these laments look for all the world like molds for later feminist castings. Indeed, one of the greatest surprises — both for feminists who have little patience for Scripture or its traditional interpreters, as well as for defenders of Christian tradition who have little interest in feminist theology or exegesis — is just how much common ground contemporary contextual critics (especially feminists) have with these precritical commentators. Both are remarkably close readers of the text. Both are concerned for readings that offer moral instruction and even spiritual edification for readers. Both are dissatisfied with the sort of historical-critical exegesis that explains a text in terms of historical causes but never addresses the meaning or impact of what the text says.[9] In the pages that follow, I will attempt to show how the difficulties and obscurities and even scandals of some Bible passages are actually made more accessible, not less, by consulting the commentators of our distant past.

The Roadmap for This Study

Each of the following chapters studies the history of interpretation of a particular difficult text or a thematic cluster of texts, tied to a discussion of related issues in contemporary faith and life. Although many of the chapters and themes are related, readers should feel free to use each chapter as an essay in its own right. Together, the nine chapters attempt to work out some broadly-related themes, including:

- texts of *violence and abuse,* including the stories of Hagar's exile, Jephthah's daughter, Gomer, the imprecatory psalms, patriarchal misdeeds, and stories of rape in the Old Testament;

- texts that address *domestic relations,* particularly divorce;

- texts that bear on the politics and polity of *women in church leadership,* including the question of women and prophecy (1 Corinthians 11 and 14) and the arguments about women teaching (1 Timothy 2).

Chapters will usually unfold in three parts, beginning with a summary of insights from contextual and other contemporary interpreters that will underscore just why the text or topic at hand remains problematic for readers today. The middle part will then survey in some detail the history of how the biblical text or topic has been interpreted by precritical commentators. These sections will necessarily be longer: there is no meaningful or substantial way to present the views of commentators through much of Christian history without actually presenting some of the details. Moreover, it is not to be expected that such details will always be pretty. If there are shallow and tendentious interpreters today, it is no recent development, and sometimes the value of knowing the past will be not to imitate historical patterns or judgments, but to repent of them. The concluding section of each chapter will attempt to distill these historical details, good and bad, and reflect on their implications for interpreting the Bible's hard texts. A final chapter will then try to make a case for why history, and particularly the history of the Bible's interpretation, is a crucial ingredient in the thoughtful practice of the Christian faith. To that end, I have also supplied this book with a "finding guide" that inventories exegetical sources available in English, along with a glossary that identifies the writers mentioned here.

On Reading with the Dead

*   *   *

Without a doubt, there is something counterintuitive in suggesting that we don't fully know what the Bible *means* until we know something about what the Bible *has meant*. Particularly for Protestants, it may seem rather curious, if not risky, to suggest that a correct understanding of the preeminent authority of the Bible will actually drive us *toward* a deeper knowledge of Christian tradition and the history of interpretation, not *away* from it.

Nonetheless, there is a twofold urgency about these suggestions. First of all, in its necessary conversation with secular culture and with the "unconverted" among its own adherents, Christianity is constantly tempted to compromise with culture, tempted to round off the angularities of its own beliefs and practices in order to broaden its appeal. There is therefore every reason to want to reconnect the church and its members with Christian tradition as a means of forming Christians in beliefs and practices that the church has always guarded. But at the same time, the call to a renewed awareness of Christian tradition must be more than just a return to the Bible, for the Bible itself can be endangered by our careless reading — as when we read the Bible only for its supposed therapeutic effect, or when we read only the texts and stories with which we are already comfortable.

I do not intend this book to serve as a critique or exposé of the shallowness of the church or its exegesis. Far more, it is an attempt to "stock the shelves" of anyone who reads the Bible, especially those who stand in the pulpit to offer the "whole counsel of God" week by week, with some vital information from our forebears. In a word, the *wager* of each chapter of this book is that the Bible is better read and preached when the legacy of traditional interpretation is taken into account, so that the faithful interpreters of the past can guide and challenge readers and hearers today.

Chapter One

Hagar in Salvation-History

Victim or Villain? Symbol or Saint?

Hagar's story is divided fairly evenly between two chapters of the Bible, Genesis 16 and 21 — two chapters that can be seen by turns as both attractive and repulsive for the preaching task. On the one hand, they tell of the miraculous but excruciatingly delayed fulfillment of God's promise to Abraham and Sarah that they would receive in their old age a son, Isaac, through whom their descendants would be as numerous as the stars. God's gift of descendants to Abraham is a tangible and necessary counterpart to the narrative's earlier declaration that, on account of his faith, Abraham was reckoned as righteous before God. The account of Abraham's faith in Genesis 15:6 is the whole focus of Paul's account of justification in Romans 4. Indeed, Paul's understanding of how Abraham was justified by faith could be seen as the essence of Paul's gospel, even as Paul's theology could be seen as the definitive and lasting interpretation of the teachings of Jesus himself. It is obvious that in the birth of Isaac there is a great promise to proclaim.

On the other hand, these chapters also harbor a fair share of stumbling blocks. Although a son is promised to Abraham and Sarah as early as Genesis 12, no son appears for a very long time. In Genesis 16, Sarah and Abraham take things into their own hands, so to speak, using the Egyptian slave girl Hagar as a surrogate for the supposedly barren Sarah. In other words, the "first parents of faith" conspired to commit polygamy, and did so, it would seem, as a colossal act of unfaith.

Things get worse. Even before Ishmael was born, Sarah and Hagar quarreled, and Sarah evidently mistreated Hagar to such a degree that the handmaid preferred to take her chances in the wilderness rather than face her mistress. And even though an angel of the Lord intervened, sending Hagar back to serve Sarah, chaos returned to the household some years later. Sarah, angry at seeing Ishmael playing with her young son Isaac, directed Abraham to "cast out this slave woman with her son, for the son of this slave woman shall not be heir with my son Isaac." A passive and hesitant Abraham, bolstered by a direct word from God, did what his wife asked. Hagar was sent off to the wilderness once more, with her son but without much by way of provisions.

Given Hagar's marginal and marginalized role, it is easy to see why one feminist writer has characterized Hagar as "a throw-away character among the matriarchs."[1] Perhaps the "easiest" way to preach through the story of Abraham, Sarah, and Isaac would be to treat these three as heroes, especially Abraham, and to ignore or vilify Hagar and Ishmael. In fact, ignoring Hagar was the traditional approach of lectionaries; only in 1992 did the Revised Common Lectionary recognize that the story of Hagar and Ishmael was a major omission from the 1983 Common Lectionary and restore it to the cycle of readings.[2] To vilify Hagar, however, might be seen as the "canonical" approach, insofar as this seems to be the strategy adopted and commended by the Apostle. Having once been driven out, Hagar and Ishmael are recalled in Galatians 4, only to be redrawn in dismal imagery as signifying the bondage and futility of the law.

Why Is Hagar Important?

If one were to take Paul's allegory in Galatians 4 as comprehending all that one needs to know about Hagar and Ishmael, the "throw-away" character of Hagar could be simply thrown away — passed by as a villain who dared to obstruct the triumphant unfolding of God's promise to her betters, Sarah and Abraham. Unfortunately, the practices of preachers and commentators have not always differed much from this caricature. Readers can easily succumb to the temptation to "read for the center," reducing the biblical narrative to what seems to be the red thread of heroes and victors of the faith.

Such readings, however, miss some amazing details not found in Galatians but clearly important for the book of Genesis. Much of the credit for recovering these overlooked details ought to go generally to the pioneering studies of feminist interpreters, among which — in the particular case of Hagar — Phyllis Trible's 1981 Beecher lectures were a watershed. As Trible and later writers have argued, a close reading of the biblical narrative reveals that Hagar's résumé is both distinguished and distressing, as we may summarize in a few paragraphs.

The observations and criticisms that feminist readers have registered with respect to Genesis 16 and 21 have two or three primary dimensions, and all of these observations can sharpen our own. There is, first of all, an abiding concern to recognize and recover the dignity, eminence, and even the exemplary character of Hagar. As Trible pointed out in her original study, Hagar was the first person in the Bible to be visited by an angel (16:7), as well as the first to receive a formal annunciation (16:11-12), much like that of Mary and other biblical women later on. Unlike any of these other biblical women, however, Hagar is promised innumerable descendants (16:10). She stands out also in the details of her encounters with God in the wilderness. Accordingly, in Genesis 16:13 she is bold enough to bestow a special name on God, calling God "the living one who sees me."[3] Others have noted that Hagar is unique among biblical women in choosing a wife for her son.[4] Somewhat more loosely, some feminist and womanist writers have lauded Hagar as a pioneer in asserting her own autonomy against the oppression of her master and mistress.[5] All of these elements of the story — the sheer fact of her being addressed by deity, her reception of an amazing divine promise, the mark of eminence signaled by her being rescued by God and by her commemorative responses — testify to Hagar's worth and interest. More to the point, all are elements that feminist critics have pressed upon us as having been ignored, neglected, or forgotten by commentators until recently.

A second dimension of feminist exegesis takes an opposite tack. If Hagar possessed an unusual degree of eminence among biblical women, she also ought to be recognized for what she suffered, as well as for her courage under fire. Along these lines, feminist commentators have called attention to her various sufferings and undeserved mistreatment. These elements are not too hard to find: entering the narrative as a slave, she is quickly press-ganged as a surrogate mother for Sarah, then finds herself despised for her success — so despised that she runs away rather than bear further mistreatment. Although she is rescued by the angel of the Lord, it remains that the divine messenger's mission was to send Hagar back to the very servitude she had hoped to escape. And if things went well for a while afterwards, the exile that followed hard upon the birth of Isaac threatened to end Hagar's story on a horrifying, even mortal, note. Critics have been understandably quick to point out the remarkable inhumanity that is perpetrated upon Hagar by both Sarah and Abraham. As Trible put it, Hagar also had the dubious distinction of being among the first biblical women to experience "use, abuse, and rejection."[6] Womanist and other African American critics have been especially troubled by the resemblance between Sarah's mistreatment of Hagar and the similar misfortunes of so many black slave women at the hands of white mistresses.[7] To be sure, Abraham is also indicted for his ethical shortcomings: even setting aside his polygamous relationship to Hagar, he is hardly to be praised for his work as a mediator between the mothers of his two sons. And there is nearly universal outrage over the terms of departure, when (according to the biblical text) he sends off Hagar and Ishmael into the desert supplied with the barest of provisions, nothing more than bread and a skin of water (21:14).[8] Obviously, leveling such charges on behalf of Hagar does not change the narrative as it stands, but it is the understandable interest of feminist critics to chronicle the injustices done to Hagar — not only as a salutary warning for our own day, but also to restore some sort of moral balance to a biblical setting that seems woefully undersupplied in this respect.

A third dimension of the feminist analysis of this story has attended to what one might call the sins of the narrator. Guided by a hermeneutic of suspicion,[9] it is not hard to find subtle clues that undercut the dignity of Hagar and that, arguably, betray the patriarchal bias of the narrator. Thus both Sarah and Hagar suffer from the typical stereotypes applied to women as petty, quarrelsome, and untrustworthy. They thereby seem blamed for their own unhappiness while Abraham is implicitly exonerated.[10] Similarly, many recent writers have wondered over the curious wording at Genesis 21:16-17, where, although it is Hagar who weeps, the text says that God heard the voice of the *lad*. Was Hagar somehow unworthy to be heard? Finally, in the eyes of many readers today, the "sins of the narrator" reflect also the sins of the deity. After all, Hagar's return to servitude and her later exile are orchestrated and ratified by God. How can God be so cruel to her? Why doesn't God at least censure Abraham and Sarah for their meanness? Why should Hagar not think that God is her enemy?[11] And why should we, today, think any differently?

Feminist readings of the story of Hagar challenge us not only to read more carefully, but also to read through the eyes of those whom the text does not seem to privilege. These readings challenge us to look not only at the center of the narrative, but also at the margins. Indeed, the composite testimony of feminist, womanist, and Latina commentators urges us to remember Hagar not just as an overlooked biblical character but also as a point of identification for so many in the world today who are themselves deemed minor or marginalized figures, far from the global centers of power. And to the extent that the church has allied itself with such centers of power, with the oppressor, and has neglected Hagar and others like her — both in the biblical text and in the world outside the text — the church and its interpretation of Scripture is found wanting by this trenchant feminist critique.

Has the Church Neglected Hagar?

If feminists urge the church to read the text more closely than usual, they also challenge the church to live up to its own profession, namely, to care for the stranger and sojourner, the poor and the weak. In the abstract, there is nothing controversial about such an exhortation. The question that will concern at least some Christian readers, however, is whether the feminist challenge truly arises from the text or whether it is being imposed on the text. Or, to put the matter somewhat differently, there is a danger that some Christian readers will regard feminist concerns for Hagar as both neglected and oppressed as just a culture-bound fad of the late twentieth and early twenty-first century. Are feminist concerns really new? Is concern for Hagar no more than an expression of political correctness? If the central concern of Scripture is salvation, after all, why shouldn't we "read for the center"?

The short answer to these objections is that these supposedly recent and "feminist" concerns have more in common with traditional Christian readings of Hagar than one might suspect. In other words, feminists are not really raising new questions about these passages. "Modern" readings of Genesis and the forceful proclamation of the text can each be greatly fortified by an awareness of how our forebears received and read the story of Hagar. Although the literature that bears on Genesis is vast, Hagar's later "career" among biblical commentators can be summarized in terms of the main developments in ancient, medieval, and Reformation exegesis.[12] This chronological division loosely corresponds to three questions raised by feminists that can appropriately be addressed to these traditional interpreters. First, did Christian commentators allow the allegory of Galatians 4 to impose a harsh judgment upon Hagar and Ishmael in Genesis? That is, did they read the historical Hagar in terms of the Pauline allegory? Second, when interpreters did attend to the character of Hagar in Genesis, did they worry about her severe treatment, or did they just "blame the victim"? Did they tend to exonerate Abraham at any cost? Finally, was Hagar treated as merely a disposable foil for the events surrounding Abraham, Sarah, and Isaac, or have commentators ever found her an interesting and even sympathetic figure in her own right?

The Trajectories of Ancient Exegesis:
Did Paul's Allegory Win?

The typology fashioned by the Apostle in Galatians 4 was actually not the only allegorical option available to the earliest interpreters. Hagar also figured prominently for Philo, a Jewish contemporary of St. Paul living in Alexandria, Egypt. Philo wrote many works of philosophy and exegesis. For him, Hagar was not a symbol of the old law or a doctrine of justification by works. Instead, she designated the "preliminary teachings" that the wise will study with diligence on their way to attaining true wisdom. In other words, though she is not the equal of Sarah, Hagar is not to be despised, for she represents a necessary station on the way to philosophical maturity. Ideally, after mastering preliminaries, one will move on to higher matters, which are represented by Sarah. The danger, for Philo, is that one will remain stuck, wedded to the preliminary teachings as if nothing were better or higher. In that case, one achieves or "begets" no true wisdom but mere sophistry — and sophistry is personified by Ishmael.[13]

Philo's influence on early Christian views can be seen in the works of other Alexandrians, including Clement, Origen, and Didymus the Blind. Writing in the third century, Origen is of particular interest, for he mixes the influence of Philo with that of the Apostle Paul. In his sixth homily on Genesis, he draws on Philo first of all to solve the embarrassing problem of Abraham's polygamy. How can it possibly be edifying to read such a tale? Easy: for Origen, Hagar represents not a literal wife or a fleshly union, but rather the virtue of wisdom. Accordingly, Abraham acquired not a second *wife* but another *virtue* — and a man can never have too many virtues! But in the next homily, Paul takes over from Philo, and Origen proceeds to use Galatians 4 to explain what Paul says in 2 Corinthians 3:6 about how "the letter kills but the spirit gives life." Although one might expect Origen's remark here to work against Hagar, insofar as she is now associated not only with the law and servitude but also with the "killing letter," Origen moves off in an unexpected direction. Fixing his attention not so much on Hagar's inadequacies as on the "bottle of water" that ran dry in the desert (21:15), he contrasts the insufficiency of the synagogue of the Jews, who rely on the law and literal exegesis, with the abundance that flows from the sort of spiritual interpretation practiced by the Christian church. Indeed, he writes, Hagar is just like the Samaritan woman: both had their eyes opened to see a well of living water, which in each case was Jesus Christ. Just as in Galatians 4, the line between the literal Hagar and her allegorical twin is very thin for Origen. But the payoff for the literal Hagar is huge, if subtle. In the space of only two homilies, she has gone from being a symbol of virtue, to a symbolic association with "carnal" exegesis and futility, only to end by becoming a symbol (if not a forerunner) of what Origen regards as the remnant of *faithful* Jews.[14]

Christian polemic against the synagogue continues to be common in early treatments of Hagar, as is the Philonic theme of Hagar as emblematic of some lesser form of wisdom or virtue. These two ingredients can be found in both Didymus the Blind and Ambrose of Milan, but with quite contrasting results. Writing a century after Origen, Didymus further illustrates how allegory can erode back into literal exegesis. In making his own case for how Hagar symbolizes the "introductory studies," Didymus goes well beyond Origen to treat her as much more than an allegorical cipher. Hagar can *symbolize* the virtue of these introductory studies largely because she is depicted in the narrative as possessing such virtues in a *literal* way — as is evidenced by her good behavior and her worthiness to receive heavenly visitations. Didymus even invokes Matthew 5:8, "Blessed are the pure in heart, for they shall see God," suggesting that since Hagar saw God, she also must have been pure in heart.[15] What has happened here? In effect, while Didymus retains the Pauline allegory later on, he has clearly pondered details not found in Galatians, particularly Hagar's vision of God, and these details he regards as too suggestive to ignore.

Ambrose was Didymus's Latin contemporary. But at his hands, allegory worked the other way — and the literal Hagar was greatly diminished. Ambrose knew and used both allegories, the Philonic and the Pauline, so one might even say that Hagar thereby lost twice. When Ambrose employs the Philonic allegory, Hagar symbolizes not so much the necessary "preliminary studies" as merely the artificial wisdom of this world. When he invokes the Pauline allegory, Hagar symbolizes not only the bondage of the synagogue but also the bondage of *all* heresy. More important still for later Christian interpretation was the way Ambrose used the allegorical status of Hagar to erase her historical particularity. Worrying over the scandal of Abraham's polygamy, Ambrose ventured to say *not* that there was no such polygamous marriage, as Origen had suggested, but rather that the polygamous marriage between Abraham and Hagar was divinely arranged precisely so that it would serve later on as the allegory found in Galatians 4. Polygamy is undoubtedly a scandal, but this particular polygamy was impelled not by lust but by God, in order to prefigure how the church would eventually supplant the synagogue.[16] What may be described as Ambrose's "providential typology" proved to be rather popular in the Latin West as a means for explaining away the immoralities of the patriarchs in general. Most of the insights of Ambrose were taken up in short order by Augustine, who found in the unruly Hagar not merely a figure of generic heresy, but a particular adumbration of the Donatists of his own day — the North African "schismatics" whom Augustine approached with the same harshness that he defended also on the part of Abraham and Sarah.[17]

By the fifth century, then, the Latin exegesis of western Christendom looks for all the world like it will continue to impose some rather stark symbolism on the figure of Hagar, reducing her either to the benign but inferior status granted by Philo or to the more suspect position described by Paul. To be sure, some Greek Christian interpreters saw more depth in the person of Hagar as described in the book of Genesis — notably, Didymus the Blind, but also John Chrysostom, whom we'll examine later. But in the West, Ambrose and Augustine seem to have submerged the text of Genesis all but completely beneath these two allegorical agendas. It comes as a surprise, then, that the early medieval interpreters offer only a casual acknowledgment of the views of Ambrose and Augustine. What surfaces in early medieval writers such as Isidore, the Venerable Bede, and Raban Maur smacks much more of Origen and Didymus the Blind. Yet the Origenistic allegory evolves at the hands of these writers: more and more attention is focused on something like the literal Hagar, while the Hagar of Galatians 4 moves into the shadows.

In the case of Isidore, bishop of Seville from about the year 600, one finds the usual polemic against the synagogue, but a new element is added. In Genesis 21, where Hagar casts her son "under a tree" lest she see him die, Isidore identifies the tree as prefiguring the "tree" of the cross. Hagar and Ishmael are suddenly no longer figures of rejection, but of repentance and salvation. Isidore has thereby amplified some of the elements found in Origen and Didymus, leaving the reader with a remarkably optimistic picture of Hagar.[18]

About a century after Isidore, the English monk who has come to be known as the Venerable Bede also expressed an interest in the Pauline allegory and voiced his own share of anti-Jewish polemic. But Bede's use of Paul, lodged wholly in connection with Genesis 21, seems perfunctory when juxtaposed with his remarks on Genesis 16 and Hagar's theophany. There, he not only acknowledged the marvel of her vision of the living God, he also attributed to her an amazing degree of spiritual insight. Indeed, he says, "she understood the sublimity of the divine substance, always living and remaining without end or beginning, and from it she believed the well ought to be similarly named."[19] These are words of highest praise, and they stand in highest contrast with Hagar's role in the Pauline allegory. In all likelihood, Bede's appreciation for what might properly be called Hagar's literal virtue and spirituality has functioned as a catalyst, so that the apostolic portrait of Hagar as an allegory of rejected Jews is increasingly countered with Origen's and Isidore's allegory of Hagar as figuring repentant or faithful Jews — Christians, in other words.

The notion that there is an allegorical transition underway in the West in the early Middle Ages is corroborated by the remarks of Raban Maur in the first half of the ninth century. He, too, wields the Pauline allegory as an instrument of anti-Jewish polemic, only to interrupt himself with a new alternative: perhaps, he writes, Hagar is better understood as a figure of the church of the gentiles, so that it would be Sarah who symbolizes the synagogue. If so, then the angel's command to Hagar to return to Sarah and submit would admonish gentiles, "lest they boast at the expense of the Jewish people." Raban Maur is unsure about this interpretation, but he is clearly also fascinated by it. Consequently, some of the shock value is removed from a second surprise to be found in Raban Maur, when (like Bede) he explains Hagar's vision of God in Genesis 16:13 as somehow comprehending all kinds of wonderful things, including a glimpse of the coming incarnation of Christ, as well as Hagar's apparent fulfillment of the great commandment to love God and one's neighbor, which is the prerequisite of successful contemplation.[20] This is another amazing encomium. Hagar has become not only the antitype of gentile Christians, but also a practitioner of the highest spirituality.

It would be too much to claim that Bede and Raban Maur definitively influenced later exegesis. Only some of their insights actually made it into the *Ordinary Gloss,* the great compendium of Bible commentators that was compiled in the twelfth century and remained popular through the sixteenth. But there are enduring echoes of this transformed reading of Hagar, a reading that resisted the reductionism one might derive from Paul's allegory and that attended much more to the literal details in the text of Genesis 16 and 21. Some such echoes may be heard in the comments of Nicholas of Lyra in the fourteenth century as well as Denis the Carthusian in the fifteenth. By the eve of the Reformation, debates over just what it was that Hagar saw in her encounters with the angel of the Lord had become commonplace in commentary literature, along with some sense of Hagar's relative worth to receive such visitations. And while Protestant Reformers were reluctant to endorse allegorical exegesis, much less coin their own, the attention that medievals had increasingly paid to Hagar as both virtuous and blessed by God guaranteed (as we will see later on) that Reformation commentators would not overlook these details, either.

Medieval Christians and Rabbis: Abraham on Trial

Another spur to the "close reading" of Genesis that led also to a "humanizing" of Hagar arose wherever interpreters worried over the ethical behavior of the characters in the story. Remarkably, the Bible is itself rather silent here, for although Genesis 16:4-6 implicitly rebukes Hagar for her insolence and Sarah for her harshness, Genesis 21 simply reports without comment the odd provocation — Ishmael "playing" with Isaac — that led to Hagar's banishment. Indeed, the text seems to suspend the moral question by insisting that the event was directed and confirmed by God. That was enough of an explanation for some, but questions still lingered for many.

The earliest worries over Abraham's behavior in expelling Hagar and

Ishmael are to be credited to the rabbis. The "great midrash" on Genesis, known as *Midrash Rabbah,* documents a diversity of rabbinic views as of the late fourth or early fifth century. The point of greatest interest to Christian writers usually concerned the "playing" attributed to Ishmael — an action that the Apostle himself seems to have regarded as persecution. Here, the rabbis offered an intriguing study of the Hebrew term used in Genesis 21:9, *mĕtzachēq,* a word capable of all the ambiguity of the English "play." For the rabbis, however, the term was associated with some shameful deeds, including the accusation of Potiphar's wife that Joseph had attempted to "make sport" with her, the "playing" of the Israelites who fashioned the golden calf in the wilderness, and the tournament in 2 Samuel 2:14 that turned into a battle. In other words, Ishmael's "play" with Isaac might have consisted of fornication, or idolatry, or attempted homicide.[21] Although modern readers seldom see such dire threats so clearly embedded in the text of Genesis 21:9, these rabbinic worries are actually a quite understandable attempt to reconcile the otherwise innocent behavior of Ishmael with the stunningly harsh actions of Sarah and Abraham. After all, what did Ishmael or Hagar do to merit being disowned, driven out, and abandoned — perhaps even to die in the desert?

The first Christian writer to take note of these rabbinic views was probably Jerome, writing at the end of the fourth century. In a work on the meaning of Hebrew words, Jerome reports most of the rabbinic suggestions above, though without naming his sources.[22] Owing largely to Jerome's eminence as a scholar of Scripture, his report was widely disseminated in the following centuries. But even where the more obscure implications of Ishmael's "playing" were not known or mentioned, the disparity between crime and punishment could still be raised. John Chrysostom, preaching on Genesis in the late 380s, attributes great reservations to Abraham over the severity and oppressiveness of Sarah's plan to evict Hagar and Ishmael. A few years later, preaching on Galatians, he makes some similar moves, arguing that only the stirrings of divine providence can account for this event, for otherwise the penalty would be vastly more serious than Ishmael's mere brashness warranted.[23] Other writers of the period, including Theodoret of Cyrus and Procopius of Gaza, also worried over Abraham's actions in Genesis 21, recognizing the exile's grimness and the apparent stinginess of the patriarch in denying Hagar and Ishmael provisions, pack animals, or servants.[24]

Rabbinic discussions of Abraham's ethics did not end with *Midrash*

Rabbah, however, and new strategies to explain the text emerged, most of which either heightened the flaws of Hagar and Ishmael or downplayed the austerity of Abraham. Accordingly, Rashi reported that Hagar's "wandering" in Genesis 21:14 may have implied her *moral* wandering into idolatry, while Abraham Ibn Ezra insisted that later on, after Sarah's death, Abraham lavished gifts upon Ishmael's children. None of the rabbis, however, nor any Christian commentator can equal the blunt confession of Rabbi Nachman, writing in the thirteenth century: "Sarah sinned in afflicting her, and also Abraham for permitting it. God hearkened to Hagar's cry, and as a result her descendants persecute and afflict the seed of Abraham and Sarah."[25]

The remarkable confession of Nachmanides may well be a high-water mark with respect to recognizing the injustice done to Hagar. Nonetheless, if later Christian writers still labored to excuse Abraham, they did so with a growing awareness of the urgency of the case against the patriarch. Focusing on the sixteenth century, we may single out four or five commentators for recognition.

Thomas de Vio (later Cardinal Cajetan) was one of Luther's earliest Roman Catholic opponents, but he spent his last years commenting on most of the Bible. At Genesis 21, Abraham's behavior becomes a major concern: "How was it fitting," Cajetan asks, "that Abraham, who was so wealthy, provided for his wife and son so sparingly — or rather, so miserably! — that he should give his wife only as much bread and water as she could carry on her shoulders?" For Cajetan, the solution lies in taking "bread and water" as shorthand for "all kinds of victuals," and he goes on to infer that Abraham would never have sent his wife and son away without all these things and much more, including pack animals, attendants, and even a tent.[26] Given the doggedness with which Cajetan also defends Hagar and Ishmael from a variety of traditional rabbinic attacks, he cannot be said to blame the victim here; nor is he intent on excusing Abraham at any cost. Cajetan reads the text to favor *all* the characters, ameliorating the injustice to Hagar by insisting that the spareness of the narrative should not be allowed to conceal what must have really happened — namely, that decency reigned all around. However much it may break our rules of exegesis to smuggle so many extra facts into the biblical text, it cannot be denied that Cajetan is deeply exercised by Abraham's injustice to Hagar.

Responses equally visceral, and possibly just as creative, are found in

24

many of Cajetan's contemporaries. Conrad Pellican, a popular teacher of Hebrew in Zurich from 1526, emphasized that Abraham acted not from inhumanity but in obedience to the divine command, so that the exile of Hagar was a great trial of faith for the kindly patriarch. Obviously, if Pellican had portrayed Hagar as a villain, his claims about Abraham's trials would seem hypocritical, but we will see in a moment that Pellican holds Hagar, too, in high regard.[27] A similar line of argument was followed by Wolfgang Musculus, reformer of Augsburg and Bern, who added that Abraham's treatment of Hagar violated Deuteronomy 15:13-14, that servants must not be set free without provisions or a stipend.[28] By contrast, Peter Martyr Vermigli, lecturing in Strasbourg in the 1540s, showed his distress over Abraham's behavior more by his own confusion. Vermigli offers three different (and incompatible) explanations, admitting in one place that Abraham did treat Hagar and Ishmael "a bit inhumanely," but asserting that the hard eviction was a useful corrective.[29] Again, if Vermigli had seen Hagar as nothing but an evildoer, his confusion might be deemed simply mean. But Hagar also earns Vermigli's admiration, and it is clear that his confusion really signals unresolved dissonance over how one biblical model has treated another.

Martin Luther is another witness to how seriously sixteenth-century commentators wrestled with the ethical problems of Hagar's eviction:

> Abraham simply sends away his beloved spouse, she who first made him a father, along with his firstborn son, giving them only a sack of bread and a skin of water. . . . But does it not seem cruel that a mother burdened with offspring should be dismissed so miserably, and that, to an unknown destination, indeed, into a vast and arid desert?[30]

It does seem cruel, Luther admits, desperately so. "If someone wanted to rant against Abraham at this point, he could make him the murderer of his son and wife. . . . Who would believe this if Moses had not recorded it?"[31]

Because of their presuppositions about the inspiration and integrity of Scripture, none of these precritical commentators is inclined to hang Abraham without a trial. On the contrary, one of their priorities is to find a way to harmonize the characterizations of the biblical actors while remaining within the confines of the narrative. If some appear to have worked overtime to exonerate Abraham, they never lost sight of the seriousness of the charge against the patriarch nor brushed aside the terror inflicted on Hagar and her son.

Reformation Exegesis: Stereotypes . . . and Sympathy

A large part of feminist and womanist concern for Hagar focuses on the way that traditional, patriarchal exegesis has locked her into a petty and stereotypical role and ignored both the injustices done to her and the anguish of her abandonment. Nonetheless, the commentators examined here don't quite fit this billing. They are admittedly patriarchal, albeit in an unconscious way, and they are capable of succumbing to gender stereotyping, but they show a surprising tendency to rise above these traits in pursuit not only of "literal" exegesis but also in defense of Hagar.

A compassionate interest in Hagar does not begin with the Reformation. In the previous section, we noted some earlier writers who clearly wondered at her hardships, including John Chrysostom, Theodoret, and Procopius, to whom one might add a variety of later figures, including Rupert of Deutz, Nicholas of Lyra, and Denis the Carthusian.[32] But the commentators of the Reformation tend as a group to heighten the moral issues that bear on Abraham, Sarah, and Hagar, in ways both predictable and surprising.

Probably the earliest Reformed commentary on Genesis was derived from the publication of students' notes of lectures given in 1527 by Huldreich Zwingli. The remarks of Zwingli are peppered with just the sort of gender slurs that make modern readers cringe. Hagar, accordingly, is both "womanish" and "servile," even as Sarah is jealous and proverbially impatient. Abraham, of course, has none of these flaws. However, none of these judgments seems to prevent Zwingli from characterizing Hagar during her first flight as actually a humble and pious woman, even obedient in response to the angel. And when Zwingli comes to the moment of Hagar's exile, he reads the story like the father of four that he was: the banishment of Hagar and her son was "inhumane, cruel, and severe," and he marvels — surely speaking also for himself — at the "violent emotions" that must have filled Abraham. Zwingli then reads the end of the story through the eyes of Hagar, observing with sympathy that her actions were governed by both a sense of despair and an overwhelming maternal affection.[33] Not everything in Zwingli's account coheres, but his empathy for Hagar and Abraham is unfeigned.

Conrad Pellican, a colleague of Zwingli, also offers his share of gender stereotypes, but these are likewise upstaged by his portrait of Hagar in Genesis 16 as a model penitent and as one of "God's own." Hagar's piety also marks her behavior at the point of her exile, and even when the water runs out and Ishmael is about to die, "she prayed to the Lord with her heart, with her faith, and with her tears; she cried out in loudest prayer."[34] Naturally, a suspicious reader may wonder if Pellican is merely forcing Hagar into yet another gender stereotype, that of the submissive Christian wife. Perhaps he is. Yet it is equally likely that he does so out of a sincere admiration for the character of Hagar and from a desire to extend to her the highest compliment he knows.

An even stronger defense of Hagar emerges from the lengthy 1554 commentary of Wolfgang Musculus. Like other Protestants of the day, he does not shrink from a few words of rebuke directed at Hagar for her malice, but he goes on to describe her as an exemplar. Musculus is sure that in Hagar's first encounter with the angel of God, she was not only brought to repentance and humility but also must have experienced an amazing conversion and kindling of faith through this divine messenger. More striking still is how he internalizes Hagar's feelings at the moment of exile. Although she accepted her fate without murmur, Musculus believes she had every reason to complain:

> She could have turned back and said, "Am I therefore being ejected without cause? And am I being evicted empty-handed, destitute of food and supplies? Are you driving Ishmael your firstborn into exile? What evil did he do? Are you giving him to me to raise? But he's yours more than mine! Why are you placing all the care for him on my shoulders? How will I bring up the son who belongs to you when I've been driven out and dismissed with empty hands? Where will I take him? If you must eject *me*, at least save your son!"[35]

Obviously, Musculus is scripting for Hagar with his heart, but he's not finished. He continues to ponder the "accumulation of misery and calamities" that Hagar and Ishmael face, praising Hagar's self-control and piety while chronicling her grief and tears. Musculus even grants that Hagar would not have sinned had she voiced some of her complaints. After all, Job and Jeremiah offered laments, and even Christ cried out from the cross, "My God, my God, why have you forsaken me?" It would be hard to frame a stronger acknowledgment of the anguish of Hagar than to compare her feelings of abandonment with those of the Savior — and it is a response that finds an almost perfect parallel in the epitaph imagined by Phyllis Trible.[36]

If Musculus's subjective engagement with Hagar is dramatic, so too are the earlier musings of Luther. Lecturing on Hagar in 1538 or so, he casts Hagar as a Christian exemplar. "Most of us are like Hagar," he writes, not only in our various faults but also in having to follow the familiar path trod by Hagar that leads from humiliation to faith and repentance. Luther then proceeds to extol in detail the godliness of "saintly Hagar."[37] But it is in his account of Hagar's exile that Luther displays his passionate identification with all the members of this cast — indeed, one may truly say that Luther loves these characters deeply. He dwells at spectacular length on the sadness of the episode and on the broken hearts of all. "Trial follows upon trial," he writes, "and tears force out other tears."

> Surely this is a piteous account, which I can scarcely read with dry eyes, that the mother and son so patiently bear their ejection and wander into exile. And so Father Abraham either stood there weeping, following the wanderers with his blessings and prayers, or else he hid by himself off in a corner, where he cried over his own fate and that of the exiles.[38]

Nonetheless, in the midst of all the grief and fear that Luther sees, he makes another observation that is perhaps the most arresting of all. For Luther, the banishment of Hagar was not merely a physical trial, though it was that, too. Rather, Hagar's greatest anxiety would have stemmed from the perfectly reasonable conclusion that, in being cast out of Abraham's household, she was also rejected by God — indeed, Luther thinks Hagar's plight looks for all the world as if God has become her enemy. Luther, too, knows the dark night of the soul, and he knows that such terrors represent the harrowing way God teaches mortals to trust his promises rather than their own sight. When some today ask why Hagar should not believe that God hates her, one can imagine Luther voicing his sober agreement, though — by faith — he would not allow the paragraph to end just there.

Hagar in Church and Pulpit

What payoff can be derived from these old commentators for reading and preaching Hagar's story? Do they help us? I think there *is* a payoff that ought to be passed on to readers and congregations today. But first, a caveat.

It would be a mistake to conclude from the descriptions and excerpts above that traditional commentators of the patristic, medieval, and Reformation eras were secretly inclined toward feminism, as if they could easily have anticipated such a development. All these commentators operate with patriarchal instincts, to one degree or another, and — like most moderns — they view their world through the stereotypes of gender, class, and culture. There were, moreover, traditional writers who had no patience for Hagar. "Cast out the slave woman and her son," was, after all, the proof-text by which Pope Urban II launched the First Crusade.[39] For Augustine, Hagar was never much more than a symbol for his opponents, and even John Calvin (who may be regarded as conspicuous by his absence from the foregoing account) refused to allow anyone but Paul to have the last word. For him, Hagar and Ishmael were always emblematic of his own papal opponents, and his hunch that the slave woman and her son were destined for reprobation would not bode well for Calvin's Roman Catholic contemporaries.[40] But Augustine and Calvin stand out as curiously untouched by the various expressions of interest and empathy that most commentators drew from this biblical text. In their own minds, most of these more empathetic interpreters would have seen themselves not as *feminists* but certainly as *humanists*, insofar as they endeavored to live up to the radical demands of the commandment to love one's neighbor — including, often, the "neighbors" to be found in the stories of Scripture.

Bearing in mind, then, the dangers of selectively recruiting voices from the past to reinforce one's presuppositions, a fair hearing of these traditional commentators offers at least four insights into the story of Hagar, and all are lessons worth hearing.

1. HAGAR IS IMPORTANT. *Any incursion into the patriarchal narratives that treats Hagar as the lectionary has mostly done, excising the dubious deeds of Abraham as well as Hagar's own triumphs and travails, is at once a betrayal of the integrity of the biblical text and the squandering of a rich homiletical opportunity.*

29

Why is Hagar important? Clearly, she is important enough to the narrator of Genesis to be the focal point of two significant stories in chapters 16 and 21. She is important within the plot of Genesis not only because she complicated the promises given to Abraham and Sarah, but also because she received her own promises from God, along with twice being the subject of a divine epiphany and a remarkable rescue. She is important to readers today, moreover, because of her dignity in the face of her mistreatment. But is Hagar important to the church? If we grant a fair hearing to our forebears, she ought to be, because we learn from them that *honoring Hagar is nothing new.* It is nothing new to recognize Hagar as a complicated character, yet clearly honored by God. It is nothing new to wonder at her encounters with angels, or to be moved by her astounding trials. And it is nothing new to see in Hagar not only an example of grace under fire, but also an identification point for so many in our congregations today: for all those who have been unjustly afflicted; for those who have been abandoned or driven out by the powers that be, or even by the church; and for those who feel that even God is against them.

2. HAGAR'S STORY IS TERRIFYING. *Nothing is gained by "reading for the center" so as to pretend that Hagar's misfortunes did not happen or that they weren't so bad after all, given the happy ending that came her way.*

There are, arguably, two ingredients in any "text of terror": atrocity and silence. Hagar's trials are made terrifying — for her, but also for any sympathetic reader — precisely because of the near-silence of Scripture with respect to the behavior of Abraham and Sarah, master and mistress of this Egyptian slave girl. Where is the intervention? Failing that, where is the word of censure? Failing even that, the Bible's silence begins to look like a conspiracy of the powerful against the weak. We cannot change the words of Scripture any more than we can change the sad events of the past, and we cannot always understand why the Bible — why God — remains so silent in the face of so many atrocities. Nonetheless, we need not remain silent ourselves, for *naming Hagar's terror is nothing new.* We ought to have taken a warning from feminist interpreters. How much more should we be willing to learn the same lesson from our own forebears? Truly, worrying about injustice in the Bible is nothing new. Feminists may not always be as interested in reconciling Hagar's woe with the command that came to

Abraham, but there is still this common ground between traditional and contemporary readers, namely, that congregations need to know *why* this is a text of terror for many readers.

3. HAGAR IS MORE THAN A SYMBOL. *Despite the precedent offered by Paul's allegory of Hagar as a figure or type of those who foolishly sought justification through the law, Galatians 4 should not erase or upstage the compelling portrait of Hagar in Genesis.*

True as it is that the allegorical depiction of Hagar in the epistle to the Galatians furnished the church fathers with the occasion for a more general and anti-Jewish polemic, it is also true that the more they found allegorical details in Genesis, the more they tended to value the positive attributes of Hagar that they found there. Among later interpreters, even Protestant commentators (who would have been most committed to the Pauline doctrine of justification) rarely used the symbolic denigration of Hagar in the New Testament to mount a similar attack on her in Genesis. Instead, as Luther and others explained, there was room for both a literal, sympathetic Hagar *and* an allegorical counterpart. Each has a role to play in history and theology. Neither should be left in the shadows.

4. HAGAR IS CONNECTED TO US BY OUR OWN TRADITION. *If it is dysfunctional to ignore Scripture's silences, it is hardly better for preachers to suppose they can fix the Bible alone, by exercising their own authority or creativity. Instead, congregations ought to be reconnected to Christian tradition by being reminded of the witness of past interpreters.*

In our own engagement with the troubling stories of Scripture, we may be reassured and challenged by the witness of past interpreters, who also faced the silence of Scripture. They worried, and they wrestled. Sometimes they were glib or unfeeling. At other times they found something to say by bringing to bear not only their sympathy and imagination, but also a profound moral compass. So far as concerns Hagar, it would be wrong for congregations to read through this section of the Bible and not recognize her story as a source of both sorrow and encouragement. But it would be equally wrong for readers to linger over Hagar, growing either proud or angry or curious, as if they were the first to know or care about this Egyptian woman. The story of Hagar is a powerful text when thoughtfully read or proclaimed. But it is more powerful still when congregations hear that their own caring is but part of "a cloud of witnesses" who have traditionally worried about Hagar, and all those like her.

Chapter Two

Sacrificing Jephthah's Daughter

The Life and Death of a Father's Only-Begotten

I remember when my daughter was in fourth or fifth grade, and she came home from Sunday school looking worried and perplexed. "Daddy," she asked, "is there really a story in the Bible where a girl is killed by her father because he made some kind of promise?" Reading her face, I was pretty sure she was hoping I'd say no. I was also pretty sure that I didn't want to say yes.

Anyone who has read through the Old Testament can scarcely forget the story of Jephthah and his daughter. The son of Gilead by a prostitute, Jephthah was banished by his stepbrothers, only to be sought by them as a leader and a deliverer when Israel was attacked by the Ammonites. Jephthah tried to negotiate peaceably with their king, but failed. As he prepared for war, two things happened. First, "the spirit of the LORD came upon Jephthah" (Judges 11:29). Second, Jephthah vowed to the Lord that if he were victorious in battle, he would offer in sacrifice whatever first came to greet him from his own house on his return (11:30). The story flips from triumph to tragedy: Jephthah was victorious, but his only child, his daughter, ran out to greet him. Jephthah tore his clothes and exclaimed how his daughter had now brought "great trouble" upon him, for he could not revoke his vow. Even so, the daughter affirmed the vow, asking only for two months to mourn her virginity. When she returned, the Bible says, her father fulfilled his vow, and every year thereafter the daughters of Israel mourned for her, four days out of the year.

33

What Really Happened? What Went Wrong?

Although there are plenty of stories in the Bible in which there are silences crying out to be explained, this narrative has more than its share of puzzles. For our purposes, it will be helpful to distinguish two sets of problems in the story of Jephthah's daughter. One set comes from *traditional interpreters,* for whom the story has raised questions such as these:

- How does Jephthah's anointing with the spirit of the Lord relate to his vow? Did one lead to the other? Did God therefore approve of Jephthah's vow? Or was his vow misguided?

- What did Jephthah intend to sacrifice? What or whom was he expecting to meet, a sheep? Surely he didn't intend a human sacrifice — or did he?

- Might Jephthah have been influenced by Abraham's near-sacrifice of his only son, Isaac, as a precedent? Might he have expected God to intervene for him as he did for Abraham?

There is another set of problems, however, and these are raised by *feminist interpreters.* Some of them are actually the same as the questions above, while others follow similar lines. Consider these:[1]

- Why was Jephthah's *daughter* actually sacrificed, when in two other cases, *sons* designated for sacrifice were freed or released? Isaac is one such example, saved when an angel intervened, but there's another story like his. In 1 Samuel 14:24-46, King Saul rashly vowed that no one should eat until the Philistines were defeated. Unaware of his father's oath, Jonathan ate some honey and would have been killed. However, the people of Israel intervened to ransom him. So why are sons rescued from human sacrifice, while this daughter is not? Indeed, why didn't she resist or run away?

- Why is it that, although it is Jephthah who makes the rash vow, it is his daughter whom he blames? "Alas, my daughter! You have brought me very low; you have become the cause of great trouble to me." This looks suspiciously like "blaming the victim," as if it were the daughter's fault for greeting her father.

(Unfortunately, we ourselves are all too familiar with those who blame the victim of rape for somehow "asking for it," but stigmatizing or punishing victims happens in other contexts, too. My hometown newspaper once reported about the difficulty battered women faced in securing safe housing, because landlords feared their properties would be damaged by the battering husband or boyfriend — so these women were living on the street. Little wonder, then, if feminist readers think they have met men like Jephthah before!)

- How is it fair, or even conceivable, that Jephthah should end up on the list of heroes of faith in Hebrews 11:32, despite his cruel and foolish deed, while his faithful and obedient daughter is not listed there, and no one even remembers her name?

It is true that virtually all interpreters of Judges 11 have to wonder over the silences in the text, but feminist readers have raised the problems with particular acuteness. And although the questions posed by feminist readers highlight their common distress over the *patriarchy* of the text, we will see in a moment that the supposedly patriarchal commentators of the distant past were often just as distressed over what happened to Jephthah's only daughter.

Who Remembered Jephthah's Daughter? And Why?

Even the most casual survey of traditional commentaries will quickly resolve at least one feminist concern, in that Jephthah's daughter is by no means ignored or forgotten. Despite the relatively small number of commentaries and sermons on Judges that survive from ancient, medieval, and Reformation writers, Jephthah's daughter makes regular appearances. Approaches to her story range from moralism to allegory and on to typology and casuistry. We cannot examine all the treatments of her story in this chapter, but a decent silhouette — and a variety of answers to the questions listed above — can be traced from the following half-dozen vignettes.

Origen and the Mystery of Martyrdom

The first of these is the story of how Jephthah's daughter fared at the hands of Origen, the third-century Alexandrian writer who was so often criticized by the early Protestants for his excessive allegories. We no longer have his homily on Judges 11, but we do have a passing remark on Jephthah's daughter in his comments on the Fourth Gospel. At John 1:29, where the Baptist proclaims that Jesus is "the Lamb of God," Origen labors to explain the significance of the symbol and of sacrifices in general. He suggests that the deaths of martyrs bear a similar significance to the Old Testament sacrifices that prefigured the death of the Lamb of God. Cruel as it seems of God to demand martyrdom, somehow (Origen writes) these deaths *do* in fact contribute to the defeat of evil. It is in this context that Origen makes his brief comment about Jephthah's daughter. She too was a martyr, he implies, for it was by her willing death that Jephthah triumphed over the Ammonites.[2]

I will confess that the first time I read Origen's account, it made me angry. It struck me as artificial, as forcing Jephthah's daughter to recruit Christian martyrs for Origen's own purposes. But as I continued to read Origen, my conscience began to bother me about dismissing him. No one can accuse Origen of being naive about martyrdom. His own father was martyred when Origen was but a teenager. We're told that the young Origen was stopped from following his father only because his mother had hidden the boy's clothes. When he was fifty, persecution resumed, and he responded by composing *An Exhortation to Martyrdom,* perhaps the best-known treatise on martyrdom ever written. And you may know that Origen practiced what he preached: his own life was ended some twenty years later, as an effect of the torture he suffered under Emperor Decius.

What is most remarkable about Origen, however, is his clear denial that martyrdom is a visible triumph of any kind! Martyrs *do* contribute to the defeat of evil, Origen says, but this is not something we see — it's something we believe. Indeed, were we to believe what we *see*, we'd have to conclude that God enjoys it when Christians suffer cruel and senseless deaths. No, the martyr's crown is visible only to faith. The true significance of these cruel deaths remains, for now, one of those secrets or mysteries known only to God.

Thus, when Origen says that the death of Jephthah's daughter does indeed look and feel senseless, he's not treating her as just a problem to be solved. No: he's filling in the silences, extrapolating from Israel's defeat of the Ammonites and the selfless virtue of the daughter in order to make sense of the story. Amazingly, Origen (himself a would-be martyr) admits that martyrdom — *all* martyrdom — looks senseless. And God, too, does *seem* heartless and cruel. Nonetheless, where sight fails, faith thrives. The martyr's crown may be visible only to faith, but it *is* visible to faith.

Origen doesn't really differ from any other commentator. He tries his best to find some sense, by asserting that Jephthah's daughter did not die in vain — even though that's the way it seems! Whatever you think of Origen's exegesis, this much can be said: he has not neglected Jephthah's daughter. Neither has he failed to praise her virtue, weigh her death, or mourn her passing — even as he commends her as a saint beloved by God.

Ambrose: Blaming Jephthah and His Daughter

Origen was not the only one to see Jephthah's daughter as a martyr of some sort.[3] But the puzzles in Judges 11 were not always solved to the daughter's advantage. Writing in the late fourth century, Ambrose (bishop of Milan and Augustine's teacher) mentions Jephthah's daughter in no fewer than six of his writings. Curiously, his interpretation of the story is not at all consistent through these works. In some places, Ambrose harshly condemns the father's vow, even as he lauds the daughter's obedience and piety. But the account I want to highlight is found in one of his treatises on virginity. There, Ambrose reflects at length on why God intervened to stop the sacrifice of Isaac, yet allowed the holocaust of Jephthah's daughter to proceed. Out of the blue, he declares that the solution must lie in the *character* (not in the *gender*, one should note) of the individuals involved. That is to say, while Abraham and Isaac were prompt in obeying God's command, Scripture tells us that Jephthah and his daughter hesitated for a full two months. Accordingly, Isaac's obedience and devotion merited a ram to be offered in his stead: for, as Ambrose says, "mercy is large where faith is prompt."[4] But Jephthah grieved and his daughter mourned, so (Ambrose implies) they suffered in turn for their flaws.

Ambrose's contrived solution contradicts his other, more favorable accounts of Jephthah's daughter, but it is of interest precisely because it *is* such a departure from the norm. His rebuke is echoed by only one other major commentator I found — Procopius of Gaza, who wrote in the early sixth century.[5] It is true, then, that there have been Christian writers who "blamed the victim" of Jephthah's vow. But it is of equal significance to note that this is the *rarest* of exegetical conclusions. And even in Ambrose and Procopius, there are explicit indications that they also entertain other views.

Augustine: There Must Be a Lesson Somewhere

Jephthah's daughter actually drew the attention of many well-known writers of the third and fourth centuries, including Jerome, Jovinian, and Ambrosiaster in the West, and Methodius of Olympus, Ephrem the Syrian, Gregory of Nazianzus, and John Chrysostom in the East, among others. But the greatest legacy was that left by Augustine, whose seven volumes of more than 650 *Questions on the Heptateuch* devoted more attention to Jephthah's daughter than to any other single issue.[6]

Augustine established a number of precedents that would be used and refined by his medieval readers. Prior to Augustine, Judges 11 was introduced either as a literal account of the father's error or the daughter's virtue, or else for its figurative or typological value in commending virginity. Augustine combines a literal reading of the story with his search for its figurative meanings. But both aspects of his agenda are complicated by other ingredients. Augustine begins by taking up a traditional worry over the vow's careless wording. It's possible, after all, that Jephthah could have been met by an unclean animal — his dog, say, or worse. In Augustine's Latin Bible, Jephthah's vow literally promised to sacrifice not "whatever" met him, but "whoever." Jephthah was grief-stricken, Augustine suspects, because he was met by his beloved daughter when he had expected his wife! The suspicion that Jephthah had intended a human sacrifice all along leads Augustine to consider next whether Jephthah meant to imitate Abraham, and whether such imitation was lawful or criminal. And in the course of this deliberation, Augustine comes to ask whether the vow's fulfillment was not only permitted but perhaps even *directed* by a secret leading from "the spirit of the Lord" that had anointed Jephthah. His suggestion is truly a wild card, for virtually every commentator after Augustine will wrestle, always inconclusively, over whether Jephthah had special divine permission — as well as over whether the tribute to Jephthah's faith in Hebrews 11 is proof of God's approval.

In any case, Augustine concludes that, whatever Jephthah had in mind, divine providence intended two lessons for us. First, on the level of literal exegesis and ethics, there is a degree of moral closure, for if Jephthah's deed was sinful, everyone ever after was warned not to imitate him by the way he was justly punished in the person of his daughter. To be sure, the comfort of this lesson is likely to be lost on most moderns, however much we try to allow for our more individualistic values. Second, on the level of allegorical or typological meaning, Augustine thinks God meant not only to teach his people that human sacrifice was unlawful but also to offer them a foreshadowing of the sacrifice of Christ. Accordingly, the daughter is offered up by Jephthah — a man obscurely born, rejected by his brethren but later their deliverer — even as the church (as the virgin daughter of 2 Corinthians 11:2) is to be offered up by Christ, as in 1 Corinthians 15:24.

Augustine extracted his lesson by applying the same "providential typology" that Ambrose[7] had used to shield Abraham from the scandal of his polygamy with Hagar. What looks like a crime really isn't, because the story's scandals are actually serving a higher, divine narrative. Even so, though the daughter is certainly upstaged by her father in Augustine's long treatise, the father does not really escape censure. One could wish for more, but it is clear that Augustine spills so much ink precisely because he finds the whole tale so disturbing.

Abelard: Jephthah's Daughter as Tragic Hero

In a moment we'll say a bit more about the legacy of Augustine's typological account of Jephthah and his daughter, but notice must first be given to Peter Abelard, who left a remarkable portrait of Jephthah's daughter. A theological prodigy and popular lecturer in twelfth-century Paris, Abelard attained notoriety with Heloise when, hired to be her tutor, he became instead her lover. Instead of marrying, the two took monastic vows. Abelard's reflections on Jephthah's daughter survive in his later correspondence with Heloise, as well as in one of the liturgical laments he wrote sometime after 1130 for her convent's use.[8]

Abelard's *Lament of the Virgins of Israel over the Daughter of Jephthah the Gileadite* is not easily summarized. The four-part poem begins and ends with choruses voiced by the "virgins of Israel," in which Jephthah is excoriated as demented, as the "father yet enemy of your people," while his daughter is lauded and remembered for her courage and nobility. The second section reenacts her confrontation with her father, in which she urges *him* to be brave and expresses the jarring hope that though God refused Abraham's offering of the boy Isaac, God will accept her, a girl. A third section depicts her musings during her two months' mourning, comparing her impending death to the marriage she will be denied.

The *Lament* of Abelard does many things. It movingly tells of the daughter's heroism, her strength and nobility — as well as her doubts, courage, and loss. It bluntly censures her father as weak and wrong. Less apparently, it serves a complicated agenda for Abelard. It is indeed exegesis and commentary of a sort, for it discloses Abelard's convictions that the father's deed was a crime *and* that the daughter's virtue transformed a senseless catastrophe into a tragedy, something bearing marks of nobility and redemption. But the poem embodies other things, too. Addressed to Heloise, it tells of her sacrifice for Abelard, even as it hints at the many misfortunes that befell Abelard himself. And, as the other references to Jephthah's daughter in Abelard suggest, the poem reflects the sort of advocacy for monasticism seen earlier in Ambrose and other writers.[9] Finally, though it would be hasty to claim Abelard's *Lament* as evidence of his own feminism,[10] it offers ample proof (even amidst the many strands of its complicated agenda) of Abelard's *humanism* — his perception of the daughter's dignity and mortality, and his ability to identify imaginatively and passionately with what she gained and what she lost.

The Climax of Typology in the Later Middle Ages

Even as Augustine's long treatise on Jephthah's daughter featured literal and figurative readings of the story, later interpreters were just as prone to distinguish and combine these two approaches, commonly described as literal and spiritual exegesis. For our last two vignettes, we'll first look at some commentators of the Middle Ages to see how they developed "spiritual" readings after Augustine. We'll then conclude with an overview of Reformation interpreters that explores their greater interest in literal exegesis and the ethical problems of the story.

Usually, the impact of Augustine in the theology and exegesis of western Europe can be assumed. However, though many parts of Augustine's unwieldy treatise were incorporated into later commentaries (sometimes the entire treatise was attributed to later writers), Augustine's typology of Jephthah and his daughter as figures of Christ and the church was not without rivals. Indeed, an alternate typology from Isidore, the seventh-century bishop of Seville, was just as influential. Isidore continued to see Jephthah as a type of Christ, but his daughter represented not the church but Christ's "virgin flesh," which he offered up on behalf of his people.[11]

Some modern writers have found Isidore's depiction demeaning to the daughter, insofar as it seems to absorb her and her sufferings into her father, leaving Jephthah as the sole actor in the story.[12] The concern is not misplaced, though medieval writers probably embraced Isidore's typology more because it seemed to account so well for both players in the drama. But there was also a lesser-known typology offered by one of Augustine's younger contemporaries, in which Jephthah moves to the margins and the daughter fully represents Christ and his sacrifice in herself. Indeed, the daughter's period of mourning anticipates the anguish Christ experienced as he prayed in Gethsemane.[13] This fuller typology reappears in the later Middle Ages. It also corresponds to a more deliberate interest in the daughter and an increased affective identification with her, as can be seen in the comments of a fifteenth-century monk, Denis the Carthusian.

Writing more or less at the end of the Middle Ages, Denis is useful especially because he summarizes so thoroughly the views of his predecessors. He usually provides two full expositions of any given chapter of the Bible: one will be a commentary on the literal or historical sense of the text, the other a commentary on the text's "mystical" or spiritual meaning. When he expounds the literal meaning of this story, Denis displays not only a good deal of sympathy for Jephthah's daughter, but also a remarkable sensitivity to the daughter's suffering and virtue. Three points may be noted here. First, Denis seems to understand the value to the daughter of being surrounded by her friends — the value, that is, of the companionship of women with other women. Second, Denis sees and dislikes the way the father blames his daughter for "deceiving" him, and he defends her from being so blamed. Third, Denis does not hesitate to compare the daughter's goodness and obedience to that of Isaac, and again he underscores her innocent suffering.[14]

Denis's figurative or "mystical" exposition is also rich. He's clearly aware of Augustine's old typology, where Jephthah represents Christ and his daughter represents the virgin church that Christ offered up to the Father, but he is also aware of the alternative whereby the daughter fully represents Christ himself. What is striking about Denis's adaptation of the latter typology is the way he illustrates it with five biblical references to the sufferings of the messiah. Among the texts that he finds to apply equally to Jephthah's daughter and to the messiah are, first of all, Romans 8:32: "God did not spare his own Son, but gave him up for us all." He goes on to quote Isaiah 53 as it might have been spoken by God the Father to the suffering servant: "I have stricken him for the transgression of my people." He then cites two messianic psalms, 69 and 88, as well as Acts 3:18, all of which spotlight the parallel he sees between the sufferings of Jephthah's only daughter and those of Jesus, the only-begotten Son.[15]

Some modern readers will assuredly like Denis's typological reading of Jephthah's daughter as a figure of the sacrifice and sufferings of Jesus. Others may dislike it, either on the grounds that only "literal" exegesis counts, or simply because they find it unappealing or unpersuasive. The point, however, is not to adopt Denis's typology, but to see how the history of the interpretation of Jephthah's daughter — as one of Phyllis Trible's "texts of terror" — is relevant for how we today should read such stories, whether on our own or in the pulpit. What is crucial to see and remember, then, is Denis's *sympathy* for Jephthah's daughter and her sufferings, as well as the *instinct* by which he tries to relate her sufferings and sacrifice to what happens on the cross. At the same time, we can also learn from his willingness to embrace the continuities (if not ironies) between the sacrificial death of Jephthah's daughter and that of Jesus Christ. Indeed, Denis prods us to recall the epitaphs that Trible composed for Hagar and Tamar, which likewise drew on Isaiah 53.[16] One could write off those epitaphs as merely an eccentricity of postmodern or feminist exegesis, but that would be to waste a significant insight. Many readers besides Trible have wondered why the church has cared so much about the suffering of Jesus yet neglected the sufferings endured by so many biblical women. The question begs for a reply. Denis's moving typology offers one.

Reformation Exegesis and a Host of Ethical Concerns

Although it is common to read that the Protestant Reformers not only "returned" to the authority of the Bible in its literal meaning but also completely rejected all non-literal exegesis, such a characterization is really a caricature. Although the Reformers rejected what they regarded as capricious allegory and changed the way they described the "spiritual" or "practical" meaning of the Bible, there is greater continuity between medieval and Reformation exegesis than often supposed.

In the case of Jephthah's daughter, it would be preposterous to credit Protestants as if they were the first to discover the moral and ethical problems in the story. Rather, they are much in Augustine's debt here, even as Augustine was far from original in his own ethical worries.[17] Still, there is an offshoot in sixteenth-century exegesis that was widely regarded as new, though really it was only newly publicized. Sometime around the end of the twelfth century, Rabbi David Kimhi reported his father's novel view of Jephthah's vow. Although Judges 11:31 was usually translated, "whatever comes forth . . . shall be the LORD's, *and* I will offer it up," Kimhi suggested that the Hebrew conjunction could also be read disjunctively: ". . . *or* I will offer it up."[18] In other words, Jephthah meant to offer a burnt sacrifice if greeted by a suitable victim, but if met by a person, he would "devote" that individual to the Lord, presumably as a perpetual servant of the temple. Thus, his daughter was not killed; instead, she remained unmarried, "devoted" in the service of the Lord.

Kimhi's "survivalist" interpretation was slow to spread. A century later, Nicholas of Lyra's popular *Postils* reported Kimhi's conclusion (that the daughter was not killed), but none of its grammatical basis. Some Christian writers liked the suggestion, but many thought it farfetched. Only in the 1530s, when the argument's grammatical details were set forth for Latin readers by Sebastian Münster, did the case for the survival of Jephthah's daughter draw serious attention.[19] Given their commitments to finding the Bible's literal meaning, sixteenth-century commentators were already disposed to focus on matters of morality more than on allegorical symbols. The "survivalist" argument, where known, mostly added fuel to these ethical discussions.

Martin Luther is one of those early writers who knew only Lyra but finds the survivalist reading unpersuasive. In some little-known lectures from 1516 and also in his table talk, Luther marvels at this tragedy of errors, wondering how Jephthah could have been so ill-informed. Without a doubt, the father sinned mortally against his innocent daughter. Equally marvelous to him, though, is that the sacrifice was actually carried out. If Jonathan was released from his father's vow unharmed, Luther argues, Jephthah's daughter deserved no less — the very complaint one finds in several feminist writers.[20]

There are three later Protestant commentators, all skilled in Hebrew, for whom the survivalist argument demanded serious attention. Conrad Pellican (a Zwinglian) and Johann Brenz (a Lutheran) both wrote commentaries on Judges in the 1530s, and while neither had a firsthand knowledge of Münster's account of Kimhi's exegesis, each favored the survivalist argument.[21] As a result, the stakes are lowered: Jephthah's vow no longer risks his daughter's life, only her marriage and his prospects for grandchildren. Jephthah is therefore not quite such a villain, though Brenz concedes that had he *meant* to offer his daughter in sacrifice, that would truly be cruel and impious. What does not change, however, is their estimate of the daughter. She is still extolled for her nobility and obedience — particularly, for Brenz, since no daughter is obliged to submit to a vow of celibacy against her own will. Brenz thus ratifies a concern registered by feminists today, who decry the daughter's loss of autonomy.

Two decades later, a third Protestant Hebraist, Peter Martyr Vermigli, is even more explicitly aware of Kimhi's survivalist argument. Unlike Brenz and Pellican, he is unreceptive to it, and he is proportionately more hostile to Jephthah as well. The daughter, however, is more than exonerated. Like his Protestant colleagues, Vermigli praises her and insists she was free to veto her father's vow, whether she knew it or not. And Vermigli commends the annual mourning for Jephthah's daughter for its value not only as a warning to other parents against foolish vows, but also as a remembrance of this "great matter" of the daughter's death.[22]

There are many more historical details that would enrich our understanding of Jephthah's daughter, but we will end with a look down the road to a sermon preached by the Puritan Richard Rogers sometime before 1615. He has only the highest possible words of praise for the courage, obedience, and grace of Jephthah's daughter. But what makes his remarks even more striking is his unexpected allusion to Hebrews 11. Earlier, we noted that some feminist readers find it a bitter irony that Jephthah should be praised in Hebrews 11:32, while his daughter is forgotten. Rogers, by contrast, looks forward to Hebrews 11:34 and proclaims that the praise in that verse for those "who by faith grew strong" surely applies to Jephthah's daughter.[23] In effect, this Puritan preacher has given to Jephthah's daughter the place on that roll of heroes that she had previously been long denied. Rogers goes on to tell his flock that the annual lament described at the end of Judges 11 is a fitting custom — and "it should not be forgotten."

Remembering Jephthah's Daughter Today

In his attempt to trace how Jephthah's daughter has inspired literary, musical, and artistic responses, Wilbur Sypherd reckoned to have found more than 300 plays and poems, over 170 musical compositions, and nearly a hundred artistic representations of this story and its motifs.[24] But there is an equally impressive roster of more properly exegetical and theological responses, only a few of which we have sampled here. Clearly, many have remembered Jephthah's daughter, and for diverse reasons. How might an awareness of the history of biblical interpretation shape our own reading of this enigmatic story, the tale of a foolish vow gone bad? Here are three suggestions:

1. JEPHTHAH'S DAUGHTER SHOULD BE REMEMBERED. *There is every reason to resist the lectionary's unfortunate omission of this story. The tragedy of Jephthah's daughter offers pastoral and homiletical opportunities on a number of levels.*

There is no small irony in the message of Judges 11:40, insofar as it tells us of a perpetual remembrance for Jephthah's daughter that endured neither in Israel nor in New Testament times. All that survives is this verse, as an unobserved memorandum. If feminist writers of our day deserve credit for awakening us from our forgetfulness, equal credit should go to those writers of the past who were by no means neglectful of Jephthah's daughter. Many remembered her as a role model for the religious life; some recalled that her action was voluntary, not coerced. Most remembered her as genuinely pious, loyal to her father and her people; some even saw her as a martyr like Jesus, without forgetting that martyrdom is painful and usually beset by ambiguities of its own. Though it is understandable that preachers today can be intimidated by the tragedy, pathos, and ambiguities of this tale, we should be encouraged, if not embarrassed for ourselves, by our forebears' willingness to grapple publicly with such tough material.

2. JEPHTHAH'S DAUGHTER IS AN EXEMPLAR AND WARNING FOR US. *Nearly everyone who has commented on Jephthah's daughter has recognized her as the story's real protagonist. And even when interpreters try to find some rationale for the father's actions, they universally condemn his mortal deed and labor to rule him out as a precedent for anyone.*

45

Some modern readers have properly worried about casting Jephthah's daughter in the patriarchal role of the "dutiful daughter," as if our own children too should offer their parents a prompt and slavish obedience. Their worry is not without basis. Monastic commentators were sometimes capable of such authoritarian counsel, urging children to honor the vows by which their parents had joined them to convents or monasteries. We know today that child abuse in the home correlates in a disturbing way with a family's authoritarianism and religiosity.[25] There is something profoundly right, then, when we find in later commentators a dogged insistence on the limits of parental authority in matters of vows, betrothal, and marriage, not to say matters of life or death! Much as these later commentators wanted their own children to know that even young people could face death with courage, they were equally concerned to warn parents and children that no one has the right to force such a destiny on anyone else.

3. THE CHURCH HAS OFTEN FILLED THE BIBLE'S SILENCES WELL. *Judges 11 probably raises fewer problems by what is said than by what is left unsaid. Nonetheless, the ways commentators have filled in these silences tells us much about how to read this text in the light of the Bible's larger witness to the value of human life.*

Did God secretly approve of Jephthah's sacrifice? Does Jephthah's place among the heroes of Hebrews 11 validate what he did to his daughter? Was he right to blame his daughter? Would she have fared differently if she'd been a son? These are gripping questions that the Bible simply does not resolve. Once asked, they won't go away. The good news, I think, is that traditional commentators did not shy away from them. Accordingly, while they puzzled over just what "the spirit of the Lord" was up to in Jephthah, they overwhelmingly testified that God does not approve of child sacrifice. Even Augustine's startling suggestion that the death of Jephthah's daughter was a divinely-directed object lesson was meant to repudiate imitation, not encourage it. While Jephthah's appearance in Hebrews 11 certainly complicated how his rash vow was evaluated, the consensus is that he was listed as a hero of faith despite his vow, not because of it. Nor did anyone ever endorse his outburst of blame against his daughter. Finally, there were many traditional commentators who saw the incongruity between the death of Jephthah's daughter and the escape of Isaac and Jonathan, and wondered, *why?* Their bafflement over this discrepancy may make them seem unsophisticated by our standards, but it also testifies to their conviction that this girl should not have died, and that daughters are as valuable as sons.

There is little doubt but that the story of Jephthah's daughter is a difficult text, truly a text of terror for many readers. Its silences and ambiguities are challenging for any interpreter. But there seems little reason to tackle it armed only with our own exegetical tools and cleverness, when we could also bring to bear so many centuries of reflection on this text. If God has anything to do with the church, there is surely some wisdom to be found in Christian tradition. We ought to be in the habit of seeking out the counsel of the past.

Sooner or later, I had to answer that question my daughter asked me about Jephthah's daughter. Here's what I said: "Yes, there is such a story in the Bible. It's about a girl who was the daughter of a man named Jephthah. It's very sad, and there's a lot the Bible doesn't seem to explain. But let me tell you also about how the church has remembered her over the years."

Chapter Three

Psalms and Curses

Anger Management, on Earth as It Is in Heaven

I f the story of Jephthah's daughter is rarely featured in the pulpit, the same case surely obtains for the imprecatory psalms — the psalms of lament that often showcase not just the painful predicament of the psalmist, but also various hopes and prayers for revenge. Take, for example, Psalm 137, which poignantly recounts the taunting that was borne by the exiles in Babylon: "Sing us one of the songs of Zion!" But how, the psalmist exclaims, "how could we sing the LORD's song in a foreign land?" More piercing still are the psalm's closing lines:

> O daughter Babylon, you devastator! Happy shall they be who pay you back what you have done to us! Happy shall they be who take your little ones and dash them against the rock!

The anger here is raw. Few of us have likely heard these lines preached in our churches, though the odds of hearing them read, at least, have recently improved. These verses were strategically omitted from the Roman Catholic Liturgy of the Hours in 1970, as "somewhat harsh in tone" and as presenting "difficulties."[1] In 1983, the Common Lectionary followed suit, but in 1992 the Revised Common Lectionary restored them.[2] Nonetheless, many similar psalms have lost snippets to lectionary architects. Here are five to consider:

- *Psalm 28:4-5:* Repay them according to their work, and according to the evil of their deeds; repay them according to the work of their hands; render them their due reward. Because they do not regard the works of the LORD, or the work of his hands, he will break them down and build them up no more.

- *Psalm 58:6-10:* O God, break the teeth in their mouths; tear out the fangs of the young lions, O LORD! . . . Let them be like the snail that dissolves into slime; like the untimely birth that never sees the sun. . . . The righteous will rejoice when they see vengeance done; they will bathe their feet in the blood of the wicked.

- *Psalm 69:22-28:* Let their table be a trap for them, a snare for their allies. Let their eyes be darkened so that they cannot see, and make their loins tremble continually. Pour out your indignation upon them, and let your burning anger overtake them. May their camp be a desolation; let no one live in their tents. For they persecute those whom you have struck down, and those whom you have wounded, they attack still more. Add guilt to their guilt; may they have no acquittal from you. Let them be blotted out of the book of the living; let them not be enrolled among the righteous.

- *Psalm 79:10-13:* Why should the nations say, "Where is their God?" Let the avenging of the outpoured blood of your servants be known among the nations before our eyes. Let the groans of the prisoners come before you; according to your great power preserve those doomed to die. Return sevenfold into the bosom of our neighbors the taunts with which they taunted you, O LORD! Then we your people, the flock of your pasture, will give thanks to you forever; from generation to generation we will recount your praise.

- *Psalm 139:19-22:* O that you would kill the wicked, O God, and that the bloodthirsty would depart from me — those who speak of you maliciously, and lift themselves up against you for evil! Do I not hate those who hate you, O LORD? And do I not loathe those who rise up against you? I hate them with perfect hatred; I count them my enemies.

Of these five examples, the Revised Common Lectionary wholly omits Psalms 28 and 58, cites only earlier verses from 69 and 79, and includes all the soaring and graceful verses of Psalm 139 except for the four above,

50

which intrude such a note of vehemence shortly before the psalm's serene ending, "Search me, O God, and know my heart."

The Divided Mind of Lectionary Design

The tendency of lectionaries such as the Liturgy of the Hours and the Revised Common Lectionary to avoid "harsh" passages is understandable, but ironic. Understandable, in that bathing our feet in the blood of our enemies seems hopelessly at odds with the sort of footwashing that Jesus enjoined upon his disciples in John 13. Ironic, in that lectionaries are usually drawn up so that readers and preachers might *broaden* the scope of their reading and preaching, not narrow it. Yet there can be little doubt but that modern lectionaries have effectively sanitized the Psalter in the name of something like niceness.

Directly or indirectly, psalms have always been the backbone of Christian worship and liturgy. They have been chanted, sung, read responsively, versified, and paraphrased. They have inspired not only poems and classic hymns, but also praise choruses and Christian rock and roll. But what shall we do with the imprecations, these disturbing curses? Should we follow the lead of the lectionaries and skip them? Or should we play them up? On the one hand, it is hard to miss that we live in a bewilderingly angry world, with a proliferation of crime, injustice, battering, road rage, terrorism, genocide, assassinations, bullying, impatience, unkindness, and revenge. Don't the Psalter's imprecations speak to this world? On the other hand, these verses seem to model, if not warrant, an unchecked expression of the worst human sentiments. Do we really want to find a license for our anger in the Psalms, so that Christians can more freely join the volatile ranks of those who are ready to lash out at everything?

The impulse that has led lectionary designers to bury the imprecations is but one of the approaches to the Psalter today. Other recent voices — ranging from evangelical Christians to feminist revisionists — have argued instead for a re-appropriation of these powerful verses. Although one might begin with these newer arguments for some sort of utility to be found in the imprecations, this chapter will unfold somewhat differently. We will eventually look at how some modern writers are returning to these "censored" parts of the Psalter, but first we will examine the varied places our exegetical forebears gave to the psalmists' curses and enemies.

"Christianizing" the Psalms: Preliminary Issues

The Psalms have benefited from an avalanche of attention over the centuries, which is simply what one might expect, given the historic centrality of the Psalms for worship, prayer, and piety. Since this chapter is intended as a supplement to other exegetical literature, not as a substitute, there are many issues that we cannot address here — including the historical origins of the Psalms, textual and translation problems, the various genres of psalms, liturgical uses in the past, and so on.[3] All of these topics may help readers and preachers, but our concern is necessarily more narrow. With respect to the imprecations, then, only two "technical" issues require immediate attention. First, who is being cursed in the Psalms? Second, what happens when Jesus cites or is otherwise associated with a psalm?

Where Did These Curses Come From?

Even though modern scholars often discount the accuracy of the superscribed titles that identify various psalms as authored by David (or Asaph, or the Korahites, or Moses), Christian readers from antiquity through the Reformation were not inclined to doubt these ascriptions. Consequently, when they considered the imprecations within any given psalm, it was often important to try to understand the psalmist's anger in light of the probable historical situation that provoked such outcries.

The impulse to care about the "historical" meaning of a psalm is really twofold. On the one hand, to know David's extremity of circumstance could itself function as an apology for his rage: extremes of anguish naturally give rise to extremes of expression. On the other hand, an accurate identification of David's enemies might also make his desire for their punishment or extinction less shocking: perhaps they really *did* deserve what the psalmist prayed for! As we will see, this sort of historical concern marked especially the reading and exegesis of the Reformation, but there were also precedents among the church fathers and medieval writers.

Where Are These Curses Going? The Messianic Complication

As often as not, the interest of early Christians in the historical origins or meaning of the Psalms was upstaged by a more recent development. The writers of the New Testament were quick to recognize in Jesus the embodiment or fulfillment of many of the Psalms' most dominant themes, foremost of which is the "royal" status of Jesus as the anointed one of God, followed closely by Jesus' identity as the "righteous sufferer" who gives voice to many of the laments and imprecations. The recognition was facilitated, naturally, by Jesus' own use of the Psalter. Thus, in the Gospels, Jesus alludes to various psalms in the Sermon on the Mount, in conversations during Holy Week, at the Last Supper, and, of course, in the words he uttered from the cross. Beyond Jesus' direct statements, however, the gospel writers found still other messianic anticipations in the Psalms, as did St. Paul and the author of the epistle to the Hebrews.

Jesus' use of the Psalms presents a double complication. Not only are some psalms applied to Jesus Christ messianically, as fulfilling the roles of Davidic king and righteous sufferer, but this same Messiah also taught that *we* should love our enemies. You can see the tension: Jesus taught an ethic of love, yet he also fulfills a Davidic role, so that David's sufferings *and* David's prayers against his enemies are transferred to Jesus. Christians rarely feel compelled to adopt *David's* stance toward the Philistines, the Ziphites, or Doeg the Edomite, but they usually take more seriously those who look like enemies of *Jesus*. In the early church in particular, considerable industry was devoted to figuring out who, among their contemporaries, should be reckoned among the enemies of Jesus that these Psalms seem to mention.

How the Church Fathers Learned to Curse from the Psalms (or Not)

If the Psalms constitute a large and complex book, the literature on the Psalms is vastly greater. Two dozen or so patristic commentaries survive in whole or part, and that's just the beginning. No short survey of the history of the interpretation of the imprecations can hope to be very detailed. For my part, I will attempt to tell the story in only four movements, with a final coda for considering how some of our own contemporaries are thinking about imprecations and laments. The first three movements correspond to the various "senses" or levels of meaning that Christians have traditionally seen in Scripture: allegory, typology, and the literal or historical sense. We'll trace these through the three main currents or schools of patristic interpretation, then turn (in the fourth movement) to see just what changed in late medieval and Reformation exegesis. As much as possible, we'll focus on a handful of psalms with imprecations that are unambiguous — if not notorious.[4]

Origen: Embarrassing Texts and the Allegorical Imperative

To read the Psalms with an eye on the imprecations quickly brings one to the origins of allegorical exegesis. For the earliest Christians, the Bible was of course the inspired word of God, but some texts and stories were problematic. The Bible was given by God to guide and edify believers, but how were Christians supposed to derive guidance or edification from texts that seem to model immorality? A brilliant teacher of the third century, Origen of Alexandria responded to this challenge by suggesting that the offensive meaning on the surface of the narrative was not the real meaning God intended. Instead, there were other meanings that might be found by the spiritually mature — meanings about the moral life of the soul, and even subtler meanings about invisible realities and our spiritual life, now and in the future.[5] Thus, narratives that seem offensive are really not so. Just the opposite: such stories actually conceal wonderful lessons in morality, as well as a glimpse of the life to come. We saw this in an earlier chapter: Abraham's marriage to Hagar urges us not to polygamy but toward the acquisition of virtue. Of course, finding helpful allegories in otherwise embarrassing or problematic texts was not invented by Origen (though he was both admired and despised as a master of the form); it was an approach generally favored by interpreters in the so-called "Alexandrian" school since the first century.

Although Origen wrote extensively on the Psalms in a variety of forms, only nine homilies survive in translation, along with a fair number of Greek fragments. Even from these glimpses, it is possible to sketch something of his typical moves. Although the curses in the Psalms are directed at literal, human enemies, Origen reads them as targeting the enemies of the moral or spiritual life — our vices, in particular, but also our spiritual (demonic) opponents. In Psalm 23, the "enemies" in whose presence a table is set are the various afflictions Christians bear. In Psalm 137, the exiles' taunting captors remind Origen of demons, who (he recounts) mock Christians when they sin; to dash the "little ones" of Babylon is to use the teachings of Christ to destroy one's own evil thoughts.[6] Origen's allegories are practical: the Psalms, it turns out, are filled with metaphors for one's pursuit of piety, spirituality, and morality. Similar readings were widely adopted by other Christian writers, who found this sort of "internalizing" of the imprecations a good way to reconcile the harsh words of the psalmist with the higher morality taught by Jesus.

A century after Origen, another Alexandrian wrote not only his own set of expositions of the Psalms, but also a short treatise on the interpretation of the Psalms for devotional use. For Athanasius, the Psalms are a mirror of the soul's emotions[7] — a characterization that will recur in many later writers, including Augustine and Calvin. Accordingly, it is scarcely surprising that Athanasius, too, sees the enemies of the Psalms in terms of his own *spiritual* opponents. But if Athanasius's list of enemies began with his own vices, he was perfectly capable of branding his literal human opponents (particularly followers of the Arian heresy) as enemies of Christ and the church as well as his personal enemies.[8] Indeed, in his letter to Marcellinus, which purports to focus on the devotional use of the Psalms, Athanasius frequently imagines his Christian reader beset by literal enemies or slanderers and prescribes specific psalms as antidotes. The vehement pleas of Psalm 58, for instance, can be applied to one's foes — albeit "for their humiliation" and not, apparently, for their demise.

As a younger man, Jerome was much enamored of Origen's exegesis, but the controversy over Origenism led him to distance himself in later years. Jerome's homilies and short commentary on the Psalms remain good examples of moral interpretation mixed with a moderate use of allegory. The imprecations are variously handled. When he finds a psalm of lament to be clearly about Christ, "enemies" are read in terms of the historic or present opponents of Christ and the church. Psalm 109, cited in the New Testament passion narratives, incites a long and bitter polemic against Judas but especially against the Jews. Yet the ending is conciliatory: however much this psalm foreshadowed the mistreatment of Jesus, the imprecations of v. 29 are pronounced not against the Jews, but on their behalf, leading them to repentance. We, too, are not to curse the Jews but pray for them.[9] A similar move is made at Psalm 79:12, while Psalm 140:9 is taken not as a curse per se, but as a prophecy of what happens to evildoers. Psalm 137 is the most properly allegorical of this sample, and Jerome follows Origen here, taking enemies as "vices" but adding a typological twist (derived from 1 Corinthians 10:4) to prove that the "rock" against which such "little ones" are dashed is Christ himself.[10]

Jerome illustrates two points that will be even clearer in Augustine. First, "spiritual" or figurative readings of the Bible often interweave allegories of individual morality with typological readings that focus on the person or work of Christ. Second, while the church fathers were not slow to identify their enemies, they were usually reluctant to curse them or to establish precedents for other Christians to do so.

Augustine & Typology: Finding "the Whole Christ" in the Psalms

It would not be fair to treat the Alexandrian allegorists as only moralists of the Psalms, for they were also apt to find messianic references, as Jerome's treatment of Psalm 137 illustrates. Nonetheless, no one was more influential on the theology and exegesis of the Latin-speaking West (including Protestant Europe) for the next thousand years than Augustine — despite the smallness of his claim to originality, for his writings on the Psalms frequently draw on Jerome and other predecessors, and perhaps Origen as well.

In any case, Augustine's comments and homilies conveniently illustrate a typological reading of the Psalms — a reading that makes Christ the subject of the *entire* Psalter, not just of the psalms quoted in the New Testament. Usually, *On Christian Doctrine* is seen as his definitive account of the interpretation of Scripture. There, he says that building up love — love of God and love of one's neighbor — is the end or purpose of the Bible, without which no passage has been correctly understood.[11] But his homilies on the Psalms refine that account; according to one scholar, "Augustine consistently routes the interpretation of the frequent psalm title, 'unto the end *(finis)*, a psalm of David,' through Romans 10:4, 'Christ is the end *(finis)* of the law,' that is, its fulfillment or purpose."[12] In other words, the end or goal of reading the Bible is not to read about love in the abstract, but rather to find Christ and faith in Christ, who models love in his incarnation and crucifixion, bestows love on his body the church, and leads us to love rightly God and our neighbor.

Consequently, though Augustine might note that a psalm was composed by David, he rarely lingers over that historical point but moves quickly to a Christological, prophetic reading. Yet if Christ is the focus of every psalm, he plays various roles.[13] Sometimes Christ is spoken to or about, while in other texts he speaks in his own voice, either as the suffering, crucified one or as the triumphant and resurrected Lord. As the "second Adam," Christ can also speak in the Psalms to or in the name of fallen humanity[14] or redeemed humanity — that is, Christ can speak *to* or *as* his body, the church.[15]

The Christological/ecclesiological preoccupation that Augustine cultivated dictates his approach to the imprecations. While he recognizes the anguish of those who suffer persecution and deals pastorally with such pain (mindful as he is of the martyrs of the church's not-so-distant past), he rarely worries about the circumstances of David or Israel that gave rise to these laments and curses.[16] Augustine's own hearers are far more perplexed by the tension between the psalmist's cry for vengeance and Jesus' command to love one's enemies.[17]

Augustine addressed that tension by drawing on several stock ingredients. First of all, he tried to see the "enemies" of the psalmist as Jesus would, that is, as the spiritual enemies that Christians should fear most because they wound not the body but the soul. Such enemies are often one's own vices, though they may also be such spiritual threats as heretics, schismatics, or the devil himself.[18] Psalm 137 is a classic instance, and Augustine is happy to recycle the allegory used by Origen and Jerome, reading the psalm as a tale of our own captivity at the hands of the devil and his angels:

> Who are the little ones of Babylon? Newly-born evil desires. There are some, to be sure, who struggle against a desire that is full-grown. So when a desire is born, before evil habit gives it strength against you, when the desire is little, by no means let it gain the strength of perverse habit! When it's little, dash it! But are you afraid that though you've dashed it, it won't die? Dash it against the rock! "The rock, however, was Christ."[19]

Israel's Babylonian enemies are, allegorically, our enslaving, diabolical sins. Yet where Jerome's exposition (originally delivered to monks) spoke mostly in terms of individual or personal morality, Augustine's account is cast as a lament of the body of Christ. If sin now holds us captive in Babylon, there is yet the hope of freedom in Jerusalem, a figure of the church as it will be. The theme of captivity provokes him not only to call for individual repentance but also to recall the persecutions the church has endured at the hands of its enemies.

Against declared enemies of Christ, one would think, there is no reason not to utter curses, but — again, like Jerome — Augustine buffers even this insight by insisting that what look like prayers or curses against an enemy are really prophecies. In other words, the psalmist is merely *predicting* the judgment of God, not wishing for it or calling it forth.[20] But there is another way Christians can wish for vengeance. In Psalm 139:22, the psalmist (speaking as the body of Christ) declares his "perfect hatred" for the enemies of God. Augustine reminds his hearers here (as also elsewhere) of what is a commonplace even today, namely, that we should hate the sin but love the sinner.[21] The sort of vengeance that Christians are supposed to seek, then, consists in their enemies' *conversion*, not destruction. Of course, these prayers for vengeance also foretell the just judgments of God, whether they come sooner or later. However, "our enemy is to be loved in such a way that we are not dissatisfied with the divine justice that punishes him; yet our satisfaction in that punitive justice must derive not from the bad consequences for the offender but from the goodness of the judge."[22]

In sum, Augustine deals with the imprecations in their historical context mostly by ignoring the imprecations' origins and context. At the same time, he plays up these laments and curses for their enduring ability to capture the spiritual grief that accompanies persecution — whether our own sufferings or those of Christ. Thus, Christians may truly have real enemies in this life, but those enemies are rarely "earthly" opponents. Instead they are magnified as threats to one's eternal soul or even threats to the survival of the church. Yet they are also placed at a distance, insofar as vengeance in any usual sense is reserved for God alone.

There are two distinct worries we may wish to air with Augustine. One has already been noted: his lack of concern for the historical context of the imprecations. However much a typological reading may allow Christians to appropriate them without retaining their apparent venom, are we not obliged to acknowledge that the origins of these curses may not have been so pure? Equally troubling, however, are Augustine's own applications of these curses. However much Augustine may have succeeded (or not) at "hating" *his* enemies perfectly, that is, with an eye to their conversion and repentance, it remains that he was not slow to identify them. The enemies of Christians are not only demons, vices, and lusts; they also include persecutors, heretics, and schismatics. For Augustine, imprecatory psalms are most commonly populated by Jews and Donatists, who are obviously enemies of Christ and his church.[23] And while he does not encourage his pa-

rishioners to curse them or take their own vengeance, there is nothing ambiguous about their status as hell-bound enemies of Christ and his church.
Granted that Augustine saw himself in the midst of a contest for the survival of the church, one may still take exception to such charged rhetoric.
By his own admission, Augustine was committed to allow God to be the
sole judge. Why, then, did he feel so constrained to demonize his opponents in advance of that divine and eschatological judgment?

Avoiding Allegorical Enemies: Imprecations in Antioch

We may begin the third part of this tour of the imprecations by recalling
that the Greek-speaking church fathers were not all advocates of Alexandrian, allegorical interpretation. To the north, in Asia Minor, there flour-
ished the school of Antioch, which opposed the arbitrariness of allegory
and urged instead a careful adherence to the letter of the text. Several of
the leading Antiochene interpreters wrote on the Psalms, including
Diodore of Tarsus, Theodore of Mopsuestia, John Chrysostom, and
Theodoret of Cyrus. An examination of the latter two will make clear that
focusing on the original sense of a psalm doesn't necessarily resolve the
mystery or scandal of the curses.

John Chrysostom preached through much of the book of Psalms in
Antioch in the 380s or 390s, before he became the Patriarch of Constantinople in 398.[24] Although he certainly recognizes the messianic significance
that the New Testament cedes to some psalms, his reluctance to proceed
without the warrant of the New Testament emerges from his exposition of
Psalm 109. For Jerome, that entire psalm was directed against Judas (as per
v. 8b, cited in Acts 1:20) and, by extension, against the Jews in general.
Chrysostom, though usually hostile toward the Jews, sees Judas as the object of the curses (uttered prophetically by David) only in the first half of
the psalm; the rest pertains to someone else.[25] Even then, Chrysostom
scarcely rails against Judas. Instead, his remarks are notable in two other
ways. First, he seems quite impressed with the speaker's vehemence:

> Goodness me! How extreme his anger, when not even the untimeli-
> ness of orphanhood may meet with mercy. . . . Do you see his lan-
> guage brimming with wrath, nowhere reaching its peak? . . . What
> he is anxious to say is this: kill him, slaughter him, do away with

59

him. . . . Do not the words astonish the listener? Are you not anxious to hear who is this person condemned like this?[26]

Second, though the betrayer of Jesus would seem an ideal candidate for such wrath, Chrysostom softens these curses for his hearers. They are really predictions, he says, couched as curses for rhetorical effect. Indeed, they signal how "God's unspeakable rage" always hangs over "such people," who bring this end on themselves. Moreover, the call for shaming in v. 29 suggests that the psalmist even hopes for his enemies' correction. Chrysostom takes the same position in Psalm 139, translating v. 19 as "If only you would kill sinners, O God," and adding the qualification that "he asks for it to happen, not to destroy the existence of the people but to change them from sin to righteousness. He did not say, note, 'If you kill people,' but *sinners*."[27]

Psalm 137:9 illustrates still further Chrysostom's discomfort with imprecation. To his credit, he appreciates the invective as expressing the captives' "intense anger" against the Babylonians. Yet he will not allow such an expression as worthy of the psalmist himself; it is rather, in effect, a quotation.

> The inspired authors, after all, say many things not on their own account but to describe the feelings of others and bring them to the fore. . . . When he tells of the sufferings of others, he depicts their anger, their pain, . . . bringing to the fore the desire of the Jews, who let their rage extend even to such a young age [that is, to the "little ones" of Babylon]. The teaching of the New Testament is not like that, however: we are bidden to give food and drink to our enemies, to pray for those who abuse us.[28]

True as Chrysostom means to be to the historical sense of this psalm, it remains that the psalm's original meaning is now obsolete. Jesus' teachings are more lofty than what the Jews knew, even as Christians are called to a higher righteousness, to love their enemies rather than curse them — as even the psalmist seems to have suspected.

Theodoret penned his commentary on the Psalms about half a century after Chrysostom. Despite his affinities for Antiochene exegesis, he saw himself as following a middle path, between those who read the Psalms allegorically and those who focused so exclusively on the historical meaning that they made "a case rather for Jews than the household of the faith."[29] His treatment of Psalm 137:9, however, models his literal, Antiochene tendencies. There is no moral, much less any allegory, only the historical explanation of the psalmist's outburst as an anticipation of how Babylonian atrocities would be repaid against their own children when the Persian king Cyrus defeated Babylon and freed the Jewish exiles from their captors (in 539).[30]

Psalm 137 signals how Theodoret will read the curses generally, as predictions of punishments to come. Thus, at Psalm 28:4 ("Repay them, O Lord") he warns, "Let no one think, however, that the righteous person is cursing his enemies: the words are a mark not of cursing but of a just verdict" that will one day come to pass.[31] Similarly, some threats are uttered to provoke repentance, as at Psalm 55:15, even as Theodoret can elsewhere make Augustine's point that we should hate the sinner but love these same individuals as fellow humans and mourn over their wickedness.[32] In his remarks on Psalm 109, the "traitor" psalm, he notes the tension between the form of the imprecations and the commands of Jesus:

> Let no one who hears the Lord imposing the obligation to bless our persecutors consider the prophecy to be in opposition to the obligation: the inspired word in this case does not proceed by way of cursing but by foretelling the punishments coming both to Jews and to Judas. This prophecy is expressed as a prayer, as is very much the custom everywhere in the divine Scripture.[33]

In sum, despite Theodoret's arguably more historical interest, his approach to the imprecations is marked by few departures from Chrysostom, or even from Augustine. Granted, he resisted a homiletical application of these curses against allegorical enemies, but *all* the fathers recognized some psalms and imprecations as linked to Christ and his enemies. In turn, these curses implicated the visible enemies of the church along with the spiritual enemies faced by individual Christians. Nonetheless, when coupled with the Sermon on the Mount — again, a move made by *all* the fathers — the imprecations were inevitably hobbled and transformed. Though their messianic content forced them into the church, to be redirected against enemies visible or spiritual, these passionate cries still had to be sanctified. Read most often now as predictions, the curses were stripped of subjectivity and venom. All the ill to come could be seen as deserved, providential, inevitable, and just — and perhaps remedial, even salutary. But one thing changed above all: they were no longer curses.

Curses & Enemies in the Reformation

Psalm commentaries did not disappear during the Middle Ages, of course, but some of the old answers did grow pat. Thomas Aquinas can resolve the tension with the Sermon on the Mount with a quick and formulaic aside: "All the curses read in the prophets can be understood in three ways," either as a prediction or pronouncement of what will follow; as an expression of divine justice; or as a "'spiritual' denunciation," in that (he explains) "when sinners cease to sin, they die and cease to be sinners — something we should always pray for."[34]

Nonetheless, a fresh look was taken at many familiar texts of the Bible during the tumultuous sixteenth century — that time of religious and theological renewal as well as persecution, flight, and war. As is well known, Protestant Reformers sought to recover the plain and literal meaning of the Bible by freeing it from extraneous traditions and capricious allegorical inventions. Such an agenda did not mean they ignored the views of their predecessors. Nor, given the New Testament's use of the Psalms to interpret both the kingship and sufferings of Christ, were they likely to discard the typological reading of certain psalms.

Martin Luther and the "Curses of Faith"

Luther commented on the Psalms several times during his career, beginning with early lectures in 1513-16, again in 1518-21, and a shorter series in 1530-32, along with many other sermons and expositions of selected psalms.[35] The legacy of a typological reading of the imprecations looms large in Luther, who was much influenced by the approach to the Psalms advocated by Jacques Lefèvre d'Étaples, his older contemporary.

Lefèvre not only took Augustine's view that Christ is the focus of the entire psalter, but also insisted that to read the psalter as speaking of Christ — *not* David — was the only true *literal* reading.[36] In his earliest lectures, Luther was quick to echo Lefèvre, and if his later lectures and sermons restored considerable historical significance to David and Israel, Luther's exposition remained preoccupied with the enemies of Christ.

> Just as the *apostles* in their day applied the Psalms against their enemies the Jews, the *martyrs* in their day against their persecutors, the

teachers in their day against heretics (as blessed Augustine demonstrates almost everywhere), so also today *we* should pray and apply them against half-Christians who serve the Lord carnally, with lip service alone.[37]

Luther's approach to the curses is shaped by his "two kingdoms" ethic, which carefully distinguishes between faith and love. God wants our faith and trust, not our works of love. It's not that good works aren't *good:* true, they cannot save or justify us, but they are perfectly appropriate and welcome when we use them to meet our neighbor's need. By extension, it is the *church's* calling to proclaim the gospel and thus awaken faith (which cannot be coerced), while the *state* is charged to keep order in society (which often requires coercion). *Faith* requires me to trust God for my own protection against enemies, but *love* requires me to protect my neighbor. It is a disastrous error to confuse these two realms and protocols, whether the confusion is on the part of the individual Christian, the church, or the magistrate.

Building on this distinction, Luther raises the problem of curses in Psalm 109, a psalm David composed about Christ, who pronounces "terrible curses" upon Judas and "everyone of Judas's ilk," including "Judaism as a whole" as well as "all schismatics and persecutors of the Word of Christ." But why, Luther asks, does Christ utter such curses here, when in the Sermon on the Mount he prohibits cursing?

> In brief, the answer is: *Love* does not curse or take vengeance, but *faith* does. . . . When the wicked persecute the Gospel, . . . this strikes at God and at His cause. We are not to bless them or wish them luck when they do this. Otherwise no one could preach or write even against heresy, because that is impossible without cursing. . . . These I would call "curses of faith.". . . Before faith would permit the Word of God to be destroyed and heresy to stand, it would prefer that all creatures be wiped out; for heresy deprives one of God Himself. The cursing of Christ in this psalm, then, is not on account of His person but on account of His office and His Word, because the error of the Jews is seeking to establish itself and to beat down the Gospel. . . . In short, it is permissible to curse on account of the Word of God; but it is wrong to curse on your own account for personal vengeance or some other personal end.[38]

In his advice here, Luther does several things well. He preserves the character of these psalms as curses, not merely predictions; he repudiates using these psalms to justify a personal vendetta; he recognizes that there are real enemies of Christ and his church, and as such they are not to be accommodated. What makes it harder simply to adopt Luther's views today, of course, is the likelihood that we no longer agree with his assessment of just who the enemies of Christ were, much less still are.

John Calvin: Only Reprobation Makes an Enemy

Calvin's exegesis of the Psalms recalls the historical approach of the Antiochene school. As happened to some of the Antiochenes, Calvin's restraint in finding Christ in the Psalms drew accusations that his reading of the Old Testament was too Jewish, too uninformed by the New Testament, and thus sub-Christian.[39] The charge was undeserved: Calvin is quite capable of recognizing Christological references, usually those cited in the New Testament, but he refuses to lose sight of David's authorship. Moreover, he regularly sees David acting or speaking as a representative of Christ.

Calvin's exposition of the imprecations relies heavily on the link between David and Christ to maintain both its theological and its historical character.[40] The imprecations are harsh, Calvin admits, as at Psalm 79:6 ("Pour out thy fury upon the heathen"), where he notes that this prayer seems "inconsistent with the rule of charity," for the faithful ought to seek unbelievers' salvation, not their destruction.[41] How, then, can such prayers for revenge stand in the Scriptures? For Calvin, the solution lies in the office, character, and discernment of the psalmist — usually, David. As for *office*, Calvin claims in Psalm 41:10 ("raise me up, that I may repay them") that David acted lawfully not only as king and judge (and thus not as a private person) but also as representative of Christ. As for David's *character*, Calvin is sure that as also representing the person of Christ, David "cherished in his heart pure and holy affections," neither indulging "his own angry spirit" nor speaking "from an impulse of the flesh."[42]

As for the psalmist's *discernment*, Calvin frequently imputes to David (and other writers of psalms) the ability to distinguish which of his or God's enemies are beyond repentance. Only those who are, in fact, incapable of repentance — in other words, those who are truly to be numbered among the eternally reprobate — are liable to the kinds of curses we find in the Psalms. Calvin doesn't mind working backwards here: wherever he finds such vehement curses, there he assumes the psalmist has discerned, and now declares, the outcome of divine judgment. Thus Calvin reads Psalm 137 as simply a further indication of the punishments against Edom promised in Ezekiel, Jeremiah, and Obadiah.

> To pray for vengeance would have been unwarrantable, had not God promised it, and had the party against whom it was sought not been reprobate and incurable; for as to others, even our greatest enemies, we should wish their amendment and reformation.[43]

Calvin often reformulated his threefold characterization of David for congregational use, so to speak, in Geneva. The point to be taken was that anyone who wishes to echo David's curses against his enemies should also possess his calling and piety. In other words, prayers of cursing are not to be employed by private persons for personal vengeance; such prayers are to be offered on behalf of the whole church, usually by those who are called by office to offer such prayers. In addition, one must be free from angry passion and possess the wisdom of the Holy Spirit. Calvin regularly cites Luke 9:54, where Jesus rebuked James and John for wishing to call down fire from heaven upon the Samaritans. Christians should pray for their enemies, not give in to misplaced zeal.[44] At the same time, Christians may also pray for some display of God's "fatherly love," by which Calvin seems to hope for some sign of how the death of his servants is precious to God. But Calvin is keenly aware that today's enemies may repent tomorrow, and he insists that unless one has assurance that one's enemies are reprobate and beyond hope, one may not pray for their destruction.[45] In fact, as anyone who knows Calvin's teaching on predestination will recall, while the elect may be assured of their own election, *no one* can know the reprobation of another — not even one's own.

Calvin's warnings here might seem to remove the imprecations from being appropriated at all, but that is not so. Rather, his intent is to retain them, albeit with prudence and restraint, as evidence that God cares for believers who suffer and that justice *will* come.

> By proclaiming vengeance against the ungodly, he subdues and restrains our perverse inclinations, which might lead us to injure a

fellow-creature. By imparting comfort to us, he mitigates and moderates our sorrow, so that we patiently endure the ills which they inflict upon us. . . . And as we cannot distinguish between the elect and the reprobate, it is our duty to pray for all who trouble us; to desire the salvation of all; and even to care for the welfare of every individual. At the same time, if our hearts are pure and peaceful, this will not prevent us from freely appealing to God's judgment, that he may cut off the finally impenitent.[46]

There are plenty of Christians, even in churches with Calvinist roots, for whom predestination is a strange and threatening notion. Here is a fine opportunity to see it used as Calvin intended: to remind Christians of their need for faith, humility, and neighbor-love, even when a neighbor is unjust; but to remind them even more that their heavenly Father reigns, and injustice is doomed.

What Are They Saying about Imprecations Today?

Curiously, although lectionaries and hymnals have often excised the imprecations, writers today are of a much more mixed opinion, and many call for a recognition of the proper place of these psalms in the life of faith and worship. Before turning to some suggestions about what may be learned from the history of interpretation, it will be useful to see some contemporary reflections on the imprecations as a backdrop of sorts. Three observations may be made here.

First, it is common for writers today to note the traditional problem — the offense — of the curses in the Psalms, usually in tandem with an acknowledgment of Jesus' command to love one's enemy. The ferocity of the curses is rarely dodged, and most writers acknowledge the problem of their public use: the curses have made the Psalms a "closed book to many" and some psalms are "almost impossible to use in Christian worship."[47] Accordingly, "we are occasionally justified in omitting certain sequences" or in distinguishing "between the use of these prayers as liturgy and as scripture."[48]

Second, even the writers just quoted, who worry greatly about the public reading of the imprecations, still look for other ways to use or understand these passages in the church. Reasons vary, however. Most of these writers — perhaps in contrast to lectionary editors — think Christians, especially in the West, need reminding that enemies are real, as are evil and injustice.[49] To be sure, virtually everyone has *felt* wronged at some time and has named someone as an enemy, and William L. Holladay warns against an easy self-righteousness.[50] Yet many Christians (and others) truly do suffer, or are wronged and persecuted, and there is something in the rage of these psalms that they can identify with and draw comfort from. But even if these psalms do not speak for us, they ought to be retained as speaking for others in the world. As Walter Brueggemann writes, "vengeance is an urgent agenda in our society," and he finds Psalm 109 — avoided by so many — to be an eloquent brief on behalf of those who are denied justice today.[51] Another poignant example, not really so recent, is the "rite of healing" written by Rosemary Radford Ruether that juxtaposes a letter from a battered wife with laments drawn from Psalm 22 — a jarring arrangement seen earlier in the epitaphs composed by Phyllis Trible.[52]

Third, the quest to find some place for the imprecatory psalms in the life of the church has led many contemporary writers to draw on traditional solutions. C. S. Lewis is more sanguine (though not uncritical) about retrieving moral allegory as a "second meaning" found in psalms such as 137, read introspectively,[53] but there is an even greater move toward a typological reading of sorts. For Bernhard Anderson, "the psalmists' cries for vindication" are recapitulated in the death and resurrection of Jesus Christ, and transformed.[54] For Patrick Miller, it is Jesus who both fulfills and relativizes the imprecations in these psalms:

> The ultimate act of divine vengeance/vindication is in the cross where God receives the world's hatred and overcomes it. The mode of overcoming, God's self-giving and suffering love in Jesus Christ, means that *the curse prayers do not finally teach us how to pray or stand as models of prayer for us.* They may give expression to the thoughts and words and feelings that we cannot let go except as they are let go to God in prayer.[55]

Similarly, although Holladay was willing to omit some of these brutal passages, he later returned to the topic to suggest — explicitly crediting the fathers and Reformers — that a Christological reading of such psalms be combined with a spiritualized understanding of evil in terms of self-destructive and socially malevolent forces. "Jesus Christ," he concludes, "is the only person who may safely pray the Psalms that speak of the evil that dwells in the enemies."[56] Brueggemann also makes a contribution. In his exposition of Psalm 109, curiously, he ignores the propensity of precritical commentators to take the citation of v. 8 in Acts 1:20 as a warrant to read the psalm as a prophecy of Christ's betrayal by Judas. But Brueggemann is not ignorant of the logic at work in such readings. He sees an essentially Christological pattern in the Psalms as a whole, in that the psalmic categories of orientation-disorientation-new orientation mirror the death and resurrection of Jesus Christ. Thus he can conclude that "the Christian use of Psalms is illuminated and required by the crucifixion."[57]

How Should *We* Read the Curses and Enemies in the Psalms?

Against the backdrop of these contemporary voices (admittedly, barely sampled here), and bearing in mind the selectivity and omissions of the lectionaries, what suggestions can be taken from precritical commentators about how to read and appropriate the imprecations? It seems to me that at least four items emerge for our agenda — three suggestions and one warning.

1. GOD CARES ABOUT INJUSTICE AND SUFFERING. *The imprecations and laments directed against enemies in the Psalms, whatever they may say about the character of the psalmists, are always seen as disclosing God's commitment to justice and concern for those who suffer unjustly.*

The history of the interpretation of the imprecations is largely a record of worry: over the character of the curses as expressions of hatred, and over their discrepancy with the teachings of Jesus. For this reason, Christian commentators have often tried to soften them by recasting them as predictions or proverbial wisdom, or by redirecting them introspectively against one's own sinfulness. None of these ameliorations, however, was ever intended to weaken the psalmists' testimony to God's faithfulness in matters of justice and equity and to God's compassion and solidarity for the poor, the weak, and the abused. For many of these commentators, the heat and hatred of the psalmists is uncomfortable, but God's response is sure and full of comfort for the psalmist and for contemporary readers and hearers as well.

2. ONLY JESUS IS FIT TO LAMENT AND CURSE ABSOLUTELY.
There is universal apprehension among the teachers of the church,
both ancient and modern, lest the Bible's curses be kidnapped to set-
tle private scores.

Here is another point where many modern and postmodern writers agree
with the ancients. No one wants to license the curses in the Psalms for general consumption or general use. Indeed, the troubled conscience that led
traditional commentators to hold these curses at arm's length implicitly
suggests that though they, too, knew the pain that could provoke such hatred, they were disinclined to trust themselves (much less their readers or
hearers) to wield unbridled passion. God may not be fast at delivering justice, but precritical commentators believed God to be very good at it nonetheless, largely because they trusted the justice they saw lived and proclaimed by Jesus. By contrast, they also knew that human beings, even
Christians, are far too hasty with justice — and far too often very, very bad
at it. Holladay's assertion that only Jesus Christ can be trusted with impre-
cating his enemies is actually a very old insight. It can be found in Augustine, but it may be more accessible still in Calvin, whose appeal to the doctrine of election underscores that there are indeed radical enemies and
radical evil in the world around us, but we are ourselves too infected to be
trusted with final judgment.

3. LAMENTS AND IMPRECATIONS MUST BE APPROPRIATED.
Precritical commentators believed these harsh passages must be read
and known not only because they are scriptural, inspired, and some-
how authoritative, but also because they are useful — even if also
enigmatic.

Modern commentators have their own reasons for returning to the imprecations, some of which apply psychological insights to matters of anger or
spirituality that surface in these psalms, while others focus more on the
dynamics of justice, injustice, and complicity in society today. Such analy-
ses were probably not of existential interest to the psalmists, but they connect us to these laments by way of analogy. In similar fashion, precritical
commentators drew readers and hearers into the psalmists' world. We
know, for instance, that later Calvinists were greatly formed in their piety
and practice by the Genevan Psalter — so much so that Huguenot soldiers

often rallied by singing psalms, to the terror of Catholic opponents, and Huguenot martyrs recited psalms at their deaths, including the imprecatory Psalm 79.[58] Indeed, it's highly likely that many lay readers will inevitably take the Psalms as theirs to own; the only question is how, and how well? Returning these passages to the lectionary and to pulpit use affords an occasion to shape Christian piety by the wider considerations that commentators of the past and present have regularly voiced.

4. LAMENTS AND IMPRECATIONS MUST NOT BE MISAPPROPRIATED. *The history of Christian anti-Jewish exegesis — along with other variations that have come and gone, by which the enemies of God or Christ are identified among our contemporaries — ought to stand as an object lesson of what* not *to do with the Psalms.*

Finally, a warning. However urgent it is to appropriate the laments and imprecations of the Psalms today as a means of recognizing the godlessness of injustice and evil and enlisting against it, the witness of history also urges us to do so self-critically — and in two ways. Traditional interpreters were quite capable of seeing their complicity in evil as individuals; that's largely what Origen meant when he allegorized the "little ones" of Babylon in terms of our own illicit desires. But there is also danger in uncritically identifying the enemies of Christ with the enemies of our church, or (more likely) our part of it. It would be churlish to scold Christians of the past — say, the martyrs — because they prayed for vindication from lethal enemies. In many cases, having identified their enemies, Christians were content to leave vengeance to the Lord. In other cases, the enmity was mutually mortal, as in the French wars of religion. If Calvin was concerned to remind his hearers that today's enemy may be tomorrow's penitent, the point may have been unaffordable to his Huguenot colleagues in the press of bloody battle. Nonetheless, the supposed enemies of the church in past days — and, truly, they may have been such! — are not necessarily to be demonized in perpetuity. They may have repented. We may have been wrong. In recovering the imprecatory psalms, we must be skeptical of our ability to know for certain who our real enemies really are, when it's enough to know that God is our ally.

Chapter Four

Patriarchs Behaving Badly

How Should We Follow Saints Who Lie,
Cheat, Break Promises, Commit Insurrection,
Endanger Women, and Take Extra Wives?

In the introduction to this book, I recounted the tale of a pastor whose strategy for upholding marriage included a remarkable bit of advice for the Christian wife, namely, that she should submit to her husband no matter what he might ask, even if her conscience should object. His proof-text was the example of Sarah, who submitted to Abraham's scheme to lie and tell everyone that his beautiful wife was really his "sister" — whereupon she was taken by Pharaoh to be betrothed, or worse. What a loyal wife!

Or, what a cowardly husband. I wish I could say that my tale of the cavalier pastor was the *only* time I've heard of someone appealing to a patriarch's unusual, not to say immoral, deeds in order to justify some equally dubious act, but I can't. In fact, it is nothing unusual for readers' curiosity to be piqued when the great characters of the Bible bend or break the rules. My colleagues who teach the book of Genesis tell me that students are always eager to see how these pre-Christian "saints" can be got off the hook. But the history of exegesis also testifies to the abiding interest in these stories. After all, most of the big names in the Old Testament are cited in the New Testament, usually as examples of faith for us to follow. How intriguing, then, when these exemplars act like cads or scoundrels!

Instances of such behavior on the part of the patriarchs of the Old Testament abound. In Romans 4, Abraham is praised by Paul as the father of those justified by faith. That evidently did not stop him from deceiving

71

Pharaoh about Sarah; indeed, the lie was so successful that he repeated it, some years later, to King Abimelech of Gerar, upon whom Isaac tried the same trick still later. Lot is called "righteous" in 2 Peter 2:7, despite having offered his daughters to the men of Sodom and later committing incest with them. Jacob is praised for his faith in Hebrews 11, but the rest of his résumé was a string of lies and sharp dealing: he took advantage of his brother Esau, deceived his dying father, and traded swindles with his father-in-law by clever sheep-breeding. Jacob's sons, patriarchs of the twelve tribes, were scarcely better. Along with their collective treachery toward the Shechemites, whom they slaughtered after having made treaty with them, one may recall Judah's incest with Tamar and Joseph's deception of his brothers. Sometimes the patriarchs' misdeeds are less obvious to modern readers, as when Abraham took up arms against the four kings who had kidnapped Lot. But earlier readers wondered how Abraham, a mere nomad, had the right to wage a war. Holding unrivaled fascination for traditional readers, however, was the apparent endorsement of polygamy that seemed to shine forth from the behavior of Abraham and Jacob, not to mention the later actions of David and Solomon.[1]

Silence Isn't Always Golden

In the case of the patriarchs, none of these deeds is explicitly censured by the Bible itself. Once again, what Scripture does *not* say creates a bigger problem than what it *does* say. Throughout the ages, enquiring minds have wanted to know: if the saints of the Old Testament can do these things, why can't we? Just as often, Christian commentators (themselves usually pastors, too) have burned the midnight oil to bar these stories against such casual imitators — and not without cause! We'll have occasion below to note how some Bible readers thought the patriarchs' example of polygamy — never clearly condemned by the Bible, after all — might be worth reviving in their own day. But even as this chapter was being written, the State of Florida put to death Paul Hill, an anti-abortion activist who shot and killed a doctor at a women's clinic in 1994. The story of Abraham's self-authorized defense of Lot against the four kings — approved, apparently, by the absence of any scriptural word to the contrary — was a significant warrant for Hill's decision to kill in cold blood.[2] Is the silence of Scripture meant to be as permissive as this?

Certainly, a "boys will be boys" attitude would seem vastly out of place here. Over a hundred years ago, contributors to *The Woman's Bible* were quick to note how some of these misdeeds occurred at women's expense, including the "cowardice" and "reprehensible conduct" represented by Abraham's endangerment of Sarah.[3] To the extent that the patriarchs' behavior did put women at risk, one has to wonder if the women mattered to them, or to the narrator. Were these men to be excused at any cost? More to the point for us, however, is a subsequent question. Did later Bible commentators — ancient, medieval, Reformation — conspire to perpetuate the Bible's seeming indifference to such endangerment, as well as its apparent indulgence of immorality when practiced by Old Testament heroes?

In Search of Inspired Excuses

The question of how traditional commentators dealt with the patriarchs' dubious deeds is complicated. Not only is Scripture mostly silent about the ethical significance or precedent to be found in what are generally recognized as scandalous acts, the acts themselves are diverse, as are the approaches and attitudes of commentators. In this chapter, I will try to blend two agendas. One priority is to survey the various Bible passages that tell these tales of indiscretion. I'll do that by grouping them in four categories: lying and deception; endangering the chastity of a wife or daughters; polygamy; and insurrection, or any unauthorized use of force. A second priority is to keep track of the varied arguments commentators invoke to explain the patriarchs' actions and often to excuse or ameliorate their deeds. By and large, "excusatory" arguments are of only two sorts: either these Old Testament saints were acting in accordance with a special or secret divine permission or inspiration; or else there were extenuating circumstances, perhaps easily overlooked by us, that cast a different light on matters. We'll track these natural and supernatural excuses as we look at each of our four categories.

Lies and Deception

Lying is common in the book of Genesis. The best-known patriarchal lies are Abraham's and Isaac's dissimulation regarding the true identities of their wives; Jacob's deception of his father, in which his mother really served as mastermind; and Jacob's manipulation of Laban's flocks to maximize his own. There are, to be sure, other patriarchal lies, but we'll have to restrict our survey to these few.

Although there are many instances of deceit in the Old Testament and many analogies to those listed above, the interpretation of the patriarchs' lies is complicated in two more ways. First, these men are supposed to be heroes, the good guys of the history of Israel and thus of the Christian church. As already noted, many of them are accounted as such in the New Testament, and commentators have traditionally expected them to be especially holy. Writing in the fourth century, Ambrose found in Abraham, Isaac, and Jacob "a pattern of how to live," that we may "follow in their shining footsteps along a . . . path of blamelessness opened up to us by their virtue."[4] But not all of their footsteps prove to be equally shiny! Second, in many cases there are few if any clues in the text to indicate whether these lies were a good idea, divinely approved, or if they were wrong.

Lying as the Lesser of Two Evils?

All commentators were disturbed by the patriarchs' lies, but a high-water mark of worrying was established early on by Augustine, who wrote not one but two treatises on lying.[5] Augustine pondered all sorts of lies, ranging from those told merely as jokes to those meant to help or harm, but he concluded fairly quickly that virtually all lies are evil and endanger the soul of the liar. Where he came nearly to a standstill, however, was over lies told in the hope of avoiding a greater evil. This particular ethical dilemma came to be known as *compensatory evil*. It's concisely stated in a rhetorical question scorned by Paul in Romans 3:8: "Why not do evil that good may come?" But the dilemma is also framed by the familiar if excruciating twentieth-century question: If a Nazi soldier came to your door and asked you if you knew where any Jews were (and you did), what should you say? Unfortunately, the world continues to witness endless variations of this "tragic moral choice," not only in episodes of genocide and ethnic cleansing but also in personal moral decisions. Understandably, Augustine wavered. Lying is evil, without a doubt. But Augustine knew as well as we do that there are so many other horrifying evils that can be done to oneself or to others, including forced idolatry, sexual abuse, and torture. Nonetheless, after making and unmaking his mind more than once, Augustine concluded: all lies are always evil.

Not surprisingly, all the commentators concurred with St. Paul and Romans 3, if not with Augustine — at least in theory! Indeed, the Apostle's sarcastic dismissal of the question virtually mandated agreement. And so, when these interpreters commented on the behavior modeled by the holy patriarchs, they could not easily commend these lies. Instead, they had to add some kind of qualification. Let us turn to the stories to see what they did.

Abraham's Charade: Lying by Permission, or as a Mission

No one thinks it a good idea to endanger one's wife by telling the sort of lie that Abraham and Isaac used. But the scale of ethics changes when God becomes a factor, that is, when or if God were to issue a special command. God, after all, is the lawgiver; and the lawgiver — in the eyes of traditional commentators, at least — is above the law. Accordingly, some set forth as an unimpeachable defense that Abraham acted with God's permission. So argued Huldreich Zwingli in the 1520s, but it was no new idea that Abraham secretly had God's approval or that he had been assured (on the basis of a special revelation) that Sarah would be protected from Pharaoh. This argument was advanced in one form or another in the patristic era by Augustine and Chrysostom, reiterated for medievals by Nicholas of Lyra and Denis the Carthusian, and adopted by several Reformation interpreters.[6] The problem for all these writers, though, was in finding textual evidence to support the claim.

Consequently, many commentators found ways to repackage the bare assertion that Abraham had special permission or a secret revelation. Three variations may be noted, all of which sidestepped the missing evidence. One variation derives from Augustine (inspired by Ambrose and Origen), who heralded *the prophetic or typological role* the patriarchs often played. The argument draws an analogy from Galatians 4, where Paul argued for the allegorical significance of Hagar. Augustine and Ambrose, however, added what Paul did not: that Abraham's polygamous union was divinely arranged for the sake of the later allegory. We'll revisit the question of polygamy below; the point here is that Augustine could make the same case for Abraham's dissimulation. Thus, when Abraham hid the truth that Sarah was his wife, he offered us a prophetic foreshadowing of the church, which is the "secret spouse" of Christ.[7] Such divine lessons allegedly resolve moral offenses by changing them into symbols.

A second variation credits the patriarchs as having a *special divine mission*. As Chrysostom described it, Abraham's "mission" was to spread true religion, and to this end God drove him from place to place and led him into all sorts of scrapes so that, by rescuing and vindicating him, Abraham's virtue was made conspicuous and the fear of God was instilled in all who heard of it.[8] In effect, Abraham's intention (even when driven by fear) was superseded by the divine plan, which overrode lesser moral concerns, as if *means* are a minor issue when the *end* is directed by God. Excuses based on Abraham's special mission were invoked in the late Middle Ages by Paul of Burgos and Denis the Carthusian, and in the Reformation by Conrad Pellican, Johann Oecolampadius, Peter Martyr Vermigli, Wolfgang Musculus, and Martin Luther.[9] John Calvin, however, was not a member of this club.

A third variant calls attention not to the patriarchs' special mission, but to their *special gifts*. After all, in Genesis 20:7 the Lord told Abimelech that Abraham was a prophet. This argument was also suggested by Augustine, but it was amplified by Lyra and Burgos, who claimed Abraham foreknew that his ruse would result not in Sarah's violation but in her deliverance and his. Hence he is scarcely to be blamed, since nothing was risked. Although Pellican and Vermigli also adopted this line, most Reformers did not. Indeed, Luther, Musculus, and Calvin seem deliberate in rejecting it.[10]

Abraham's Charade: Lying as a Form of Prudence

Not all excuses prized by commentators had to discover divine approval. There were other, more common explanations ready to hand. Of course, not all these *explanations* served as *excuses:* for instance, some commentators were content to say that Abraham lied simply because he was afraid.[11] Others note the obvious point that Abraham didn't so much lie as tell a half-truth, since Sarah *was* his sister, though in a more distant sense than usual.[12] Some assert that despite the formal deception, Abraham's intention was not at all malicious.[13] Alert readers may complain that all three of these options look like forms of compensatory evil, in that Abraham chose a less-than-virtuous path regardless of why. The observation is sound, for although many commentators thought his fault was reduced by considering his motive or wording or intention, most still held his lie to be a moral fault.

The most interesting of the non-supernatural explanations, however, is the appeal to the obligation of *prudence*. As this argument goes, God gave human beings the gift of reason and judgment so that they might use it. To fail to act with prudence and to presume on some sort of divine rescue or intervention verges on the serious sin of tempting God. Accordingly, Abraham was simply doing what he could to avoid disaster, and trusting God for the rest. Who could fault that? But Abraham's prudence was actually better gauged and less fear-driven than one might suppose. On the one hand, he was quite right to worry about the loose morals of the Egyptians. On the other hand, he had good reason to think that Sarah would be in no immediate danger of joining Pharaoh's harem, at least not until a twelve-month period of purification had passed. These bits of "inside information" from Josephus and Jerome were cited by many as significantly reducing the scandal by enhancing Abraham's prudence. (The purification is not mentioned in Genesis, of course, but inferred from the book of Esther.) Some commentators liked this amelioration; others found it farfetched.[14]

Abraham's Charade: Lying as a Form of Sin

There is yet one more line of argument regarding the lies told by Abraham and Isaac: they sinned. They may have been filled with fear or they may have had reason to think lying was a shrewd strategy, but it was wrong. Of all the commentators I've read, this conclusion is argued most forcefully by John Calvin and Wolfgang Musculus, though Luther sometimes inclines to this view. Musculus and Calvin dismantle all the would-be ameliorations offered by other commentators, especially the appeals to prudence that would seem to be easiest for us to appropriate. For Musculus, prudence is obliged only where it does not act against God, against another's well-being, or against decorum. Abraham violated all three! "It's no work of faith," Musculus wrote, "to do what is unjust and dishonorable in order to obtain the promise of God."[15] Even if, by the grace of God, Abraham's plan turned out well, his actions remain sinful. Calvin, too, faults Abraham: not for his supposedly great faith but for his unbelief — for *not* casting his cares upon God. Far from modeling prudence, Abraham acted rashly and with presumption. In short, Abraham did not *avoid* tempting God, for ultimately he *did* tempt him.[16]

The exasperation of Musculus and Calvin should probably be read as a rebuke of their predecessors. But it would be wrong to think that *only* Musculus and Calvin were worried about casual imitators of Abraham and Isaac. The exegesis here is constantly disturbed by dissonance. Traditional commentators are disposed to admire Abraham and the other patriarchs. They don't want to set them up as villains. But neither do they want to foster what we would call copycat crimes. Consequently, while we ought to concur with the harsher judgments of Calvin and Musculus here, we should not ignore what else is intended by even the more improbable excuses offered above, namely, that Abraham's excuses — whether extraordinary or fragile — are almost certainly not available to us. Precritical commentators do hope to excuse Abraham, but not at any cost.

Jacob the Trickster

Although there are many things not to like about Jacob, his most notorious misdeeds are the deception that he perpetrated on his dying father in order to receive the blessing meant for Esau, and his use of peeled sticks (Genesis 30:37) to manipulate the flocks of Laban, his father-in-law, so that the speckled and spotted sheep Laban had granted him would be more numerous and stronger.

In both cases, most of the excuses offered on behalf of Abraham's lie are also extended to Jacob, including various appeals to divine permission, typology, good intentions, and the obligation of prudence. The scheme of Jacob and his mother, to be sure, benefits from the oracle to Rebekah (Genesis 25:23) that "the elder will serve the younger." Some take this as implicitly granting her divine permission to redirect her husband's misplaced affection for Esau. Luther's bold comments are of particular interest. Comparing Jacob's lie to the Israelites' spoiling of the Egyptians on the eve of the exodus, he asserts that "to take from another by deceit what God has given you is not a sin," but rather (if done by divine command) "a saintly, legitimate, and pious fraud." Indeed, he compares Jacob's trick to the deception which Christ practiced upon the devil and by which we were redeemed.[17] Calvin, by contrast, is disinclined to excuse Jacob at all.

Luther is equally outspoken, and perhaps equally worrisome, in his account of Jacob's sheep-breeding. In his view, the ploy was "necessary" on account of Laban's "unjust rapacity," and he adds that looking after one's own family is a matter of both divine and human law. (Several commentators cited 1 Timothy 5:8 for the same point.) Did Jacob really cheat Laban, then? Yes, but Luther provides three excuses: Jacob is excused by *human right,* as well as by natural and civil law, according to which those who serve unjust masters without pay may recover what is owed to them, so long as they do not act to their master's detriment. Jacob is also excused by *divine authority* and by what Luther terms *extreme necessity,* essentially a corollary of the first excuse. In a postscript to these excuses, Luther belabors Jacob's hardships and his benefits to Laban so as to stress how rare Jacob's circumstances were — and how unlikely it is that anyone else would ever have cause to take him as an example. Nonetheless, the appeal to natural rights implicitly furnished a rationale for resisting oppression that, once spoken, Luther could neither deny nor call back.[18]

Once again, Calvin writes in contrast to Luther. While he, too, knows that our duties to our families are prescribed by Scripture — that is, by divine law — he frets over the quick application of "natural rights" to Jacob's case, for the Bible also says we are not to avenge ourselves. Although Calvin does excuse Jacob in this instance, he prefers to think God led Jacob to this plan, as seems implied by the dream Jacob narrated a few verses later.[19] Still, one may wonder whether Calvin is worried more by Luther here than by Jacob.

Pandering and Endangerment

To some extent, the chief instances of endangering another person's chastity — specifically, Sarah's and Rebekah's — have already been introduced. Nonetheless, these particular patriarchal misdeeds elicit other comments that go beyond the question of lying and deception. And there is also the notorious incident in Genesis 19 to consider, where Lot offered his daughters to be ravished by the men of Sodom.

Exposing a Wife to Adultery

What should be added to our earlier account of the deception practiced by Abraham and Isaac in calling their wives "sisters" is some notice of the greater gravity attributed to sins against chastity. Luther again serves as a case in point, for while he might be willing to excuse Abraham's lie, he refused to excuse him for exposing Sarah to adultery.[20] Writing in another context, Luther stated categorically that "the Holy Spirit does not move or impel anyone to fornication and incest."[21] Luther was not alone in abhorring sexual crimes and infidelity. Writing against Peter Comestor's assertion in the twelfth century that Abraham received a dispensation to adultery, Denis asserts that no one in Scripture was ever dispensed to adultery by God.[22] It's no surprise, then, that with respect to Abraham's endangerment of his wife, Lot's willingness for his daughters to be ravished, and the incest later committed by Lot and by Judah, almost no one will posit a special dispensation per se, despite the common assertion that these misdeeds served good ends.[23]

Acting as a Pander for One's Daughters

When commentators turned to Lot's offer of his daughters to the men of Sodom, they were uniformly astounded and scandalized. In the face of Lot's repugnant act, they were driven to look for some amelioration only by two items of contrary testimony: first, despite this deed, he was deemed worthy of angelic rescue; and, second, 2 Peter 2:7 calls Lot — probably in light of his rescue — both "righteous" and "godly." In other words, Scripture itself seems to get Lot off the hook. But was his endangerment of his daughters (not to mention his incest later on) therefore commendable? Or even understandable?

As already noted, virtually no one suggests that Lot was in any way divinely prompted to offer his daughters to be raped. God may be rescuing Lot, but risking his daughters' chastity was clearly his own idea. And not a good one! So the best that commentators can do for the "righteous" Lot is to ameliorate his misdeed. Some conjecture that Lot hoped the very outrageousness of his offer would shock the townsmen into shame and a change of heart.[24] Others impute to Lot a monumental faith in providence, that God would intervene.[25]

Of special interest, however, is Augustine. His two treatises on lying were mentioned earlier, but it's worth noting his deliberations on Lot, which are peculiar — and shifting. In the first treatise, Augustine addresses the view of Ambrose, one of the few commentators who excused Lot by appealing to compensatory evil. Ambrose's logic could scarcely be more offensive to modern readers: Lot did well, risking a lesser evil to avoid a greater, for it would be less unnatural for women to be defiled by the men of Sodom than for Lot's male guests to suffer the same.[26] Although Augustine does not dispute Ambrose's judgment that it is more evil for men to be raped than women, his first treatise does reject Ambrose's defense of Lot and concludes that Lot did, in fact, sin. What makes the second treatise so striking, then, is that Augustine *begins* by setting aside Ambrose's "lesser evil" defense and eventually settles on what we would call a plea of insanity: "[Lot's] mind was so disturbed that he was willing to do that which God's law declares must not be done. By fearing other men's sins, he was so perturbed that he did not attend to his own sin and willingly subjected his daughters to the lusts of impious men."[27] This is a radical shift! Augustine has abandoned all arguments from prudence. Lot's horrible deed, at best, signals a mental breakdown. At worst, it is merely "his own sin," and totally unexcused.

Feminist writers have had a field day against the assumption of Ambrose and Augustine that women's bodies are of less value than men's — and rightly so.[28] Although the assumption is rooted in deeper notions about how "nature" embodies the teachings of divine law, what really lurks behind the curtain is a deep-seated fear on the part of Ambrose, Augustine, and most Christian writers of homosexual intercourse. The point to be taken here, however, is that while some later writers agreed that Lot must have been deranged to make this offer, the argument was not meant to excuse — only to explain.[29] Augustine himself asserted that Lot had no "paternal" right to force such evil on his daughters.[30] Later commentators agreed, rejecting the appeal to compensatory evil and, moreover, condemning Lot's deed as shameful, unlawful, a great and atrocious crime, even though (as Pellican observed) the Bible does not condemn Lot.[31] Luther liked to think that Lot possessed a great faith, but Luther's feelings were undisguised: "Lot failed abominably in his duty toward his daughters, whose honor he should have defended from danger with his own life."[32] Calvin was sharper still. Lot acted unforgivably, "pandering his own daughters as prostitutes." Better he should have "died a thousand times" at his doorstep than to try such a thing![33]

In the case of Lot's endangerment of his daughters, the inclination of precritical commentators is clear: despite their often convoluted deliberations, they are scarcely interested in excusing Lot's behavior. They are vehemently opposed to seeing him imitated. He may have been righteous in some other way, but his treatment of his daughters was *no* part of whatever righteousness Lot possessed.

Polygamy

Although Genesis 4 reports that the first polygamist was Lamech, a direct descendant of Cain and evidently a murderer as well, it is the polygamous marriages of Abraham and Jacob that draw the most attention. Unlike these patriarchs, Lamech is not taken as a model of Christian behavior. In their attempt to reconcile the patriarchs' multiple wives with their role as exemplars, most commentators use the same lines we have already examined, especially the idea that they had special permission from God. Now if their exegesis of these texts were nothing more than the boilerplate application of standard excuses, we could simply note that fact and move on. But under this heading we'll actually discover both surprises and complicating factors. First, there are provocative variations on the appeal to secret permission. Second, the issue of patriarchal polygamy proved to have much more urgency than one might ever expect. For us, polygamy is rarely more than an occasional headline or the substance of a banal joke. For some of our forebears, the precedent offered by the patriarchs was fraught with religious and political consequences.

Excuses for Polygamy: The Usual Suspects

We saw earlier that it was exceedingly rare to claim that God simply permitted Abraham to take a second wife — particularly since there is no sign of such permission being sought or received. Given that commentators were much more disturbed by sexual crimes than, say, by lying, those who appealed to a special dispensation as excusing Abraham's polygamy almost always added other considerations.[34] Augustine publicized many of these factors, including a case for finding special permission implied by the typological significance of Abraham's polygamy.

> The patriarchs and prophets . . . understood by the revelation of the
> Spirit of God . . . how God appointed all these sayings and actions
> as types and predictions of the future. Their great desire was for the
> New Testament, but they had a personal duty to perform in those
> predictions.[35]

In other words, Abraham's polygamy was *staged,* for the sake of the allegory that Paul would construct from Sarah and Hagar in Galatians 4:24.

Augustine's suggestion drew followers even among Reformation writers, but there were other arguments, too. Chrysostom asserted that Abraham was merely obeying the original command to "increase and multiply," a command that Ambrose found especially relevant after the Flood had depopulated the earth.[36] Augustine, never short of arguments, amplified these insights by suggesting that the patriarchs lived in an age before Christ, that is, back when polygamy was neither forbidden by law nor driven by lust — as it would be were *we* to revive it. Augustine also voiced an argument that Luther especially liked, that the patriarchs' polygamy was driven by their knowledge that eventually the promised Messiah would be born of their line. Polygamy was a way to hasten that blessed day.[37] All of these arguments had in common that they posit a world or a culture where the divine imperatives or laws worked differently than they do now. Consequently, none of these excuses could possibly apply to us today, and that is clearly why commentators liked them.

Motives: Defending the Bible, Coping with Monarchs

As peculiar as some of these lines of excuse or amelioration seem, it would be wrong, again, to suppose that precritical commentators were trying to exonerate the patriarchs at any cost. We've already seen that some excuses were dismissed as invalid, even as some actions were virtually impossible to defend, no matter who committed them or what the Bible might say elsewhere in defense. Any discussion of patriarchal misdeeds would inevitably also be a course in Christian ethics for the readers of these commentaries. When interpreters interrupted the flow of their exegesis with lengthy digressions on patriarchal morality, their motivations were always *pastoral,* at least in part, because prudent congregations and readers always wanted to know the standards by which God would judge their own behavior.

However, other motives were also at work. Much of Augustine's defense of the patriarchs' behavior was crafted less as pastoral care or catechism than as *apologetic* — specifically, as part of his response to the slanders of Faustus. Writing sometime around 390, this Manichaean bishop severed the Old Testament from the "true" Christianity of the Manichaeans, indicting the deity portrayed there as a fraud and charging the patriarchs, Moses, and the prophets with carnal immorality. Augustine's burden was to refute Faustus and retain the character of Christ and Christianity as the fulfillment of the Old Testament, not its repudiation. To this end, he felt compelled to portray the patriarchs in as favorable a light as possible.

Something quite different was at work in the sixteenth century. The 1530s saw three separate scandals in which the polygamy of Abraham and Jacob was invoked as a precedent. First was the "great matter" of Henry VIII of England, whose quest for a male heir led him to ask the pope either to annul his marriage to Catherine of Aragon or allow him to take a second wife. Another such petitioner was Philip of Hesse, Luther's prince, whose unhappy marriage had not saved him from frequent infidelities nor from a deservedly anguished conscience. Between these two fell the short-lived seizure of the city of Münster by Anabaptist radicals in 1534-35, who revived polygamy as part of a restoration of the kingdom of Christ in which Münster was to be the New Jerusalem. To a profound degree, Protestants and Catholics alike were forced to reckon with the *political* implications of patriarchal polygamy. While many commentators were inclined to defend the patriarchs, some also argued (more or less after Augustine) that polygamy was not outside divine law, even if current laws and customs had come to reject the practice. It will be instructive here to poll three such commentators, including Cardinal Cajetan, Martin Luther, and Martin Bucer — Catholic, Lutheran, and Reformed.

Cajetan's views emerge in his commentaries, but he also may have been consulted by Pope Clement VII over the problem of Henry VIII. Cajetan opposed divorce but took the patriarchs as proof not only that having a second wife was not contrary to divine law, but also that no special divine word was required.[38]

Luther, too, had been asked to advise Henry. Like Cajetan, he was opposed to divorce and advised bigamy,[39] but other details reveal him as more cautious. In particular, Luther's exegesis of Genesis tried to balance excusing the patriarchs with minimizing the potential for imitation. So while the patriarchs acted with good intent (to obtain the "promised seed," Christ), and in accord with custom, and with special dispensation, none of these considerations apply to us. Yet Luther also warns of violating equity in the name of consistency — hinting that he might allow polygamy in the present.[40] In fact, the guarded remarks in his commentary are fully consistent not only with his advice to Henry VIII but also with earlier statements, including his 1526 response to Philip of Hesse (long before Philip's bigamous marriage came to pass early in 1540). There, Luther said that polygamy is not to be generally re-instituted: it is allowable only as an exception in case of "necessity" (say, if one's wife were leprous), on the condition that one has a special word from God as the patriarchs had, or as a means to avoid a greater evil such as divorce or unchastity.[41] The last factor was decisive in his reluctant approval of Philip's bigamy.

The messy affair found Luther in close agreement with Martin Bucer, also a trusted advisor to Philip. Bucer embraced the same assumptions as Luther, listed above, and added that Old Testament practices and privileges were permitted to Christians unless explicitly forbidden. It's no surprise, then, that Bucer had also advocated bigamy over divorce for Henry VIII, at least in his preliminary opinion.[42]

Both Bucer and Luther were effectively trapped in their words, then, when Philip of Hesse claimed, late in 1539, that his salvation and conscience were in danger from his own unchastity and begged them to endorse his planned bigamy. Luther was thereby implicated in the resort to compensatory evil that he elsewhere condemned. Indeed, desperate to keep the bigamy secret, both Reformers urged Philip to tell "a holy lie" like the one Abraham used (Bucer) or simply "a strong lie" (Luther). The threat was greater than merely the scandal of bigamy, for Philip — leading prince of the Protestant faction — threatened to withdraw from leadership and seek rapprochement with the Catholic forces of Emperor Charles V. Neither Luther nor Bucer wanted to change the marriage laws and customs of Europe in favor of plural marriage — though they worried that Philip might do so. Yet they did give Philip's conscience the final say. The "special word from God" that Luther would have liked to hear proved to be something mediated wholly by Philip's own conscience and reports of his heartfelt prayer. No other evidence was sought or demanded.[43]

We cannot go far into the aftermath; suffice it to say, the damage was immense. Luther and Bucer were accused of Münsterite ways, and Catholic writers discredited Protestantism in general. It's especially worth noting that the scandal was a catalyst for later exegesis. Bullinger attacked these modern defenders of polygamy in his 1542 commentary on Matthew,[44] and Vermigli's remarks on polygamy may also have been shaped by this affair.[45] Bucer himself may have joined his own critics, adding "proofs" for monogamy in his late lectures on Ephesians.[46] And Calvin, beyond his peers, dismissed virtually every defense offered by his predecessors. Not only did he argue that monogamy has always been the divine order,[47] but he also contradicted Henry VIII's "advisors" by asserting that polygamy is a worse crime than divorce — *not* vice versa.[48] Thus, though the patriarchs did commit polygamy, Calvin says "it was not therefore lawful."[49] However much Calvin might have agreed with Bucer that what God permitted to the patriarchs is that much more permissible for us, his point is that God never permitted polygamy to anyone.

The polygamy scandals of the 1530s found commentators torn between exegesis and pastoral worries, between the silences of Scripture and the realities of politics. Some took an absolutist stand, faulting both the patriarchs and their modern imitators. Others compromised, hoping to preserve at least some biblical values while bending others. But though the latter group theorized that the Bible's silences were to be read permissively, they cringed when faced with the demand for such permission, discovering the hard way that the patriarchs' examples precipitated only disaster, not deliverance.

Insurrection and Self-Authorized Violence

In the United States, it's impolitic to speak against the American revolution — the war against Britain for life, liberty, and the pursuit of happiness that has shaped so much of American identity. But what now looks like such a justified and heroic emancipation from tyranny could have been described in far different terms in 1776 — terms that indicted colonists for rebellion, insurrection, and the overthrow of divine order. After all, Romans 13:1 says that "there is no authority except from God, and those that exist have been instituted by God." Wouldn't this have applied to King George III? Indeed, in the face of today's terrorist threats, calls to "resist tyranny" seem suddenly unpatriotic when we hear them directed against America.

Abraham's Private War

The controversy over resisting tyranny is nothing new, and even the patriarchs are implicated. The best-known Old Testament precedent is probably Moses, but he was only one in a parade of biblical deliverers that stretches to include Gideon, Jephthah, Samson, and even Deborah. For a few commentators, however, the procession began not in the book of Exodus with Moses but much earlier — in Genesis 14, where Abraham wars against Lot's captors. Compared with the drama of the exodus, Abraham's rescue of Lot seems modest. But when he armed his household, Abraham faced the same moral dilemma as Moses would. The traditional Christian doctrine was echoed by all the early Protestants: private individuals have no right to take up arms against an oppressive ruler, for rulers are appointed by God. So what gave Abraham or Moses the right to oppose or overthrow a legitimate ruler?

Few commentators lingered over Abraham's private status in his war against the four kings. Chrysostom, Pellican, and Musculus ascribed Abraham's victory to providence but did not address his right to declare war. Only for Luther, Zwingli, Vermigli, and Calvin was the patriarch's morality at issue.[50] Zwingli's remarks were unguarded, to say the least. Finding neither impropriety in Abraham's retribution nor any special divine impulse, he portrayed him as an excellent example for Christian warfare: "those who wage war . . . to free the oppressed from injury and violence . . . not only do not sin, but undertake what is most pleasing to God."[51]

By contrast, Luther was at pains to prove that Abraham was *not* an example; in fact, had Abraham *not* had a special command in this case, he would have sinned. If Luther reluctantly accommodated Philip on the matter of patriarchal polygamy, he was consciously reactive here. Abraham's victory should be seen as a miracle, not an example, Luther says, then adds that this was Thomas Müntzer's error — to take passages like Genesis 14 as a model or warrant.[52] Müntzer, a disaffected follower of Luther, added much fuel to the peasants' war of 1524-25. That tragic rebellion was an embarrassment to Luther because the peasants had credited his writings as their inspiration. Luther wanted no part of Müntzer or his applied exegesis and later warned his students that "you have more and greater examples which testify that one should *not* slay a magistrate."[53]

Abraham's little war weighed heavily upon Calvin, for the patriarch appears to have done what no private person should do: he took it upon himself to initiate a public war. Calvin was worried enough that he offered not one but two possible excuses. First, Calvin thinks Abraham acted in obedience to a secret prompting of the Spirit, "armed with a heavenly command, lest he transgress the bounds of his vocation." This traditional excuse would occasion no comment, were it not for the fact that Calvin almost never invokes it.[54] His second excuse is more subtle. It's not necessary to see Abraham as a private person, says Calvin. After all, Canaan was promised to Abraham and his seed, making Abraham the legal ruler of that realm, even if no one knew it yet. As the king (that is, the king-to-be) of that region, he was fully within his right and office to undertake a war.[55]

From Public to Private Resistance

Aside from Zwingli's rash remark, there is a consensus among these Reformers that Abraham offers no precedent and that private resistance is normally unlawful. (Zwingli, too, espouses this view in other writings.) Calvin's comparison of Abraham to Moses is of special interest, since in sixteenth-century discussions of tyranny, "Moses" was a code-word for the divinely-sent help that oppressed Christians of private status might pray for but which was not theirs to initiate.[56] Significantly, while Calvin was willing to justify Abraham on the basis of special dispensation, he clearly preferred to cede *public* office to Abraham and avoid the problem of *private* resistance altogether. Calvin did not deny that deliverers might arise from the private realm,[57] but he clearly hoped to see Protestants in France freed not by private avengers but by the intervention of a public body such as the Estates General. Calvin's reluctance to resist tyranny on any other than constitutional grounds puts him in the company of most Reformers of his day, as Luther and Vermigli illustrate. Thus the patriarchs, like Moses and the judges, turned out to be as circumspect about their private status as Calvin and his colleagues would have been. This is surely no coincidence.

Obviously, sometime between Calvin and 1776, things changed. Actually, theories of resistance and views of patriarchal precedent changed very soon. As the situation of Protestants in France worsened, and especially after the St. Bartholomew's Day massacre in 1572, there was a profound shift in "political exegesis." A hint of the change can be seen in the comment of Calvin's successor, Theodore Beza, that the Israelites were delivered by extraordinary means only because "they were too stupid to see that they might have resisted tyranny without it."[58] Beza thus expanded the list of excuses based on prudence so as to include new ideas about what made a monarch legitimate. Nonetheless, this more permissive reading of patriarchal precedent was accompanied by the bloody European wars of religion, as well as later revolutions. Its continuing use as a religious pretext by individuals bent on resorting to violence might suggest that the older exegesis deserves to be respected and reconsidered.

Negotiating Excuses and Exceptions

The traditional commentators examined here do not wholly agree on how to appropriate or apply the Bible's reports of patriarchal misdeeds. They range from maximizing excuses (Augustine) to a principled resistance to what are deemed simply sins and cautionary tales (Calvin). None of these writers was eager to see these dubious deeds break out in their own churches, yet no one — not even Calvin — would dare to say that God is not free to direct something similar today.

Consequently, these pastors and preachers also thought about how they might test claims to such exceptional privilege. We've seen some of these criteria, such as possessing a special call or word from God. Sometimes Luther could leave this qualification to be verified by one's conscience, but at other times (as in his dealings with the peasant uprising) he would demand exceptional claims to be corroborated with signs and wonders — the same demand some Catholics made of Calvin to verify his claims and teachings.[59] (One corollary is the demand for success or results: if Müntzer was really raised up by God, why did he fail?) We have also seen excuses that appeal to prudence, necessity, "lesser evil," or the principle of equity or natural right. Commentators generally disliked such appeals, especially when they served to justify some act that was otherwise clearly wrong. Nonetheless, as Luther and Bucer illustrate, they sometimes found themselves on the horns of exactly that ethical dilemma.

The criterion that was probably of greatest weight in evaluating morally suspicious actions, however, was Scripture itself. Were there other passages in the Bible that might clarify, contradict, or trump the idea that one might be specially permitted to engage in some improper act? This criterion is sometimes described as the *rule of faith* or the *analogy of faith*.[60]

The first phrase looks for conformity to the apostles' main teachings; the second phrase takes the whole Bible as a standard, interpreting unclear passages by those that are clearer. The analogy of faith was at work in Luther's and Denis's flat denial that God ever permits incest or adultery.[61] Calvin, too, was precise on this point: "whatever is opposed to the nature of God is sinful."[62] For Luther, conformity to right doctrine was an even stronger proof than performing miracles.[63] But Calvin, as usual, could go further: "These days, God does not reveal the future by [oracles or] miracles. The teaching of the law, the prophets, and the gospel . . . is abundantly sufficient for the regulation of our course of life."[64]

Following the Patriarchs and the Commentators

The disturbing deeds of the Old Testament saints offer a unique window into how earlier commentators and pastors approached the problem of divine intervention as well as questions of biblical ethics. Certain as it is that we will find something in these commentators to disagree with, there are still lessons to draw from the history of interpreting these passages that add to the lessons of Scripture itself.

1. NOT ALL OF THE BIBLE IS A MODEL FOR US. *The narrative and descriptive portions of Scripture need to be handled with care, even when heroes and saints are the leading characters, lest exceptions or sinful deeds become the basis for a bad rule.*

The disastrous peasant rebellion that Müntzer helped inflame and the coercive polygamy in Münster had complex causes. Both sympathetic and hostile retellings are possible. But there can be little doubt that both affairs ended badly, and that neither was well-served by the use of patriarchal examples as warrants for violence or polygamy. The sixteenth-century understanding of biblical "exceptions" was given a pair of lasting scars by these contemporary examples of applying the texts permissively. It's hard to think differently today about instances of self-authorized violence, particularly in the name of religion. For that matter, while the question of how the gospel applies to polygamous cultures has been a perennial problem, there are also Christian advocates of polygamy in North America today who are quite happy with these Old Testament examples.[65] If there are lessons to draw from the commentary tradition, one would surely include a profound skepticism towards any uncritical or unchecked appropriation of such examples, particularly when (as Luther reminds us) there are so many other examples — and explicit teachings and commands — to commend conduct that differs from the patriarchs' misdeeds.

2. THE SILENCES OF THE BIBLE SHOULD BE FILLED *BY* THE BIBLE. *The principle of reading unclear passages of Scripture in light of Scripture's clearer passages is solidly endorsed by traditional commentators.*

In one sense, the problem of the patriarchs' misdeeds is a dilemma that is both raised and (potentially) resolved by Scripture itself. If you only knew the patriarchal narratives, or if you only knew the moral teachings of the Bible, there would be no problem. The problem arises largely because one part of the Bible collides with another. What the Bible instructs is not always what it models. (The conflict between Genesis 14 and Romans 13, mentioned earlier, is just one example.) There is therefore much to be said in favor of a solution that allows the Bible to correct itself, so that rules and pastoral counsel are derived from passages *intended* as rules rather than from one-of-a-kind exceptions. There is no need to fabricate implausible rules or hidden scenarios simply to get the Bible's heroes off the hook. As Calvin generalized, "whenever the faithful fall into sin, they do not desire to be lifted out of it by false defenses, for their justification consists in a simple and free demand of pardon for their sin."[66] In other words, it is better to construe such silences in terms of the Bible's well-known pattern of sin and forgiveness, rather than invent a completely new pattern of biblical ethics or conclude that God or the Bible is hopelessly unreliable.

3. EXEGESIS CAN BE MISLED BY POWER, POLITICS, AND PRESTIGE. *Although "God shows no partiality" to those supposedly of repute (Galatians 2:6), we often do. Our best exegetical instincts about right and wrong can run aground when our esteem for someone — whether in the Bible or in our congregation — distracts us from the facts of their behavior.*

However slow we should be in passing judgment on the mistakes of our forebears, it's hard not to conclude that Luther and Bucer erred in encouraging the bigamy of Philip of Hesse and in failing to challenge his conscience to cling to the clearer teachings of the Bible rather than its more obscure examples. That's not just a modern perspective; it's also the view of Luther's contemporaries, and possibly the view of Luther and Bucer in hindsight. Unfortunately, Luther himself also allowed — in his theory and through his practice — that faults could be indulged in leaders that were intolerable in ordinary folk. He saw it in his own day, even as he saw it portrayed in the Bible. Modern society, too, is well acquainted with (if not fascinated by) the vices of the rich and famous. But this is not the pattern of biblical ethics to which we are called. In the genealogies of Jesus, the patriarchs fit in nicely next to other men and women of checkered reputation. Special deference to them, or to anyone of power or prestige, is unwarranted — as the best commentators of the past have illustrated in their own successes, as well as through their failings.

Chapter Five

Gomer and Hosea

Does God Approve of Wife Abuse?

A lthough women are scarcely prominent in the many books that make up the latter prophets, their few cameo appearances and the prophets' regular use of feminine imagery and metaphors have met with protests from many contemporary readers. Their objections are not surprising. At issue is not the *quantity* of women represented, but the *quality* of that representation. In a word, it seems that the prophets never mention women, whether real or metaphorical, except to serve as villains and bad examples.

Of all the women in the prophets, none is better known than Gomer, the wife of the prophet Hosea. Her story is easy to outline, if only because there are so few details. According to the book's opening lines, Hosea's first oracle was directed to himself: "Go, take to yourself a wife of harlotry and have children of harlotry, for the land commits great harlotry by forsaking the LORD" (1:2). Gomer was that "wife of harlotry," who bore to Hosea a son, a daughter, and another son — prophetically named Jezreel, Not-pitied, and Not-my-people. All three names signal impending judgment against Israel, even as the oracle in 1:10–2:1 goes on to anticipate a time when a repentant nation will again be prosperous, pitied, and worthy to be called God's people.[1] Gomer, on the other hand, continues to figure through much of the rest of the book as the unnamed woman and mother who is guilty of harlotry and adultery — a figure of Israel's political, moral, and religious infidelities. And yet if Gomer/Israel is destined for punishment, she is also the target of God's affectionate and vigorous courtship.

The book of Hosea is a study in contrasts, if not divine mood swings. In Hosea, God is a jealous God. He is a husband who cannot suffer a rival and who berates his wife's foolishness. Yet he is also an affectionate lover: "Behold, I will allure her, and bring her into the wilderness, and speak tenderly to her" (2:14). At times the prophet's words depict an agonized inner dialogue, a kind of divine bipolarity:

> How can I give you up, Ephraim! How can I hand you over, O Israel! . . . My heart recoils within me, my compassion grows warm and tender. I will not execute my fierce anger, I will not again destroy Ephraim; for I am God and no mortal, the Holy One in your midst, and I will not come in wrath. (11:8-9)

Echoes of Hosea can also be heard in the New Testament, often in unexpected places, but usually recalling God's love or deliverance. Matthew 2:15 sees Jesus as a fulfillment of Hosea 11:1, "When Israel was a child, I loved him, and *out of Egypt I called my son*." Exulting over Christ's resurrection in 1 Corinthians 15:55, Paul alludes to Hosea 13:14: "O death, where is thy victory? O death, where is thy sting?" It's clear in Hosea that God is loyal to his people, vehemently so, even when they're as unfaithful as Gomer. Why, then, do some find the portrait of Gomer so very troubling?

Gomer and Her Wicked Sisters

One clue might be found in the Revised Common Lectionary — or in what it omits. Naturally, the lectionary has to leave something out of every book, and Hosea is not exactly brief. But in view of the lectionary's dislike of controversy, it's predictable that its selections should skip from the promise of restoration in 1:10 to the "wooing" of Israel in 2:14. Lost are the intervening details of Gomer's dalliances and the punishments to come: "lest I strip her naked and make her as in the day she was born. . . . I will uncover her lewdness in the sight of her lovers."

Although the metaphor of the unfaithful wife was crafted by the biblical author to indict the apostasy of *both* sexes in Israel, many readers today find such metaphors less than reassuring about the character of God. Hosea is not the only prophet to vilify Israel as an adulteress and to extol God as her nemesis. A few examples from two other prophets will sharpen the problem. In Ezekiel 16, for instance, the prophet rages on and on against the idolatry of Israel:

- You trusted in your beauty, and played the harlot because of your renown, and lavished your harlotries on any passer-by. . . . Yet you were not like a harlot, because you scorned hire. Adulterous wife, who receives strangers instead of her husband! Men give gifts to all harlots; but you gave your gifts to all your lovers, bribing them to come to you from every side for your harlotries. (vv. 15, 31-33)

- Wherefore, O harlot, hear the word of the LORD: . . . I will gather all your lovers, with whom you took pleasure, all those you loved and all those you loathed . . . and will uncover your nakedness. . . . They shall stone you and cut you to pieces. . . . They shall burn your houses and execute judgments upon you in the sight of many women; I will make you stop playing the harlot, and you shall also give hire no more. So will I satisfy my fury on you, and my jealousy shall depart from you; I will be calm, and will no more be angry. (vv. 35, 37, 40-42)

In Ezekiel 23, the prophet goes on to indict Samaria, Israel's "sister," for equally abominable idolatry, including child sacrifice:

- She increased her harlotry, remembering . . . when she played the harlot in the land of Egypt and doted upon her paramours there, whose members were like those of asses, and whose issue was like that of horses. Thus you longed for the lewdness of your youth, when the Egyptians handled your bosom and pressed your young breasts. (vv. 19-21)

- I will direct my indignation against you, that they may deal with you in fury. They shall cut off your nose and your ears, and your survivors shall fall by the sword. They shall seize your sons and your daughters, and your survivors shall be devoured by fire. They shall also strip you of your clothes and take away your fine jewels. (vv. 25-26)

- Do not men now commit adultery when they practice harlotry with her? For they have gone in to her, as men go in to a harlot. . . . But righteous men shall pass judgment on them with the sentence of adulteresses, and with the sentence of women that shed blood; because they are adulteresses, and blood is upon their hands. . . . Thus will I put an end to lewdness in the land, that all women may take warning. (vv. 43-45, 48)

In Jeremiah 2:23-24, Israel is likened not to a promiscuous woman, but even worse: to a female camel or wild ass in heat.

- How can you say, "I am not defiled, I have not gone after the Baals"? Look at your way in the valley; know what you have done — a restive young camel interlacing her tracks, a wild ass used to the wilderness, in her heat sniffing the wind! Who can restrain her lust? None who seek her need weary themselves; in her month they will find her.

Once again, all these are lines that users of the lectionary will never read, ponder, or proclaim. The lectionary editors would probably classify them simply as "harsh." But in the last quarter-century, some feminist critics have had another analysis. For them, these passages are not just harsh; they are also *pornographic.*

Reading through the Eyes of Gomer

To label parts of the Bible as pornographic is to use "fighting words" — at least for those who want to resist the feminist reading. Nonetheless, before we look at Gomer in the history of interpretation, we need to note the current controversy over the Bible's representation of women (and, metaphorically, of Israel) as harlots or adulteresses.

Possibly the earliest protest against the Bible's use of such imagery appeared in a 1985 essay, "Prophets and Pornography: Female Sexual Imagery in Hosea."[2] The original argument has been amplified by later writers and complicated by quarrels over what exactly constitutes pornography, but the central assertion has remained unchanged. Despite the fact that Hosea and other prophets employ the image of the sexually unfaithful *wife* as a metaphor for *people or cities* who have been politically or religiously unfaithful to God, this metaphor (it is alleged) looks and functions a lot like pornography. Feminists decry pornography for degrading and humiliating women, for presenting women as objects, for assuming women are made for male subjection and domination, and for expecting women to internalize a perspective that serves only the male and treats a male-constructed fiction as if it were a universal norm or objective reality.[3] When the prophets brand Israel as an unfaithful wife or harlot, destined to be stripped naked, shamed and humiliated, mutilated, exiled or killed, they may intend to bring Israel to repentance. But these graphic woes seem to "luxuriate obscenely in every detail of a woman's humiliation."[4] Even Robert Carroll — who contests the underlying feminist analysis — grants that in such texts, "the fantasy about mothers, wives, sisters and daughters has run riot" and is "out of control."[5]

The accusation that the prophets were deliberately pornographic is, of course, impossible to adjudicate. The term itself is modern, and proving authorial intent is tricky. On the other hand, few would contest the truism that the prophets were men of their time, conditioned by the attitudes of the day: Israel was, after all, a male-dominated society. But if we shift our focus from the author's *intent* to the text's *effect,* the feminist protest becomes more understandable. Explaining the rhetoric of prophetic speech, Renita Weems says that "the first task of a prophet is to arrest the imagination of one's audience."

> The most useful function of this kind of language is its highly emotive impact. For what was the case in ancient Israel remains the case in modern times: talk about sex and sexuality tends to provoke, rouse, humiliate, and captivate people. Such language certainly arrests the imagination.[6]

Nonetheless, she continues, we must also "consider the consequences of such imagery" — especially those that may be *unintended.*

In Weems's analysis, the Bible's image of the unfaithful wife has wonderful potential. It captures God's love for a wayward people, and it often denounces injustice, abuse of power, social and moral decay. Yet it is also "a metaphor gone awry."[7] Metaphors are powerful means by which values are formed or cemented; they are sometimes our "first lessons in prejudice, bigotry, [and] stereotyping."[8] One could add that the imagery of metaphors can live in our subconsciousness, often undetected but still powerful. In the prophets, they invite the audience "to imagine plausible . . . ways of treating women."[9]

The problem, as Cheryl Exum puts it, is "the ideology that informs this imagery." Women's bodies are viewed as "the property of men." Subliminally, men are taught to exert authority; women, to submit. "Because most readers are likely to read *with* the text's ideology and privilege God, the abusive husband's behavior is not open to question."[10] Some find a troubling ambiguity even in the happy ending that the book forecasts for Israel: "The reader who is caught up in this joyous new betrothal and renewed covenant overlooks the fact that this joyous reconciliation between God and Israel follows the exact pattern that battered wives know so well,"[11] namely, "periods of mistreatment . . . followed by intervals of kindness and generosity" — a strategy that "reinforces the wife's dependence on the husband" only so that "the cycle of abuse" can begin again.[12] Other feminist writers are reluctant to see Hosea as an ideal husband. Gomer, after all, "is denied the right to name [her children], is appropriated as a symbol, and is literally stripped, trapped, and pressed into conformity."[13]

Such observations and generalizations are, of course, contested. For Carroll, it seems sufficient to note that metaphors, even metaphorical women, are only metaphors; so in Ezekiel 23, the narrative isn't about two women, it is only about two cities — Jerusalem and Samaria.[14] For Raymond Ortland, these images do not "insinuate a negative judgment upon the moral character of women as opposed to men, or seek to manipulate opinion against women, as opposed to men."[15] At fault for him is not the Bible but feminist readings of it, which "[take] offense where none is given." For him, a hermeneutic of suspicion is "simply unfair," especially when it reads the prophets' figurative language — itself intrinsically ambiguous and risky — in light of implications and entailments the prophet never intended.[16]

Carroll and Ortland nicely sketch the impasse from the other side. While feminists usually recognize that declamations against the unfaithful metaphorical wife do indict the real women *and men* of Israel,[17] the problem of the metaphor's *unintended* effects remains. It is not enough for many readers and hearers to be told, upon hearing such shocking and brutal language, that the rape or torture just portrayed was (no worries!) "just" a metaphor — particularly when the real brutality suffered by some parishioners instantly upstages whatever the biblical point may have been.[18]

Is there a way between these opposing points of view, some sort of middle path? Is there anything to be learned, positive or negative, from the history of the interpretation of Gomer and Hosea?

With Gomer in the School of the Commentators

The history of the interpretation of Hosea 1–3 has been sketched in part by John Farthing, who reports the views of many patristic and Reformation writers as digested in the 1558 lectures of Jerome Zanchi, and partly also by Yvonne Sherwood, who gives more attention to rabbinic exegesis as well as to commentaries of the last century or so.[19] We'll draw on both surveys and occasionally supplement them with other, less accessible material.[20]

The issue that preoccupies most precritical commentators, and later commentators as well, is the scandal of a prophet marrying a harlot. Commentators generally adhere to one of three views.[21]

The Literal-Historical View: Real Marriage, Real Harlotry

We usually think of the church fathers as more allegorically inclined and credit the Reformers as champions of literal and historical exegesis. Not so here. The most "literal" reading of the marriage of Hosea and Gomer is also one of the earliest, and can be discovered in the anti-heretical writings of Irenaeus. His larger point is typological: Hosea's marriage prefigured Christ's union with a fornicating people. Christ sanctifies these sinners, just as Paul declares that "an unbelieving wife is sanctified by the believing husband" (1 Corinthians 7:14). But in making that point, he also characterizes Hosea's marriage as an *action* that stands in contrast to mere visions or words.[22] The same typology is argued by Augustine, who labors to defend a host of Old Testament figures against the slanders of Faustus. Augustine reminds him that Jesus reckoned harlots ahead of the Jews of his day in entering the kingdom of heaven. Significantly, Augustine also assumes Gomer repented of her fornication and became a chaste wife.[23] Jerome, however, falls in this group only with qualification. In the preface of his commentary on Hosea, he insists that the prophet's narrative of his marriage was an allegory, because "God commands nothing but what is honorable." Nonetheless, Jerome's later remarks suggest that though he'd prefer to think Gomer was merely part of a prophetic vision, reading the story as history is also an option.[24]

The literal-historical view was embraced by many commentators. Cornelius à Lapide lists Basil the Great, Cyril of Alexandria, Theodoret, Hugh of St. Victor, Aquinas, Denis, Arias Montanus, and himself.[25] Matthew Poole also joins this group, though not without some waffling.[26] And, as Zanchi and others report, this view has its weaknesses as well as strengths. In its favor is the rather obvious point that recounting a vision would scarcely have had as dramatic an impact on Hosea's contemporaries as an actual marriage with a prostitute. On the other hand, as Jerome said, surely God would not command anyone, especially a prophet, to violate the moral law. After all, Leviticus 21:7 forbids priests from marrying harlots, and 1 Corinthians 6:16 is aghast at the thought of a Christian joined to a harlot. Of course, as Zanchi points out, God is above the law — an argument frequently invoked to excuse the patriarchs' misdeeds. In any case, Irenaeus and Augustine found ways to blunt most of the objections: they protected Hosea's reputation (and God's) simply by presuming Gomer's repentance and insisting on the sanctifying effect of her marriage to the godly prophet.[27]

The Visionary-Metaphorical View: No Marriage, Allegorical Harlotry[28]

A second view has already been glimpsed in Jerome: Hosea didn't marry a prostitute; he merely had a vision (or told a parable or allegory) in which he did so. Though Zanchi doesn't name the adherents of this view, except for *Targum Jonathan,* he claims that "almost all the Hebrews" and "many of the most learned among us" embrace this view.[29] Of the rabbis best known to Christian interpreters of the day, Abraham Ibn Ezra reduces Gomer to an allegory, while Maimonides casts her in a dream sequence. *Targum Jonathan,* an ancient Aramaic paraphrase, also employs allegory, but Gomer is stricken from Hosea 1:2; likewise, the text of 3:1 is changed from "Go again, love a woman who is beloved of a paramour and is an adulteress," to "Go and speak a prophecy concerning the house of Israel, *who are like* a woman loved by her husband, but she betrays him."[30] The neutralization of offense is obvious in the Targum, as it is in Rashi, who alters the text to read not "Go, marry," but "Go, teach." Such ameliorations seem driven by Ibn Ezra's concern: "It is inconceivable that God should command one to take a harlot and conceive children of harlotry."[31]

Visionary readings were common among Christian interpreters, too, just as Zanchi said. Zanchi himself was one, and he tried to paraphrase what Hosea might have said to the people of Israel: "The Lord appeared to me in a vision and commanded me to take to myself a harlot. . . . You know, of course, that I did not actually do this."[32] Zanchi doesn't name the Christian adherents of this view, but Lapide counts the followers of Origen, Haymo, Isidore of Seville, Paul of Burgos, and François Vatable; Poole puts Oecolampadius on the list; and a glance at seventeenth-century commentaries in English quickly adds three more Protestants.[33] Few of these are household names anymore, but their arguments all converge: a literal marriage with a prostitute would defile the prophet, discredit his ministry, conflict with other biblical laws and morality, unfairly defame his children, and (in a pragmatic turn) delay the urgent indictment of Israel — assuming, that is, that Hosea couldn't begin preaching until Gomer bore and weaned three children! The rebuttals from the advocates of a "real" marriage almost always argue, among other things, that God is above the law. But equally insightful is the observation (noted by Poole) that it is hardly less dishonorable to imagine or envision an immoral action than it would be to enact such a deed.

The Rhetorical View: Real Marriage, Staged or Parabolic Harlotry

A third view derives from Luther and Calvin and looks a lot like the visionary view. Luther sets forth his interpretation in a few words:

> Don't take her whoredom in the active sense, but understand that his wife allowed herself to be so called, along with her children and husband, on account of the people and in the presence of the people: "I am *called* a whore — and my husband, a whore's knave — because you all *are* whores and knaves." See how great a cross they endured in those shameful names for the sake of the word of God![34]

For Luther, the dramatic marriage with a harlot is openly fictitious. So also Calvin, who thinks Hosea received no vision, only a straightforward command to set forth a similitude or a parable. Like Zanchi, he can imagine what Hosea said: "The Lord places me here as on a stage, to make known to you that I have married a wife, a wife habituated to adulteries and whoredoms, and that I have begotten children by her." Of course, Calvin adds, everyone knew Hosea had done "no such thing" but was speaking only for effect.[35] Although Luther's account is unusual for extending some empathy to both the prophet and his wife, as they pretended to merit undeserved scorn, Calvin barely admits that Hosea might have a real wife or children at all.[36] And if it's hard to know why Luther adopted his view (partly because we have only student notes to go on),[37] Calvin's rationale is the common one: to protect the dignity of the prophetic office.[38] At the end of the day, there is little practical difference between these last two views, the visionary and the rhetorical.

"Spiritual" Readings of Hosea: Mysteries and Morals

In addition to these three strategies for explaining (or explaining away) the prophet's startling marriage with a prostitute, precritical commentators found other layers in the text. Allegorically, Hosea fulfills a twofold Christological type.[39] First, just as Hosea was joined to an unfaithful and sinful wife, so was Christ united in the incarnation with our adulterous and sinful flesh. Second, Hosea's marriage also foreshadowed the marriage between Christ and the church, particularly the gentile church. Like our sinful flesh, the church is an image of something unholy that is transformed by this unlikely union with the divine. All the biblical marital imagery, from the Song of Solomon to Ephesians 5, can be summoned to reinforce the point.

Protestants drew the same connections, despite their usual avoidance of allegory, for the book of Hosea is amply represented in the New Testament. Romans 9:25-26, for instance, sees the church of the gentiles as fulfilling the prophecy of Hosea 1:10: "Those who were not my people I will call 'my people,' and her who was not beloved I will call 'my beloved.' And in the very place where it was said to them, 'You are not my people,' they will be called 'sons of the living God.'" The promises made to and about Israel, as well as to and about Gomer, are fulfilled in the grafting-in of the gentiles — whose ungodliness, idolatry, and infidelity correspond to Gomer's and Israel's harlotries. In other words, the church that aspires to be the bride of Ephesians 5:25-30, "without spot or wrinkle," is by definition also a church in need of being cleansed and sanctified by Christ.

Whether allegorical or moral or typological, these "spiritual" readings are significant because they enable at least traces of Gomer and her story to survive elsewhere in the canon as well as in the realm of Christian piety and pastoral practice. Indeed, Gomer's wanderings and chastisement reminded many that they, too, have deserved God's enmity. More on this in a moment.

Mixed Results and Second Thoughts

In the case of Hagar (Chapter One), there were precritical commentators to be found who were clearly capable of reading the Bible through her eyes. Gomer seems to find no such champion. Should we therefore conclude that Gomer is despised by these traditional readers, or that they would countenance such harsh treatment of a harlot or even an unfaithful wife? To answer that question, we must look at the commitments that precritical commentators bring to the playing field.

Although they would never have thought to put it like this, precritical commentators are committed to remain "within" the text — unlike many historical critics and feminist readers, who do not hesitate to challenge the authority and autonomy of texts from outside. One could also say that traditional interpreters read for *coherence*. The Bible is a providential communiqué, a saving word from a sovereign God, so it must make sense in its main outlines. These readers often looked to guides such as the rule of faith, the rule of love, and the analogy of faith — three reference points from which the unknown territory of divine revelation could be mapped by triangulating from the basic teachings of the apostles, the great commandments to love God and one's neighbor, and the likelihood that the unclear parts of Scripture will be illumined by a careful reading of the clearer parts.[40]

One way or another, most of these readers thought the command for Hosea to marry a prostitute fell among the unclear parts. Consequently, many embarked on a search for a clearer passage from elsewhere in the Bible that would clear things up. Here's where dissent entered the ranks of our precritical commentators, resulting in some truly mixed exegetical results. Which biblical text or teaching best explains the unprecedented affair of Gomer and Hosea? There are two answers, each with its own logic, perspective, and agenda. One finds clarity in analogous doctrines, the other in analogous narratives.

A Doctrinal Analogy: Protecting the Ministry

Although some readers thought Hosea's marriage looked a lot like other startling commands (as when Abraham was told to sacrifice Isaac) or like other bizarre prophetic actions (as when Isaiah wandered around naked for three years), many were not inclined to invoke *any* unusual *narrative* as a means of clarifying Hosea. Indeed, some doubted that Isaiah really did walk around naked, even as they worried that some might foolishly imitate Abraham's offering of Isaac. (As we saw in Chapter Two, Jephthah may have been just such an instance of foolish imitation when he offered up his daughter.)

Instead, these readers found Hosea clarified by biblical *precepts,* such as the law that forbade priests to marry a prostitute, or Paul's demand that bishops be the husband of one wife. How much more should prophets set a good example! The conclusion was obvious: the prophet did not really marry such a woman, because such a marriage would have violated a divine command. The account must therefore be understood as a vision or a parable.

If such readers were accused of protecting male interests in this text, they would surely say that the issue is not protecting *men,* but protecting the *ministry,* protecting the dignity of the word of God by defending the integrity of God's ministers. That's a good thing to do, but the year this chapter was written regularly saw headlines decrying clergy sex abuse scandals — scandalous in no small part because these men had often been sheltered from investigation. Yet when ministers are mostly male, protecting ministers or the ministry can easily *look* just like protecting men.

One could imagine there being evidence to the contrary, some sign that Gomer is more than a scapegoat. In our look at Hagar in the history of exegesis, we saw how Reformation commentators described Hagar and Sarah as "womanish" or petty, yet dropped these gendered stereotypes as Hagar's character developed.[41] In Gomer's case, the results are different, perhaps because the evidence is so thin. Although Hosea 2 presents a few words attributed to her, the speech is a rhetorical device, not a quotation. Gomer as a character scarcely appears in the book at all, and when she does, it is strictly in her role as a prostitute and a symbol of a particular kind of vice — idolatry, actually — not as Everywoman. Unfortunately, even Gomer's status as a *symbol* of the unfaithful nation decays in the hands of some commentators. Though most understand that it is the *na-*

tion that is being threatened, not Gomer the symbol, some draw a line from Gomer to women in general. In a long excursus on the moral of Hosea's marriage, Lapide stresses the importance of a wife's character: "The vices of parents, especially mothers, are transferred to their children."[42] Thus Solomon's polygamy may have derived from his adulterous mother — a prejudicial account of Bathsheba, to say the least!

As we assess this preoccupation with the prophet's dignity at Gomer's expense, it does not help that the minds of so many commentators seem to have been long made up. Surely something prodigious is signaled when so many take evasive action against the Bible's literal wording. John Downame, a prominent Puritan of the seventeenth century, illustrates something of the contradiction when he faults Catholic expositors for reading Hosea's marriage as factual. Their mistake, he generalizes, is to interpret things that were actually done as if they were allegories, but to read biblical allegories and parables as if they actually happened, "though innumerable absurdities follow thereupon." Thus, in the case of Hosea's marriage, "the litterall sense . . . implieth a grosse absurditie, and contradicteth other places of Scripture, . . . therefore it is to be understood typically and as a parable."[43] Ironically, this Protestant commentator echoes here the exact reasoning Origen offered for his own allegorizing — Origen, the epitome of capricious "Catholic" exegesis, who was held in such contempt on this score by Luther and Calvin. But how, one must ask, does Downame *know* such a marriage is absurd? Given Jesus' notorious association with prostitutes and sinners, and given Augustine's well-known emendation (that Gomer repented), one wonders why the prophet needs such protection — unless it is to protect these commentators' and pastors' sense of propriety against a God who is not always polite or predictable.

A Narrative Analogy: God Is No Respecter of Dignity, Including His Own

A commitment to the coherence of the Bible could lead in other directions, too. Sometimes commentators — some of them the same writers just described! — found Hosea's marriage illumined not by particular commands but by the grand narrative of the history of salvation. The "spiritual" readings noted earlier, in which Gomer images our own spiritual infidelity, are noteworthy not because they indicate a modern sensitivity to gender issues, but because they provide a snapshot of precritical commentators attempting to indwell language that is "gendered" against them, so to speak. Gomer's story was not always applied as a chronicle of someone else's failings — the Jews, say, or the "Papists." Sometimes Gomer's story was read as the story of the infidelities of Christians and their church — *our* story.

Farthing's study of Zanchi, like this chapter, was carried out in dialogue with feminist exegesis. "As a man of the sixteenth century, Zanchi could hardly have engaged in a radical feminist criticism of Hosea's gender-stereotyped metaphor," Farthing admits. But he properly calls attention to the ease with which Zanchi embraces Gomer's role as his own. Indeed, the trials and chastisement that Hosea sets for Gomer in the second chapter are read by Zanchi as an expression of God's "severe mercy" toward the elect. Only those specially loved by God are so tried and so constrained by sufferings, lest they be abandoned to the futility of their own pleasures.[44] Other precritical commentators write in similar fashion: they direct their rebuke not against women as such, but against the women *and men* of Israel, and even more urgently against their own complacent churches and complacent selves. Calvin's account of the painful threats against Gomer in Hosea 2 is yet another case in point: having described in detail God's provision and Israel's ingratitude, he ends with a prayer that puts himself and his hearers in the place of the prostitute and penitent: "Almighty God, . . . *we* have by our ingratitude renounced your great benefits, and you know the defection and unfaithfulness of which *we* are all guilty and for which you have justly rejected *us*. . . ."[45]

Nothing that Zanchi or Calvin wrote will alter how Hosea's harsh rhetoric may be heard today, and it may well be true that identifying with Gomer in this way does more to ratify the male prerogative to chastise and control women than to challenge it. Nonetheless, one may still learn something about the complex *intention* of some precritical readers, and their commitment to read Gomer's story more with an eye to rescue and redemption — hers, Israel's, and ours.

Like all readers, precritical commentators were more than just the sum of their exegetical opinions. It's easy to see that they did not read Gomer's story from a feminist perspective, nor could they have. But that doesn't tell us everything we would like to know about the issues Gomer's story raises for us. Sometimes these writers mustered a surprising advocacy for women. In looking at Jephthah's daughter, we saw Reformation exegetes protest the notion that a daughter's life is at her father's disposal. In the same way, neither does a wife belong absolutely to her husband, and there are times when she may have to invoke a version of Acts 5:29 and "obey God rather than" her husband.[46] If the *rhetoric* of a wife as the husband's possession survived in their day, the *reality* was clearly in flux, for many Protestant readers had rediscovered an "egalitarian" side of St. Paul in 1 Corinthians 7:3-5. As pastors and teachers who often wielded civic influence, they used Paul to argue against the common double standard whereby husbands might divorce an unfaithful partner but wives could not. Calvin lobbied his city council for fifteen years before the double standard was finally taken off the books in Geneva.[47]

There is a similar "back story" to be weighed regarding spousal abuse. Medieval and early modern families are sometimes caricatured as unrestrained in matters of corporal punishment, but sixteenth-century marriages were probably far more companionable.[48] Certainly the forms of penance divinely visited upon Israel in the person of Gomer were not embraced as household advice, particularly by the Reformers. The Protestant church in Lyons followed the lead of Geneva by instituting a "consistory" that looked into the behavior of everyone, including Christian spouses. In response to the new rules, one man reportedly lamented that he wasn't allowed to beat his wife anymore.[49] Calvin himself, though not much interested in the character of Gomer, could still display his awareness of how the world works. When women turn to prostitution, he writes, it's often the case that they blame their husbands for "too much severity" or unkindness. Calvin's point is that this wasn't true of Gomer, who (the text says) was beloved by her husband. But *our* point should be to notice that, wherever Calvin got his information, he knew that a cold or abusive marriage can drive a wife to devastating extremes.[50]

Returning Gomer to the Pulpit

Gomer was a prostitute married to a prophet who alternately shamed her in public and courted her with kindness. Despite the foul deeds of Israel that Gomer is intended to symbolize, and despite an ostensibly happy ending, the graphic details can make Gomer's story a hard one to tell. The same may be said of similar passages in Ezekiel and Jeremiah. What should we do with biblical texts like these?

107

At the end of her pithy essay, Cheryl Exum discusses how to deal with texts that use sexual abuse as a model of divine action. She urges us to pay attention to the different ways such texts may be heard by male and female readers; to recognize that "prophetic pornography" has an undeniable, detrimental impact on readers; and to read such texts "resistantly," looking for alternative and suppressed perspectives within the text. To be sure, Exum's interest is not in supporting biblical authority; for her, the Bible is "an important part of our cultural heritage" but shouldn't be privileged on that account.[51] Across the divide, Raymond Ortlund offers a different prescription. For him, the feminist critique is part of the postmodern drift toward "nihilistic hermeneutics" and "radical subjectivism." But "a misogynist reading of the biblical text takes offense where none is given," he writes. "The abuse of women is real, . . . [but] it is not true that the metaphor of the harlot is 'verbal violence' toward women." The prophet's message is true just as it stands, though one can recognize this only if one is born again and illumined by the Holy Spirit.[52]

Once again, these are the two polarized readerships of our own day. Earlier in this chapter I asked if there were any middle ground between these two positions that might be indicated or illuminated by the history of this text's interpretation. Here are some concluding theses that point in that direction.

1. ALL READERS LONG TO FIX THE STORY OF GOMER AND HOSEA. *The precritical commentators we have looked at most often want to fix the story by protecting the prophet. Were we to look at later accounts, we would see that other readers fixed Gomer instead. Our own use of this text must be aware of the ways other readers have been offended by it.*

We wouldn't know this from exegesis alone. Rather, it's in the melodrama of how precritical commentators maneuver to avoid or change Gomer and protect the dignity and credibility of the prophet that we see how easily readers can impose their will upon the text. Any amelioration simply confirms Sherwood's assertion that even traditional interpreters read resistantly when they "resist elements of the text that displease them."[53] Her next question (and it's not impertinent) is, *whose ideology will be favored* by such resistance or amelioration? If the story of Gomer makes us uncomfortable, if we have a hard time imagining the vivid details of her life told from the pulpit, we are obliged to ask ourselves why. Why do we want to protect the prophet from the taint of a harlot, when God commanded this union? Why might we wish the story could be toned down? Who or what interest might we be protecting? And how will others hear this tale?

2. A HERMENEUTIC OF SUSPICION IS NOT ALWAYS A BAD THING. *As a tool for understanding the implications of a text, suspicion can and should cut two ways. The Bible was written by human beings who were also sinners, so we shouldn't be surprised if it displays some of the limitations and ambiguities of human language — even as the Holy Spirit can work through the medium of that language. By the same token, every reader of the Bible is also a sinner and ought to fall under suspicion as prone to misuse, distort, and twist Scripture.*

Does it damage our understanding of the authority and inspiration of the Bible if we acknowledge that the human authors of Scripture were finite and sinful? I think not. Instead, such a recognition can prevent us from thinking of the Bible as a magic book, filled with formulas that brook no ambiguity and no exceptions. (Indeed, this book examines the very texts that seem most ambiguous and exceptional!) Suspicion is also important, however, insofar as it leads to a recognition that, as sinners, we too are inclined to misread and misapply the Bible. Why should we be surprised if feminist critics accuse Christian interpreters of reading the Bible in a way that perpetuates their own privileged status — whether as European, educated, emancipated, or male? How could sinners easily do otherwise? There is a great opportunity to be had, delivered by the harshest feminist critics, to turn suspicion upon ourselves and ask how we may have filtered out aspects of Scripture, or aspects of our society's or congregation's realities, that displease us. Naturally, suspicion will run the other way, too, as it ought; but humility, like charity, should begin at home.

3. WE MUST DISTINGUISH THE BIBLE'S INTENTION FROM ITS EFFECT. *Traditional Christian theology has always known that God accommodates revelation to human capacity. In like manner, our proclamation of Scripture will be effective only if accommodated to the aptitude and receptivity of our hearers.*

However true it may be, as Ortlund writes, that the truth of Scripture can be recognized only through the inward working of the Holy Spirit, the "scandal" of the gospel ought to be enough on its own, without needlessly adding other offenses by the way we read or proclaim Scripture. In other words, inspired and authoritative words from the Bible can still have unintended consequences for various readers or hearers. Preachers are obligated to know their audiences and to try to remove every obstacle. It's not enough simply to blame the hearer for misperceiving the text's intention or to tell her to "get over it," particularly when the Bible's forms of speech are or have become inflammatory. The graphic descriptions in Hosea and other prophets were surely intended to shock the men and women of Israel, but they can also inflict collateral damage, so to speak, on some hearers today.

A similar case could be made with respect to descriptions of "the Jews," say, in the Gospel of John. Writing at the end of the first century, John the evangelist could scarcely have intended or foreseen the eventual persecution of Jews by Christians throughout European history. But John's innocent intention is not enough to cancel out the way such sharp rhetoric is heard by Jews today, even when nothing is added to the words of John's Gospel. Some recent versions of the Bible have attempted to counteract the anti-Semitic potential of such texts by translating "the Jews" as "the Jewish leaders."[54] That's a strategy that ought to instruct us here as well. It takes nothing away from the intention of an authoritative scripture when we recognize, in the course of preparing and delivering a sermon or lesson on this text, that the vehement language of the prophet will raise painful issues for some of our hearers.

4. WE MUST READ HOSEA AND GOMER DIALECTICALLY. *We musn't lose sight of the prophet's intended meaning, with its promises and threats. Neither should we lose sight of the text's unintended effects, especially its potential misuse as a precedent or model for the denigration or abuse of women.*

This is a lesson gleaned also from our consideration of the misdeeds of the patriarchs. We might grant, as did some precritical commentators, that the patriarchs' dubious actions — their lying or polygamy — might have expressed great faith or good intentions. But we would probably hasten to add, also with many precritical commentators, that these same actions offer no precedent for contemporary readers or hearers. The promises held forth by Hosea's oracles as a testimony to God's inextinguishable love are further canonized by the New Testament and should be cherished by all. Conversely, the threats uttered against Gomer and Israel and us are also deserving of a sober appreciation: God is God, the one who gives life and takes it away. That can be both good news and bad. We ought to cultivate the tendency of precritical commentators to read themselves into the story of Gomer, directing an appropriate suspicion against themselves as having any fidelity or righteousness worthy of their Christian calling.

However, we are also justified — indeed, mandated — to wonder and worry about the effects of the prophet's charged and gendered rhetoric. One justification comes from the blind spots of many precritical commentators, who fretted about how their congregations or readers would be affected if they thought one of God's prophets got away with fornication (their description, not mine). Yet they did not think to ask what other prejudicial models might be hidden in the book of Hosea, despite the fact that they would have been opposed to domestic violence and even took steps, during the Reformation, to address this social ill. If patristic, medieval, and Reformation writers strike us as a bit naive with respect to the pervasiveness of domestic violence, we today have no excuse for remaining so. We must see this other dimension of the prophet's words, granting the distinction between intention and effect, then name abuse as the sin it is.

Chapter Six

Silent Prophetesses?

Unraveling Theory and Practice in 1 Corinthians 11

I came to faith as a college junior, having dabbled for a few years in the youth counterculture of the late 1960s. I didn't yet know much about the Bible, but I was instantly fascinated by the piety and apparent purity of the Christian women I'd begun to meet. A friend of mine, seeing my interest in one young woman, remarked that I could really impress her if I memorized her favorite Bible verse, which he just happened to know — 1 Corinthians 11:14. Eagerly I flipped through my Bible, only to read, "Does not even nature itself teach you that if a man has long hair, it is a dishonor to him?" Still wearing my hair at shoulder length, I was crestfallen. He just grinned. He'd set me up, of course, as only a friend can.

You can sometimes tell a lot about how a particular church reads the Bible just by looking at people's heads in church — particularly if you notice that all the men have short hair and every woman wears a headscarf of some sort. Feelings about how the head and body should be covered (or not) can run just as strong today as they did in the third century, when Tertullian raged against Christian women given to adornment as "the devil's gateway."[1] The apparel and public demeanor of Christian women is the concern of a number of New Testament texts, including the so-called "household codes" found in Ephesians, Colossians, and 1 Peter, but also the familiar passages that bar women from public leadership, such as 1 Corinthians 14 and 1 Timothy 2. In a later chapter, we'll take a look at these latter two passages and their prohibitions against women speaking in church and teaching men. In this chapter, however, we'll sort through the many theological, exegetical, and practical questions bearing on gender roles that arise in the short space of 1 Corinthians 11:2-16.

A Snarl of Questions about Practices and Explanations

The Apostle's instructions about the proper demeanor of women who pray or prophesy are part of a series of exhortations about Christian behavior and morality. In chapter 10, Paul warns the Corinthians against sexual immorality and explains how a Christian's freedom of conscience might bear on eating meat offered to idols. In the second half of chapter 11, he addresses problems in the way the Lord's Supper was being observed. The first half of chapter 11, however, focuses on something Paul did not like about the practice of worship in Corinth, and he offers a variety of what we might call "theoretical" arguments to explain his concern and change their practice.

The practice that Paul disapproved seems clear enough: he did not think it proper for a woman to pray or prophesy with her head not covered (11:5). Of course, just what sort of covering is not quite so clear, but neither are other elements of his argument — such as his appeal to the angels (11:10), his assertion about what nature teaches (11:14), and his references to tradition and custom as warrants of some sort (11:2, 16). The arguments he draws from the creation of woman are clearer (11:8-9), though these assertions still raise problems (some of which we'll reserve for our later look at 1 Timothy 2). Perhaps the most vexing question of all is found in 11:7, where Paul extols the man as "the image and glory of God," but calls woman "the glory of man." The description is oddly unbalanced. Does he mean to imply that a woman is *not* God's image? Such an inference draws on silence, though many readers did so infer. But could Paul really have meant to deny that women also bear the image of God?

The exegetical problems raised by Paul's abrupt style continue to trouble the best interpreters today. It's easy to see why lectionaries might look elsewhere for liturgical texts! But as we'll see, it's also nothing new to hesitate over these difficulties. There may be something well worth learning from our forebears' deliberations on the theory and practice of women's ecclesiastical roles — even if we learn only that this is an old and knotty problem.

As we survey the history of the interpretation of 1 Corinthians 11, we'll discover that precritical commentators often agreed about the theory or theology that informs what the Bible says about gender roles, but disagreed about how the theory was (or ought to be) applied or practiced. We'll also see how a commentator's practice of exegesis can reveal things otherwise unannounced about his "real" exegetical theory or working presuppositions. Since we'll be using these terms throughout this chapter to clarify how Paul's words have been understood and used, let me add a comment on theory and practice.

When we distinguish theory from practice, sometimes we think of "theory" as a grand but untested *predictor* of some outcome. However, it's probably better to think of theory not so much as a predictor of results, but more as systematic *reflection* on practice. Such reflection might tell us that a practice has broken down and needs to be restored to what it was meant to be. Or it might tell us that the theory itself — that is, our previous reflection on practice — was wrong. In either case, it's artificial to insist that theory precedes practice, for the best theories are honed by a cycle of practice and reflection. One way to read 1 Corinthians 11:2-16, then, is as Paul's "theoretical" or theological reflection on what could be seen as the new practice of women prophesying. The passage shows how he uses theological reflection to correct a practice as well as how his theological exhortations (especially in vv. 11-12) are informed by what he observes. In sorting out the arguments and observations embedded in 1 Corinthians 11:2-16 as they have been understood over the centuries, we'll begin with an account of the practices Paul is addressing, both approved and otherwise, then work backward (so to speak) to describe his theory or theology of gender roles along with his supporting arguments.

"Practice" in Corinth: What *Were* Those Women Doing?

There are really two practices to be noted in 11:2-16. One is the practice that the passage takes for granted, namely, that women in Corinth were praying and prophesying, presumably in public worship, just as described in chapter 14. The other practice was a mode of the first, in that the women in Corinth who were praying and prophesying evidently did so without proper headcovering. The first practice is scarcely noted by Paul, neither contested nor interdicted. Instead, the passage is all about the "practice" of a woman's headcovering, whether understood to indicate her veil, her long hair, or some sign of the man's authority (vv. 5, 10, 15).

It might seem logical, therefore, to skip the prophetic activities of these women and go straight to the controversy over *what* they should wear on their heads, and *why* — except for the fact that in the history of the interpretation of this passage, exegetes have not agreed about what it was that the Corinthian women prophets were actually doing. Precritical commentators ranged among three or four positions.

The Corinthian Prophetesses Were Listening to God's Word

The most restrictive interpretation was voiced by three commentators, all ministers in Zurich in the 1520s and 1530s: Huldreich Zwingli, Heinrich Bullinger, and Conrad Pellican.[2] Prophecy, according to Bullinger, consists not only in proclaiming and expounding divine things, but first of all in *understanding* them. The "prophesying" of women in the Acts of the Apostles represented the last option: such women were "wholly devoted to prophecy, that is, to the word of the Lord," in that they listened to proclamation and understood it. Indeed, in 1 Corinthians 11:5, "Paul plainly uses the word *prophesying* for *listening to prophecy*."[3] And how does Bullinger know this? Because Paul — nay, the Lord! — so clearly forbids women to teach, as is proved by 1 Corinthians 14:34 and 1 Timothy 2:12. Thus, whatever the women were doing in 1 Corinthians 11, it could not have involved public speaking or teaching.

The position staked out by these teachers in Zurich is significant for at least two reasons. First, it was a view that found few imitators. Second, it illustrates a tendency, noted also in the case of Gomer, to let scriptural commands resolve the ambiguities of other passages. Equally, it exemplifies a determination to hold to a particular *theory* despite the possibility that the first-century *practice* did not always fit. Nonetheless, for Bullinger, 1 Corinthians 14:34 forbids women to speak in church, and that command *defines* what 11:5 ambiguously *describes*.

The Corinthian Prophetesses Proclaimed God's Word, but Not in Public

Bullinger's definition of prophecy, wherein the prophetic gift could be manifested as a purely passive understanding of the word of God, was not the norm. For most commentators, prophets not only understood God's word, they also proclaimed it — as revelation, exposition, exhortation, or teaching. So argued John Chrysostom, who was much impressed with women of the New Testament, including the prophet Priscilla but also Junia, whom he freely acknowledged as holding the title of apostle. But Chrysostom still had to reconcile the offices of these women with 1 Timothy 2:12. He did so with a one-word gloss: women were forbidden to teach *publicly,* so they must have carried out their instruction in private.[4] This was no new argument. Early in the third century, Origen had denied any public role to biblical women as part of his refutation of the Montanists, who (he fumed) honored their prophetesses Priscilla and Maximilla more than Christ.[5]

Other church fathers held the same view,[6] as did many medievals. Aquinas was especially influential. He freely allowed that women may have the gift of prophecy, that is, they may *receive* divine revelation. They may also *announce* what is revealed to them — but not in public, that is, not "officially" or in the name of the church. Women may openly prophesy or teach only among women, as in convents. But even if Thomas was less strict in applying other parts of 1 Corinthians 11:2-16 (for instance, men needn't uncover their heads for private prayer or when teaching in school disputations), it remained true for Aquinas that women really may "prophesy" and what they receive really is a divine gift. Indeed, elsewhere it emerges that he is much less concerned to bar women from *prophetic* office than to make clear that they are utterly disqualified from *priestly* ordination.[7]

Aquinas was closely followed in the next three centuries by most Catholic writers, including Nicholas of Lyra, Denis the Carthusian, Cardinal Cajetan, and Claude Guilliaud, among others. Cajetan is of special note for reading the two crucial verses as progressively restrictive: 1 Corinthians 11:5 forbids women to pray or prophesy *bare-headed*, while 14:34 adds that they may not do so *in public*. Cajetan may be suggesting that Paul was trying to curtail a prevailing and more permissive practice, whereby "public prayer or reading or teaching" had not yet been forbidden to "the holy women of that time" — thinking, perhaps, of Priscilla or Philip's daughters in Acts 18 and 21.[8]

By and large, Protestant commentators also liked the distinction between public and private contexts that patristic and medieval writers had long favored. While most of them held views that are complex and often mixed, sooner or later most of them granted that the apparent scandal of women prophesying is reduced if that action took place in private or only among other women. That is one of the readings offered by Calvin, for example, in his exposition of the Acts of the Apostles and 1 Corinthians 11:5. Priscilla and Philip's daughters would have exercised their gifts in this way, as would the Corinthian women prophets: "at home, or in a private place outside the public meeting," and Calvin even allows that there may have been men present.[9]

The Corinthian Women Were Public Prophets, but Only in Emergencies

One of the complicating factors for early Protestant commentators in considering prophecy by women, as well as prophecy in general, is that they were largely cessationist in their theology. That is to say, they believed that what we call the "charismatic" gifts of the Holy Spirit had long since ceased. For the Reformers, everything that the New Testament said about the office of prophet was to be applied in their own day not to the office of soothsayer or seer, but to the more ordinary office of teacher — the very office occupied by most of these Protestant commentators.

The threat of self-authorized prophets or teachers was taken seriously by all of the Reformers, and no less so when they imagined the office being claimed by a woman. All the more remarkable, then, that a handful of commentators can, in fact, imagine such a scenario. Sixteenth-century interpreters who held this view — if reluctantly, and with alternate explanations — include the moderate Catholic exegete Jacques Lefèvre d'Étaples, the Strasbourg reformer François Lambert, Martin Luther, and John Calvin. But none of these writers was as clear and sustained as Peter Martyr Vermigli. For Vermigli, prophecy is normally a public action in the sacred assembly; while some women may have prophesied in private, not all did so. Indeed, if it is more common among precritical commentators to subordinate 1 Corinthians 11:5 to 14:34 and to use Paul's silencing of women to minimize the significance of the Corinthian women prophets, Vermigli worked in the opposite direction. For him, 1 Corinthians 11:5 proves that "it was lawful for a woman both to speak and to prophesy in church."[10] To be sure, 1 Corinthians 14:34 does have force, as does 1 Timothy 2:12, but these verses state the ordinary rule that bears on ordinary women. But the office of prophetess is by definition an extraordinary calling.

In making this last point, Vermigli is found in the company of Lefèvre, Luther, and Calvin. Like Vermigli, these three also believed that women should not aspire to prophetic office, for which women are not normally suited or called. Nonetheless, there are too many examples of women prophets in the Bible to ignore. In fact, it seems to be the biblical pattern that God raises up women prophets especially when the church is in disarray (as in the early Reformation) — sometimes to shame men, but sometimes just because there is no man around who can do the job. Calvin admitted as much of Deborah: "If at some time women served as prophets and teachers, . . . raised up by the spirit of God, He who is immune from every law could do this. But because this is an exceptional case, it does not conflict with the constant and usual arrangement."[11] Yet Calvin did not quite restrict such exceptions to the past. Instead, he held a line close to what Vermigli explained at greater length:

> When a Church is being planted for the first time and there are no men to preach the Gospel, a woman may serve at first, provided that, after she has taught for a while, some man from among the faithful be ordained who from then on will minister the sacraments, teach, and pastor faithfully.[12]

For the sake of brevity, I've focused more on Vermigli than on the other four mentioned above, each of whom offers a unique testimony — again, often marked by some reticence. Nonetheless, it is clear that some significant sixteenth-century churchmen found themselves compelled to admit, if not argue, that the strictures against women speaking or teaching in church were not absolute. Instead, there were exceptions — exceptions impelled by biblical examples and correlated with reflection on contemporary experience.[13]

Today, these sixteenth-century opinions may seem like too much or not enough. The notion that women may at best be *emergency* ministers smacks of the sexist and racist notion from a more recent Christian past that women are adequate to teach the gospel on the mission field to ethnic nonbelievers, but they have no such status or credibility at home. In its time, however, the suggestion that women might teach men, and teach them in public, was as radical as it was biblical. Born of the tension between two parts of Paul's letter to the Corinthians, it was an exegetical solution that attempted to acknowledge the *theory* of male preeminence that these chapters presuppose, yet reconcile that theory to the equally biblical *practices* these commentators found scattered throughout the Old Testament and the New. Indeed, Luther's allowance for women as emergency ministers may well have contributed to their eventual ordination in Germany, when the "emergency" of the Second World War saw pastors' wives and other women filling pulpits left vacant by Lutheran ministers imprisoned or conscripted — and filling them well.[14]

Paul's Agenda: What Did He Want Men and Women to Wear?

So far, we have simply been mapping disagreements over what was really going on among the women of Corinth — a discussion complicated by what the Corinthian practice might imply for what women may do today. Given the range of disagreement, we should probably expect similar dissent over the lesser matter, namely, what should women who pray or prophesy have on their heads, and why?

What makes this passage fascinating, however, is that the Apostle doesn't speak only to women. He also addresses what *men* should or shouldn't wear in church, and he grounds his exhortation not only in biblical allusions but also in appeals to tradition, nature, and custom — all for what might seem a small and culturally-relative matter. Paul describes the problem from various angles: *veils* are theologically linked to a woman's long *hair,* and both seem to symbolize the *exousia* (usually read as "authority" in v. 10) that a woman should have on her head "because of the angels." The resulting argument is undeniably difficult. Small matter or not, Paul's instructions raised as many questions as they were intended to resolve.

Perhaps the crucial observation with which to begin is this: Paul affirms the prophetic speech of women without adding any qualifications, but he is quite vexed over the matter of headcoverings. More often than not, precritical commentators reversed Paul's priorities. They all worried lest women speak "prophetically," but many felt the church was free to adapt Paul's instructions about dress and hairstyles to changed times and circumstances. But if Paul's stipulations could be altered or suspended in the one case, why not also in the other? In studying these commentators, we want to see how they came to regard some parts of the apostolic injunctions as either inapplicable or less than fully binding. In so doing, we may discover how we too have come to adapt or disregard parts of Paul. We'll look at a number of commentators, beginning with the least flexible, then work our way toward those who found more room to negotiate with the Apostle.

Bullinger and the Scandal of Bareheaded Women

Protestants usually found Paul more flexible than Catholics did, but Bullinger is a stark exception. He was no more open to unveiled women than he was to women serving as prophets in any significant sense. The custom of women covering their heads is to be defended behind "a wall of bronze," and it was Bullinger's conviction that Paul's commands here are linked to the Old Testament prohibition of cross-dressing. That proof-text may explain the vehemence of his opinion, so strong that elsewhere he invoked Matthew 18:6 to underscore the scandal of such women, who would be better off drowned than to come to church so dishonorably arrayed.[15] Yet the Old Testament law does not explain the double standard whereby Bullinger held *women* strictly accountable to have heads covered in church, but relaxed the rule by allowing *men* to wear hats for warmth in winter. Nonetheless, Bullinger insisted these rules weren't meant legalistically but only to serve decorum and moderation. After all, to expose men to such chills would be inhumane, truly against the law of God and nature.

Roman Catholic Exegesis

For Thomas Aquinas and most Catholic writers, the details of this text were not troubling — largely because Paul's appeals to tradition and custom in vv. 2 and 16 dovetailed with Catholic understandings of ecclesiastical authority. For Thomas, the Apostle was merely modeling a precedent that Augustine enunciated: "In all things in which nothing certain is de-

121

fined by the holy Scriptures, the custom of the people of God and the practice of the majority is to be considered law."[16] Thomas was also happy to grant divine authority to the teachings of nature. But he still had to reconcile Paul with the practice of cutting the hair of nuns when they took their vows. The solution was close at hand: espoused to Christ, nuns are thus promoted to male dignity. Moreover, their shorn hair symbolizes the perpetual penitence associated with monasticism.

Despite its conservative tendency, Catholic exegesis presented other interesting variations. Denis the Carthusian defended Paul's rules just as they stand, but he admitted that the overall goal is simply propriety, and standards of propriety do vary with circumstances.[17] A century later, Cardinal Cajetan also didn't challenge these standards, but he did regard Paul's exhortations more as an admonition than as a command. Indeed, Cajetan felt the question of women's behavior in church was fully settled not by Scripture but only by the authoritative custom of the church, just as Paul anticipated in v. 16.[18] After Cajetan, in the years leading to the Council of Trent, this argument hardened against Protestants. Jean de Gaigny, Claude Guilliaud, and Ambrosius Catharinus Politus, commenting on Paul from 1539 to 1552, singled out the authority of church custom in this passage, predictably enough, as a perfect model for the church of their day.[19]

Erasmus and the Early Reformers

The Catholic commentators just named had ample provocation for drawing a line in defense of custom and tradition, based on writings from earlier in the century penned by Erasmus, Luther, Melanchthon, and Pellican. None of these four really objected to the arrangements described by Paul, at least with respect to women, but in the early days of the Reformation, they were especially alert against the encroachment of human traditions.

The *Paraphrase* of Erasmus is a case in point: he does not advocate any change in the restrictions of 1 Corinthians 11:2-16, but he does say that the entire passage pertains to *externals,* matters that vary according to time and place and that do not pertain to the heart of the gospel.[20] Luther followed a similar trajectory, arguing (as did Denis, above) that Paul's goal in 1 Corinthians was decency and order, and his specific rules must be accommodated to local custom — which was why Luther said he tolerated the

German custom of not veiling unmarried women, despite what Paul said.[21] Melanchthon actually incorporated such observations in Article 28 of the Augsburg Confession (1530), arguing that a woman does not necessarily sin if she appears in public with head uncovered. And although Conrad Pellican was Bullinger's colleague in Zurich, his views are much more Erasmian — indeed, he cites Erasmus verbatim. But Pellican also liked Bullinger's allowance for men to wear hats in winter, and he added this gloss to 1 Corinthians 11:4: "it is a disgrace for a man to pray with his head covered" could mean "covered *for the whole time.*"[22]

Later Protestant commentators — including Vermigli, Musculus, and Calvin — copied Pellican's suggestion that Paul's rule was sufficiently honored if the preacher doffed his cap at the beginning of the sermon, then put it back on. Clearly, it was a bold stroke in their day to set one's practice even slightly at variance from the apostolic precepts. In our day, when so few churches care what Paul said about headcoverings, their token gesture looks more like a case of scruples.

Protestant Readings of the 1540s and 1550s

We will end this part of our survey with the later Protestants just mentioned, who deliberate at even greater length to frame a sophisticated rationale for "accommodating" apostolic precepts to local circumstances.

Possibly the best account is that of Vermigli, who opens with the problem acutely framed: in Paul's day, men wore their heads bare as a sign of authority, but in our day (he writes), men remove caps as a sign of submission to authority. Vermigli then makes the first of several important distinctions: headcoverings merely *symbolize* the status of men and women, and symbols are relative to a particular time and a particular church.[23] In considering the force of 1 Corinthians 14:34, he adds a further distinction. Paul's assertion there that "women are not permitted to speak but should be subordinate, *as the law says*" is not explicitly found in the Old Testament. It is therefore an example of a "derived" precept — in this case, derived from the explicit command for woman's subordination in Genesis 3:16. Explicit precepts are in a sense the rules for judging the validity of derived precepts, which are to be retained only if supported by reason, common sense, universal consent, and the word of God.[24] In effect, Vermigli has carried into this context a distinction commonly observed in 1 Corinthians 7:12, 25, between apostolic doctrine and apostolic polity — between what Paul taught as a divine command and what he imparted as merely personal advice. It was not unknown to distinguish between primary and derived doctrines, but Vermigli is unusual in applying it to Paul's teaching about women's silence — even though he is not inclined to challenge the general practice.

The remarks of Musculus and Calvin make many of the points already covered by Vermigli, but they add interesting insights about the role of nature as a teacher of doctrine — particularly because they so strongly disagree over the details. Although Musculus would agree that the goal of Paul's regulations is order and decorum, these ingredients contribute to edification and so bear indirectly on salvation. Musculus is more inclined than Vermigli to present Paul's precepts as *divine* constitutions, and therefore also *fixed*. Consequently, he takes the teachings of nature somewhat as Aquinas did, as a guide to divine order, *if* nature is properly understood. So although there were times and cultures where men wore long hair and women went bareheaded, Musculus passes judgment against such cultures for favoring their customs over the teachings of reason and nature. Paul's advice is meant to counter the error of Christians in Corinth, who had wrongly adopted the Grecian tradition of "soft men and impudent women."[25]

Calvin took Paul's appeal to nature quite differently. He reports that there were many times in the past when long hair was accepted on men. Indeed, when Paul wrote to the Greeks in Corinth, men in France and Germany did not yet cut their hair and would have found it disgraceful to do so. So when Paul cites what *nature* teaches, he's simply appealing to the "common consent and usage *at that time*" to reinforce his presentation of what is proper and decorous.[26] Calvin's apparent recognition of the cultural relativity of men's hair lengths, however, seems at odds with what he said earlier, that a woman with a shaved head is "a loathsome, indeed an unnatural sight."[27] Women were therefore to wear their hair long and, lest they show off its beauty to attract onlookers, add another covering as well. Although patristic and medieval exegetes identified the "angels" of v. 10 as priests or bishops, Calvin dismisses that notion as farfetched. These angels are simply witnesses, with Christ, of any woman who casts off her headcovering.[28] But despite the seriousness with which Calvin takes Paul's words about veils, Calvin can also recognize that veils, like all matters of polity, should not be treated as if essential to one's salvation. His position thus resembles Melanchthon's, for he denies that piety or religion is destroyed if a woman forgets her shawl and he allows that customs vary. Still, Calvin really can't imagine any local custom that wouldn't honor the words of 1 Corinthians 11:5.[29]

So, What Did Paul Want?

For the first-century church in Corinth, Paul presumably wanted men to have short hair and women to wear long hair and some sort of covering. Though they defended exceptions in the case of nuns, later Catholic commentators were happy not only with Paul's specific injunctions but also with Paul's example of how ecclesiastical traditions and customs have a defining authority over against Scripture alone — a view sharpened against Protestant readings in the course of the sixteenth century. For Catholics, Paul's appeal to "nature" simply anticipated the view of Aquinas and others, that the law of nature and divine law are fundamentally one. Many Protestants would have shared that high view of natural law but were not inclined to invoke it here. For them, and for moderate Catholics such as Erasmus, the customs and natural practices of first-century Corinth might express order and decorum, but they weren't necessarily universal, nor did they represent more than the externals of the faith. The Reformation was itself a reaction against spurious religious traditions and laws. Most Protestant interpreters were moving in a tentative but determined way to discern differing levels of authority and fixity even in apostolic, scriptural precepts. Their goal was to defend salvation by faith, not works, and to protect Christian freedom and Christian consciences from the tyranny of unbiblical demands. So if their Catholic opponents read 1 Corinthians 11:2-16 as affirming the authority of ecclesiastical custom, Protestant readers saw instead an affirmation of custom's provisional and flexible character, as well as its dependence on the prior authority of Scripture. This new reading was revolutionary in its potential, even if, outwardly, Protestant and Catholic women would have looked about the same.

Filling in the Gaps of Paul's Theory

The practices Paul addressed in 1 Corinthians 11:2-16 express his underlying theory of gender relations, which could be fairly described as a combination of subordination and equivalence.[30] The practice of women prophesying looks like a mark of equivalence, but the practice of women wearing a covering is a sign of subordination to male preeminence or authority. We've already observed several of Paul's lesser arguments and articulations, which marshal tradition, custom, and nature to support or illustrate his theory. Now we'll examine how commentators grappled with the argument that woman's subordination stems from her creation, focusing particularly on whether women bear the image of God. Once again, we'll see that readers were exercised as much by what Paul did not say as by what he did say.

Arguing from Silence

Precritical commentators would have had no problem with the Bible affirming male preeminence, but they *did* have problems at 1 Corinthians 11:7 — because Paul's affirmation there seemed too strong! The crux lay in what Paul *didn't* say. The verse argues that men should have heads uncovered for prayer or prophesying on the grounds that man is "the image and glory of God." Woman, however, is "the glory of man." As noted, the formula is unbalanced. One might have expected Paul to say that woman is the *image and* glory of man, but he doesn't. He also doesn't say that woman is the image of God — nor does he deny it! So, on the one hand, Genesis 1:27 says both male and female were made in the image of God. On the other hand, when Paul says here that *men* are the image and glory of God, he means also to *deny* something about women. But what?

A Very Old Question: What Is the Image of God?

It's a commentator's job to fill the obvious gaps created by Paul's silence. Did Paul mean to overturn Genesis 1:27? In what way is or isn't woman the image of God? We'll answer these two questions by clarifying, first, how the image of God has been understood, then how that understanding was applied to 1 Corinthians 11:7 through the history of interpretation.

"Image of God" occurs about a dozen times in Scripture (including seemingly parallel constructions such as "image of the heavenly one" or "image of the Lord"). The phrase is probably best read as having three distinguishable references. Sometimes it denotes something universal about us as human beings, as in Genesis 1:27. In other cases, it's applied to Jesus Christ as uniquely an image of his heavenly Father. Yet another application is eschatological, in that the sanctification of Christians entails conformity to the likeness of God or Christ. Unfortunately, precritical commentators were often hampered by a misplaced quest for one definition that would suit all applications.

Through the era of the Reformation, three or four definitions of the image of God were at play. Probably the most influential view was that of Augustine, who argued that the image of God is situated in our mind or soul, particularly in *the rational part of our soul,* whose most noble function is to contemplate God (as opposed to the "lower" aspect of the soul, which is occupied with caring for the body).[31] Another common reading, often credited to Chrysostom, was to identify the image of God as the *dominion over creation* that God entrusted to our first parents. Yet another interpretation derives from Ambrosiaster, the unidentified fourth-century author of a commentary on the Pauline epistles long attributed to Ambrose, as well as of a treatise on the Old Testament. Ambrosiaster argued that the image of God was a matter of *headship,* in that God is imaged foremost by Adam: even as all things are from one God, so also are all human beings from one man, Adam. All other men share in Adam's original function of imaging God in this way. A fourth understanding of the image of God was especially favored among Protestant commentators. Their rediscovery of salvation by grace fed a strong Christocentrism, which in turn fueled their interest in the work of Christ. They preferred to define the image of God in Genesis 1:27 both by the excellence they saw in Christ and by what he imparts to Christians by way of restoration. Thus, many Protestant definitions tacitly built upon the medieval idea of *original righteousness,* the moral perfection that our first parents lost but which is displayed in Christ and restored in us by him.

A Very Hard Question: How Do Women Image God?

Of these four definitions of the image of God, only Ambrosiaster's was drafted with 1 Corinthians 11:7 in mind. Indeed, it's probable that he wanted not just an allusion to the hierarchy of headship represented by the succession in 11:3 — God : Christ : man : woman — but a definition calculated to disqualify women from bearing God's image and from the authority it connoted.[32] So for Ambrosiaster the solution was easy: woman is *not* God's image, as 1 Corinthians 11:7 "proves" — though when he came to other "image" texts, his definition faltered precisely because some of them, such as Colossians 3:10, clearly speak in an egalitarian and universal way of the image as renewed in us by Christ. Consequently, while medieval theologians knew his definition, they invoked it sparingly. The only ones who were truly fond of Ambrosiaster's definition were medieval canon lawyers, perhaps because it was part of their job description (so to speak) to exclude women from exercising ecclesiastical authority.[33]

Augustine's account is more difficult, largely because it looks like he is prepared to diminish woman's share of the image of God, yet his intention is just the opposite.[34] For Augustine, both men and women truly do possess the image of God, because the image pertains to the soul, while sex pertains to the body. But our souls have two parts, one more noble and the other less so, and these parts are *symbolized* by male and female. Our higher, rational soul contemplates God and eternal truths; our lower, affective soul ministers to the needs of the body. Reason commands; the affections obey. The analogy may confuse, however, because both sexes *have* both parts of the soul, though each sex *symbolizes* only one of the parts. If traditional gender expectations survive at the level of the symbolic — men command, women obey — there is still a somewhat egalitarian agenda at work. Real women may contemplate God, just as real men, too, must care for their bodies. And both have or bear the image of God.

For Augustine, then, 1 Corinthians 11:7 is speaking not about actual and complete men and women but about the two parts of the soul, which are symbolized by the two sexes. In other words, in v. 7, Paul is saying that our higher rationality (symbolized by men, but found in both sexes) is the image and glory of God, while the affections and desires of our "lower" soul (symbolized by women, but found in both sexes) are the glory of man. Let me risk a paraphrase: our rationality at its highest ought to reflect the divine, just as our desires at their best should reflect our rationality. Subtle? Yes. But what's really striking is Augustine's motive — to *avoid* saying that women do not bear the image of God, an implication that he fears readers of Paul could easily but mistakenly draw. Women don't symbolize the image, Augustine concludes, but they are made in it and renewed in it by Christ.[35]

Not surprisingly, Augustine's subtlety was largely missed by later readers. Indeed, no matter how they read other passages about the image of God, when they came to 1 Corinthians 11:7, medieval and Reformation readers often defaulted to Chrysostom's view — that the image consists in the exercise of dominion, a privilege that women either do not possess, or possess in a lesser degree. A few examples will suffice. Like most medievals, Denis the Carthusian followed Augustine by identifying the image of God with rationality, possessed by both men and women. For Denis, 1 Corinthians 11:7 says women are not in God's image — because reason is much stronger in men *and* because man *rules* over woman. Denis is obviously trying to salvage his preferred definition of the image from a text where it doesn't fit, so he adds an appeal to dominion as a fall-back.[36] This dilemma ensnared Catholics and Protestants alike. Luther, for example, defined the image mostly in terms of righteousness, understood not as a faculty but as a right relationship with God. But at 1 Corinthians 11:7, he identified "governing" as the "public" aspect of the divine likeness.[37]

Some drew another strand from Augustine, by which a woman images God only as joined with her husband. Musculus wrote:

> The woman also shares the image and glory of God insofar as she is the flesh of the man . . . ; [but] she does not share [it] if she is considered separately, insofar as she is subject to the man as her head. What is read in Genesis pertains to the first sense, but what is stated here by the Apostle . . . fits with the latter sense.[38]

Wolfgang Capito, Bullinger, and Catharinus used similar notions of a woman's "incorporation" with her husband to argue that she does share in the image of God, but she does so in some lesser or subordinate sense, and that explains Paul's words here. Vermigli supplied what was missing from Paul's text by applying a slightly different explanation. Woman bears God's image because she has dominion over *lesser* creatures. To them, she is therefore the image of God — but not to her husband, to whom she is subordinate.[39]

Calvin may serve as a final example. Like all his Protestant colleagues (save Musculus), Calvin preferred to avoid defining the image in terms of dominion. But his solution to 1 Corinthians 11:7 still took recourse to dominion. Without a doubt, woman was created in God's image, Calvin argued, but "in a secondary degree":[40]

> When he speaks about the image here, he is referring to the conjugal order. . . . Paul is not dealing here with innocence and holiness, which women can have just as well as men, but with the preeminence that God has given to the man so that he might be superior to the woman. The glory of God is seen in this higher degree of dignity even as it is reflected in every superior authority.[41]

Paul's concern here isn't with what could be called the "internal" image of God, but with the manifestation of that image's "external" polity or arrangements — with the "conjugal order." The spiritual equality of the sexes that Scripture affirms elsewhere, most strongly in Galatians 3:28, is not to be confused with the external ordering of family, church, and society. The spiritual kingdom does not overthrow or disrupt civil affairs. Thus, a husband and father is like a king, Calvin wrote: "He reflects the glory of God because of the dominion which is in his hands."[42] In effect, Calvin corrected Paul, adding what he saw as some needed precision. Despite what 1 Corinthians 11:7 might suggest, women *are* in God's image. But on account of their eminence, men are much more so — so much more, in fact, that Calvin saw God as more glorified in the birth of a boy than in the birth of a girl.[43]

Privileging Theory over Practice?

Paul has more to say about sex and gender roles in this passage. I've deliberately given short shrift to vv. 11-12, where Paul's assertion of the preeminence of man (in vv. 8-9) is counterbalanced by an affirmation of mutuality between the sexes. Many commentators took the latter verses as the Apostle's attempt to offer women a modicum of comfort after the difficult words that went before. Few, however, lingered over the question of mutuality or allowed it to do more than sweeten the overall exhortation, almost as an afterthought.

That's not to imply that these commentators held the mutuality of the sexes in contempt, but rather to recognize that their interests usually lay elsewhere. What precritical commentators seem most interested in, and surest of, is the preeminence of men over women. What is of interest to us, however, is how they see that theory working out in practice — and what they're *unsure* of along the way.

Although there are other ways to analyze 1 Corinthians 11:2-16, we have surveyed the history of this passage's interpretation by distinguishing two practices in Corinth, along with one theory. The observable practices were (1) women praying and prophesying, and (2) women doing so with heads uncovered. In the background one may assume that there were also men praying and prophesying. What is less clear is whether the men of Corinth also ran afoul of the Apostle by praying with heads covered or wearing their hair long, or whether they are only rhetorical counterparts to the women. The theory that serves to explain and authorize Paul's exhortation is the headship of man over woman, of which it seems a corollary that a man is the image and glory of God while woman is the glory of man.

What is remarkable about traditional exegesis of this passage is the extent to which outside texts are brought to bear to shift Paul's focus or to explain Paul's silences. Take the first practice we looked at. That women in Corinth were praying or prophesying is a practice that Paul doesn't really address, but *all* the commentators do! Why? Because in the very same epistle, in 1 Corinthians 14:34, Paul says women should keep silent in church — and silent prophecy would seem to be an oxymoron. The history of interpretation here is dominated by attempts to reconcile a plain reading of 11:5 with a plain reading of 14:34. Something had to give. Often, interpreters denied that the women of 11:5 prophesied *in public* (and, sometimes, at all) in order to avoid a breach of 14:34. But there were other options, because there were other models. In particular, there were models — in Scripture *and* in the contexts and cultures of precritical commentators — of women who were called by God to lead and to proclaim a divine word. None of these commentators envisioned the ministry of proclamation as regularly falling to women, but some in the era of the Reformation went so far as to authorize women's temporary ministry on the grounds of necessity, without a miraculous calling, signs, or wonders.

Paul's great concern for the *veiling* of women was also a concern among precritical commentators, but nowhere near as great. Commentators were much more worried about women serving as teachers or preachers than about what women wore on their heads. And yet they did worry about that, too. The history of the interpretation of Paul's instructions about headcoverings again reveals the diversity among exegetes, ranging from the angry outbursts of Bullinger (or Tertullian) to the measured recognition of Luther, Calvin, and others that men and women are not saved or lost by what they wear or fail to wear on their heads. And yet, even among the more flexible interpreters, the allowance that there are situations where women might go bareheaded never became a standing permission. There is an odd tension here. Even though some Reformation commentators insisted that Paul's instructions are external matters, things not bearing on salvation and therefore liable to change with time and circumstance, their conviction stopped short of implementation. An obvious sort of suspicion is raised when these male pastors fail to imagine changes in the headcoverings of *women*. But a rather different sort is raised when even the exceptions they grant to *themselves* are so tentative. Five Swiss commentators of the sixteenth century agreed that a preacher might wear a hat to keep warm in the pulpit. Yet for most (if not all), propriety still needed a brief and token removal of the preacher's cap during the service.

There was greater assurance among commentators when they came to consider Paul's account of male headship and preeminence. Clearly, this made sense to them. What made less sense, however, was Paul's disturbing overstatement — again, that pesky implication drawn from silence — that seemed to deny that women bear God's image. Taken at face value, 1 Corinthians 11:7 upsets almost all the definitions of the image of God found elsewhere in Scripture. To deny that woman bears that image is potentially to deny her humanity and her salvation. No one wanted to allow that implication, and everyone labored to fix this seeming defect in Paul's argument. In many cases, commentators were forced to adopt definitions of the image of God that they found theologically problematic and were otherwise inclined to disfavor. Nonetheless, even if they couldn't account for every obstacle in the text, they still tried to make the rough places smooth.

Allowing Practice to Complicate Theory Today

Texts like 1 Corinthians 11:2-16 are often read in order to extract absolute statements about the way men and women are or what they must do or be. As such, they provoke strong responses from readers, and lectionaries pass them by. But the history of exegesis suggests that these strong responses are not homogenous. Some saw women prophesying as inconsistent with Paul's later injunction against women speaking in church and therefore denied or vetoed their calling to prophesy. Others saw the practice as consistent with instances of women who prophesied in Scripture, and later. Both views ran into biblical continuities *and* discontinuities. What can *we* learn from their struggles?

1. NOT EVERY ARGUMENT OR COMMAND IN THE BIBLE CARRIES THE SAME WEIGHT. *Many precritical readers recognized that Paul's words — like all effective speech — were accommodated to his readers' culture and circumstances. They also saw Paul as concerned less for specific rules than for the order and decorum such rules served, so that Christian freedom might be preserved and consciences protected by love of neighbor.*

It's an ancient notion that some acts or behavior are ethically neutral, neither right nor wrong. The traditional term for such matters is *adiaphora,* "indifferent" things. Christians applied the concept also to matters neither commanded nor forbidden by Scripture, and sometimes to matters that did not bear on salvation one way or the other. The notion took on a new life in the sixteenth century, however, as the early Protestants reclaimed freedom of conscience — often voiced as freedom from papal tyranny or freedom from human traditions — against a plethora of ceremonies and regulations that they found nowhere in Scripture. Even in what the Bible teaches, not all is binding on the conscience, particularly in the case of *polity* — the rules that may pertain to the good ordering of a church's life, but which certainly do not bear on salvation. The Reformers we've seen who granted more latitude on hats and veils are in the first wave of this growing awareness, as their tentative openness testifies. The same awareness appears in the recognition that Paul's appeal to "nature" is really an appeal to local custom; it's less a universal truth than a rhetorical corroboration of his point. *Our* customs, as Luther and Calvin noted, may differ — for better, or worse, or just different.

The cautious flexibility modeled by Luther, Calvin, and other Reformers offers a lesson for today. Even though Christians in the West rarely worry about headcoverings, one can still find groups and congregations (and, of course, websites!) where the issue is important — sometimes for good reasons, sometimes not. The yardstick we'd do well to use is the same one early Protestants found in Paul: What is the local custom, and what practice best serves the goals of order, decorum, freedom, and charity that Paul himself envisioned?

2. WHEN ANALOGIES ARE DRAWN FROM SCRIPTURE, MORE IS BETTER. *The women who prophesied in Corinth set an example that commentators sought to explain by appealing to texts that were*

arguably clearer. Some took the rule in 1 Corinthians 14:34 as proof that women never really prophesied; others found parallels in texts such as Acts 21:9, where Paul himself met Philip's four daughters, all with the gift of prophecy. The best commentaries anchored their clarifications in both kinds of text.

The commentators' problem here is similar to their problem with Hosea's marriage. Namely, in clarifying an obscure text, which cross-reference ought to trump its rivals? The problem with Bullinger's redefinition of prophecy as merely *hearing* the word with understanding is that it forced an unnatural reading upon a host of passages (in both testaments) that depict women in a prophetic and, often, apparently public role. The common alternative, that women prophesied "in private," may still be untrue to the reality in Corinth, but it's at least an attempt to bring a broader biblical witness to bear. The same may be said with respect to the peculiar "slighting" of women as bearing God's image in 1 Corinthians 11:7. Few interpreters besides Ambrosiaster allowed this text to eviscerate the implications of so many other passages in which the image of God clearly evokes the humanity and regeneration of both men *and women.* The plain sense of a text is a good thing, but the plain sense of the whole counsel of God is better.

3. THE PROCLAMATION OF THE GOSPEL IS MORE IMPORTANT THAN THEORIES ABOUT GENDER HIERARCHY. *Traditional commentators were patriarchal and they easily found their views mirrored and warranted in Paul. Nonetheless, they knew there were limits — doctrines and practices where gender roles had to take a backseat.*

In offering this as a lesson of the history of interpretation, I certainly do not mean to understate the degree to which precritical commentators resisted departing from what they saw as the biblical norm in general polity and practice, much less the gender roles that most of them saw as fixed by Scripture for as long as this life shall last. Nonetheless, few if any saw these roles as eternal! That conclusion emerges in a number of places, including from the strategies by which they tried to sort out the implications of 1 Corinthians 11:7 for women as bearers of the divine image.

Precritical commentators saw in the Apostle what modern readers often see: a collision of sorts between two agendas and two kinds of text. On the one hand, Paul can write in a radically egalitarian vein, grounded in our redemption, as in Galatians 3:28: "there is no longer male and female, for all of you are one in Christ Jesus." On the other hand, Paul can write of male headship and female subordination, grounded in creation, as in the supporting arguments of 1 Corinthians 11:2-16 (as well as in 1 Timothy 2:11-15, which we'll examine later on). These male commentators are keen to preserve the theory of male preeminence and leadership that vv. 3 and 7 describe, but they offer two crucial qualifications that ought to be ours as well.

First, there's a higher "theory" at work in the corpus of Pauline writings and in the New Testament as a whole — a theory that relativizes the doctrine of male headship. As we saw in the exegetical distress surrounding the apparent exclusion of women from the image of God in 1 Corinthians 11:7, precritical commentators interpreted the "lesser" imaging of God by women in terms of the external realm. As demeaning or paternalistic as that seems, it is also a backhanded affirmation of Galatians 3:28 and of the spiritual equality of women with men. In many ways, Paul's theory of spiritual equality is also at work in the background of 1 Corinthians 11:2-16, tacitly guiding many of these exegetes and preventing the erasure of the Corinthian women prophets.

Second, whatever one makes of the theory of male headship that is meant to inform Paul's desire that women pray with heads covered, that theory does not challenge or check the practice of women prophesying (even if it does inform what they wear). Whatever Paul meant by this theory or doctrine, he did not intend to censure women for fulfilling a call to pray or prophesy. Rather, he meant to facilitate that practice and ensure its success. Scrupulous as precritical commentators were with respect to the polity of gender roles, they were more scrupulous still with respect to divine sovereignty. As Lefèvre, Lambert, Luther, Calvin, and Vermigli began to glimpse, if God calls women to proclaim the gospel, even for a short time, who are we to object? These five commentators would surely agree that we must always be ready to revise our theoretical understandings when God's surprising practices intervene.

Chapter Seven

Divorce

Moses, Jesus, and Paul on the Proper End of Marriage

I n an earlier chapter, we saw something of Martin Luther's generosity of spirit toward his prince, Philip of Hesse, whose marriage had grown cold but whose libido had not. Luther was among the first and fiercest Protestant defenders of marriage, and he hated divorce. In fact, it was Luther's hatred of divorce that drove him to commend to Philip that surprising alternative: not to put away his wife but to take a second one, and to keep the whole arrangement a secret. Luther and Philip naively hoped Philip's first wife — and her mother — would be happy to go along. They weren't.

Although the Reformation is usually remembered for its ardent defense of justification by grace through faith and for its assertion that "Scripture alone" was the final authority for belief and conduct, early Protestants had other concerns, too. Less often recalled is the revolution they fomented in the way Christians thought about marriage — a veritable sea-change, in which marriage was taken out of the hands of the church and given over to civil authorities. No small part of their motives for "secularizing" marriage was their conviction that the Roman church had distorted the biblical view of divorce, adding tangles of restrictions and exceptions that were impossible to unsnarl except with the aid of a good lawyer and, better still, some political influence. Like Luther, all the Reformers hated divorce. No one hoped to see *more* divorces among their parishioners. But prevailing laws governing marriage and divorce seemed unbiblical and out of control. Theirs was a quest to bring the pendulum back to center.

In our own day, the divorce pendulum has swung its full arc and back, scattering the churched and the unchurched all along its path. In my own lifetime, American society has gone from stigmatizing divorce to the once-controversial notion of "no fault" divorces, and on to the idea of a "good" divorce that harms no one, or the "expressive" divorce that looks to end a marriage for the sake of personal growth. More lately, psychologists, social workers, and others have begun to react against the fallout of these broken marriages and families, looking at divorce's "unexpected legacy" and indicting what one writer has called our "divorce culture."[1]

Churches have tracked these swings and reactions in diverse ways. Roman Catholicism has moved little if at all in what it teaches and practices with respect to divorce, and one may find Protestant voices that mirror a similarly absolutist position. But many denominations, mainline and otherwise, have significantly accommodated society's changes.[2] The Westminster Confession of Faith (part of the constitution of my own Presbyterian denomination) originally allowed divorce and remarriage only on the grounds of adultery or desertion, and went on to condemn the proclivity to look for other causes as a sign of "human corruption."[3] Nonetheless, both northern and southern Presbyterians softened this passage in the 1950s. The southern church went further, recognizing that a "gross and persistent denial of the marriage vows" or "unfaithfulness (spiritual or physical)" can indeed cause a marriage to "[die] at the heart," leading to separation or divorce — and adding that divorced persons should pray about not remarrying, given the obvious failure in their first marriage.[4] Such wording sounds moralistic and antique only half a century later, when discipline for marital breakup in the Presbyterian Church has all but disappeared and divorce has come to be viewed as statistically normative and inevitable, however regrettable.

What does the Bible say about divorce and remarriage? More to the point of our study, what have Christians *said* the Bible says about divorce and remarriage, and what can we learn from the history of the interpretation of these texts? In this chapter we'll look at how the exegetical components of this issue have been variously weighted and understood by a sampling of Christian commentators. Along the way, we'll point out some of the developments in Roman Catholic marriage law that Protestant leaders variously affirmed and contested. But first, we need a quick tour of the exegetical difficulties.

Moses vs. Jesus vs. Paul

The key texts in this discussion are attributed to Moses, Jesus, and Paul, but no small part of the problem lies in the divergence among these biblical authorities. Moses' chief contribution was the "writ of divorce" mentioned in Deuteronomy 24:1-4, which seems to allow a man to dismiss his wife for fairly trivial objections. The text is well known because it is denounced by Jesus[5] as having been permitted by Moses only "because of the hardness of your hearts, . . . but from the beginning it was not so." Obviously, Jesus censured such divorces, but how does that work out in practice? Matthew 5 also criticizes those who, by lusting, commit adultery in their hearts; yet we still take actual fornication as a greater sin than mental imaginings. Should all our laws be revised or tightened in light of Jesus' critique? Was Moses wrong to allow this concession, or was Jesus just recalling an ideal?

The words of Jesus may conflict not only with those of Moses, but also with his own. While Matthew, Mark, and Luke all report Jesus as teaching that "whoever divorces his wife and marries another commits adultery," only Matthew (in 5:32 and 19:9) inserts a qualifier with huge implications: "except for unchastity." Is it problematic that the words of Jesus differ among these Gospels? Many think so. Either Mark and Luke carelessly abridged Jesus' words, thereby escalating his teaching into an absolute prohibition; or else Matthew highhandedly relaxed the stricter teachings of the Lord. So when pastors teach or preach on these texts, which edition of Jesus should they follow?

In 1 Corinthians 7, Paul adds to the complexity by allowing something like divorce when an unbeliever is unwilling to remain with a Christian spouse. Though Paul hopes such mixed marriages will survive, he permits these partners to separate — the so-called "Pauline privilege."[6] But how is the permission granted by Paul to be squared with what Jesus taught? Was Paul paraphrasing Jesus? Or was he saying something new, adding to Jesus' "unchastity" clause so as to offer desertion, too, as grounds for divorce? These varied possibilities are raised by the curious way in which Paul presents some instructions as if they were the very words of Jesus, as in v. 10: "I give charge, not I but the Lord," while other matters are framed more modestly, as in v. 25: "I have no command of the Lord, but I give my opinion as one who by the Lord's mercy is trustworthy." Some of Paul's teachings are attributed to the Lord Jesus, then, even if they do not bear a verbatim resemblance to the Gospels. Other advice is attributed not to Jesus but to Paul — though if Paul speaks as the Lord's apostle, aren't his "mere" opinions inspired, too? In any case, Paul's instructions about divorce here seem more detailed than anything attributed to Jesus and weave Jesus' authority together with his own.

One more complication arises at Romans 7, where an analogy from marriage is used to explain Paul's point about "dying to the law."

> A married woman is bound by law to her husband as long as he lives; but if her husband dies she is discharged from the law concerning the husband. Accordingly, she will be called an adulteress if she lives with another man while her husband is alive. But if her husband dies she is free from that law, and if she marries another man she is not an adulteress. (vv. 2-3)

Paul is discussing freedom in Christ; marriage is just a handy illustration. But is there an authoritative note about marriage here anyway? Did Paul mean to modify Jesus' teachings in the Gospels? As we will see, some traditional commentators have thought so.

The confusion generated by these exegetical problems would not amount to much if Christian marriages never foundered. However, not only has the church perpetually struggled with *understanding* these texts, but Christians have also struggled with *remaining married* — and it proved impossible for many commentators to exclude their pastoral concerns from their wrestlings with Moses, Jesus, and Paul. As we look at some vignettes from the history of interpretation, we'll focus on these questions: What is divorce? Is it ever allowable? If so, on what grounds? And is a divorced spouse ever allowed to remarry?

Early Rigorism — and Early Second Thoughts

A thorough survey of the writings of the church fathers on the topic of marriage and divorce would leave two distinct impressions. On the one hand, the fathers generally affirmed that marriage was *indissoluble*. In other words, despite the seeming exception Jesus allowed for adultery as grounds for divorce, marriage was seen as binding until the death of one partner. On the other hand, there were notable voices among the fathers that inquired whether such rigor was what Jesus or Paul intended, and whether it was wise.

Rigorism: Marriage Is Indissoluble

How did it come to pass that the church fathers saw no dissolution of marriage except by death? From what we can know of the earliest writings, it is certain that this was the majority view, affirmed in various ways by Hermas, Justin Martyr, Athenagoras, and Clement of Alexandria in the second century; by Tertullian and Origen in the early third; and by Ambrose, Augustine, Jerome, and Chrysostom (among others) in the fourth and fifth.[7] To teach that marriage is indissoluble was distinctly countercultural: Greek and Roman law, as well Judaism, normally recognized at least some form of divorce with right of remarriage. But the doctrine also reflects the ascetic tendencies of early Christianity: the apologist Athenagoras, for example, heralds the sexual restraint of Christians even within marriage, as if the fact were public and well known.[8]

Nonetheless, the origins of this rigorous view of marriage bear the marks of various New Testament texts. A second-century work known as *The Shepherd* includes the conversation of a Christian prophet named Hermas with "the angel of repentance" (in shepherd's guise) about what to do in the case of an adulterous wife. According to the shepherd, if the wife is unrepentant, the husband sins if he remains with her. Instead, "he should divorce her . . . and live alone" — for he would also sin were he to marry another.[9] Although the shepherd does not cite Jesus or Paul, his instructions combine the two in the same way that Origen, a century later, would make explicit.[10] That the husband may divorce or dismiss his wife for her adultery surely depends on Matthew 5 and 19; that the bond of marriage persists even after separation, so long as one's spouse lives, probably reflects Romans 7. The shepherd, however, added a rationalization for not remarrying: an adulterous wife might, in fact, repent — in which case the husband sins if he does *not* take her back.

The "indissolubilist" view described above was embraced by many later church fathers, including Jerome and Chrysostom. But there were other fathers who could be more rigorous still. Athenagoras, cited above, believed that *all* second marriages were "veiled adultery," even for those who had been widowed. Indeed, to make his point he cited the words of Jesus *without* the exception clause, implying that Christians simply do not separate, much less remarry. Tertullian held to a similar view in his later writings.[11]

Origen: Second Thoughts on Divorce

The general practice of the early church effectively tightened up the already austere words of Jesus by forbidding even the innocent partner to remarry after separating from an adulterous spouse. But the church fathers occasionally considered other views, and these too had exegetical implications.

In a commentary written sometime after 244, Origen addressed problems raised by Matthew 19 and many other passages. The conclusion toward which Origen builds is not only that celibacy is easier than marriage — especially in view of "how many possible accidents may arise in marriages" and its "great hardships" — but also that celibacy is a gift God will give to anyone who asks.[12] Origen's advocacy of celibacy would become the usual view in the following centuries, but his exposition is unusual for voicing some second thoughts.

To begin with, even though Jesus seems to have criticized Moses for allowing divorce, Origen sees a parallel between Moses and Paul. Just as Paul could link his personal "judgment" with having the Spirit of God (in 1 Corinthians 7:40), so might it be that Moses permitted divorce on the strength of his own judgment yet also not without the Spirit of God.[13] Why this rehabilitation of Moses? Because Origen wants to read Moses' permission for divorce "spiritually," so that Christ himself is seen as having given Israel, his former wife, a "bill of divorcement." He is now married to another — the church.[14] However much the divorce between Christ and the synagogue is a "spiritual" reading, Origen implicitly recognizes its rectitude, even if Christ seems to be the last beneficiary of Moses' permission.

Origen's general recognition of the indissolubility of marriage is complicated by other considerations as well. Just as Moses permitted divorce as a concession to human weakness, there are similar concessions under the New Covenant, including Paul's various "permissions" in 1 Corinthians 7. As Origen continues to muse, his own pastoral disposition emerges. Thus, even where he expresses wonderment at certain contemporary "rulers of the church" who "have permitted a woman to marry, even when her husband was living" (and despite the prohibitions in Romans 7:2 and 1 Corinthians 7:39), Origen supposes that such concessions must have been made in order to avoid something worse.[15] Pastors do run into difficult and exceptional cases.

In the very next paragraph, Origen reveals more of his thoughts about such exceptions. He intends to argue — against an imagined Jewish opponent — that Jesus' threshold for allowing divorce (that is, for adultery or fornication) is higher than that of Moses, who seemed to have allowed divorce "for any cause." But he wanders into a longer consideration of whether there are other sins in a wife that might reasonably warrant the dissolution of a marriage. For example, poisoning, infanticide, murder, and pillaging her husband's house all appear to be "monstrous," and

> to endure sins of such heinousness, which seem to be worse than adultery or fornication, will appear to be irrational; but again on the other hand to act contrary to the design of the teaching of the Savior, everyone would acknowledge to be impious.[16]

He concludes with two astonishing concessions. First, it is left to the *reader* to weigh the merits of allowing divorce for poisoning and the like. Second, even though his discussion has focused on an erring *wife*, Origen can imagine that her husband may himself be the cause of the wife's adultery — either by failing to supervise her activities, or by failing to satisfy her desires. Indeed, such a man may be "more culpable" than one who has separated for other reasons.

Origen was not the only church father to harbor second thoughts over the prevailing notions of marriage as indissoluble and remarriage as forbidden until the death of one's partner. Ambrosiaster believed remarriage was possible after separation; so did Epiphanius, if more reluctantly.[17] But Origen's worries are probably the most developed. Although he did not want to allow remarriage after the dissolution of a marriage, he was aware that it sometimes happened. And although he did not want to depart from the words of Jesus or Paul, he was aware that they did not address every conceivable case.

Augustine: On the Road to a Sacrament

Augustine was by no means the first to argue for marriage as an indissoluble bond, but he is fairly credited with cementing such a view in the mind of the Western church and for pioneering a sacramental understanding of marriage. Both points are advocated in several of Augustine's writings, all of which grapple with exegetical issues.

Augustine's conviction about the indissolubility of marriage was in place by around 393, when he commented on the Sermon on the Mount. Harmonizing Paul and Jesus, he argues that 1 Corinthians 7:11 ("if she does separate, let her remain unmarried or else be reconciled to her husband") clarifies Matthew's account, so that Jesus is to be taken as allowing separation but *not* remarriage. In other words, while Jesus allows separation in the case of "fornication," Paul makes it clear that separated spouses are not free to marry anew. There are only two options — separation or reconciliation — and Augustine is not much perplexed by this restriction.[18]

Where he is perplexed, it seems, is over the meaning of *fornication* in Matthew 5:32. As Augustine knows, infidelity can be carnal or spiritual in nature, but his concern (again) is to harmonize Paul and Jesus.

> If it *is* allowable to dismiss an *unbelieving* spouse (although better not to do so), and yet *not* allowable, according to the commandment of the Lord, to dismiss a spouse except on account of *fornication*, then unbelief is itself also fornication.[19]

Thus, Paul and Jesus were not at odds but spoke as one. With similar reasoning, Augustine goes on to add other forms of "fornication" that justify marital separation, including idolatry, covetousness, and more. (Late in life, Augustine wondered if he was correct to maintain such "general and universal" grounds for separation: "What is to be understood by [fornication] and . . . whether because of it one may put away his wife is a most obscure question."[20]) Equally obscure, however, is the inconclusive note on which Augustine's remarks end. Like Origen, he can imagine some really tough cases. Suppose a barren wife permitted her husband to take some unmarried woman as wife. Would he be charged with fornication? The case is obviously that of Sarah, Abraham, and Hagar — and though Augustine escapes by asserting that we now live by "greater precepts" (presumably the teachings of Jesus), he never really answers his question. Yet it was still his intention, as a pastor, to prepare for the unexpected.[21]

Although Augustine clearly held to the indissolubility of marriage in his commentary on the Sermon on the Mount, his assertion of the sacramental character of marriage emerged later on. In a treatise "On the Good of Marriage," written in 401, he attempted to counteract Jerome's dismissive account of marriage by establishing that there are three "goods" or benefits of marriage: it is ordained by God for the production of offspring, for the cultivation of fidelity between husband and wife, and as a sign or sacrament. In this treatise, the "sacrament" of marriage signifies "that in the future we shall all be united and subject to God in the one heavenly city."[22] In later treatises, Augustine built more explicitly on Ephesians 5:32, which in English translations describes marriage as a great *mystery* of Christ and the church, but which the Latin Bible would have translated as a great *sacramentum*.[23] Even though Augustine did not develop this notion of marriage as a sacrament, the correlation was clear enough to endure: couples are to be as permanently united in wedlock as Christ is indissolubly united to the church. The bond of matrimony, then, endures even when a couple separates — just as the character of ordination persists in a priest even if he fails to gather a congregation or is removed from his office for misconduct.[24]

Augustine thus combines a rigid adherence to the indissolubility of marriage, so that remarriage is never an option until one's first spouse dies, with a modest flexibility in both theory and practice. Though he allows at most for separation (rather than divorce with right of remarriage), he broadens the scope of the immorality or "fornication" that might warrant such a separation. He recognizes, too, that the standards for Christian marriage are stricter than prevailing secular law — or Old Testament law, for that matter.[25] He can imagine complicated cases that test the best pastor and exegete, and he approaches moral dilemmas with a hierarchy of values by which he can imagine plausible excuses. Remarriage after separating from an adulterous spouse *is* a sin, but Scripture is "obscure" enough on the point that one who did so might be regarded as "pardonably mistaken" (suggesting a lesser or "venial" sin).[26]

From the Church Fathers to the Reformation

The theory and practice of marriage in medieval Roman Catholicism reached a stable form by the twelfth century — a consensus that was scarcely modified by the Council of Trent in the 1560s, despite the many changes introduced by Protestantism. Before we skip ahead to consider the changes that accompanied the Reformation, however, a few historical notes must be added by way of background.

Christian Emperors and (Christian) Roman Law

Despite widespread recognition among the church fathers that marriage was indissoluble, early Christian emperors did not simply legislate the words of Jesus. To be sure, prevailing (pre-Christian) Roman law was fairly permissive. Constantine, who came to power in 312 as the first Christian emperor, was less so, but divorce with right of remarriage was still allowed not only in cases of adultery but also where a spouse was guilty of homicide, poisoning, procuring, or violating graves.[27] Justinian I, Christian emperor in the sixth century, undertook a major revision of Roman law — revisions that were doubly potent, affecting not only his own day but also the Christian Europe of later centuries, for which the Code of Justinian served as a model. Indeed, the sixteenth century saw a widespread revival of interest in Justinian. Nonetheless, Justinian still allowed divorce for adultery and concubinage, in cases where a spouse wished to take a religious vocation, and in cases of presumed death. Curiously, Justinian at one point allowed divorce by mutual consent, but abandoned the policy; Justinian II, his successor, reintroduced the permissive policy in the face of popular demand.

Canon Law and Consistency

Despite their explicit commitments to the Christian faith, these Christian emperors framed policies at variance with the church fathers and the church of their day. Of course, the church of the early Middle Ages was itself not yet consistent in demanding a doctrine of indissolubility. Divorcing an adulterous spouse with right of remarriage was allowed by various church authorities at various times, including by a synod called by Pope Eugenius in 826. But through the course of the ninth century, this permissiveness disappeared from both secular and ecclesiastical contexts.[28]

One factor in the standardization of marriage doctrine and law was the gradual standardization of church law that took place in the early Middle Ages, largely as a result of the attempt to gather and collate the rules or canons adopted by councils (such as the Council of Nicea in 325) with bodies of church legislation (such as Hippolytus's *Apostolic Tradition* from the early third century), and with papal letters and decrees, and so on. A milestone in the growth of this body of church or "canon" law was Gratian's massive *Concordance* (*c.* 1140), which was more comprehensive and therefore more authoritative than any collection yet produced. Given the growing consensus that marriage was dissoluble only by death, a key contribution of canon law was to settle the definition of marriage, that is, that marriage was constituted not by a ceremony or sexual intercourse but by the *consent* of the two parties.

One Sacrament among Seven

The Roman Catholic doctrine of marriage was further settled about this time as a consensus was reached also about sacramental theology. Although Augustine had associated marriage with the *sacramentum* or mystery of Ephesians 5, he did not work out a general theory or even enumeration of the sacraments. Only with the writings of Peter Lombard in the 1150s were the sacraments definitively numbered at seven; and only with Aquinas, a century later, was marriage seen as a sacrament like the others, that is, a sign that actually dispensed grace to the recipients. These developments only strengthened the indissolubility of marriage by its association with the exclusivity and permanence of the union it signified between Christ and the church. Yet to define marriage as a sacrament and as a means of grace was not to accord it the seat of honor. As a sacrament, marriage was upstaged by the nobler sacrament of priestly ordination; as a vow, marriage was upstaged by the arguably more demanding vows of religious or monastic profession, which usually entailed lifelong celibacy.

Dying for a Divorce? Separation and Annulment

Strengthening the indissolubility of marriage and establishing its sacramental status also did not eliminate abusive or loveless or faithless marriages. But the indissolubility of marriage meant that pastoral intervention was limited to separating warring spouses — "divorce," yes, but only "from bed and board." Remarriage was never an option so long as one's spouse survived. Not surprisingly, some sought to hasten the passing of an estranged spouse. In some cases, laws discouraged rapid remarriage after widowhood in order to reduce the attraction of spouse murder.[29] Homicide might go undetected, after all, and one might undergo penance later on. But remarriage while a former spouse lived was deemed adultery and thus a constant mortal sin.

Of course, if one could prove that the marriage had been invalid from its inception, the marriage might be wholly and summarily dissolved. Grounds for annulling a marriage, called "impediments," were numerous, and included (among other things) violations of free consent, prior marriages or religious vows, impotence, insanity, and marriage to someone too closely related. Henry VIII sought permission to remarry in just this way, claiming that his marriage should be annulled because he had married his brother's widow and had thereby violated the "prohibited degrees" mentioned in Leviticus. (Henry's logic might have proved persuasive if his current marriage had not already received a special dispensation from Pope Julius II — and if his wife had been anyone other than the aunt of Charles V, Holy Roman Emperor, whose forces had sacked Rome in 1527 and imprisoned Pope Clement VII!) Protestant Reformers often decried the manipulation of annulments and impediments under canon law, and Henry's maneuvers offer a case in point. Nonetheless, modern historians suggest that annulments were actually rather hard to come by.[30]

Divorce and Exegesis in the Sixteenth Century: Five Cases

Such, in brief, was the state of marriage and divorce on the eve of the Reformation. At the Council of Trent in the 1560s, the Catholic Church would defend this status quo against major changes instituted by Protestants. Reformers throughout Europe — including Luther and Calvin, but also many others — had sought above all to restore a biblical view of marriage and divorce. Usually such a restoration meant allowing remarriage if the divorce were provoked by offenses mentioned in Scripture, including adultery (as Jesus had allowed) or religious incompatibility (following Paul's "advice"). It also meant refusing to demand celibacy of those who pursued pastoral ministry, and regarding marriage as fully a godly option (if not necessity) for all Christians, pastors included. Perhaps surprisingly, Protestants also "secularized" marriage: as an order of creation rather than a sacrament, marriage belonged not just to Christians but to all. Certainly, recent history had proved how much the church had mangled and mismanaged matters of marriage and divorce. Yet, having dismantled the traditional consensus of theology and exegesis that had settled divorce practices in the Middle Ages, the sixteenth century saw little or no "biblical" consensus emerge. This brings us back to the history of exegesis, where we will look at five remarkable vignettes.

Desiderius Erasmus: A Plea for Intervention

While it is true that Protestants dramatically changed the institution of marriage, the controversy over divorce was sparked not by Luther, but earlier, by Erasmus. In 1516, Erasmus published a critical Greek edition of the New Testament that challenged many readings and doctrines that had been derived from the Latin (Vulgate) Bible. He also published a set of accompanying notes — the *Annotations*, revised and expanded through five editions over twenty years. Some of these notes are short and bear on minor matters of wording, definitions, or grammar. His longest note, however, is a fourteen-page excursus on 1 Corinthians 7:39, added in 1519: "She is free from the law to marry whom she wishes."[31] The burden of Erasmus here, as so often, is to encourage Christians to recover and return to "authentic piety," which requires us to care for the weak and broken. He concisely states the precise occasion of his long note: "We see so many thousands of people yoked together in unhappy marriages leading to mutual destruction, who might be saved were they disjoined."[32]

In contesting the prevailing doctrine of divorce, Erasmus draws on a vast array of authorities, including church fathers, popes, and canon law. He distills an impressive survey of Christian thought in support of a sustained plea to rethink our reading of Moses, Jesus, and Paul, and to fix a system of regulating marriage that was clearly broken. Of special interest, however, is Erasmus's depiction of apostolic authority. Not only does he cite examples of bishops who openly flouted the command of the Lord and of Paul,[33] he also alleges that Paul himself felt free to modify what he received from the Lord. Here, Erasmus explicitly interacts with that curious phrase, "I say, not the Lord," and Paul's other allusions to his own opinions and advice — and it makes for quite a litany of interpretative freedom.

The stage is set in the notes on v. 6, where Paul tells the Corinthians that he is speaking to them "by way of concession, not of command," and on v. 25, where, having "no command of the Lord," Paul offers "his opinion." In both places, the Apostle is depicted as teaching simply "what seems best to me."[34] Erasmus goes on to suggest that making concessions to human weakness was the stock in trade of Paul, who "often relaxed the command of the Lord" — and if Paul did so, why can't the Pope do the same?[35] Indeed, Paul would have made even *more* concessions if he'd faced the worst-case marital scenario Erasmus goes on to sketch. Accordingly, *we* ought to interpret *Paul's* words more humanely than we do today.[36]

Scattered throughout are the usual Erasmian watchwords of equity, humanity, charity, necessity — the principles of authentic piety and Erasmus's "philosophy of Christ."[37] To these principles, he assumes, Paul would subordinate his own specific commands and even those of Christ. That is the note on which his long excursus ends: for the sake of Christian charity and the salvation of many caught in this miserable bondage, Paul himself "sometimes twists the sacred letters."[38]

It is not hard to see why Erasmus would have caught his readers' attention. Traditional exegesis was committed to harmonizing Moses, Jesus, and Paul by infringing on the pronouncements of Jesus as little as possible. To portray Paul as having blunted the words of Jesus for the sake of pastoral care was simply too threatening to the usual understanding of an apostle's derived authority, not to mention the fixed ideals and practices of the church. In the eyes of his Catholic detractors, Erasmus had depicted an apostle who not only applied the commands of the Lord, but who also ventured to reconsider, accommodate, and even alter those commands. Outrage ensued, and Erasmus had to reconsider his own annotations at this point. Nonetheless, not all Protestants were scandalized. Some agreed that Paul's intention was to apply the spirit of Jesus' commands more than their letter. Most Protestants also agreed that the indissolubility of marriage was an unbiblical ideal and, for many, too heavy to bear.

Martin Bucer: Reevaluating Moses

In considering Jesus' teachings about marriage and divorce, Bucer's 1527 commentary on Matthew echoes what Erasmus had said about *equity* as both a virtue and a principle of interpretation:

> Let us learn how to interpret passages of Scripture, not by sticking fast to the letter of the text, but by consulting other passages as well, as we see Christ doing here, to ascertain what in each case corresponds most closely to the original institution of God and to his will in general, and promotes soundness and decency of life.[39]

Bucer's "Protestant" approach to the teachings of Jesus on divorce, however, would prove to be more generous than Erasmus, the controversial Roman Catholic, could afford to maintain. Yet, in trying to square Moses' writ of divorce with the words of Jesus, Bucer really reflects the classic dilemma raised by the Sermon on the Mount:[40] Should Jesus' interaction with the Old Testament be construed as a correction or contrast, or as a refinement and deepening?

Bucer's stance emerges clearly from his assertion that Jesus did not intend to condemn anything his Father had commanded. In other words, Moses' concession to hardhearted husbands may still have an application — and an unexpected, timeless rationale:

> The purpose of [Moses'] provision is to prevent [a husband] from ill-treating [his wife] twice over, both in denying her the duty of a husband, and in precluding her at the same time from being able to receive it from another. . . . There is no room for divorce among the godly. . . . But since the hearts of the ungodly are no less hard today than in the past, the magistrate should accordingly make no less provision than obtained of old for unfortunate wives. . . . It is preferable that men should divorce their wives and not subject them to life-long torment by cruelly committing adultery, rather than add to the adultery they perpetrate while not treating their wives as wives the further infliction of unending torture.[41]

Bucer is unusual in highlighting the plight of neglected and rejected wives, but his comments continue to see the heartlessness of husbands as a taproot of the problem that Jesus also indicts. Indeed, it is husbands who are on trial when Jesus said, "Let no man put asunder," a maxim directed "against men who divorce their wives, not against the magistrate, who does not so much separate as deliver from a worse plight the wife who is already separated in spirit."[42]

Bucer goes on to consider possible grounds for divorce. He cites with approval the "just causes" once allowed by Christian emperors, including murder, poisoning, sedition, harboring criminals, church-robbing, tomb-wrecking, cattle-rustling, infidelity, and wife abuse, among others.[43] At the same time, because no one should be denied marriage who does not have the gift of celibacy, divorce should be "true" divorce, not mere separation without the right to remarry. Yet divorce is not available for the asking: cases and petitions must be submitted to the scrutiny and wisdom of Christian magistrates.[44]

Bucer's long excursus at Matthew 19 also looks at St. Paul, who displays the same discernment and prudence that Jesus modeled. Thus, even though it is to be taken as "a general law of marriage" that "a wife is bound to her husband as long as he lives," Paul himself admits (says Bucer) that it "does not hold in every circumstance."[45] The rule pertains to "a woman able and allowed to be a wife," but not to those separated with "good cause." Otherwise, Paul would be contradicting the words of Jesus, which clearly do allow for divorce *and* remarriage in cases of adultery.[46]

Throughout this section, Bucer rails against the "pernicious papal laws," as a result of which "innumerable consciences are either tormented or perilously assailed." Yet Bucer is by no means complacent about divorce or infidelity. To his Catholic detractors, he replies,

> When they plead that if they were thus to permit divorce and remarriage, countless marriages would be dissolved which are now solid and secure, we must reply that if they were to do their duty and punish those who violate the marriage vows . . . this would never happen. . . . [Instead,] adultery goes unpunished, and "divorces" which force persons into fornication are recognized as valid; in addition, the innocent are debarred from just and necessary marriages.[47]

The note of necessity that Bucer strikes here brings us full circle in his exegesis, back to his conviction that Moses, Jesus, and Paul all share a common goal: not to fashion laws, but to foster justice and decency among even the weak and those who have already failed in marriage.

> Nothing can be less in doubt than Christ's unwillingness, and even inability, to deny to any sinner whatsoever the means for his advancement towards uprightness and godliness. Therefore, whatever the circumstances of a woman's divorce, if her former husband refuses to take her back, Christ did not wish her to be denied remarriage on any account, since his own testimony declares that "Not all men can receive this saying, 'It is expedient for a man not to marry'," and live free of marriage. Therefore, the man who marries such a divorced woman will not be an adulterer.[48]

Heinrich Bullinger: A Mediating View

Many Protestants were not so enamored of Erasmus, and Bucer's advocacy of such radical changes in divorce law was just as problematic — if not scandalous. Bullinger should be listed here, even though his 1534 commentary on 1 Corinthians claimed to defer to the "copious and erudite" disputations of Erasmus, then to the "pious and learned" comments of Bucer.[49] Yet whatever Bullinger owed to Bucer and Erasmus, his musings on the possible tension between Paul's advice and Jesus' commands are far from adventurous. For him, the Pauline privilege and Paul's other advice about marriage and remarriage must be regarded as authoritative, inspired, and perfectly congruent with what Jesus taught. If Bullinger preferred to ratify Paul's comments rather than expand them, it is in part because he felt that *expanding* Paul's remarks was at the heart of the "madness" of the Popes, who had forced human traditions upon the church in place of those that were divine.[50]

Consequently, Bullinger takes care to explain the seeming self-deprecation — "I say, not the Lord" (1 Cor. 7:12) — that introduces Paul's concession that a marriage with an unbelieving spouse may be dissolved. Paul's directives are virtually those of Christ himself.

> No one understands [this teaching] as if Paul made this up out of his own head, without regard for the rule of divine law. . . . Rather, the precepts of God take two different forms. There are precepts ex-

pressed by God himself in specific words, such as that which we now hear, "Let a wife not separate from her husband." Others are not expressed by God in distinct words but are inferred from them by the sure rule of faith and charity, such as he offered here regarding unequal marriages. We have many precepts of this kind in the church.[51]

Bullinger's distinction is clear: the Lord gives commands directly and indirectly, through explicit divine words but also as an *inference* from those explicit divine words.[52] So when Paul says "I say, not the Lord," Bullinger thinks that though there is no record of the Lord giving a command such as 1 Corinthians 7:12 or 7:25, Paul's words are nonetheless inspired and bear the Lord's authority.[53] Should one happen to ask *why* Paul speaks in such an indirect manner, Bullinger has a ready answer: Paul was well aware that he was commanding something "divine and sacrosanct," but he called these commands "his" all the same in order to model the prudence, caution, and modesty that befit teachers of the truth.[54]

Still, Bullinger's near-equation of Paul's words and those of the Lord is not without its problems. Indeed, he has left an Erasmian loophole or two. Granted that Paul was guided in his writing by the Holy Spirit, he still followed a rather human and discursive process in deducing these inferences — presumably, from some other explicit divine words.[55] Moreover, the principles by which Paul worked are commended to us, too. Like Paul, we should rely on "the sure rule of faith and charity"[56] — a rule remarkably like Erasmus's insistence on equity and charity as the guiding lights of biblical interpretation.

Some proof of Bullinger's willingness for Christians to appeal to the *implications* of Scripture may be drawn from his own teachings on divorce. Like a few other Reformers, Bullinger read Jesus' words in Matthew 19 as allowing divorce on grounds besides adultery. For Bullinger, adultery was the *minimum* justification, but he could imagine offenses more serious than adultery (including attempted homicide) that would justify divorce all the more. He makes this point in commenting on 1 Corinthians 7:10, but also in his remarks on Matthew:

> The Lord . . . included in fornication equal or more serious reasons. . . . Likewise the words of our Lord, "he who marries a divorced person," are not to be taken absolutely. . . . If anyone slavishly adheres

to the letter of this which our Lord says to us, let him note what Paul says, by the Spirit of God, in 1 Corinthians vii.[57]

In other words, Paul *is* a precedent for enlarging the words of Jesus — or, at least, for explicating the intentions of Jesus. Is this something that *we* should do? Apparently so, for Bullinger's insistence that there *are* such "more serious reasons" appears in his lay-oriented household manual, *On Christian Marriage*.[58] There, he approvingly reports the laws of "faithful and virtuous emperors," who added as grounds for divorce *poisoning* and *murder*.[59]

Bullinger pursued a mediating course. Disconcerted by the latitude for divorce in Erasmus and Bucer, he was further repelled by restrictive Catholic traditions. His exegesis advocated a literal reading of Jesus' allowance for divorce in the case of adultery, but Paul's advice was to be seen not as widening that allowance but as explicating it. Bullinger thus landed near Augustine, for whom "adultery" signaled a host of related grounds for divorce — except that Bullinger found no reason to deny an innocent spouse the right to remarry.

John Calvin: Ideals and Compromises

Though Calvin was notorious for not identifying his sources, he was surely familiar with the exegesis of Erasmus, Bucer, and Bullinger regarding marriage and divorce. His own strong opinions were probably provoked by the exegetical permissiveness he perceived not only in these three contemporaries but also, in a different form, in his Roman Catholic adversaries.

Like most Protestants, Calvin was convinced that Jesus allowed the innocent party to remarry after divorcing an adulterous spouse. Like Bullinger, Calvin wants to insist that Paul's "advice" in 1 Corinthians 7:12 (encouraging Christians to remain married to an unbeliever, but not demanding they do so) really adds nothing to Jesus — even though, Calvin admits, Paul's rules "seem to conflict to some extent with those which he had just given above as from the Lord."[60] Calvin is inclined to think Paul's advice is somehow derived from Scripture under the influence of "the Spirit of God," and he takes a similar approach to 7:25, where Paul has no command but offers his advice.

> The Papists infer wrongly from this that it is permissible to go be-
> yond the limits of the Word of God, whereas Paul had no thought at
> all of leaping over the boundaries of God's Word. For if anyone
> would look closer he will see that Paul introduces nothing here
> which Christ has not included in His words in Matthew [5:32 and
> 19:5-6].[61]

Calvin is at pains to tether Paul's words to a scriptural precedent.[62] If Roman Catholics erred by going beyond God's Word in demanding clerical
celibacy, Calvin took equal offense at the exegetical looseness of those who
advocated a more liberal doctrine of *divorce* — even though Bucer and
Bullinger might be numbered among his friends. Like Bullinger, Calvin
believed Paul's advice was an explication of statements found either in the
Law or in the words of Jesus. Unlike Bullinger, Calvin framed no general
principle that would correspond to what Bullinger said about "the rule of
faith and charity."

Equally striking is Calvin's minimal interest in exploring grounds for
divorce that Erasmus, Bucer, and Bullinger all raised in their exegesis of
1 Corinthians 7. Calvin does allow here for divorce and remarriage in accordance with the Pauline privilege, when a believer is abandoned or repu-
diated by an unbelieving spouse. Yet even that topic is barely explored:
while there are parallels to religious abandonment, Calvin cites them only
to dismiss them.[63] Unlike his contemporaries, he also does not agonize
much over broken marriages — apparently because he sees no way out.
Calvin's advice is curt and absolute: "If, contrary to our expectations,
things go wrong" in our marriages, he advises, "let us hope that God will
help us."[64]

What we have in his exegesis, then, is Calvin's *theory* of marriage, his
ideal for a beneficial and divine institution that needs no improvement
and from which there are few authorized exits. What we do not have there,
however, is the whole of Calvin's *practice.* Curiously, the Ecclesiastical Or-
dinances he drafted for Geneva in 1545 — while also working on his Corinthians commentary — had proposed additional grounds for divorce
(alongside adultery and religious incompatibility), including impotence
and desertion.[65] But Calvin not only framed new legislation, he also
helped arbitrate and enforce it in his capacity as a pastor and a member of
the Consistory — the church's "morals" commission that conducted hear-
ings and was empowered to mandate both counseling and catechism.[66]

Some Genevan divorces were justified on Calvin's "biblical" grounds, namely, adultery or religious incompatibility. But there were others, too, including cases in which the Consistory was able to do little more than capitulate and grant a divorce to estranged and intransigent spouses.[67] In letters of pastoral counsel, Calvin often pleaded with Protestant spouses (usually wives) to bear with their Catholic husbands, enduring abuse and even persecution as long as possible. But should the danger become too great or the Christian spouse unable to endure, Calvin allowed that the marriage might end.[68] It is significant that even in expressing his contempt for those heartless Old Testament husbands who dismissed their wives, Calvin could concede that "for women who were cruelly oppressed, . . . it was better that they should at once be set free, than . . . groan beneath a cruel tyranny during their whole lives."[69]

Catharinus: Concessions from a Controversialist

Aptly described by one Catholic historian as a "pugnacious Dominican,"[70] Ambrosius Catharinus Politus defended his church for thirty years against opponents without and within, beginning with his 1520 attack on Luther. His lifelong enemy, however, was Erasmus, whom he saw as having opened the Pandora's box from which the many evils of Protestantism emerged. When the subject turned to marriage, divorce, or celibacy, he was particularly annoyed by Erasmus's annotation on 1 Corinthians 7:39.

As a vocal opponent of Protestantism, Catharinus (predictably) defends Catholicism's traditional view that marriage is a sacrament and therefore indissoluble. Less expected are two points of dissent. First, while he does not believe a wife may divorce an unfaithful husband and marry another, he *is* willing to argue for such a right on the part of a husband with an unfaithful wife — at least, so long as the church had yet to define matters otherwise. Submitting his arguments as a brief to the Council of Trent in 1551, he was well aware that his views might be disfavored by that council — and in 1563, ten years after his death, the twenty-fourth session of Trent did just that.[71] Nonetheless, he was still willing to risk arguing on behalf of husbands aggrieved by a wife's infidelity. We may pause at the one-sidedness of Catharinus here, but he was just trying to adhere to Scripture: the exception for adultery appears only in Matthew, and Jesus speaks there only about divorcing an unfaithful *wife*. Among Roman Catholics, Catharinus was progressive on this point. By contrast, most Protestants not only allowed the innocent party — husband *or* wife — to remarry after divorcing an unfaithful spouse, they also lobbied against the double standard that penalized a husband's infidelity less than that of a wife.

Catharinus was also quick to admit the difficulty of the question of divorce and remarriage and to acknowledge real-life complications. Thus, in his comments on 1 Corinthians 7:10-12, he begins by invoking the words of Jesus to trump Paul's failure to mention divorcing an adulterous wife. But he then raises some familiar questions. What should a wife do if her husband were, say, a poisoner, or if he threatened her, or if he were a heretic? Even Jesus seems to allow her no way out.

> But if this is true, that it is not licit for a wife to depart from her husband on account of fornication or for any other reason, this could appear extremely harsh. What if there is such rivalry that she is nearly in danger for her life? It is not to be doubted but that in this case it would be licit to leave and beg for some protection or for public redress. . . . To be sure, the Apostle, by the added precept [of v. 10], prohibits her leaving. But never, in any case? Honestly, I don't think so. For if there is danger of murder, or if he wishes to induce her to adultery and faithlessness, or to compel some unusual foul deed, it is not to be held that she must remain with him.[72]

There is no reason to think Catharinus ever imagined an abused wife doing more than separating from her husband; "divorce" from bed and board was probably all he had in mind. Yet he could not avoid imagining these pastoral issues that forced him, in the end, to hedge his exegesis not only of the Apostle but of the Lord himself.

Upholding the Proper End of Marriage Today

On the vexed topic of marriage, divorce, and remarriage, there are scores of other commentators and theologians who could be surveyed (and at greater depth), even as there are further issues raised for us today not only from the standpoint of biblical research but also from the fields of ethics, psychology, and social work. Our sampling of the history of exegesis should be taken to supplement, not replace, the other considerations that pastors, therapists, and theologians must bring to bear when marriages head toward the rocks. Nonetheless, some useful reflections emerge even from this modest survey.

1. THE BIBLE'S DIVORCE TEXTS ARE HARD TO HOMOGE-NIZE. *As desirable as it has always been to look to the Bible for easy solutions to life's hardest questions, the diverse interpretations of traditional commentators testify that the hard question of divorce cannot be solved by proof-texting. We don't have to pretend these texts are easy.*

Roman Catholic reforms at the Council of Trent dogmatized the indissolubility of sacramental marriage. However, despite the doctrine's early origins, there were always some who had second thoughts about it, both as an exegetical theory and as the church's pastoral policy. There are unresolved tensions between Moses and Jesus, and between Jesus and Paul, that many found more papered over than resolved by imposing a doctrine of separation without possibility of remarriage. The first Protestants fought hard to return marriage to what they saw as the plain meaning of Scripture. To that end, they sought to discern the mind of Moses and Jesus and Paul. Their conclusions diverged, however, despite a common commitment to the authority of Scripture over human laws and traditions. We should not be surprised if our exegetical views are equally varied despite similar commitments.

2. IDEALS BELONG WITH COMPASSION AND REALISM. *Protestant views of divorce have, historically, attempted to avoid the extremes of indissolubility, on the one hand, and the laxity of "expressive" divorce on the other. Between these two poles Protestants have always sought room for the ideals framed by Jesus as well as for pastoral sensibilities.*

All these commentators had high ideals for marriage, driven by a desire to honor the whole counsel of God as found in Scripture. All were also pastors who confronted failed marriages among their flock and who attempted to navigate pastorally between the Bible and their broken, often foolish, parishioners. It was their conviction that the Bible was practical and could be brought to bear on the hardest cases. It was their experience, however, that these hard cases were at times beyond repair and had to be dealt with by way of triage. Along the way, they often asked pertinent questions. Bucer and Erasmus, for instance, still deserve an answer as to why we enforce Jesus' words against divorce with such rigor, yet so loosely construe what he says about anger, or caring for the poor, or mammon? Scripture has other commands and priorities, so why should sexual issues upstage all others? It's true, of course, that the area between legalism and laxity can be both a fine line and a slippery slope. But, as one historian has observed, when Protestants rejected the Roman Catholic doctrine of indissolubility, they implicitly conceded remarriage after divorce not just to an innocent party, but to all. After all, if the urgency of marriage is founded on the notion that not all are capable of celibacy, there is but one other option outside of promiscuity: to allow even the least justified divorce to lead to remarriage on both sides, in the hope that greater evils will be avoided this time around.[73]

3. CHARITY *AND* DISCIPLINE BELONG IN THE CHURCH. *It is possible to love the Bible and prize obedience to Jesus, yet allow divorce when a marriage has died. But such decisions should not be merely private.*

We need not anathematize those who dissent from our own particular leanings. Bucer and Calvin, for instance, represent diverse exegetical and pastoral views, but their very disagreement may serve us well. Bucer acutely wondered whether Jesus' ideals for marriage should be imposed on all, regardless of beliefs or state of grace. Calvin worried, it would seem, that lowered expectations would lead to a further decline in the state of marriage. Yet, Bucer sought no small safeguard when he insisted that the dissolution of a marriage rested finally not with either spouse but with wise judges or magistrates — perhaps a role that, today, wise pastors ought to assume. Like Calvin, Bucer by no means sought to coddle the unfaithful, but he was more concerned still for their victims. Our churches need to claim the ideals of both Bucer and Calvin: for we, too, are surrounded by those who are hard of heart — yet Christians still seek to model a better way.

Chapter Eight

Wasn't Adam Deceived?

*Deciphering Paul's Arguments about Women
in Creation, Fall, and Redemption*

When I entered seminary in the 1970s, the debate over whether women could serve as pastors was just coming into full flame, and many of my male classmates were personally concerned about the growing presence of women in their courses. One of my seminary friends, Beth, recounted to me how she had been closely interrogated in the cafeteria by a male student:

— So, are you studying for a degree in Christian education?

— No, I'm getting an M.Div. so I can serve as a pastor.

— Oh. [*Silence.*] Did you talk with your own pastor about this?

— Yes, I did. She thought it was a good idea.

The interrogation ended there, with the unexpected *she*. Beth, you see, was raised in the Assemblies of God and grew up with a woman pastor — something that male seminarian had never imagined.

The Assemblies of God were early proponents of what was to become a twentieth-century trend.[1] Especially after mid-century, many Christian denominations, including most mainline Protestants, made up their minds to open the pulpit to women. In some quarters, the ordination of women to public ministry has been greeted warmly, but the issue also marks an enduring cultural divide. The debate still rages on, not only among conservative Protestants but also among Catholics, as witnessed by a never-ending flow of books and articles along with periodic conferences, colloquies, and declarations.

Reading with a Guilty Conscience?

Even where the ecclesiastical issue has been resolved in favor of ordaining women, an understandable dissonance arises when the New Testament describes a practice that one's own church has abandoned. In the case of women serving as pastors or teachers, the key texts have always been 1 Corinthians 14:34-35 and 1 Timothy 2:11-15:

> 34 Women should be silent in the churches. For they are not permitted to speak, but should be subordinate, as the law also says. 35 If there is anything they desire to know, let them ask their husbands at home. For it is shameful for a woman to speak in church.

> 11 Let a woman learn in silence with full submission. 12 I permit no woman to teach or to have authority over a man; she is to keep silent. 13 For Adam was formed first, then Eve; 14 and Adam was not deceived, but the woman was deceived and became a transgressor. 15 Yet she will be saved through childbearing, provided they continue in faith and love and holiness, with modesty.

The lectionary itself seems to anticipate the discomfort provoked by such texts — at least, that's one way to interpret its omission of these two passages. Yet there are many Christians who have come to support women in ecclesiastical leadership who nonetheless do not wish to excise these texts, much less dismiss the authority of Scripture. Is there an alternative to reading with a guilty conscience?

Modern Exegetical Strategies

Defenders of women in ministry in our day have approached these texts in a number of ways. The extreme approach is to regard the letters to Timothy as not authored by Paul: they may have been written by a disciple of

Paul, but they are the products of a later period and they carry a lesser authority, at best. The arguments for this view are not insignificant, but they are generally rejected by conservatives, including evangelical feminists.[2]

Conservative scholars are more likely to mitigate the prohibitions in these texts in two other ways. First, they have endeavored to add precision to our understanding of the words in the text. For example, the word for "silence" in 1 Timothy 2:11 might be better rendered as "quiet," and the word for "have authority" in v. 12 might be better translated as "dominate" — nuances that might mean the injunction in 1 Timothy was addressing a specific and limited problem rather than framing a universal commandment.[3] Another way scholars have reread these prohibitions is by attempting to gauge a text's intention in light of its precise historical context. The conflict noted in an earlier chapter between 1 Corinthians 14:34 (which commands women to be silent in church) and 1 Corinthians 11:5 (which depicts women praying and prophesying) is a good example. Even if the sense of one passage seems straightforward on its own, another text may describe teachings or practices not easily harmonized. One solution is to ask if seemingly universal commands might actually be less so. Thus, 1 Corinthians 14:34 may have addressed only a subset of women in the Corinthian church, even as 1 Timothy 2:12 may pertain to what was only a local dispute, perhaps exacerbated by the religious climate of Asia Minor.[4]

These ameliorating approaches, of course, have not gone unchallenged. With equal industry, other Christian scholars and writers have attempted to counter and rebut egalitarian interpretations, verse by verse and word-study by word-study. One recent work addresses "more than one hundred disputed questions" raised by evangelical feminism: four or more of these questions arise from 1 Corinthians 14:34-35; another fifteen or more, from 1 Timothy 2:11-15.[5] The avowed intent of such voluminous refutation is to recover the "plain" meaning of the Bible when it teaches that men and women are assigned to different yet complementary roles, and to recognize the authority of all of Scripture without seeming to prize some verses at the expense of others.

Older Exegetical Worries

Readers will have to judge these current debates for themselves. The purpose here is not to review or resolve the contemporary debate over women in church leadership, either in its exegetical or theological dimensions. As with previous chapters, our concern is rather to look to the history of interpretation in order to see what consensus, or lack of consensus, might emerge among patristic, medieval, and Reformation commentators on the exegetical issues that bear upon women's ecclesiastical leadership. Having given some attention to 1 Corinthians 14:34-35 in a previous chapter, we will focus a bit more on 1 Timothy 2:11-15, which seems to state the prohibition in stronger terms and adds several supporting arguments. As we will see, even though they were inclined to defend the tradition of a patriarchal church and a patriarchal home, these interpreters still found reasons to be perplexed by what the Apostle wrote.

One Conclusion, Three Supporting Arguments

The injunction against women teaching or exercising authority over men is part of a series of exhortations directed generally at men and women. Subsequent chapters add exhortations bearing on the specific duties of overseers or bishops, deacons, widows, masters and slaves. 1 Timothy 2:11-15 is notable, however, because Paul not only frames a command but also furnishes supporting arguments. The command is found in vv. 11-12; the two primary supports for barring women from authority follow in v. 13, which appeals to Adam's preeminence as formed before Eve, and v. 14, which recalls Eve's inferiority as the one who was deceived and who violated the command in the Garden. The last verse in this passage, v. 15, supports the prohibition against women teaching only remotely: it seems mostly to soften the indictment of "the woman" in v. 14 both as "deceived" and as "transgressor." Yet it also supports the command indirectly, as part of the Apostle's general rules for women's demeanor and lifestyle.

These are terse arguments! And since the persuasiveness of a command rests on the coherence of its support, exegetes have usually felt obliged to fill in the details that these arguments seem to assume. Not surprisingly, diverse accounts have arisen to identify these details and defend the cogency of these supporting arguments. In surveying the history of interpretation, we will look first of all at these supporting arguments. Afterwards, we'll return to the commandment as stated in vv. 11-12 in order to see how traditional commentators qualified this prohibition in light of its larger context as well as by the circumstances and concerns of their own day.

"Adam . . . then Eve."
Is Woman a Second-Best Human Being?

At first glance, v. 13 looks like a simple appeal to the sequence of creation. "Adam was formed first," so Adam and all men should be regarded as . . . what? Wiser? Stronger? Just "special"?

First Come, First Served?

In fact, few commentators embraced this verse in an unadorned fashion, as if priority in time were a self-evident demonstration of anything. That is not to say that anyone asserted the simultaneous creation of Adam and Eve. Although one might read Genesis 1:26 as implying simultaneity, traditional commentators deferred to the account in Genesis 2, where the woman is described as taken from the side of Adam. Many commentators actually erased her from Genesis 1:26, inferring that she was mentioned there only in anticipation, as an expression of divine foreknowledge.[6]

One way or another, then, Adam was created first in time. But appealing merely to sequence is not persuasive. If first is best, wondered John Chrysostom, why were animals created before humans? Erasmus thought the usual order is to save the best for *last* — so the claim for Adam's preeminence here and in 1 Corinthians 11:8 runs against the common order of nature. Writing later in the sixteenth century, Ambrosius Catharinus (opponent of Erasmus and all the Reformers) conceded that an appeal to sequence looks weak, but less so if one takes the verse as affirming not so much priority of sequence as priority of *intention*. In other words, the verse signals that Adam was the head of the human race, and Eve was created to be his helper.[7]

Protestant writers also noted the weakness of the argument in its simplest form. Luther, for example, began by affirming that authority is generally given in Scripture to the firstborn, yet — in commenting on other texts — he was quick to note that God often reverses this privilege. Wolfgang Musculus also cited primogeniture, the preeminence of the firstborn, as the pattern here, only to admit that in many cases elders are not to be preferred to those who are younger. He ended his remarks in a somewhat circular fashion, insisting that the earlier creation of Adam displays man's superiority because that is what God intended to show. Peter Martyr

Vermigli felt less compelled to defend the Apostle here: the argument from sequence is "not firm enough in itself," and that is why Paul adds other arguments. Calvin echoed the thought: "Paul's argument . . . does not seem very strong," for John the Baptist, after all, came before Christ yet was inferior to him. Like Vermigli, Calvin insisted that Paul adds other arguments. Moreover, Paul intended all along to signal not just sequence but the overall reason for which woman was created: to be a help to the man, indeed, "a kind of appendage" to him.[8]

Did Woman Become Subordinate, or Was She Made That Way?

Calvin, like many others, instinctively connected Paul's appeal to Adam's prior creation with other common assumptions about male superiority and headship — assumptions often expressed in stark and absolute terms. "The first and better sex is the male," wrote Musculus, contemplating the greater mental and physical powers of men. Vermigli asserted that men ought to display greater wisdom and virtue than women — "even if this is not always the case."[9]

Expressions of male superiority could be multiplied, but it's more revealing to ask whether male superiority and the subordination of women was seen as original or as something that came later. The majority position is that women were created to be the helpers of men, subordinate and submissive to male leadership, as befits their lesser gifts and derived status. The result of sin was to worsen their condition from submissiveness to servitude. This view is held by Augustine, Ambrosiaster, Denis, Cajetan, Erasmus, Zwingli, Bullinger, Bucer, Vermigli, Catharinus, Calvin, and undoubtedly many others.[10] So far as concerns classic Roman Catholic theology, the original inferiority of woman was given a scientific basis by Aquinas, who applied the Aristotelian notion of woman as, biologically and psychologically, a "defective male" — necessary for the propagation of the species, to be sure, but "impaired" at conception so as to lack the physical and mental excellence of the male.[11] Protestant commentators did not cite Aristotle, but they retained as a working assumption that woman was created weaker in body, intellect, and temperament.[12] As we'll see, this weakness explains why Eve was approached by the serpent.

It remains, however, to describe the minority position. When addressing 1 Timothy 2:13 or related verses, some supposed an original equality of men and women. In other words, the subordination of women to men is something that came later, as an effect of sin. Here is Chrysostom's poignant paraphrase of what God said to Eve:

> In the beginning I created you equal in esteem to your husband, and my intention was that in everything you would share with him as an equal, and as I entrusted control of everything to your husband, so did I to you; but you abused your equality of status. Hence I subject you to your husband.[13]

The half-dozen Protestants who flirted with this view, though, hardly developed it — and all, in fact, also affirmed the contrary position. That was the case with Chrysostom, too, who regularly placed statements about woman's original secondary status next to affirmations of her original equality. The Protestant writer who most often affirmed Eve's original equality was Martin Luther:

> If the woman had not been deceived by the serpent and had not sinned, she would have been the equal of Adam in all respects. . . . Eve was not like the woman of today; her state was far better and more excellent, and she was in no respect inferior to Adam, whether you count the qualities of the body or those of the mind.[14]

But Luther was as inconsistent as his peers: elsewhere he observes that Eve was *not* the equal of her husband.[15]

These isolated affirmations of the original equality of Eve may therefore be mere rhetorical flourishes, meant to dramatize how much all women lost by Eve's sin. Yet they may be more than rhetoric; they may be driven by eschatology. That is to say, given the expectation that human nature will be righted and restored in heaven, and given Paul's words that in Christ there is neither male nor female, these commentators may be projecting their hopes for heaven back into the Garden. Either way, and despite their inconsistencies, they clearly do affirm that neither an original nor a future equality between the sexes should be seen as anything but a good thing — even if, for the present, such equality is not the order of the day. As Chrysostom warned his congregation, "equality of honor causes contention."[16]

"Adam was not deceived."
So, Was Eve the Only Sinner?

The argument for Adam's greater authority on the basis of his prior creation is followed by an argument for Eve's lesser authority based on her moral failure in the face of temptation. That Eve is indicted for her transgression is no surprise, of course. But the bald assertion that Adam was not deceived generates considerable discussion.

Things You Didn't Know about Eve

In seeking to explain everything the Bible does and does not say about the disaster in the Garden, few commentators neglected the resources provided by their forebears. Puzzling passages were usually accompanied by a litany of traditional questions and answers. This "exegetical lore" regarded no detail as too obscure to address. For example, which of the two, Adam or Eve, was created of a more noble substance — Adam, made of earth; or Eve, made of flesh? Did the removal of Adam's rib leave him deformed or, instead, remedy a defect with which he had been created?

One such detail that bears on Eve's culpability is the matter of how she received the prohibition against eating from the tree. After all, if her actual creation did not occur until Genesis 2:22, she would not have been present to hear God's warning to Adam in Genesis 2:17. If she knew the command at all, she would have gotten it secondhand. In fact, several commentators agree that Eve was absent when the command was given, and a few are inclined to excuse her disobedience somewhat, based on her ignorance or perhaps on the grounds that Adam would have made less of an impression than the voice of God.[17] But most who mention Eve's absence are disinclined to excuse her on that basis: to learn God's will from one's husband is, after all, what Paul presents as the right and usual order of teaching.[18] By contrast, Musculus thinks Eve *was* present at the giving of the command, but only Adam was addressed because he was the head of his wife.[19]

Eve's Weakness and Sin

One way or another, then, it was generally held that Eve was deceived by the serpent and transgressed the command because she was the weaker of the two. Typically, Eve was seen as governed less by reason than was Adam. An ancient allegory, known to virtually all these commentators, identifies *man* with the rational soul or mind; *woman* with the affections and appetites; and the *serpent* with the body or its senses. Temptation arises from the senses, but it is the appetite that leads the mind astray.[20] So it was with Eve: woman's weaker reason and unstable appetites made her prey to temptation. Most interpreters imply that Adam would have stood the test, even though they often concede that Eve's weaknesses reflect generally those of both sexes.

Traditionally, the sin ascribed to Adam and Eve is *pride,* but most interpreters discerned other sins peculiar to Eve, including presumption, impatience, curiosity, ingratitude, and so forth.[21] Musculus also criticized her for failing to consult with her husband before striking up a conversation with the serpent. Eve was further culpable for leading Adam to eat after she had partaken, according to Ambrose, who reconstructed her motive with a degree of sympathy: though Eve knew what she was doing in giving Adam the fruit, she did so fearing that "she alone" would be cast out, separated from her beloved husband.[22]

Did Adam Sin Deliberately? How to Fix Verse 14

For Christian commentators, the provocative statement that "Adam was not deceived" drives explanations of the Fall, regardless of whether a commentary purports to explain Paul or Genesis. Everyone must reckon with this bold assertion, which raises more problems than it solves. Obviously, if Adam was not deceived yet was punished along with Eve, he must have sinned, presumably with deliberation. Interpreters were quick to note that deliberate disobedience would be more reprehensible than disobedience stemming from ignorance or deception. Yet most admitted that Adam did disobey God, fully aware of his action. His motive? The opinion of Augustine was hugely influential, that Adam acted out of a misguided affection for Eve:

> Solomon . . . was unable to resist the love of women. . . . So it was in the case of Adam. . . . He did not wish to make her unhappy, fearing

she would waste away without his support, alienated from his affections, and that this dissension would be her death.[23]

At the crucial moment, Adam's mind was overcome by his heart.

Was Adam's sin therefore more heinous, since done wittingly? In theory, yes. But the question of who sinned more does not resolve so easily. Interpreters commonly wavered. Some were content to distribute equal blame; others felt obliged to explain why Eve received a special rebuke. Denis initially found Eve at fault for persisting in her intention despite having been reminded of the command by the serpent itself; yet he later faulted Adam more, because he had the stronger intellect and had been placed in charge. Denis finally concluded that Eve sinned more gravely, an inference he drew from her harsher punishment.[24] Eve was also blamed more by Jacques Lefèvre d'Étaples, who insisted that Adam ate the fruit in ignorance.[25] But Catharinus marveled at Adam's "exceptional obtuseness," suggesting that *he* deserved to be placed in subjection more than the woman![26]

Catharinus's line of argument was addressed more directly still by Musculus. If Adam sinned deliberately and thus more grievously, shouldn't he have been punished more severely and forfeit his dominion over Eve? Actually, no: dominion requires prudence and wisdom, and Eve's lapse in judgment proves that she lacked these qualities.[27] This whole discussion could amount to a lose-lose proposition for Eve and all women: to say that woman sinned *more* reinforces the justness of male dominance, but to say she sinned *less* underscores her lesser competence and gifts. In the case of Musculus, though, his commitment to defend 1 Timothy 2:14 does not upstage his pastoral insight:

> Care is to be taken that we do not extend this example of Adam and Eve further than the Apostle's proposition requires, that is, lest we make his specific [proposition] into something general and perpetual. Indeed, while Adam was not misled by the serpent's lie, the same cannot be said of every man. And what happened to Eve does not automatically happen to all women, many of whom strongly resist the lies and temptations of Satan.[28]

For Musculus, then, the "lesson" of v. 14 is not just for women.

Regardless of how culpability is to be distributed between Adam and

Eve, commentators stumbled far more over the impossible choice framed by v. 14: if Adam wasn't deceived, he must have sinned with eyes wide open. We have already noted how commentators appealed to his misplaced loyalty, but what is more surprising is their tendency to qualify the Apostle's pronouncement still further. That is to say, most commentators thought Adam *was* deceived, and those who did not think so usually attributed to him still worse sins.

The second group is the minority here. Cajetan thus asserted that Adam was not deceived, and Erasmus added that Adam *couldn't* have been deceived — as did Musculus, citing v. 14 as a proof-text but offering no further explanation. Denis the Carthusian also thought Adam did not believe the serpent, though he did retain some doubts, in addition to lying to and envying God! Pellican, too, insisted Adam was not deceived: he merely forgot or neglected God's command.[29]

Most interpreters, however, felt compelled to add an explanatory phrase to v. 14. Chrysostom set a precedent by arguing that Adam was not deceived as much as or in the same manner as Eve: she was deceived by a snake, but he was deceived by an equal. Both Ambrose and Ambrosiaster took similar views: Adam was deceived not by the devil, but by the woman. As usual, Aquinas added precision: Adam was not deceived about what was prohibited, but he *was* deceived about what would follow his disobedience. Luther offered a more existential analysis: while not deceived by the serpent, Adam was deceived by his wife — or by himself.[30] Theodoret did not "fix" the verse, but he did append a curiously weak endorsement of Paul's assertions. "One should realize that the divine apostle composed his text with current needs in mind," he wrote, probably to register that there was much more to be said about the sin of our first parents than was to be found here.[31]

Perhaps the most surprising comment is Calvin's musing that Adam might well have fallen into the same deception: "It could have been that Adam came along shortly, even before the woman ate . . . and he became entangled in the same fallacies by which she was deceived." Calvin was admittedly speculating, but he still implied his dissent from a simplistic reading of v. 14 when he describes the verse as intended comparatively: Adam was not deceived *as thoroughly as* Eve. Elsewhere Calvin insisted that "Paul does not mean that Adam was not involved in the . . . deception but only that the cause and source of his transgression came from Eve."[32] Clearly, denying that Adam had been deceived moved Calvin to discomfort, and he refused to allow that such a denial was what the Apostle had in mind.

Other Tales of Adam

Calvin was discomfited by other things, too. He vigorously dissented from those who denied that Adam was deceived, as if he transgressed "only to satisfy his wife's whim." To the contrary, Adam *did* believe Satan's lie. Paul's point here is, again, simply to indicate Eve as "the cause and source of his transgression."[33] Calvin reiterated this point in his Genesis commentary and went on to cite a crucial text for the doctrine of original sin, Romans 5:12, where Paul states that "sin came not by the woman, but by Adam himself."[34]

Calvin's scruple here highlights an obvious concern: to blame only Eve, as 1 Timothy 2:14 seems to do, is to truncate the larger biblical account. Calvin was by no means the first to notice or to supplement 1 Timothy 2 with Romans 5: Luther did likewise, as did Chrysostom long before.[35] Most commentators felt obliged, one way or another, to call Adam to account alongside Eve in order to counterweight the one-sidedness here. The search for balance is to be found even in Tertullian, who is frequently cited today only for his shock value:

> Do you not know that you are an Eve? The sentence of God on this sex of yours lives on in this age; the guilt must of necessity live on as well. You are the devil's gateway. You are the one who unsealed that tree. You were the first to desert the divine law. You are the one who persuaded him whom the devil was not strong enough to attack. It was you who so easily destroyed the image of God, man.[36]

Tertullian has amplified 1 Timothy 2:14 to a deafening degree, and many writers make him a whipping-boy for all patristic misogyny. However, the offense of his rhetoric has also led most not only to overlook his advocacy on behalf of women prophesying, but also to ignore two other texts in Tertullian in which blame for sin is attributed to both Adam and Eve, and three more that blame Adam alone.[37] We needn't admire or emulate Tertullian for rhetoric that is ungoverned and excessive by our standards, but we do well to admit that he, too, knew that the whole story of human sin was not to be found in 1 Timothy.

"Saved through childbearing"?
Not Quite, and Not Every Woman

The final verse of this section functions as a sort of bookend: it ties v. 15 to v. 9, where the discussion of women began, by repeating the exhortation to modesty. Somewhat more unexpected, however, and much more provocative, is the announcement that "woman will be *saved through bearing children, if they continue in faith and love and holiness, with modesty*." As we will see, the notion that a woman's salvation might be effected through procreation was problematic not only for Protestants but also for Roman Catholics.

Patristic Maneuvers

Anyone might guess that Protestants, deeply committed to a gospel of salvation by faith alone, would be uncomfortable with the idea that women are saved by childbearing. But there was equal resistance to a "plain" reading of v. 15 well before the Reformation. Many church fathers puzzled over how woman's salvation by childbearing could possibly fit into the rest of the biblical picture. For Ambrosiaster, the verse did not make the woman's salvation dependent on bearing children; it merely described how women may experience salvation — that is, resurrection — in the company of their children, if the children indeed persevered in their regeneration.[38] Pelagius, on the other hand, took childbearing as symbolic of *baptism:* "Let woman not despair, for she is saved through baptism, which begets sons of God."[39] That promise, of course, pertains only to women who believe *and persevere,* even as the reference to faith, love, and holiness led to a lesson for which Pelagius was well known, that "faith alone does not suffice." Writing before 410, Pelagius was no Protestant: he happily connected a woman's salvation to her demeanor, but it bothered him greatly to think anyone might be saved by the good works of another, whether one's parents or progeny.[40]

Those two fathers tried to dodge the obscure wording of v. 15 by quietly substituting their own free associations. A different solution was offered by Ambrose in his treatise *On Paradise:*

> If woman is responsible for sin, how can her accession be considered a good? . . . [It is a good] because the human race could not

have been propagated from man alone. God preferred the existence of more than one whom He would be able to save than to confine this possibility to one man who was free from error. . . . If the woman was the first to sin, . . . she was [also] the one destined to bring forth redemption. . . . Woman, we are told, "will be saved by childbearing," in the course of which she generated Christ.[41]

Ambrose's passing remark reflects a traditional Christian observation, that the men and women of the Old Testament yearned not only to have children of their own but also to bring forth one child in particular: the messiah, the "promised seed" of Genesis 3:15. (Earlier we saw this observation invoked to explain the patriarchs' polygamous tendencies.) For Ambrose, 1 Timothy 2:15a was fulfilled once and for all by Mary, the antidote to Eve and the woman by whom the Savior was born. Presumably, the exhortations of v. 15b still remain for other women.

Spiritual and Ascetic Childbearing

Other church fathers found ways to spiritualize the childbearing enjoined by v. 15. Wondering how a childless widow might be saved, Augustine opined that good works are very much like the "sons" of our life. So, when a faithful Christian performs works of mercy, this command is fulfilled.[42] More often, the occasion for spiritualizing this verse centered on consecrated virgins, who fled the carnal attachments of marriage in order to draw near to God. Gregory of Nyssa thus urged his readers to bear not mortal children but, in their place, "life and immortality." Such "deathless offspring," born of "virgin mothers" through the Spirit, truly fulfill the promise of 1 Timothy 2:15 that women will be saved by childbearing.[43] Asceticism played a huge role in pre-Reformation exegesis: married Christians might well fulfill the commands that are binding on all, but those who lived lives of celibacy aimed higher, at the "counsels of perfection" that Jesus held out as the narrow way.[44] Among patristic and medieval writers, there was considerable worry lest a command to bear children overthrow the vocation of nuns and other women who had taken vows of celibacy. (The command to "fill the earth and subdue it," by contrast, was often seen as having been fulfilled.[45])

Advocacy for the ascetic life was just as pronounced on the eve of the

Reformation and well beyond. The views of Denis the Carthusian, Cajetan, and Catharinus were thus doubly repugnant to Protestants: not only did they view childbearing as a meritorious work, they also placed monks and nuns in a privileged class with respect to salvation. Verse 15 was therefore read as pertaining only to the married; nuns were by no means obliged to procreate.[46]

The Reformation and Domestic Exegesis

In 1 Timothy 2, the references to woman's creation and fall in vv. 13-14 led many exegetes to seek an explanation also for v. 15 in Genesis, where pain in childbirth has traditionally been seen as part of the "curse" women bear for Eve's sin. Protestant interpreters are no exception. While quicker than Roman Catholics to extol the goodness of marriage and childbearing, Protestant writers still had to avoid portraying the domestic duties listed in v. 15 as works of *merit*. They did so, but the contrast with Catholics should not be overdrawn. Protestants dissented vigorously over monastic vows, but there was a closer approach to the Catholic position when Protestants explained childbearing not as meritorious, of course, but as having nonetheless a salutary, medicinal, and even atoning effect for women. A few examples will suffice.

Zwingli was bolder than most. When God said to Eve, "I will multiply your pain" (Genesis 3:16), these words imposed "a curse on women and a penalty for disobedience, which they *remove and atone for* when they are submissive and compliant with their husbands, bear children, and raise them in religion."[47] Zwingli did not seriously envision women effecting an atonement to rival Christ's, but such penitential language was common. Johann Brenz, a Lutheran reformer, called birth pains and subjection "a work of satisfaction."[48] He could have drawn the insight from Luther:

> That subjection of women and domination of men have not been taken away, have they? No. The guilt has passed away, but the penalty remains, as do the pain and tribulations of childbearing — punishments that are to remain until the judgment. Thus the domination of men and the subjection of women remain, too. You should put up with them, for you can be saved if you are also submissive and give birth with pain.[49]

175

Commentators here found a neat way to bring together many of the imperatives for women in 1 Timothy 2 under the general umbrella of subjection to their husbands. Childbearing is then a primary symbol of all that defines a woman's life. And while submissiveness is not a good work that merits salvation, it is seen as part of God's plan for women: not *contributory* to their salvation, yet *congruent* with it. Though Calvin can speak of a medicinal effect of the curse, he could also address his hearers with penitential and sacrificial imagery:

> If women submit themselves willingly and patiently to that which God has commanded of them and which their state requires, it is an acceptable sacrifice to God, and the curse which was laid upon all women in Eve's person is virtually obliterated, for God receives them into his favor and love.[50]

For Protestants, childbearing does not "save" women in the precise terms of v. 15. Yet if the verse remains imperfectly explained, these writers came close enough, in their own minds, by explaining how childbearing dovetails with the other parts of redemption. And insofar as they agreed that God is pleased to call women to these duties, Protestants and Catholics also came close to finding middle ground.

"I permit no woman to teach."
Saving Paul's Conclusion

The male commentators surveyed here all took male preeminence for granted and found that view ratified by Scripture, as well as by their culture and experience. It would be astonishing, then, to find anyone from this group who hoped to find new loopholes for women. At the same time, an undeniable dissonance emerges from the arguments supporting vv. 11-12. It wasn't the practice of patriarchy or hierarchy that bothered these commentators: Paul's *conclusion*, in other words, was not the problem. The problem lay elsewhere, in the terseness (if not weakness) of Paul's reasoning, in other Scriptures that seemed at variance with this one, and in other experiences at least some writers had of notable women in their own day. These other factors led them to frame Paul's command with significant qualifications or concessions, even as they strove to defend his conclusion.

Parentheses, Asterisks, & Footnotes

We've already seen how commentators typically added a phrase to v. 14 in order to square it with how they read the rest of the Bible. "Adam was not deceived" thus became "not deceived *by a snake*" or "not deceived *in the way Eve was deceived*." Similar moves occured at vv. 11-12, where interpreters mitigated the absoluteness of the command to silence in order to let women ask questions in the course of catechism or offer confession to a priest. Likewise, the prohibition against teaching is usually read as if Paul had written "in public" — a qualification that might be inferred by reference to 1 Corinthians 14:34-35, which doesn't address teaching but does restrict the silencing of women to "in church." It was important to these commentators that women be able to teach children, at least, frequently other women, and sometimes much more.

The passage from 1 Corinthians 14 was precisely what occasioned Origen's assertions that however women may have prophesied in the Bible, they didn't do so in church, nor did they address the people of God corporately.[51] Pelagius similarly qualified 1 Corinthians 14:34-35, but his paraphrase of 1 Timothy 2:12 said more: "He does not permit [it] in public, for she ought to teach a son or a brother in private."[52] The reference to teaching a *brother* comes unexpectedly, though, possibly arising from Pelagius's experience of learned women ascetics. About the same concern was voiced ten centuries later by Denis. To the injunction for women's silence, he added "especially in church." To the prohibition against women teaching, he added "in public or in the church," on the grounds that women are weak in reason, talkative, vain, and incite more dissipation than devotion. But he was quick to note that women may teach those who are rightly subject to them at home or in the convent.[53] Denis gave voice to the common Catholic position — a position that Protestants (including Luther and Calvin) left largely intact.[54] Yet the boundaries of this interpretation were rarely tidy: Luther had other views about exceptions (see below), and Calvin implied that women who "privately" exercised the gift of prophecy (which he viewed as a teaching function) might well have done so in groups that included men.[55]

There were other kinds of "asterisks" added to the prohibitions against women speaking and teaching in 1 Corinthians and 1 Timothy. Theodoret, for instance, pointedly introduced the injunction for women to be silent by noting the presence of prophetesses in the New Testament setting:

"Since women also enjoyed the charism of inspiration, he is obliged to give directions for it as well."[56] Instead of the usual cross-reference to the silence enjoined by 1 Corinthians 14:34, he was more mindful of the prophetesses of 1 Corinthians 11:5. Theodoret did not dissent, of course, from Paul's general assertion of male authority. But he was also unwilling to ignore the larger context of the New Testament in which women were called to prophetic roles.

Exceptions That Prove the Rule

Theodoret's mindfulness was not unique: many writers wondered how to square 1 Timothy 2:12 with their memory of biblical prophetesses. Most commonly, writers limited the context or content of what these women did, insisting (for example) that they must have prophesied in private, even if the immediate narrative does not say so. This was Calvin's approach (and that of many others) with respect to Philip's daughters, whose prophetic ministry occurred "outside the public meeting."[57]

Aquinas took the same approach to Deborah, the prophetess who also judged Israel: she did not teach or preach publicly but gave advice in private.[58] But not all commentators restricted Deborah in this way. Gratian, the great systematizer of canon law, concluded that what Deborah did was licit in the Old Testament but not in the New. Most writers, however, saw her only as an exception raised up by God, who is free to suspend the usual order, and they made no attempt to locate her calling within the frame of 1 Timothy 2:12. This was variously the view of Denis, Bucer, Luther, Brenz, Calvin, and Vermigli — again, among others.[59] Rudolf Gwalter, Bullinger's successor in Zurich, drew an explicit contrast between prophetesses such as Deborah and the "garrulous, willful" women whom Paul silenced in 1 Corinthians 14:34-35.[60]

For some Reformers, though, the more license they granted to Deborah, the more likely they were to echo Jerome's cynical maxim that God raises up women only to shame men.[61] The observation was applied to Deborah (with puzzling inconsistency) by Denis, Pellican, and Brenz; Calvin was harsher still.[62] On the other hand, Bucer and Vermigli saw Deborah as simply the means God used in an emergency. Vermigli's estimate of Deborah may also have reflected a strategic admiration for Elizabeth I of England, the Protestant monarch who at times saw herself as a new

Deborah.[63] (Calvin, too, had pondered whether an English queen might be a new Deborah, but his sour remarks on the prospect were occasioned rather by the Catholic Mary Tudor.) Even Luther, who worked so hard to portray Deborah as somehow under male authority, ended his remarks on 1 Timothy 2:11-15 by affirming prophetesses: "If the Lord were to raise up a woman for us to listen to, we would allow her to rule like Huldah."[64]

If the case of biblical prophetesses represents a "supernatural" exception to the usual restrictions on women teaching and ruling, other cases are more mundane. One such case pertains to women ascetics — the consecrated virgins or nuns we mentioned earlier. Protestants despised the practice, but many fathers and medievals saw it as the highest path of discipleship. Thus, for Jerome, the gospel holds forth the promise not only of being delivered from childbearing and its pains, but even from submission to a husband. Such benefits, of course, were held out not to the married but only to virgins and widows.[65] Jerome was one of many voices asserting the privileged and elite status of ascetics, the "spiritual athletes" of their day. By being spiritually espoused to Christ, nuns were delivered from the headship of a husband — though, practically speaking, they were still accountable to various church authorities, usually male.

Expecting the Unexpected: Rules for Exceptions

For another kind of exception, we must briefly revisit the emergency ministry of women. Granted that the Bible depicts God as breaking the rules to raise up queens and prophetesses, might this happen in our own day? Should churches expect or countenance such a development? All our commentators embraced the traditional view that the Bible teaches the subordination of women to men, yet — as we saw in an earlier chapter[66] — some sixteenth-century interpreters also granted that women might occasionally minister in this way. Luther's reference to Huldah identifies him as one such writer, but we'll focus again on Vermigli and Calvin.

Vermigli and Calvin each voiced a theory of women ministering more or less in public in extraordinary circumstances. Each also imagined a temporary (yet not "supernatural") calling for such a woman, who would speak or teach the gospel until church order be restored — that is, until she could be replaced by a man duly ordained. But how did they account for the departure from biblical teachings?

The answer is rooted in their nuanced understanding of doctrine. Discussions of how doctrine is variously derived from the Bible go back a long ways, and Vermigli's account is not novel. He takes his cue from 1 Corinthians 14:34, where woman is commanded to be silent and subordinate, "as the law also says." Vermigli knows silence is not expressly enjoined by the law but is instead a command derived by Paul from Genesis 3. Here, then, is one of Vermigli's principles: Not all "biblical" precepts carry the same weight, for *explicit* precepts constitute the standards by which *implied* precepts are to be judged.[67] In this context, Vermigli then turns to ask whether *we* have transgressed the divine command today, since we no longer use the rite of tongues and prophecy in church. His reply frames a second principle:

> Today, when the inspired and abundant gifts of God are not to be had and there is a great dearth of teachers and preachers, we do not transgress the laws of God if we deviate a bit from Paul's arrangements. Nonetheless, care is to be taken that we accommodate ourselves to them as much as possible.[68]

For Vermigli, because our circumstances differ from New Testament times, we must also adjust how we read and apply Scripture.

Although Calvin is more reluctant to offer an explanation for how exceptions work, he too distinguishes "levels" of doctrinal authority. The command for women's silence in 1 Corinthians 14:34 falls under Paul's own summation in v. 40, that the principle underlying all his detailed instructions is to do all things "decently and in order." For Calvin, Paul's instructions here pertain not to the essentials of the faith but to external matters, to "administrative arrangements *(ritus politici)*, which are not so necessary to observe."[69] In general, polity is less important and less fixed than the essential doctrines of the faith, and that is why we may, at times, legitimately deviate from Scripture.

> Paul forbids [women] to speak in public, whether for . . . teaching or prophesying. But this should be taken as pertaining to ordinary procedures, where the workings of the church are in order. Indeed, such a need can arise which requires a woman to speak.[70]

Calvin made the same point in his *Institutes:*

These are no fixed and permanent sanctions by which we are bound, but outward rudiments for human weakness. . . . Is that decree of Paul's concerning [woman's] silence so holy that it cannot be broken without great offense? . . . Not at all. . . . And there is a place where it is no less proper for her to speak than elsewhere to remain silent.[71]

By no means does Calvin desire or expect to usher women into public roles as preachers or teachers, but should exceptions to the rule of 1 Timothy 2:12 or 1 Corinthians 14:34 arise or be needed, he *can* explain why.

Living with a Divisive Text

What the Bible teaches about gender roles for church and family is hotly contested today. Within evangelical Christianity, competing views are well-defined: "complementarians" or traditionalists oppose "egalitarians," and the line in the sand often seems more like a broad, ugly ditch. No sooner has one side published a new defense of its exegesis than the other side replies with yet another detailed refutation.[72]

Is there anything to be learned from the history of the exegesis of 1 Timothy 2:12 and similar passages? Actually, mine is neither the only nor the most detailed survey of the treatment of this text. Perhaps the closest parallel is a 1995 survey by Daniel Doriani, appended to a set of essays written from a complementarian perspective.[73] That study does a good job of documenting one key point that we have also seen here, namely, that 1 Timothy 2:12 has nearly always been defended as teaching the subordination of women — at least, through the era of the Reformation. What Doriani's study does not address as well is the question central to this book, namely, does it make any difference to know *how* traditional commentators reached this conclusion, or how they weighted and applied it? I think that it does matter, and that knowing the history of exegesis here — not just the history of exegetical *conclusions* — can help Christian readers avoid a simplistic understanding of a text that isn't simple and has rarely been treated simply. I would suggest these insights as part of the payoff:

1. FEW EVER READ PAUL'S SUPPORTING ARGUMENTS AS LITERALLY TRUE. *Despite their conviction that 1 Timothy 2:12 and*

1 Corinthians 14:34 dictate the exclusive right of men to teach and rule in the church, traditional commentators wrestled with the details of these passages, which did not fall neatly in place. Our own wrestling with these details is also traditional.

Despite the literal wording of these texts, traditional commentators generally recognized that these texts were not perfectly easy to grasp or apply. In fact, Adam's prior creation was not seen as a strong argument for his precedence. Few believed that Adam was not also, like Eve, deceived; those who did often saw him guilty of worse sins. While everyone agreed that faith, love, holiness, and modesty were fine virtues, no one believed women were actually saved by having children. Few construed the strictures about women's silence without adding qualifications of time and circumstance — and exceptions. And even the prohibition against women teaching or presiding was not absolute. For many, women may teach: usually not in public, but sometimes they may teach men, and sometimes they are called to extraordinary public ministries, just as they were in the Bible — for not every commentator reduced the role of prophecy to a private, cloistered, or domestic activity. The practices described by these texts may fairly be taken as depicting an ideal embraced by traditional commentators. Yet they were usually wise enough to recognize that Paul's teachings and arguments were not handled well if reduced to simple formulas with simplistic proof-texts that brooked no opposition, exceptions, or contextualization.

2. THE COMPLEXITY OF SCRIPTURE AND GENDER IS NOT AVOIDABLE. *The Bible's inspiration and authority does not mean that every command has the same weight. Likewise, simply because the Bible speaks of men and women does not mean they are homogenous classes.*

When Vermigli distinguished between the Bible's explicit and implicit precepts, he was attempting to set forth not only the process of Paul's theological reflection but also the Apostle's humility, in that Paul invited the Corinthians to judge for themselves whether he'd properly deduced his argument. For Vermigli, implicit precepts, including Paul's, were of lesser weight, just as Calvin construed some of the Bible's instructions as polity, not doctrine. Not only is a woman not saved by childbearing, she is also not saved or damned by her subordination. If it is a mistake to ignore what

Paul says about men and women, it is a catastrophe to treat matters of polity as if they constitute the heart of the gospel by which we are saved.

It is equally counterproductive to define what it means to be a man or a woman in such a way that overrides what God may give as a charism. Luther set an early Protestant precedent when he insisted that all Christians — men and women — are prophets and priests, so that "everyone has the right to preach." (To be sure, he added that a preacher needs a good voice and speaking skills, which he thought women don't have.[74]) Other writers gauged the propriety of a woman speaking and teaching not on her gender per se, but on whether she had a *word* from God when no man did.[75] But to assume that women cannot lead or teach because of their nature, despite biblical counter-examples, is to transform a precept of polity into a statement of ontology — an assertion of the way men and women simply "are," even if some of us don't recognize ourselves in such dogmas. We should hope to be as discerning as Musculus: women are not necessarily or universally wired to replicate Eve's mistakes or character, and her bad example is just as likely to be emulated by men.

3. THE COMPLEXITY OF HISTORY IS ALSO NOT AVOIDABLE.
   To claim a historical consensus about the role of women while disregarding the ambiguities of exegesis or traditions of dissent is to falsify the past.

I teach history, and it is not uncommon for students to hope I will identify the lessons of the past for them, neatly defined and easily retained. I usually disappoint on this score. History is complicated. In the case of the history of the interpretation of 1 Timothy 2:12, that complexity is tied to a perennial discussion, within the church and without, of gender roles. There never was a "golden age" when the prohibitions against women speaking and teaching were not controversial. Some signs of that controversy have emerged on these pages. A longer book, however, or a different one, could set forth historical details that fall at greater distance from the history of interpretation — details that would tell the story of women who found ways to use their gifts and fulfill their callings despite what their brothers in the faith (and, perhaps, selected proof-texts) said they could not do.[76]

The burden of this chapter has been to sketch some of the complexity of the history of exegesis, and to argue that the way we come to conclusions about what the Bible teaches is an indispensable part of how we use the Bible. No one comes to the Bible with a blank slate. We come instead with a host of presuppositions and habits of mind, some conscious and deliberate, others products of culture, family, denomination, and our personal fallenness and finitude. The same was true of the classic commentators of the Christian past.

One of the dividing factors in this conversation about the Bible and gender roles derives from a disagreement about history and its complexity. There are diverse ways to understand history, especially the nature of the Bible as a historical book. One of the most contentious points is whether the Bible, especially the New Testament, ought to be read as perfectly homogenous or whether the Gospels and Epistles arise from a primitive church that was somewhat diverse in its experiences and practices. Insisting on an original homogeneity will force some sort of showdown between the accounts of women teaching or prophesying and the strictures against women teaching. Yet the historical reality of the early church may have embraced both without dissolving either, perhaps in ways we can, at best, conjecture.

Some Christians abhor such lack of resolution for the uncertainty it seems to impart to the Bible. As one recent writer has put it, "If Scripture does not mean what people have taken it to mean for centuries, then the Bible is obscure, and, due to its lack of clarity, it cannot possess the authority it once had."[77] Actually, the doctrine of Scripture's *clarity* usually focuses specifically on its message about salvation from sin, and it is generally conceded that not all passages of Scripture are equally clear or have equal bearing on the message of redemption.[78] With respect to the texts we have surveyed in this chapter, the musings and hesitations of many traditional commentators regarding the limitations of Paul's arguments and conclusion might suggest that these texts are, in fact, neither perfectly clear nor easy to apply. Fortunately, these are not matters that bear on salvation. And just as fortunately, as traditional commentators themselves also acknowledged, behind these matters lie guiding principles — decency and order, faith and love — that *are* clear to all.

Chapter Nine

Reading Sex and Violence

Dinah, Bathsheba, Tamar, and Too Many Others

P reachers never really want to preach on rape or adultery, do they? On a Sunday morning, to a congregation of families? Certainly the lectionary, once again, does not let us down: of the stories of Dinah, the Levite's wife, Bathsheba, and Tamar, only Bathsheba appears in the three-year cycle of readings. Of course *she* would: the story of David's rebuke by Nathan the prophet and of how David came to be the father of Solomon by Bathsheba — tied as it is to the classic penitential psalm, Psalm 51 — is simply too important and too extensive to omit. But these other women remain neglected.

The decision is not too hard to understand. Sooner or later the exposition will have to address — or sidestep — explicit deeds of sex and violence. The potential for awkwardness or embarrassment is high, as is the potential for witless disaster. A former student told me of her experience in a preaching class, in which a male classmate read the entire narrative of the incestuous rape of Tamar by her brother Amnon, dwelling on the narrative at length and in detail, only to wind up with this unlikely lesson: *How wonderful that the love of Jesus is so unlike the love of Amnon!* This student preacher had no inkling that his gratuitous retelling of Tamar's rape had scratched open a classmate's memory of her own abusive brothers. His breathless discovery that "Jesus is better than Amnon" only underscored his own insensitivity to the sort of scarring that sexual abuse brings.

How should such texts be read and appropriated? Are they simply too painful to read? Or might it be better to say that they are too powerful, precisely in their painfulness, to be used by *beginners?*

When Desire Leads to Violence

The stories of the four women named above are, without a doubt, disturbing details in the history of salvation. Each of these women is caught up in violence stemming from the men who desire them. In Genesis 34, young Dinah goes out to visit the women of the land and ends up raped and nearly married, only to witness the slaughter of Hamor and Shechem at the hands of her treacherous brothers. The Levite's wife in Judges 19 is on the way home with her husband when he surrenders her to the townsmen of Gibeah, who would have preferred to rape him but settled for raping her — over and over, until she was dead. In 2 Samuel 11, while her husband is off at war, Bathsheba is espied and bedded by King David. When David fails to pin her pregnancy on Uriah, he arranges Uriah's battlefield death. In 2 Samuel 13, David's son Amnon sets a trap to seduce his half-sister Tamar, whom he conquers by force only to reject her afterwards in contempt. David's anger with Amnon leads only to his inaction, but Tamar's brother Absalom eventually exacts a lethal vengeance.

Just as the stories about Jephthah's daughter and Gomer elicited poignant responses from contemporary feminists, so also have these tales. We need not review all the details here; the questions should be familiar by now.[1] These women are scarcely actors: instead, they are acted upon. As daughters and wives, they are assumed to belong to fathers and husbands, subject to the control of men. When that control is endangered or contested, chaos among men breaks out and the storyline leaves the women behind, damaged or dead. Yet the Bible says enough about these women for some readers to care about them and wonder about their feelings and fate. What happened to them? Why did they receive such raw treatment? Did anyone speak on their behalf or remember them? Because the Bible itself says nothing about such matters, feminist readers feel constrained to speak on their behalf. But such readers have another concern, too, equally urgent: why is it that even modern commentaries compound the injury to these women not merely by continuing to neglect them but also by adding insult? Dinah, for example, is faulted for the foolish curiosity that led her from the safety of her father's home; Bathsheba is accused of exhibitionism when bathing.[2] It's bad enough that Scripture is so silent about these women, but why fill the silences by blaming the victims? Are there better patterns for interpreters to follow?

Reading between Sympathy and Suspicion

The task of the present chapter is not to offer extensive surveys of Dinah, the Levite's wife, Bathsheba, and Tamar in the history of biblical interpretation. Instead, we'll focus strategically on a topic they all have in common: *sex*, as complicated in diverse ways by *violence* or subtler forms of coercion. Today, we tend to speak of *non-consensual sex,* a modern label that not only includes rape but might also cover David's adultery with Bathsheba. Admittedly, some have questioned just how much or what sort of coercion Bathsheba faced; a few have raised similar questions about Dinah. But there is no doubt that the Levite's wife and Tamar were unwilling victims, and it is hard to imagine that any of these women were initiators of premeditated acts.

How, then, did traditional commentators read these stories? How did they address the various misdeeds and crimes recorded in these biblical texts? Whatever else one might say about patristic, medieval, and Reformation interpreters, they were intensely interested in *morality,* particularly as the Bible might be applied to the needs of their readers and hearers. But in these stories, as in so many other passages we have examined, the obvious crimes are accompanied also by obvious *silences* — the details that were not recorded and the behavior that cries out for explanation and motive. It's common for preachers today to fill out a sermon on such texts by filling in the silences. So, how did these early writers fill them?

As we will see, traditional exegetes could be as suspicious of these women as the modern commentators alluded to earlier. But there are seeds of sympathy to be found, too. We will proceed by looking individually at these four women and their stories, concentrating on points of exegesis that have been the most provocative.

Did Dinah Have Only Herself to Blame?

Although the entire chapter of Genesis 34 describes the aftermath of Shechem's rape of Dinah, there are principally three questions that bear on Dinah herself. First, what was the moral significance, if any, of her "going out" in v. 1? Second, while Shechem is explicitly described as smitten with Dinah, was there any reciprocity, or only violation? Third, what finally happened to Dinah? Was she forgotten?

Early Worries about Dinah

Of these three questions, the first is utterly dominant. By blithely "going out" from the safety of her father's house, only to find catastrophe in the person of the first man she met, Dinah offered an uncomplicated lesson that few commentators (all of them men, and often brothers and fathers) could resist. This moral is drawn by the earliest writers. It appears in the midrash on Genesis, which repeatedly intones "Dinah went out" as the explanation for each detail of the catastrophe — and as a link to Eve's immodesty, Sarah's eavesdropping, and other instances of implicitly low or immoral female traits.[3] Clearly, women have no place "going out" from home, where they are protected by men, and bad things happen when they do. Jerome does not appear to have derived this lesson from his rabbinic sources, but his view scarcely differs. In 384, in his long letter of advice to Eustochium on the disciplines of virginity, Jerome used Dinah to warn Christian virgins against public life:

> Ever let the privacy of your chamber guard you; ever let the Bridegroom sport with you within. . . . Go not from home nor visit the daughters of a strange land, though you have patriarchs for brothers and Israel for a father. Dinah went out and was seduced. Do not seek the Bridegroom in the streets. . . .[4]

As this "lesson" grew over time, Dinah's character declined. A key contributor here was Pope Gregory I, who in 591 wrote an immensely influential book on pastoral care. In a passage on admonishing penitent sinners against overconfidence, he read Dinah allegorically:

> Commonly [our] crafty foe, when he sees the soul which he trips up
> by sin to be afflicted for its fall, seduces it by the blandishments of
> baneful security. [This] is figuratively expressed in the history of
> Dinah. . . . For indeed Dinah goes out to see the women of a foreign
> land when any soul, neglecting its own concerns and giving heed to
> the actions of others, wanders forth out of its own proper condition
> and order. And Sichem, prince of the country, overpowers it inas-
> much as the devil corrupts it . . . so that the soul, seduced by these
> deceptions, may be suspended from its purpose of penitence . . .
> [and] even rejoices in its transgressions.[5]

For Jerome, Dinah was just an example of carelessness. For Gregory, she
came to symbolize a whole series of vices that lead to destruction. Gregory's allegory also imputes to Dinah a degree of consent in this seduction:
what else could be meant when Dinah (the careless penitent) comes to "rejoice in its transgressions"?

Later commentators echoed Gregory, often verbatim, and his allegory
was enshrined in the *Ordinary Gloss* — that twelfth-century collection of
patristic comments on the Bible that was still popular in the sixteenth century. Other medieval writers added to Gregory's depiction of Dinah. Bernard of Clairvaux, in a treatise on pride and humility, identified the first
downward step as *curiosity,* often marked by wandering eyes. He cited
three examples: Eve, Satan, and Dinah.

> O Dinah, you wanted to see the foreign women! Was it necessary?
> Was it profitable? Or did you do it solely out of curiosity? Even if
> you went idly to see, you were not idly seen. . . . Who would believe
> that idle curiosity or curious idleness of yours would not be idle in
> the future, but so terrible in its consequences for you and your fam-
> ily and for your enemies too?[6]

What Shechem did was wrong, of course, but Dinah bears the brunt of
Bernard's rebuke. Victim she was, but she could have avoided her fate. The
lament for Dinah written by Bernard's contemporary, Peter Abelard, was
more sympathetic but drew the same conclusion: "Woe is miserable me,"
she cried, "ruined by my own doing!"[7]

Not long after, Richard of St. Victor added yet one more complication
in a treatise on the steps of contemplation that allegorized all the children

of the patriarchs. The children of Leah represent seven virtues or ordered affections; Dinah, the last, represents ordered *shame*.[8] The allegory was not deliberately hostile to Dinah: while indeed conquered by Shechem (identified as "love of one's own excellence") and drawn into "scandalous delight," Richard insists that she struggled and was unwilling — even if "she surrenders after being conquered by Shechem's strength." While Dinah's resistance may well be taken for granted by the biblical text, the question loomed large in the minds of many, especially in light of Deuteronomy 22:23-29, which exonerates a woman from complicity in her own rape — *if* she cries for help. Naturally, there are many places where no cry could be heard, and in these cases Deuteronomy 22:25-27 gives the woman the benefit of the doubt. What Gregory and Richard illustrate, however, is that commentators were capable of denying that benefit to Dinah by suggesting that she sinned not only by wandering out, but also by enjoying her ravishment. For modern readers, this is a problematic move and a worrisome precedent, especially when unsupported by the biblical text. But what complicates our assessment of Richard's exegesis is "Dinah's" larger role in his allegorical treatise, where she is properly praised as a *virtue:* the godly sort of shame that can soften the rage of *men* and make them commendable and lovable.

The legacy of patristic and medieval interpretation was to ascribe Dinah's ruin to her foolish curiosity. Both literally and allegorically, she offered a cautionary tale of the danger that looms for women when they stray into the public sphere, outside the home or cloister, where walls (and men) can protect them.

Dinah among the Reformers

With few exceptions, the writers of the sixteenth century continued to find fault with Dinah. "She is not excused by ignorance but accused by her curiosity," wrote Pellican, even as Vermigli stated that the occasion of her rape was "adolescent wanderlust and curiosity." Luther agreed, as did Musculus and Calvin — adding, in the case of Luther and Musculus, that curiosity is a vice to which women in particular are prone.[9] The lesson isn't subtle. Calvin, for example, urgently warns of the danger that

> hangs over weak virgins at this day, if they go too boldly and eagerly
> into public assemblies, and excite the passions of youth towards

themselves. For it is not to be doubted that Moses in part casts the blame of the offense upon Dinah herself, . . . whereas she ought to have remained under her mother's eyes in the tent.[10]

Luther identified another sin on Dinah's part, namely, that she went out "on her own without a companion," indeed, "without the permission of her father and mother" — an especially controversial issue for Protestants, who hotly opposed the way Roman Catholics granted children the right to contract marriage without parental consent.[11]

Clearly, Reformation commentators saw the place of women as firmly fixed in the private sphere of home and hearth, but some hammered on this point more than others. A prime example is Zwingli, who vented palpable anger at Dinah and her imitators. Convinced that the verb in Genesis 34:1 is best construed in the imperfect past tense, he concluded that Dinah did not go out just once, but habitually, regularly visiting the women of the city. Shechem probably saw her on one of these visits, in the course of which he "spoke to her heart" (v. 3), "so that, having at last been persuaded by him, she might be seized by him."[12] Zwingli seriously faults Dinah, but he also lambastes women who parade their rings and robes in public, who "go out" to see and be seen, indeed, prostituting their chastity. Oddly, it escapes Zwingli's notice that he has reversed the order here: Genesis 34:1-3 puts the rape first, prior to Shechem's attempted consolation. Nothing suggests that Dinah began by conniving with Shechem, despite Zwingli's insinuations.[13] Dinah's final role in Zwingli's commentary is to illustrate the strange workings of providence: for while God could have ordained to make Jacob great by allowing the pact with Shechem and Hamor to stand, the Israelites were not slated to possess the land for centuries to come. "Meanwhile, God permits Dinah to be violated so that *we* might learn about the ways of young men and the wantonness of young girls."[14]

If there are any words of sympathy to be found for Dinah, they are probably to be found in Luther's remarks, which have received more study than most.[15] Luther writes as a father, and his sympathies lie largely with Jacob. Nonetheless, as Joy Schroeder observes, Luther was not only the father of daughters, he himself had lost a daughter of about Dinah's age not long before he wrote on Genesis 34.[16] So while Luther can recap the usual stereotypes about women's levity and curiosity that Dinah epitomizes, he is also emotionally engaged: directly with Jacob, indirectly (but still deeply) with Dinah.

Two of Luther's observations will have to suffice here. First, he takes with utter seriousness the extra measure of suffering both Jacob and Dinah endured on account of their sense of divine abandonment. We saw earlier, in his account of Hagar, how Luther could speak so movingly of the "godless" dimension of such tragedies, and of how no aspect of suffering brings as much anguish as feeling deserted by God.

> Who is watching here? Is anyone keeping awake? God and his angels wink and look the other way. God pays no attention and acts as if he does not know or see the daughter being snatched away to be raped. Indeed, he permits this to happen while the angels sit and do nothing.[17]

Admittedly, Luther has focused on Jacob's grief here, but Dinah is by no means out of sight. She is sorrowful, grief-stricken, and inconsolable. And it is further typical of Luther to involve her entire family in tears and anguish — including Jacob's wives, servants, maids, and shepherds.[18] Here is a crucial contrast between Luther and Zwingli. Both writers saw this tragedy as wrought by providence and as bearing a lesson for us. But where Zwingli saw a lesson about the faulty morality of others, Luther found a lesson vastly more immediate:

> Why does God permit such a godly patriarch to be burdened with this cross, as if he were not pious, pleasing, and dear to God? This happened for our sake, so we might learn patience, be consoled in adversity, and restrain our own mouths if similar calamities happen to us. I mean, we are no better than these great men, so we should not aspire to special treatment. Instead, we should get used to such exercises and tests of our faith, consolation, and patience.[19]

A second remarkable aspect of Luther's exegesis is his constancy in defending Dinah. Granted that she sinned through foolish curiosity, she is still the one wronged. There is no need for further severity. As Schroeder observes, Luther refused to suggest, as some medievals (and contemporaries) did, that Dinah had not only been treated like a harlot (v. 31), but had acted like one as well.[20] Instead, Luther reserved his contempt for the impenitent presumption of Shechem and his father. And it is a further mark of his "fatherly" concern that Dinah does not soon disappear from his comments on Genesis 34, or from Genesis at all. She is mentioned often, eventually receiving from Luther what few ever gave her: a happy ending of sorts, or even an ending at all. Feminist critics have observed not only that Dinah's fate is left unrecorded (implying that, like Tamar, she was ever after "a desolate woman"), but also that her brothers' rampage destroyed the sole prospect of marriage she would ever have, to Shechem. Yet Dinah reappears in Genesis 37:1 and 43:5 — not in the Bible, but in Luther's comments — where we learn not only that Jacob brought Dinah and Joseph to the aged Isaac to keep him company, but also that she accompanied Jacob to Egypt, serving as the mother of the household after the death of Jacob's wives.[21] It is no small irony that in penning this imaginative ending to Dinah's story, Luther has joined some unlikely company: for despite the rabbis' hostile critique of Dinah, there is a strand of midrash that also associated Dinah with the sojourn to Egypt — not as Jacob's housekeeper, but as the mother (by Shechem) of Asenath, Joseph's "Egyptian" wife.[22]

Was the Levite's Wife Being Punished?

No story of violence to an individual in Scripture can be more grisly and horrifying than the gang rape, murder, and subsequent butchery of the Levite's wife in Judges 19. It is an obscene event that triggers a civil war that reportedly leads to 65,000 deaths, along with the slaughter of the city of Jabesh-gilead, except for 400 abducted virgins, and the abduction of another 200 virgins from Shiloh. Among these details, three questions bear on the Levite's wife.[23] First, why did she leave her husband (19:2), and what does that suggest about her? Second, when the house of the Levite's host in Gibeah was surrounded by townsmen, clamoring to have sex with the Levite, can any justification be found for his act of forcing his wife into their hands? Finally, was his wife's horrifying death somehow a providential punishment?

Sanitizing the Story: Josephus, Ambrose, and Jerome

The tale's repugnance may be argued from the reluctance with which it is mentioned by commentators. Among the church fathers, only Ambrose, Jerome, and Sulpicius said anything at all. Even Augustine fell mute: having addressed a huge set of questions on the first seven books of the Old Testament, he abruptly ended with Samson, at Judges 15. The silence of Augustine, in turn, may well have paralyzed many medieval commentators, who habitually borrowed wholesale from the Latin father. Amazingly, the silence would be broken only in the fourteenth century, when Nicholas of Lyra publicized some "new" information.[24]

The modest comments that we do have prior to Lyra often seem shaped less by the biblical text than by a paraphrase of the story that Josephus produced in the first century.[25] Josephus sanitized the tale, recasting it as a patched-up lovers' quarrel that met a tragic end when the men of Gibeah seized the husband's beautiful wife. After a night of abuse, she died, less from bodily injury than from her grief and shame. The story remains tragic, but Josephus has removed the reference to same-sex rape and endowed the Levite's wife with the classic female virtues of modesty and shame.

Josephus's influence is clearest in Ambrose, who digressed deeply into the story of the Levite's wife in the course of two letters written around 380, advocating virginity and defending a Christian virgin named Indicia from an accusation of unchastity.[26] Ambrose's long retelling of Judges 19 was meant to illustrate the importance of character, though it seems an odd excursus. In any case, Ambrose followed Josephus in ignoring questions of homosexual rape and in focusing on the woman's beauty as the cause of the frenzy. Likewise, the Levite does not expel his wife; she was rather seized by the mob, only to die of humiliation the next morning.

The paraphrases of Judges 19–21 in Josephus and Ambrose recur in a few later writers,[27] but the silence of Augustine dominates: the *Ordinary Gloss* is remarkably barren, mustering little more than a few definitions.[28] What is easily missed, however, is that all these patristic and medieval writers were blinded, even when they were silent, by a special kind of ignorance. All of them were working from either the Latin Vulgate or the Septuagint (the Greek version of the Old Testament) — neither of which reports what the Hebrew Bible says of the Levite's wife at Judges 19:2. Where the Vulgate and Septuagint say that the Levite's wife "became angry" with her husband and left him, the Hebrew version states, instead, that she "played the harlot" and left. This is truly an inflammatory bit of information, and highly prejudicial to the Levite's wife. Along the way, it is a mystery beyond explanation that Jerome, who translated the Vulgate from what he liked to call the "Hebrew truth," seems to have preferred the

Greek reading here. But what Jerome left hidden emerged at last in Lyra's "literal commentary" on the whole Bible — a work that quickly upstaged the *Ordinary Gloss,* largely because of Lyra's facility in Hebrew and his extensive use of otherwise unknown rabbinic sources.

The "Hebrew Truth" Unveiled: Lyra and the Reformers

Lyra was well aware, then, that the Levite's wife wasn't just angry. Rather, as the Hebrew Bible says, she was an adulteress, so she probably left her husband either because he threw her out or because she ran off with a lover.[29] It is therefore all the more surprising that Lyra did not linger to rebuke her but moved on to other ethical issues in the passage. One of these is the shocking offer made by the host in Gibeah to give his daughter to the mob at his door, an offer fulfilled by the Levite when he pushed his wife outside. Where earlier writers equivocated or emended the storyline at this point, Lyra condemned the offer for what it is: *a mortal sin.* Lyra thus ruled out any excuse based on the notion of *compensatory evil*[30] — the idea that a lesser sin (the rape of a woman) may be permitted to avoid a greater sin (the "unnatural" rape of a man). Centuries earlier, Augustine pondered this question when Lot offered his daughters to the men of Sodom in Genesis 19, a tale that mirrors Judges 19. Though he rejected the appeal to compensatory evil, Augustine left a precedent for thinking that the bodies of men are of greater value than the bodies of women. But Lyra countered Augustine's interpretation with a sober and sophisticated analysis of the situation, for the angry men of Gibeah may well have "abused" the Levite's wife by subjecting her to "unnatural" intercourse — what we usually call *sodomy.* So the Levite would *not* necessarily have avoided any greater evil by abandoning his wife.

Lyra's knowledge of Hebrew and rabbinic traditions remained of great interest for the next two centuries, but his findings were often disputed. By the sixteenth century, Christian scholars had come to regard a working knowledge of Hebrew and Greek as indispensable for commenting on the Bible, and many now read the sources for themselves. These later scholars were uniformly of the opinion that the "Hebrew truth" was more authoritative than Greek or Latin versions of the Old Testament. Consequently, all agreed that Judges 19 told not of a marital spat, but of adultery — and someone was to blame.

Readers today may be caught off guard by the vehemence with which early Protestants despised adulterers. But for Pellican, Brenz, Bucer, and Vermigli, the adultery of the Levite's wife introduced a volatile issue. Several wondered, for example, why she hadn't already been put to death. That may seem harsh, but were they really out to get her? No, they were merely trying to be good commentators. Elsewhere the Bible tells us that the punishment for adultery is death by stoning, except for the daughter of a priest, in which case the punishment is death by fire.[31] As a part of Old Testament history, the events in Judges ought to have been governed by Old Testament law. That the laws of Moses were not enforced alerts us to the anarchy of the day, when "there was no king in Israel," and "the people did what was right in their own eyes" (21:25). These Protestants, moreover, knew what anarchy was. For them, the Reformation had brought not only the glorious restoration of the gospel, but also civil strife, persecution and bloodshed — and accusations that telling people they were saved by "faith alone" would lead to loose morals. Unfortunately, sometimes it did. So it was with a grim satisfaction that all four of these writers concluded that the death of the Levite's wife was also providential: a gruesome but fitting punishment for someone who had violated God's law of marriage. Bucer's comments are probably the starkest:

> As she sinned by her own lust, so with the lust of another did the adulterous woman pay a penalty both more savage and more shameful than according to the law. . . . God compensates for the lateness of a well-deserved punishment with severity, and he converts into punishments those very things by which pleasure was sought for against God.[32]

It would be wrong, however, to draw either of two possible conclusions. First, it would be wrong to infer from their determination to see the Levite's wife punished that Bucer and his colleagues were specially hostile to women. Indeed, they were quite aware that the Bible's punishment for adultery applies to both sexes, and these four Reformers would also be numbered among those in the sixteenth century who contested the double standard by which men were usually favored in matters of adultery and divorce.[33] Second, it would be wrong to conclude, on the grounds that it was *God* who punished the Levite's wife by means of the mob of Gibeahites, that those rapacious men were in any way excused.[34] The men at the door, like those who assaulted Lot's guests in Genesis 19, were vilified by all commentators in terms as dire as imaginable: they were cruel, filthy, children of Belial, foul and monstrous, reprobate, brutal, wicked, "altogether hateful and detestable to God and men."[35] And if we read on to see what these writers said about the chaos that followed the rape of the Levite's wife, we would find that they continued to excoriate the men of Israel for avenging the Levite so savagely, by means of a serial brutality inflicted too often upon innocent women and children.

What about the actions of the Levite and his host in Gibeah, who imitated Lot in offering women to be raped, but who did not have the benefit of angels to defend them? The appeal to compensatory evil that Augustine described and rejected continued to interest writers in the sixteenth century. (Indeed, it continues to interest us today, because we too may face moral choices of which even the best seems ethically tainted.) Pellican, Brenz, and Bucer all make a case that the Levite may have acted to avoid a greater evil than the rape of his wife; Cajetan, their Catholic contemporary, did likewise. By and large, they agreed with Augustine that homosexual rape is a greater crime than heterosexual rape. But the consciences of these commentators are clearly uneasy: Pellican looks for another way out; Bucer equivocates, insisting one cannot judge these matters in advance. Vermigli, however, is unambiguous in condemning the Levite and his host: no sin should ever be committed under the pretense of avoiding a greater sin. More remarkable still is the conclusion reached by both Cajetan and Vermigli that, regardless of any claim to have avoided a greater crime, no wife or daughter is ever the "possession" of a husband or father in a way that gives him the right to endanger her. The old man in Gibeah therefore had

> no right to prostitute his daughter or his guest's wife. For a father does not have his daughter so in his power that he may expose her to the lusts of others. Nor is the daughter herself obliged to obey in anything that is sin, even if her father . . . commands it.[36]

Were we to compare the parallel story of Lot, similar results would be obtained: Luther, Calvin, Musculus, and Vermigli reject any appeal to compensatory evil. They find Lot's endangerment of his daughters disloyal and execrable, vicious and detestable, unlawful and unfaithful. Like Vermigli, Musculus insists that no father has the authority to make such an offer, and no daughter is bound to obey.[37]

Postscript: Where Is the (Hebrew) Truth Today?

A sea change in the interpretation of the Levite's wife occurred when the Hebrew wording of Judges 19:2 — and the wife's alleged adultery — came to the attention of Christian commentators. At that point, opinion swung from empathy for her to suspicion and hostility. But when the Hebrew text says she "played the harlot," must we picture literal infidelity, or might this be a way of branding her for abandoning her husband on her own initiative?[38] Might the Greek Old Testament actually be not a distortion of the Hebrew, but a less charged way of saying the same thing? Today, most English Bibles follow the Hebrew text, but the RSV, NRSV, and New Jerusalem Bible give more credence to the Septuagint here: *she became angry, these Bibles state, and she left.* How might Lyra and later commentators have written about the Levite's wife if they had shared these critical textual judgments?

Did Bathsheba Set David Up for Seduction?

Bathsheba appears in two biblical scenes. In 1 Kings 1–2, she collaborated with the prophet Nathan to ensure that Solomon would succeed David as Israel's king; here in 2 Samuel 11, she plays a more passive role. Among the details of her encounter with David and his arrangement to do away with Uriah, his faithful subject and her faithful husband, three are of special interest. First, there is David's voyeurism in 2 Samuel 11:2. Was Bathsheba bathing immodestly, so as to contribute to the adultery? Second, commentators differ over v. 4. The NRSV reading, "she was purifying herself after her period," construes the text as proving that the pregnancy reported in v. 5 had to be by David, not Uriah. But the ancient versions — Hebrew, Greek, and Latin — are all less clear about the purpose of her purification and its timing. Third, when v. 26 says Bathsheba "made lamentation" for Uriah, some wonder if she was sincere, or if she was wrong to accede to David when "he brought her to his house" (v. 27). In the history of exegesis, however, these questions emerged rather gradually.

All about David

Given the historical, liturgical, and messianic shadows that David cast over the entire Bible, it is no surprise that Bathsheba and Uriah are commonly treated as props in a drama all about the king. Particularly in light of the traditional ascription of Psalm 51 to David, "after he had gone in to Bathsheba," commentators eagerly read 2 Samuel 11–12 as the tale of a mighty man who became a model penitent. The classic account may be Ambrose's *Apology for the Prophet David,* in which the enormity of David's crime corresponds to the depth of his repentance and God's forgiveness.[39] Bathsheba's only role is allegorical: she symbolizes the church of the gentiles, rescued by Christ (David) from the devil (Uriah). The basic features of Ambrose's allegory recurred constantly, extending from Augustine to Gregory the Great and Isidore, and on to Raban Maur and the *Ordinary Gloss.*[40] Edifying as the allegory may have been, there was no intention to excuse David, as Augustine explained:

> The literal David, then, was guilty of a heinous crime, which God by the prophet condemned in the rebuke addressed to David, and which David atoned for by his repentance. On the other hand, He who is the desire of all nations loved the Church when washing herself on the roof, that is, when cleansing herself from the pollution of the world . . . ; and after commencing an acquaintance, He puts to death the devil, whom He first entirely removes from her, and joins her to Himself in perpetual union. While we hate the sin, we must not overlook the prophetical significance; and while we love . . . that David [= Christ] who in His mercy has freed us from the devil, we may also love the David who by the humility of his repentance healed the wound made by his transgression.[41]

The church fathers did not excuse or minimize David's crimes. Yet they were scarcely interested in the literal Bathsheba. And while the parable of "the poor man's lamb" with which Nathan confronted David (12:1-4) seems to foreground his abuse of power, the fathers saw David's adultery more as a private sin precipitated by his inability to resist Bathsheba's allure.

Bathsheba's Secrets

David never leaves the stage, but various observations bearing on Bathsheba were raised from time to time. One of these goes all the way back to Josephus, who thought Bathsheba must have sent word to David as soon as she realized she was pregnant, "asking him to contrive some way to conceal her sin," lest she be stoned to death as an adulteress.[42] Curiously, despite their use of Josephus, the fathers do not feature her as conspiring in this way. Later writers do note the vagueness of Bathsheba's "purification" in v. 4. Writing in 1179, Peter Comestor offered three explanations: it may mean merely that she bathed after intercourse; or that her menstrual flow ceased because she was now pregnant; or that it ceased "when she was touched by the king" (presumably one of the lesser-known powers of royalty).[43] Three centuries later, Denis the Carthusian added other possibilities, including the view of some that, since Bathsheba had borne no children, she may have been "purified" by being healed of sterility. Denis actually wondered how the Bible can say she was purified, since her adultery really left her more impure than before. Yet he saw nothing scandalous in her bathing (in v. 2): she may have been cooling off, or just attending to menstrual cleanliness. Denis is generally sympathetic to Bathsheba: although some think her lament for Uriah was feigned and that she really rejoiced because her husband's death allowed her to escape the punishment of stoning and marry the king, Denis was inclined to think that "her heart wept for the fallen husband whom she loved."[44]

What complicated any assessment of the morality of both David and Bathsheba in the later Middle Ages was (as so often) the inside information that Lyra gleaned from the rabbis. In this instance, Lyra learned from Rashi that before a soldier in the Old Testament went to war, he would give his wife a provisional writ of divorce. If he fell in battle, his wife's divorce would be calculated from the time he gave her the writ.[45] Thus, even though David committed adultery while Uriah was alive, the writ of divorce Bathsheba allegedly received was effective as of Uriah's initial departure for battle. Technically, David did not commit adultery: he rather had sex with a widow, properly (if retroactively) divorced. This elaborate construct is perfectly tailored to exonerate David (and, incidentally, Bathsheba) from any crime — an odd agenda, given the evidence of Psalm 51 as David's confession of sin. Christian commentators generally dismissed this amazing bit of background information as a fable, not least because of its refutation later in the fourteenth century by Paul of Burgos — a Christian convert, former rabbi, and Lyra's self-appointed "corrector."

Bathsheba as Victim and Conspirator

Protestant exegesis rode the rising tide of humanist scholarship, with its intense interest in original sources and languages. But the Reformation was also an intensely moral movement, one that implemented widespread reforms against the prevailing laxity of Catholicism and society in general — reforms and concerns reflected also in exegesis. The Bible's silences were usually unpacked with worries about ethical behavior in mind, only to be reassembled with added lessons and exhortations. Many commentators simply assumed that biblical characters harbored the same vices they found or feared in their congregations.

The Reformers' skeptical portrait of Bathsheba may well be the product of such presuppositions, even if that portrait fails to satisfy in many respects. Bathsheba received only modest attention in the sixteenth century, but ample comments survive in lectures Vermigli gave in 1557 and in Calvin's strikingly similar sermons, delivered in 1562. Both indicted David unsparingly and at length. Calvin classed him as a "monster," devoid of scruple or remorse, who committed "whoredom" and treated his servants as pimps. David was just like all princes, who "do not worry much about the death of their subjects." His crime, moreover, was not only a private sin but a failure of office. "David the King is not the guardian of the law, but its violator," cried Vermigli, for "he does not uphold modesty but assaults it."[46]

Clearly, Bathsheba was wronged by David, who used his servants to seduce her and "to draw her into such perdition that she would have been . . . lost if God had not . . . had mercy on her."[47] But she was no model saint, much less a martyr. To be sure, Vermigli and Calvin did not condemn her for bathing, and Vermigli insisted that there is nothing wrong with a woman's beauty, which is a gift of the Creator and even part of God's image. But both felt she should have shown more discretion and modesty, and taken greater care not to be seen. Both also compared her to Susanna, a matron (in the apocryphal additions to Daniel) who was overtaken by two evil elders while bathing in a garden and who preferred death to defilement. Vermigli therefore wondered why Bathsheba offered no resistance. Maybe she was overwhelmed by the king's dignity. Maybe she was ambitious and hoped to become queen. Or maybe she thought David could somehow decree her divorce — "Weak women often think such things."[48]

It is no surprise, then, that Vermigli and Calvin met Bathsheba's purification with suspicion. Neither connected her act with menstrual impurity. Instead, Calvin was sure she was in the grip of guilt over her adultery: "there is no doubt" that her act was the ritual sprinkling performed "after someone had been soiled by some sin." But Calvin was also sure she let herself off too easily:

> In what sense was her purification real? It was nothing but a shadow, full of hypocrisy. . . . That she felt she was guilty before God was in itself a good beginning. But she did not continue. . . . She thought that she had been properly absolved when she sprinkled herself as required by the Law, but she only considered the external appearance.

Vermigli said much the same. Bathsheba went back to life as usual: "she worshiped on the Sabbath, joined the sacred assembly, and purified herself as did others. . . . But it all came from hypocrisy."[49]

More distrust greeted Bathsheba when she lamented the death of Uriah (v. 26). Vermigli seems to agree with those who saw her grief as a cover for her greater desire to be freed from suspicion of adultery, which could never happen while her husband lived. Calvin branded her mourning as "fiction" and a "farce," granting that "perhaps she was touched" by Uriah's death but ultimately concluding that her grief was feigned. *How did Calvin know this?* Apparently he deduced this, and more, from Bathsheba's return to David's house (v. 27):

> We also see how she personally profited from the situation. For she should have hidden herself, but instead, she went on to place herself in an eminent position so she could be seen from afar. And what could one have seen? Here was an adulteress, who was the cause of the death of her husband, going around brazen-faced, and giving herself a good time with her adulterous partner, with a murderous and disloyal individual. Well, when she consented and willingly agreed with such a villain, what could one judge but that both had conspired in the death of this poor man? . . . She readily went with

David to live in his house, forgot the death of her husband, and paid no attention to the villainous and detestable outrage which had been done to him. Without argument, she joined herself to him who put the sword in the hand of the enemies of God in order to put Uriah to death.[50]

It's entirely possible that Bathsheba possessed all these crass motives, just as Calvin claimed. But it remains to note that Calvin found her vices in a verse that merely says, "David sent and brought her to his house." The actor in this scene was David. All the rest is silence.

Remarkably, neither Vermigli nor Calvin hesitated to endorse the happy ending the Bible provided for David and Bathsheba in the later birth of Solomon. According to Calvin, David exhorted Bathsheba to join him in repentance, and mutual accord and divine consolation followed. Vermigli mused seriously and with some feeling over Bathsheba's trials: "She knew she had sinned, she saw God's anger, she knew God had caused the death of her son. As the greatest good is to have pleased God, so the greatest evil is to know that God is hostile and angry with us." Vermigli then tried to imagine David's words at 2 Samuel 12:24, which reports that "David consoled his wife." Vermigli constructs a tender speech for David. It culminates in an unexpected but traditional promise, that the Messiah would be born through the line of David and Bathsheba, two sinners now graciously restored.[51] David seems to have heard this news from Nathan and passed it along to his wife — an inference Vermigli found in a rabbinic source, but which he surely used because it was already embedded in the genealogy of Jesus in Matthew's Gospel.

What Was Tamar Thinking?

The story of how Amnon entrapped and raped his half-sister Tamar is viewed by some commentators as an inversion of the story of Dinah: both women were violated in acts of passion, but whereas Shechem came to profess abiding affection for Dinah, Amnon's love turned to passionate hatred. In both cases, brothers intervene on behalf of a wronged sister, with equally dismal results: an unmarried daughter is left in desolation. In considering Tamar, three exegetical elements are crucial. The story in 2 Samuel 13 is bracketed, first of all, by Amnon's crime and its punishment — or lack thereof. How do interpreters deal with his treachery and cruelty? More telling, perhaps, how do they deal with David's stunning passivity in v. 21, where his anger leads only to inaction?[52] Next, Tamar's speech in vv. 12-13 comes under scrutiny for urging Amnon to ask for her in marriage rather than taking her by force. Yet she and Amnon had a common father in David. Was she proposing an incestuous marriage? Finally, Tamar's responses to the rape — a second speech in v. 16 and her lament in vv. 18-19 — are studied by those who want to know why she claimed that her ejection by Amnon was a worse deed than rape, and why she cried aloud after the rape but (apparently) not before. Our survey will move quickly through patristic and medieval writers in order to spend a bit more time with writers of the Reformation.

Lessons from Tamar: Watchfulness, Prudence, Tenacity

Patristic commentary on this text ran largely along familiar lines. Jerome offered a moral reading, warning nuns and monks to guard their virginity even in the presence of close relations.[53] Others allegorized the names of Amnon ("giving"), Tamar ("bitterness"), and Absalom ("father of peace"), but the moral was about the same: he who *gives* himself to desire will fall into the *bitterness* of sin and deliver himself to an enemy disguised as a *father of peace*.[54]

Medieval writers, however, began to worry about the ethical implications of the text. Tamar's plea that Amnon seek permission from David to marry her is of constant interest. Peter Comestor subscribed to the old opinion of Josephus that Tamar's plea was not sincere but rather a subterfuge designed to buy time. Indeed, he added, marriage between siblings is unlawful — except there are "some" (not named by him) who say that this Old Testament law pertains only to those of the same race. Amnon's mother was an Israelite, but Tamar's mother was a gentile, taken by David in war, so perhaps such a union was licit after all. Lyra added another wrinkle to this line of exegesis. According to his rabbinic sources, not only did David take Tamar's mother as a spoil of war, she was at the time pregnant with Tamar by her previous husband. Tamar was thus *not* David's natural daughter, and she was but a *half*-sister to Absalom. Since she was unrelated to Amnon, she was free to marry him — and her suggestion to Amnon was therefore without fault.[55] Unfortunately, these little-known details were nowhere to be found in the Bible. A century later, when Denis considered whether Tamar and Amnon were too distantly related for the laws of incest to apply, he ignored Lyra altogether and eventually dismissed even Peter Comestor's version of the argument. Instead, Denis sided with Josephus: Tamar's speech was a ruse.[56]

Lyra also asked about David's response to Amnon's deed. The question was obvious. Rape is a capital crime. In some circumstances, both rapist and victim may be put to death. So why didn't David punish his son? Lyra frames the question without favor to David: "It seems that David sinned gravely" when he refused to chastise his son, much less consider executing him.[57] But Lyra gets David off on a series of technicalities. The law about the rape of a betrothed virgin in Deuteronomy 22:23 doesn't apply because Tamar was not engaged. And while the law in Deuteronomy 22:13-19 might be used against Amnon, he could not be convicted of an unwitnessed crime without a complaint from Tamar and some physical evidence — but 2 Samuel 13:20 says she kept silent on the advice of Absalom. Lyra goes on to speculate that David did punish Amnon, but not immediately, because Amnon was still weak and infirm. David's failure to punish Amnon would have fueled Tamar's hatred for Amnon, and her hatred would explain why David did not force Amnon to marry her (again citing Deuteronomy 22:19).

Lyra's defense of David's inaction is checked by Denis's skeptical rebuttal. As various Old Testament texts argue, if a father is called to correct an erring son, how much more is it the duty of a judge! And while it is proper to defer punishment if time and circumstance are inappropriate, Denis is not persuaded that Amnon was weak and infirm. If he had the strength to force himself on Tamar, he was well enough to bear punishment. Indeed, David should have realized that Amnon's show of illness was fakery. And when Scripture says Tamar kept silent, Denis thinks Absalom would have urged her to complain to David if he'd had any hope that Amnon would have been put to death. Denis thus sees nothing but culpable indulgence on David's part, and nothing like repentance or sorrow on the part of Amnon. David's love for Amnon was, in short, "carnal and corrupt."[58]

Denis paired his case against Amnon with a modest defense of Tamar. In addition to vindicating her plea to Amnon in v. 13 as a ruse — indeed, an "officious" lie and scarcely a sin — he also considered the question from Deuteronomy 22:24 that has perennially burdened victims of rape: Why didn't she cry out? After all, she was in a palace — surely help was nearby! But Denis was still ready to excuse her. Perhaps she was actually trying to *save* her brother Amnon by this ruse, lest he receive a death sentence for his deed. In any case, Denis was sure she defended herself vigorously, even manfully *(viriliter)*, and this may be why Amnon's desire turned to hatred: Tamar may have wounded him in the struggle, as "the Hebrews" suggest.[59]

Good Girl / Bad Girl: Tamar in the Reformation

The contrast that emerged between Lyra and Denis finds a more detailed counterpart in the sixteenth century. However much Vermigli and Calvin agreed regarding Bathsheba, they were at odds in the case of Tamar.

Before looking at Tamar, however, it is important to see that they were by no means soft on Amnon or David. Calvin regarded Amnon as detestable, not least for having "nurtured this evil within himself." Amnon's act was "grossly immoral," "against nature," and disgraceful. He "wallowed in" his lust, and there is no sign "that he was displeased with himself over his evil, nor that he was fighting against it." Both Calvin and Vermigli offer a fine analysis of Amnon's craftiness, especially the way his references to Tamar change to serve his deception. To Jonadab, his co-conspirator, he refers to "my brother Absalom's sister," Calvin notes, "as though . . . not at all related to him!" But before David, he innocently calls her "my sister," as if "to cloak his fornication."[60] Another instance is cited by Vermigli at v. 17, where Amnon heartlessly tells his servant to "put this woman out." Amnon "does not call her by her own name, nor by 'sister.' You see three grave crimes: first is rape; another is incest; a third is hatred of his sister. He publicizes his wickedness as much as he can."[61]

David, too, comes under fire. While Calvin credits him for teaching his children right and wrong (unsuccessfully, in Amnon's case), it is David's failure that he "let his daughter be corrupted."[62] Both Calvin and Vermigli dismiss those who would excuse David for not punishing Amnon. For Calvin, "David's sin" here was exceptionally scandalous because, as king, he "ought to have maintained equality in justice." Of course, this whole tragedy was the fallout of David's adultery with Bathsheba, and Calvin opines that he

> ought to have foreseen the evil, and even if he had not condemned his son to death, still he ought at least to have subdued his body; he

ought to have held him in prison and in stocks — either for a time
or for life. . . . It is certain that David was given a sentence of con-
demnation here for not having punished the misdeed of his son.[63]

Vermigli is equally unpersuaded by the defenders of David's inaction. To
counter Lyra's claim that Amnon could not be prosecuted without Tamar's
testimony, Vermigli insists that David — like any good judge — should
have undertaken an investigation even if no witnesses came forward.
There was, after all, plenty of evidence to be seen, including Amnon's ejection of Tamar and her public lament; and there are precedents in the Bible
and elsewhere for legal proceedings even where there is no direct complaint. To Lyra's suggestion that David punished Amnon later, in secret,
Vermigli simply says, "That was not enough." David's inaction provoked
Absalom's homicidal wrath, adding to David's disrepute and inciting blas-
phemy against God.[64]

What about Tamar? Here is where Calvin parts company with
Vermigli. Calvin's sharp indictment of Amnon and David leaves one un-
prepared for his coolness toward Tamar at two points. First, where
many read Tamar's appeal to the king in v. 13 as a ploy, Calvin will have
nothing to do with it. Not only does he rebuke the rabbis for speculating that Tamar and Amnon were more distantly related, he is angry with
Tamar for a suggestion that would violate divine laws against incest. But
wasn't it just a ruse? Wasn't she deferring judgment to her father, knowing he would overrule her unlawful plan? It might have been so, says
Calvin, "but she was not well enough instructed to have been able to
figure this out." Tamar was thus only partially prudent: she knew incest
was wrong, but she embraced the plan anyway.[65] Tamar fares no better
in her second speech, where she pleads with Amnon not to cast her out,
bewailing that rejection as worse than being raped. Calvin is appalled:

> In wanting to persist, she clearly showed that she was badly taught
> in the Law of God, and . . . that she was more concerned about her
> own reputation than . . . about what was legitimate for her.

> . . . She was content with squatting in her filth and being the wife of
> her brother! In this way, she reversed the whole order of nature. She
> wanted to pervert the sanctity of marriage; she wanted to persist in
> this evil to the very end.[66]

For Calvin, there is no way to redeem Tamar's plea to remain with Amnon, and he spends a third of one of his sermons railing against her for caring more to avoid public shame than to observe God's law. Somehow Calvin knows she is a hypocrite, "motivated only by superficial appearances." However, when Calvin's sermon goes on to find a moral or two for his congregation from Tamar, his lessons may have been more homegrown than usual. Early in 1557, the wife of Calvin's younger brother Antoine was banished for repeated improprieties with another man, conducted even in Calvin's own house. Could Calvin's reading of Tamar and Amnon — not to mention Bathsheba — have been unaffected by his own family's scandal, five years before?[67]

Tamar and her speeches met with greater kindness from Vermigli, beginning with his long analysis of her attempt to dissuade her brother from violating her. Vermigli's sympathy is unmistakable.

> He has arranged that she be led into his chamber; he is ready to use force against her; she sees herself trapped, and he the stronger one. What should she have done? She resorts to the weapons she has, she fights back with arguments. "No, my brother," she says. She recalls this word to his mind: he's her *brother*. "You're not supposed to be my corrupter! You should rather have been the one to protect me if others had wished to violate me!"[68]

Vermigli seems impressed with Tamar's quickness: she goes on to draw an argument from the law, then appeals to Amnon's self-respect, pleads on behalf of her own future hopes, and finally, "lest she lose all hope," desperately urges him to ask the king for her in marriage. It is no problem for Vermigli that Tamar has invoked this ploy, but (he suspects) Amnon never really wanted her for a wife.

Vermigli then returned to the old question of why Tamar did not cry for help. His first observation is that while the law in Deuteronomy 22:24 technically protects only betrothed virgins, we should extend it to cover also those not espoused, including Tamar. That she did not cry out, however, still does not prove she gave her consent to Amnon. As Denis had suggested, she may have been trying to protect Amnon; or she may have thought David did have the power to relax the prohibition against such a marriage.[69] (It is worth noting that while Calvin and Vermigli agreed that divine law cannot be relaxed, Luther had registered his dissent decades earlier. For Luther, Tamar illustrates how such laws may be overruled by the dictates of faith and love. Luther also interpreted Deuteronomy 22:24 on behalf of Tamar, who would have cried for help "but did not dare, for fear of death. A fair reading of the law, however, will take the view that she did cry out," even though she was in the city, not out in the fields.[70])

Tamar's second speech to Amnon is also paraphrased by Vermigli: "If, having been violated, I'm now evicted, I'll be like an obscene woman, a prostitute. Evicted in this way, I'll be unfit for marriage when this crime is made known. No one will want me for a wife."[71] Probably she wanted to form some plan with Amnon, now that he had brought her to ruin, but what she really needed (Vermigli suggests) was some *consolation*. Amnon gave her only hatred, as often happens after an affair like this. Vermigli then wondered, poignantly, if Tamar thought of Dinah, who was also raped by the son of a king but who was afterwards comforted by him. Amnon, alas, "did no such thing." So Tamar could only lament: whatever she might do, nothing would restore her.

Sex, Violence, and Blind Spots

In surveying the readings put forward by traditional commentators, we may rightly marvel at the diversity of views. We cannot help but notice that some readings satisfy our sensibilities, while others offend. Some address the nuances of the biblical text perceptively and with great insight, while others seem to dodge the problems or foist easy lessons onto hard texts. We have just reviewed how four of the Bible's most disturbing stories have been appropriated over the course of much of the church's history. Do any patterns emerge? Might the history of the interpretation of these texts help us perceive and interpret the bigger picture of which both the Bible and we, as part of the church of Christ, are a part? Several insights come to mind.

1. LESSONS OF FAITH AND MORALS MAY BE PRESENT EVEN WHERE THE BIBLE DOESN'T SPELL THEM OUT. *Traditional commentators believed the stories in the Bible were put there for a reason — for our sake, to instruct us in what we should believe and do. Even where the text seems devoid of morals, it is worth the effort to ask such questions.*

Dinah, the Levite's wife, Bathsheba, and Tamar were assaulted by men in ways that we would call wrong. Yet in these texts, as in so many others, the Bible is surprisingly dispassionate and reserved about exactly *who* is evil or wrong in these stories — and how, and why. All of these stories could be read only for the big historical events they report, bypassing questions of right and wrong that might pertain to so-called "minor" characters. Dinah would be just a footnote to the drama of Jacob and his sons; the Levite's wife precipitates a civil war and is forgotten; Bathsheba and Tamar fill cameo roles in support of King David, one of Israel's leading men and a big star.

Sometimes traditional interpreters did "read for the center" in this way and ignore the margins. But even where they gave these women short shrift, they almost always paused to wonder what *this* text might mean for Christians of their own day. In raising that question, they often read more slowly than we do, and they looked for morals and exemplars at every turn. Usually, we too find it impossible to read such tales of lust and violence without becoming emotionally and morally engaged. The best commentators of earlier days may well be the ones who were themselves similarly affected and engaged. At their best, they attempt to bring the whole counsel of Scripture to bear on the details of the text just as they would bring it to bear on the details of their own lives. Even if we take issue with their exegetical opinions, they urge us to think with care about what it means to live one's life before a God of goodness and justice.

2. WITHOUT A CLEAR WORD FROM SCRIPTURE, OUR MORAL JUDGMENTS MUST NOT BE TAKEN AS INFALLIBLE. *Interpreters often unlock passages in Scripture by deriving explanations from other biblical texts. We do this today, just as traditional commentators did. But the disagreements among our exegetical forebears should warn us against rushing to judgment or assuming too quickly that we have all the facts.*

Many commentators approached any biblical account of rape through the supposedly clarifying lens of Deuteronomy 22:23-29, asking essentially: *Did she cry out? Did she resist?* But over the course of the history of interpretation, this question (and the exegesis of the Old Testament in general) grew increasingly complicated — and did so for the better. Denis, Luther, and Vermigli thus agreed that Deuteronomy 22:24 should not be woodenly applied to Tamar, even though 2 Samuel 13 reported no outcry. There are other circumstances, not addressed by Deuteronomy, that might explain and exonerate Tamar's silence — including a mortal fear of Amnon, or an undeserved loyalty to him. So, these three commentators mostly gave Tamar the benefit of the doubt, allowing the facts of the story to remain ambiguous.

We may learn from this precedent. Just as it seems a squandering of Scripture to read with no interest in its account of the people of God and their successes or failures of faith and practice, so too may we learn from traditional commentators — in their own successes and failures of exegetical practice — that the search for moral lessons can be taken too far. Vermigli and Calvin shared virtually the same ethical concerns and moral worries, yet their depictions of Tamar, the "desolate woman" in Absalom's house, were poles apart. Yet both cannot be correct: Tamar cannot be simultaneously good and bad, assuming we can resolve the question at all. Vermigli met Tamar with sympathy, charity, and an assumption of her innocence, however naive or uninstructed she may have been. His approach is surely preferable to Calvin's, not only because Calvin's case against Tamar lacks clear evidence, but also because we who are ourselves sinners would want the same consideration Vermigli extended to Tamar.

3. EXEGESIS CAN BE SKEWED BY STEREOTYPES AND PERSONAL PRESUPPOSITIONS. *When considering the complaint raised by feminist critics that the Bible and its interpreters are unfriendly to women and women's interests, it is a useful corrective to see firsthand just how prejudiced in favor of men these commentators were — or weren't.*

It is difficult to read the history of the interpretation of these four women's stories and come away satisfied that they have constantly been treated fairly or that justice was done. To be sure, it should not surprise us that if traditional commentators sometimes model values or behavior worth emulating, they can also harbor dispositions that should provoke our criticism and perhaps even our repentance on their behalf. It is unfair, of course, to judge a prior age by the standards of a later time. But it *is* fair to wonder why a prior age did not live up to its own standards, or why various blind spots developed as they did. Such is the case with respect to the recurring hostility of Christians toward Jews. In the context of this chapter, such is often the case with respect to how traditional commentators approached the women of Scripture — often more with suspicion than sympathy.

Blaming the victim, denigrating women by treating them in terms of prevailing stereotypes — we have seen these traits often enough to justify the protests of feminists. Calvin is not alone, but in three of the passages we have examined, he models as clearly as anyone the sort of unfriendliness to women that raises a reciprocal suspicion on the part of many women readers. That said, one must complicate matters still further. Calvin does seem ready to doubt the integrity of biblical women, but he can also be hard on men.[72] Moreover, one must mark with care just where and how the line of prejudice is crossed. For example, Calvin was not wrong to wonder if Bathsheba resisted David's imperiosity. It is a reasonable thing to ask, because the answer might go either way: she might have been a woman of virtue *or* vice. If Calvin is to be faulted, it would rather be for underestimating how the inevitable imbalance of power between men and women (as well as between kings and subjects) tilts the playing field in favor of men. That, of course, is a modern sort of observation. But it remains that Calvin's exegesis tends to tell us less about what kind of woman Bathsheba was than about what kind of pastor Calvin was. In a word, Calvin withheld sympathy for women in difficult circumstances unless they had clearly gone the extra mile in piety and defense of the faith.[73] It was not Calvin's agenda, indeed, to write about the women of Scripture; his agenda was to write about God and the church. Nonetheless, as one recent writer has observed, in the rape of Dinah and Tamar, "the crime is lost in the agenda."[74] And yet, by coming to understand Calvin's agenda, we may see the strengths and shortcomings of our own.

4. SEXUAL VIOLENCE SHOULD NOT BE COVERED UP. OLD COMMENTATORS MAY BE OUR ALLIES. *The lectionary's omission of texts that speak of sexual violence reflects our own tendency to avoid speaking of sexual sins from the pulpit or lectern. But the effects of such sins are as common in our world as they were for our forebears, who were generally more willing to name the crime and address it.*

Not every ancient commentary will provide a model for our own engagement with this topic and these texts. It is disappointing to see so many commentators think they have said enough when they blame Dinah for curiosity and for "going out." Granted, they have at least said *something:* in an unsafe world, in places where men prey upon women, husbands and fathers and brothers will continue to say things like this in hopes of protecting their wives, daughters, and sisters. It would be foolish to think otherwise. We can and should credit these writers for recognizing right and wrong, even if their comments and lessons seem too easy and shallow. After all, no one in the history of interpretation sought to justify rape. It is as *commendable* that they admitted complicating factors, sometimes in the behavior of the women in these stories, as it is *regrettable* that they did not always transcend their stereotypes about women or delve more subtly into the ways of men and power.

But not all these commentaries are alike. Some of them model how to read with sympathy, attentive to the details of plot and character, treating the text and its characters with fairness. We can see such sympathy in those who insisted that Dinah did struggle against Shechem, or in Luther's sad expectation that tragedies like Dinah's will surely befall us, too. We find a commitment to justice in the insistence of many that the Levite had no right to treat his wife, faithful or not, as a possession to be cast aside. Even though writers such as Vermigli and Calvin were wary of Bathsheba, they still rejoiced that she returned with her husband David to God's promises and forgiveness. Indeed, it is of no small moment that Vermigli took the occasion of David's adultery to argue at great length against the prevailing double standard that favored men in marriage and divorce. Finally, there is a strong consensus to condemn the unjust actions of Amnon and the inaction of David in seeking justice for Tamar. Even puzzling aspects of Tamar's speeches are usually resolved in her favor (Calvin excepted), and there are signs, especially in Vermigli, that the devastation Tamar suffered was neither minimized nor forgotten.

In calling these sad stories to the attention of Christian readers and hearers, we can imagine that among our own readers and hearers there may be some who have harmed people in analogous ways (perhaps under the modern rubric of "sexual harassment"), even as there will surely be others who have suffered such wrongs. One part of that audience needs to know that God cares about the details of justice; the other wants to know that God cares about the details of their loss and offers healing and hope — *and* that God does not favor men over women. Our calling is to proclaim both sides of the gospel: justice *and* love. In bringing forth the gospel from the pages of the Bible, we do not do well to avoid hard passages and hard questions. Despite their imperfections, our exegetical forebears remind us that we are not the first to know or care about women — of the Old Testament and of our own day — who have suffered unspeakable losses.

Conclusion

On Cultivating the Habit of History

Reading the Bible in the Presence of the Past

It's time for a true confession. When I was little, I never dreamed of growing up to be a historian, not even once. I did hope to walk on the moon. But I never thought about being a historian, and I'm sure I didn't even know what they did, except maybe to write boring books that we got tested on, and who would want to do that? Obviously, I had a change of heart some decades later, but I think the chances are pretty good that most churches are full of people who probably want to follow Jesus in *some* way, but who probably don't think they want to become historians in *any* way.

Shouldn't Christians think differently? Shouldn't an affection for the Bible and its message also lead to some appreciation for the *historical* character of the Bible — some sense of how the narratives and instructions of Scripture emerged from real persons and communities of faith, engaged in real discernment and real negotiations with God and with one another? And shouldn't Christians also have some sense for how the essentials of the gospel have come to us already much considered and much digested, through centuries of reflection and controversy within the Christian church and often even within the conscience of individual interpreters?

If we answer *no* to these questions, if we minimize the historical character of the Bible and the church by which the Bible has been preserved, interpreted, and argued over, we run several risks. Among other things, we risk thinking that we (or our pastor, or our church or denomination) have found the true center of the gospel, while all others have missed the mark. We also risk dismissing the life and witness of all Christians prior to our own day, as if they had nothing to teach us and as if they had no role in shaping (for good *and* for ill) the Christian faith and the Christian church that exist in our own day.

This book began by wagering that the Bible is better read and used when traditional commentators — the teachers and preachers of the early church, the Middle Ages, and the Reformation era — are invited to join us in a conversation about the meaning of Scripture for our own day. In particular, I have tried to illustrate how these old books and interpreters can offer us guidance with respect to some of the Bible's most obscure and difficult texts — the texts lectionaries often avoid, and pastors as well. Each of the preceding chapters has tried to highlight patterns and developments in the history of exegesis that may have affected our reading, or ought to. We've also noted how the awkward silences of certain stories were filled in by earlier readers — some with equal awkwardness or discomfort; others with a fine sense for finding hope and redemption, and sometimes a sensitivity to character, plot, and issues of right and wrong that we may learn from today. In some chapters we focused on the "backstage" discussion — on second thoughts or exegetical worries that commentators shared with their readers and that give us license, too, to wrestle with hard texts and share those second thoughts about divorce or gender roles. And we have also seen that traditional commentators had blind spots, wherein they skewed the Bible in terms of their own cultural stereotypes. We would disown such practices, yet we also see a distant reflection of our own fallibility.

In drawing this book to a close, I don't intend to repeat the observations or lessons of earlier chapters. Instead, we'll conclude by doing two things that are loosely connected. First, I'll take some of the reflections generated by earlier chapters and push them one step further, to suggest some ways Christians might want to think about the historical dimension of Christian faith and the Bible. After that, I'll offer some practical suggestions for how one's regular study of the Bible might welcome and incorporate the influence of the past, in the person of the traditional commentators we've met.

Things You Can Do with History

To say that historians write history is to beg the question of what history is. A moment of reflection, however, ought to make it clear that "history" is not the same as the *past.* The past is everything that has happened, and no account could possibly capture or record it all. So historians, like anyone who has ever tried to keep a diary, must settle for partial accounts. These accounts are partial in more ways than one. They are partial because they cannot include every detail or tell the whole story. But they are also partial because they inevitably reflect not only the past, but also the one who writes about the past. Every written history is shaped by the historian's own interests, method, sensitivities, care and depth of research, background, and so on. The nineteenth-century assertion of Leopold von Ranke, that history should describe the past "as it really was," has long been seen as at once idealistic and simplistic. Even where historical "facts" seem fixed and final, the facts about the past always spawn diverse perspectives and interpretations. So while it is easy to write history badly, it is impossible to write it perfectly or definitively.

This question of *method* is of great interest to historians, who, in addition to writing books about the past, also like to write about how they write. The twentieth century saw a huge amount written about what history "is," but the question has continuously been refined and reformulated. For our purposes, we may focus briefly on two forms of the "what is history" question. One might ask, what *purpose* is served by the writing or telling of history? And one might also ask, how does the past, or how *should* the past, shape the present? (I hope you'll begin to see that these questions are of interest to many, not just to professional historians. The "good news" of the gospel derives from certain past events, as does the identity of the church. Thinking Christians are obliged to ponder such things.)

Writing History for Fun and Profit

The first question directs us to think about the uses of history, and why people write about the past. There are many reasons. Sometimes a history is written as a *memento,* a record of past events or people meant to serve various purposes. A family history or photo album may simply keep memories alive to honor the dead or celebrate a legacy. So may a national history, though such records may also serve to protect longstanding claims to territorial rights, and so forth. There may also be an element of *entertainment* or poetry in certain episodes, and many histories emphasize the implicit *morality* of the past: virtue or vice, cowardice or bravery, wisdom or folly — behavior exhibited by individuals and nations alike.

There are larger functions of history, however. Sometimes historians have gone in search of the larger patterns of how history "works" in order to explain the past and perhaps to predict — or influence — the future. Such global theories can be highly illuminating or highly reductionistic. Some of the most influential "histories" have also been among the worst: conspiracy theories, for example, ambitiously explain everything about the world by identifying (say) Jews, African Americans, or Roman Catholics as villains and scapegoats. In fact, any use of history may also become abusive. A narrative of a people's suffering or heroism may unify a nation, but it may also target historical enemies without bothering to ask or care if there is another side to the story. In such cases, history becomes propaganda or an exercise in self-congratulation. If, as Alexander Pope said, "a little learning is a dangerous thing," a one-sided history is equally hazardous. So new histories are often written to counteract "bad" histories or to do justice to sides of the story that have been neglected or dismissed.

When history is at its best, it enhances our self-understanding without having to privilege us over others. Indeed, deeper self-knowledge may come about precisely in our encounter with the "other," that is, with the stories or histories of those who are recognizably sharers of our humanity yet by no means wholly like us. We learn not only how we have been shaped and affected by factors past and present, but also how someone else might turn out quite differently, and arguably no worse or better in the eyes of God.

Relating Past and Present

Thinking about the uses of history naturally leads to our second question, on how past and present are related. There are two opposite mistakes one could make here: either to say that the present has nothing to do with the past — an assertion of a kind of radical freedom, but very hard to substantiate in history or in one's own life! — or to say that the present is utterly dictated by the past. Some might insert here that the reality of the matter is actually beyond our ability to know, and the point is worth noting. We may take an example from our own lives. Let's assume we are sufficiently self-aware to know how our character and personality reflect our family history and temperament, to the point that we can sometimes counteract our "natural" dispositions. Yet do we not often discover that there are always more factors in the background, overlooked or forgotten, that exert a hidden influence — even though we may then (ideally!) incorporate them into our growth and self-awareness?

For the most part, people and societies operate with assumptions about human behavior that avoid asserting our utter autonomy *or* total determinism. Yet we generally recognize that our understanding of the people and circumstances of the present is deepened — sometimes crucially so — by an appreciation of the past and its effects. One might even say that we don't really know *who* or *where* we are, historically speaking, until we have some sense of *how* we got here. This minor lesson could be applied to nations or individuals, but also to churches and denominations.

Things You Can Do with the Bible

Everything said so far about the uses of history could be applied fairly directly to the particular case of the Bible. Like the past, and like any historical narrative about the past, the Bible is open to interpretations that vary according to a reader's perspective and agenda. Indeed, if it is impossible to write a perfect history, it's just as impossible to claim the perfect interpretation of Scripture — though some interpretations are obviously more off the mark than others! Nonetheless, all the uses of history in general find counterparts in the ways people have used or abused the Bible. This, too, is an oft-told tale: even as the Bible has been a means through which lives have been changed and redeemed, it has also served less noble causes. Proof-texts have been found to support the conquest of colonial peoples and the subjugation of lower classes, as well as to call for crusades, buttress the divine right of kings, and depict slavery as apostolically endorsed. Ever since the Enlightenment, writers have regularly rubbed the church's nose in its alleged misdeeds and implicated the Bible as part of the problem.

It is therefore indispensable that Christians consider with care just what constitutes the Bible's proper use. This is a controversial question, and answers will vary according to the identity of the one who asks. Let me outline an answer intended to represent the perspective of the Christian church, broadly defined. Obviously, there are other perspectives from which the question might be addressed, but the purpose of this book has been to help "churchly" readers use the Bible better. So it's reasonable to begin by recalling what the church has traditionally supposed the Bible to be good for. Even here, there are many places to start — say, with the writings of the apostles or the church fathers or medieval theologians. I'll use John Calvin as an example, but I don't think he is much at odds with his predecessors.[1]

Calvin's training in rhetoric always led him to read a text looking for the author's intent. Finding that intention entailed not reconstructing the author's mental state but, instead, discerning from the text what the writer wanted the reader to think or do. The Bible *is* a special book, but only because its diverse writers were guided in a common intention by an unseen divine hand. Like other books, the Bible is handled best when we look for what its author intended its readers to think or do in response to what they read. So, what *does* the Bible intend? For Calvin, the Bible tells of how a just and loving creator has dealt with people enslaved by sin but called to restoration and redemption. The promises of grace and mercy through Jesus Christ constitute for Calvin the *benefits* of Scripture; our responses represent the Bible's proper and practical *application*. What needs to be added, however, is that Calvin did not see this use of Scripture as an individualistic exercise. God's glory and goodness are meant to find embodiment in a *people*, remade in God's image. The Bible is thus the story of the people of God, beginning with our first parents and continuing through the New Testament into our own day. Significantly, Calvin did not bypass the church fathers or skip from first-century Jerusalem to sixteenth-century Geneva. Despite his belief in the preeminent authority of the Bible over all matters of faith and life, Calvin by no means neglected the writings that came after the New Testament. At one point, he ambitiously planned to translate the works of Chrysostom into French, for popular reading. He described the writings of the church fathers more generally as "aids" and "resources" that *God* has provided for understanding Scripture. Such writings are not to be neglected, for they are meant to function hand-in-hand with the illuminating work of the Holy Spirit.[2]

Calvin's overall approach to Scripture models two notable virtues, both of which are actually quite traditional. On the one hand, by keeping the Bible's redemptive intention constantly in mind as a key to unlock the meaning of Scripture, he offers at least one way to distinguish between the use and abuse of the Bible. Take the case of Calvin's struggle to reconcile the imprecatory psalms with Jesus' word that we should pray for our enemies, not curse them. For Calvin, God's mercy upon sinners (including ourselves, pointedly!) doesn't dodge or deny human injustice, but it also challenges the right of one sinner to exact vengeance upon another. In other words, the temptation to direct the curses in the psalms against one's earthly enemies is trumped by Scripture's larger, redemptive, divine intent. Of course, one might argue that Calvin and many others sometimes failed to keep their eyes on that larger agenda in their exegesis — say, when they read about the women of Scripture and allowed stereotypes and prejudices to run unchecked. Such failures are sad, but hardly surprising. Protestants and Catholics were serious about sanctification and changed lives, but they were still pilgrims on that holy way.

Calvin also indicates, on the other hand, a role for all the commentators and theologians who have gone before us — part of that "cloud of witnesses" of which Hebrews 12 speaks. He thereby calls us back to the second question considered above: how past and present are related. In Calvin's day, a conversation with prior interpreters was a necessity: Christian teachings and practices were being radically reconsidered in the wake of the Reformation, and it mattered to know who had departed from the trajectory of the apostles' traditions and who had not. Like most Reformers, Calvin fiercely contended that Protestants were in closer agreement with the ancient church than their Roman Catholic rivals. While the church is not obliged today to mimic every detail of the Acts of the Apostles, continuity in essentials is crucial. To this end, exegesis must be more than the dissection of chapters and verses; it must also be a conversation with the community of interpreters throughout the church's history.[3]

Things You Can Do with the History of Exegesis

Most Christians, however, have never sustained a conversation with any but the most recent of their theological ancestors. Why should they start now? The short answer is that knowing the history of interpretation has its benefits, just like knowing history in general. But let's elaborate that answer a bit.

The lessons of the history of exegesis, like those of other kinds of history, can be as simple as finding good examples to imitate and bad ones to avoid. We have seen both. Sometimes the "good" of the example to imitate has been simply the willingness of traditional commentators to think through difficult and offensive texts (often those *we* avoid) and bring them to the pulpit or lectern. But we've seen bad examples, too, where commentators explain away hard texts with interpretations that seem dysfunctional or forced — such as crafting implausible excuses for the patriarchs, or protecting Hosea's dignity by eradicating Gomer's humanity or even her very existence.

But there is another lesson, not necessarily peculiar to the history of exegesis, that should be noted before we conclude. This sort of lesson emerges from the mixture of familiarity and strangeness that we experience when reading what old commentaries have to say about well-known Bible stories. The experience of *familiarity* may be, or begin as, a comfortable sensation. Truly, it is reassuring to perceive ourselves as somehow joined to Christian readers of centuries past in a solidarity of belief and yearning as we read the Bible to find a word from God to us, today. It is rightly encouraging to confront a heart-rending story in Scripture, then discover that we are not the first to be stupefied by the cruelty recorded in the text. The same might be said of passages that bewilder not so much because they are sad *stories* but because they are difficult *teachings* — as with texts about divorce and women speaking and teaching in church. Ancient, medieval, and Reformation-era commentators do not solve these ethical and exegetical problems for us, but they do bear witness that such problems are not necessarily the by-products of a degenerate modernity and its cultural accommodations. When brought to bear on real-life situations, these texts are intrinsically difficult, and have always been so. So it may well empower us to find out that Christians of days long past at least attempted to address such ethical and exegetical issues with the sort of sensitivity we hope for today, and with just as much awareness of the problems raised by unfeeling exegesis or its formulaic application.

Inevitably, however, reading old commentaries will also evoke the *strangeness* of the past, even the Christian past. That, too, is a good thing. If reading the church fathers or medievals impresses us only with how much they anticipated our own wonderful views, chances are good we've been reading with blinders on. We should hope to find writers in the past who argue with us, and with all our contemporaries. We should also hope to lose some of those arguments, if we are at all teachable. Sometimes we'll dissent from our forebears on the grounds that they allowed their presuppositions or cultural baggage to distort the meaning of a text. At other times, our presumptions about their presuppositions will turn on us and expose our own failings. And even when we're sure *they* are in denial of an obvious difficulty, *we* should be moved to self-examination.

At the same time, however strange these old commentators may seem, however "precritical" or naively literal or fanciful, it remains that their goals are largely our goals: to read the Bible as Scripture and to derive from its message a sure knowledge of what we should believe, how we should live, and where we should place our hope. These goals represent the *quadriga,* the ancient "fourfold rule" of interpretation — the rule that led ancient and medieval commentators to search the letter of the text for figurative meanings: for allegories, morals, and indications of heaven. And even though Protestant writers complained bitterly about the capriciousness of allegory, we have encountered two other considerations along our way. On the one hand, the Protestant rejection of allegory was not absolute: allegories rejected from one text often emerged elsewhere, chastened and recast as analogies, applications, or simply as moral exhortations. On the other hand, we've seen that allegories often served multiple functions, as in the case of patristic and medieval allegories about Hagar and Ishmael. Having been licensed by St. Paul to allegorize the banishment of Hagar, traditional commentators found allegorical ways not only to edify their readers and hearers, but also to do justice to the literal Hagar of Genesis 16 and 21. Something similar happened to Jephthah's daughter, whose senseless death could not be undone except by connecting it, somehow, to the mystery of the cross. That might seem like the easy way out, were it not for the compassion and empathy that emanated from the words of those who drew this connection between God's only son and Jephthah's only daughter.

There is an undeniable strangeness about much traditional exegesis. Yet the more we ponder it and weigh the intentions of our predecessors, the more we may find that their *strangeness* is also strangely *familiar.* That strangeness may harbor surprises for us about the past, and it may offer unlooked-for readings of Scripture that draw us out of ourselves into other Christian minds and other epochs of Christian churches and Christian culture. We need such encounters and such conversations. We may return from the past unpersuaded, but we will not return unchanged.

History in Daily Doses

I'd like to end by considering how the study of the church's past and the history of exegesis can become part of the toolbox of a busy pastor, or any Christian. The joy of reading old commentaries probably looks like an acquired taste — and it is. But it's acquired easily enough by anyone whose love for the *Bible* includes some affection or respect for the *church* as the people of God through the centuries who not only preserved and transmitted the gospel, but have also witnessed to its power in life and in death. How can we not want to strike up a conversation with those who also share the fellowship of Jesus?

In order to carry on a conversation with the past, however, one has to have some actual knowledge of actual history. That also means some actual reading. One easy way to cultivate the habit of reading the Bible in conversation with our predecessors is to find one of these old commentaries and read it alongside whatever passage of Scripture you're studying, whether for personal edification or for preaching or leading a Bible study. To that end, I have appended to this book a list of old commentaries that are available in English, often in print but also in various electronic or online formats. For some books of the Bible, it may be difficult to find translated commentaries from the Reformation era or before, and there are many authors whose works are still locked away in Latin and Greek. But the translation of these classic and not-so-classic works is more than a cottage industry. More and more works appear each year, and the list I have drawn up will soon need updating.

One may also take special note of some series, mentioned earlier, that offer significant excerpts from Christian exegetical literature for virtually every passage of the Old and New Testaments. *The Ancient Christian Commentary on Scripture* (InterVarsity, nearly complete) and *The Church's Bible* (Eerdmans, just underway) attempt to harvest the best of patristic literature that bears on the meaning of Scripture, passage by passage. *The Reformation Commentary on Scripture* (InterVarsity, scheduled for 2009) promises to do the same for commentators of the sixteenth century. The downside of reading excerpts, of course, is that it is easy to miss the larger context, and any collection inevitably omits some worthwhile writers. The benefit, however, is that these projects provide a more diverse selection of authors than most readers can assemble, all between a single set of covers.

For those who would like a different approach, let me outline a plan that could be applied to further reading in the history of biblical interpretation, or more generally to church history or historical theology. Naturally, for any focused reading in history, it helps to start with an overview. Seminarians and most pastors will likely have read some survey text already, and that may suffice. But there are many general and specific surveys of church history, historical theology, and biblical interpretation that are written at a fairly accessible level, and that's where genuine beginners should start.[4] It's hard to appreciate what is being argued in a particular writer if you know neither the major events and themes in church history nor the contributions of major theologians that shaped various epochs.

Once you have a basic feel for the history of the church and its theology, consider deepening your knowledge (including your knowledge of the history of exegesis) by adopting a threefold strategy, as follows. First, *explore your roots.* That is to say, think about the particulars of your Christian identity — how you were raised, what church or denomination you joined, what theological beliefs or liturgical expressions you hold dear. Where did these things come from? Who founded your church or tradition? Who first expressed or practiced Christianity as you best know it? These writers or founders represent your roots, whether as recent as Aimee Semple McPherson, or as far back as John Wesley, Menno Simons, Martin Luther, or Thomas Aquinas. In most cases, they wrote; often they contributed exegetical opinions. You should read what they wrote in order to see how your strand of Christian tradition got its start. You may find you agree with your founding fathers or mothers, or disagree. You may find your tradition has wandered away from its roots, for reasons you embrace or reject. In any case, you'll have a better sense of how you and your tradition arrived at the present, and why.

Second, *read the writers who influenced your ancestors* — the "roots of your roots," so to speak. Even those who claimed a "sudden conversion" like Calvin, or all at once a heart "strangely warmed" like Wesley, were reading more than the Bible. It turns out that Calvin was deeply indebted to Augustine, and many of the developments in his own thinking seem to be a response to reading one church father or another. Wesley, on the other hand, was reading Luther — yet he was also conversant with the church fathers, as well as with various puritans and pietists. Reading those who influenced our founders broadens our understanding of them and helps us avoid narrowing their theology to a caricature or a party line. (One should

225

also note in passing how often the church fathers prove to be a common denominator among Protestant writers and their heirs.)

Finally, as time allows, *read the writers with whom your forebears disagreed.* There may be many to choose from, of course, including both predecessors and contemporaries. In my opinion, it is better to focus less on their arguments with those far outside the church and more on what we can charitably call in-house squabbles. Calvin's sharp rejection of medieval scholastics cries out for some assessment: were they all as evil as he suggests? Luther's contempt for Zwingli needs the perspective of as sympathetic a reading of Zwingli as one can manage. Going further back, one ought to read enough of Origen to understand why Luther and Calvin could vilify him while Erasmus embraced him. But let me add a word of caution. Reading polemical writings is not always edifying. The writers of long ago often did not play by modern rules, and it is always risky (even today) to accept uncritically what writers say about their adversaries. This is one more reason to try comparing opponents also on other grounds — that is, in different genres — and the commentary genre is especially interesting because it is often the repository of observations omitted from polemical and systematic theologies. Important as it is to know where and how Christian theologians have disagreed, it is worth discovering how much they may agree (or how subtle their disagreements are) when their focus is not on an opponent but on the interpretation of Scripture.

Connecting the Church with the Church

Although this book probably has looked like a book about exegesis, or history, or the Bible, I hope by now you've discerned that these other topics are really supporting players for the book's real topic: the church in all its fullness, from its prehistory in the Old Testament to its birth in the New, and through twenty centuries of success and failure. These days, it's common for Christians to be embarrassed by the church. Jesus is seen as lovely and profound, even worth making movies about, while the church is often seen quite differently. The church is popularly vilified as backward and repressive, an easy target for pseudo-historical novels like Dan Brown's *The Da Vinci Code.* So it is not surprising that churches today often labor to present themselves as fully in step with contemporary culture. "Traditional" worship is not a selling point for the young, for we often expect only the worst from the past.

To know something about the history of interpretation is not to whitewash the past, because the history of interpretation is not always a pretty picture. But in the preceding chapters, we have seen cases in which the commentators of the distant past have offered great insight and sensitivities to the sufferings, cruelty, and foibles of human beings in ways that we ought to emulate. Sermons and Bible studies are perfect occasions for connecting Christians of the present with their brothers and sisters of the previous twenty centuries. After all, it is common for sermons to contemporize or contextualize a passage of Scripture by connecting it with anything and everything going on in the present — local news, recent films, anecdotes, novels, national leaders, matters of poverty and justice, war and peace — as well as with Christian exemplars of recent memory. How much more should the proclamation of the word of God be connected with the largest community of interpretation possible — with the mind of the whole church as it has attempted to be faithful to the whole counsel of God?

This closing plea is *not* for the sermon to become a dry hash of the history of interpretation. But each of the previous chapters has offered reflections on the history of exegesis that surely deserve as much consideration in the preparation of a sermon as the technical data found in modern commentaries. Such reflections, as well as these commentators' specific exegetical insights, should shape how we read and interpret the church's Bible and therefore also ought to be welcomed into the pulpit.

Whether Protestant, Catholic, Orthodox, or independent, all Christians have a rich legacy of biblical interpretation that has formed us in ways beyond our knowing. To know this legacy is part of the Christian birthright. In the Reformed tradition, it is often said that the *preaching* of the word of God *is* the word of God. But preaching is also a means by which the people of God are theologically formed, so as to learn and rehearse the beliefs and practices that constitute their real human and Christian identity. The church suffers when that identity is dictated by ignorance or by secular culture. My plea, then, is this: That those who handle and proclaim the Scriptures would avail themselves of the opportunity to bring the church of the past into the present, to place us in the company of that "cloud of witnesses" and so connect us with the life of God among the everlasting people of God.

Abbreviations

The commentaries, sermons, and homilies cited in this book are usually identified by abbreviated title and a number representing either chapter:verse of the biblical text addressed or book.chapter of the work as a whole. Variations such as *annotationes* and *enarrationes* are usually cited simply as *Comm.* Because this book is intended to encourage access to exegetical literature in English, quotations and page references normally indicate translations, sometimes supplemented by original-language editions.

a, b	For double-column pages, "a" – left column, "b" = right column.
ACCS	*The Ancient Christian Commentary on Scripture.* 28 vols. in two series, designated here as ACCS-OT and ACCS-NT. Downers Grove, Ill.: InterVarsity Press, 1999-.
ACW	*Ancient Christian Writers.* 60+ vols. Mahwah, N.J.: Paulist, 1946-.
ANF	*The Ante-Nicene Fathers.* 10 vols. Buffalo and Edinburgh, 1885-96, but frequently reprinted. E-text is commercially available on CD-ROM; online edition at CCEL.
CCEL	*Christian Classics Ethereal Library,* a website dedicated to producing e-texts of public domain Christian literature: www.ccel.org
CCSL	*Corpus Christianorum, Series Latina.* 168+ vols. Turnhout: Brepols, 1953-. E-text accessible at some research libraries via *Cetedoc Library of Christian Latin Texts* CD-ROM or online (6th edition; Brepols, 2005).

CNTC   *Calvin's New Testament Commentaries.* 12 vols. Ed. D. W. and T. F. Torrance. Grand Rapids: Eerdmans, 1959-72.

CO   *Ioannis Calvini Opera Quae Supersunt Omnia.* 59 vols. Corpus Reformatorum 29-88. Ed. G. Baum, E. Cunitz, E. Reuss. Brunswick and Berlin, 1863-1900. E-text available on DVD from the Instituut voor Reformatieonderzoek (The Netherlands).

CSEL   *Corpus Scriptorum Ecclesiasticorum Latinorum.* 85 vols. Vienna, 1866-.

CSCO   *Corpus Scriptorum Christianorum Orientalium.* 600+ vols. Various publishers since 1903; currently published by Peeters (Louvain).

CTS   *Calvin Translation Society* edition of Calvin's commentaries. 46 vols. Edinburgh, 1843-55. Several reprints, but variously bound; volume numbers (when cited) are relative to specific commentaries and not to the entire set. E-text is available on CD-ROM; online edition at CCEL.

CWE   *Collected Works of Erasmus.* 86 vols. planned. Toronto: University of Toronto Press, 1969-.

EEBO   *Early English Books Online.* Digital page images of works printed in England, Ireland, Scotland, Wales, and British North America, and works in English printed elsewhere, 1473-1700. **Note:** *Editions of these early works are often keyed to STC numbers (below), which are reliable search terms for locating files in the EEBO database that can be downloaded and retained.* Accessible online at some research libraries.

ET   English translation

FC   *The Fathers of the Church.* 111+ vols. Washington: Catholic University of America Press, 1947-.

LCC   *Library of Christian Classics.* 26 vols. Philadelphia: Westminster, 1952-69.

LCL   *Loeb Classical Library.* Cambridge, Mass.: Harvard University Press. Volume-numbers cited refer to collections of individual authors.

LEC   *Library of Early Christianity.* Washington: Catholic University of America Press, 2006-.

LFC   *Library of the Fathers of the Holy Catholic Church.* 48 vols. Oxford, 1838-88. Many vols. reprinted or revised in ANF and NPNF.

LW   *Luther's Works* [= "American Edition"]. 55 vols. St. Louis: Concordia; and Philadelphia: Fortress, 1955-86. E-text is commercially available on CD-ROM from Concordia and Fortress.

MO   *Philippi Melanthonis Opera Quae Supersunt Omnia.* 28 vols. Corpus Reformatorum 1-28. Ed. C. G. Bretschneider. 1834-60; reprint ed.; New York: Johnson, 1963.

NPNF   *A Select Library of the Nicene and Post-Nicene Fathers.* 28 vols. in two series, denoted as NPNF[1] and NPNF[2]. New York: 1886-1900, but frequently reprinted. E-text is commercially available on CD-ROM; online edition at CCEL.

PG   *Patrologia Graeca.* 168 vols. Ed. J.-P. Migne. Paris, 1857-66. Digital page images commercially available and accessible online at some research libraries (Religion and Technology Center).

PL *Patrologia Latina.* 221 vols. Ed. J.-P. Migne. Paris, 1844-55. E-text available online at some research libraries as the Patrologia Latina Database (ProQuest / Chadwyck-Healey).

PML *The Peter Martyr* [Vermigli] *Library.* 24 vols. projected in two series. Kirksville, Mo.: Truman State University Press, 1994-.

PS *Parker Society* for the Publication of the Works of the Fathers and Early Writers of the Reformed English Church. 54 vols.; titles may lack volume numbers. Cambridge: Cambridge University Press, 1840-55.

Quasten *Patrology.* 4 vols. Ed. Johannes Quasten. Reprint ed.; Westminster, Md.: Christian Classics, 1983-86. Vol. 4 ed. Angelo Di Berardino.

r, v Some old books are numbered not by page but by folio (leaf). Front and back sides (pages) of a numbered folio are indicated by *recto* and *verso.*

SC *Supplementa Calviniana.* 11+ vols. Neukirchen: Neukirchener, 1961-.

STC *A Short-Title Catalogue of Books Printed in England, Scotland, and Ireland and of English Books Printed Abroad, 1475-1640.* Ed. A. W. Pollard, G. R. Redgrave, et al. 3 vols. London: Bibliographical Society, 1976-91. The STC for the later seventeenth century (1641-1700) is a separate work, identified by the name of its compiler, Donald Goddard Wing. **Note:** *Titles in the Finding Guide (below) that carry an STC or Wing number can be obtained as digital facsimiles; see EEBO, above.*

SWZ *Selected Writings of Huldrych Zwingli.* 2 vols. Pittsburgh Theological Monographs 12-13. Allison Park, Penn.: Pickwick, 1984. Vol. 1: *The Defense of the Reformed Faith,* trans. E. J. Furcha. Vol. 2: *In Search of True Religion: Reformation, Pastoral, and Eucharistic Writings,* trans. H. Wayne Pipkin.

WA *D. Martin Luthers Werke: Kritische Gesamtausgabe.* 66 vols. Weimar: Hermann Böhlaus Nachfolger, 1883-1987.

WADB *D. Martin Luthers Werke: Kritische Gesamtausgabe: Deutsche Bibel.* 12 vols. Weimar: Hermann Böhlaus Nachfolger, 1906-61.

WATr *D. Martin Luthers Werke: Kritische Gesamtausgabe: Tischreden.* 6 vols. Weimar: Hermann Böhlaus Nachfolger, 1912-21.

WGRW *Writings from the Greco-Roman World.* Atlanta: Society of Biblical Literature, 2001-.

Wing See STC, above.

WSA *The Works of St. Augustine.* 50 vols. (projected) in three series. Hyde Park, N.Y.: New City Press, 1990-.

ZSW *Huldreich Zwinglis Sämtliche Werke.* 14 vols. Corpus Reformatorum 88-101. Ed. E. Egli et al. 1905-59; reprint ed.; Zürich: Theologischer Verlag, 1983.

Endnotes

Notes to the Introduction, "On Reading with the Dead"

1. Remarkably, while some members of the lectionary task force argued for including the story of Jephthah's daughter, this did not happen — even though there was an attempt to be more inclusive of women. The issue is discussed in *The Revised Common Lectionary*, edited by the Consultation on Common Texts (Nashville: Abingdon, 1992), p. 78. Information on the deliberations over Jephthah's daughter derives from my private correspondence with a member of the task force.

2. See Ruth B. Bottigheimer, *The Bible for Children: From the Age of Gutenberg to the Present* (New Haven: Yale University Press, 1996). Some of these texts are also bypassed by the recent work of Elizabeth R. Achtemeier, *Preaching Hard Texts of the Old Testament* (Peabody, Mass.: Hendrickson, 1998).

3. Phyllis Trible, *Texts of Terror: Literary-Feminist Readings of Biblical Narratives* (Philadelphia: Fortress, 1984), p. xiii.

4. Barbara Brown Taylor, "Hard Words," *The Christian Century* 118, no. 14 (May 2, 2001), p. 24.

5. Although "womanist" could be described as feminism's African American counterpart, the term (coined by Alice Walker) claims a distinctive voice for black women over against white feminists. Similarly, *mujerista* designates not a Hispanic subset of Anglo feminism but an agenda and experience that is unique to Latina women and theologians.

6. Taylor, "Hard Words," p. 24.

7. See my essay, "The Immoralities of the Patriarchs in the History of Exegesis: A Reassessment of Calvin's Position," *Calvin Theological Journal* 26 (1991): 9-46.

8. Although "precritical" sounds derogatory and is sometimes so used, "precritical exegesis" differs from later approaches not by its ignorance of textual problems in the Bible, but by its commitment to address those problems by staying "within" the text (using tools of grammar, rhetoric, and logic, as well as all available textual, linguistic, historical, and geographical data), as opposed to the tendency of "higher" criticism to explain problems by challenging the integrity or reliability of the biblical text itself. In this study, "precritical" will be used merely as a chronological locator for pre-Enlightenment writers and writings, without presupposing what sorts of "critical" insights and methods will be present or absent.

9. These conclusions are explored in the final chapter of my book, *Writing the Wrongs: Women of the Old Testament among Biblical Commentators from Philo through the Reformation* (New York: Oxford University Press, 2001).

Notes to Chapter One, "Hagar in Salvation-History"

1. See Cynthia Gordon, "Hagar: A Throw-Away Character among the Matriarchs?" *The Society of Biblical Literature Seminar Papers* 24 (1985): 271-77.

2. Consultation on Common Texts, *The Revised Common Lectionary* (Nashville: Abingdon, 1992), p. 78.

3. Phyllis Trible, *Texts of Terror: Literary-Feminist Readings of Biblical Narratives* (Philadelphia: Fortress, 1984), pp. 14-18.

4. Sharon Pace Jeansonne, *The Women of Genesis: From Sarah to Potiphar's Wife* (Minneapolis: Fortress, 1990), pp. 51-52.

5. See Delores S. Williams, *Sisters in the Wilderness: The Challenge of Womanist God-Talk* (Maryknoll: Orbis, 1993), p. 19; Danna Nolan Fewell and David M. Gunn, *Gender, Power, and Promise: The Subject of the Bible's First Story* (Nashville: Abingdon, 1993), p. 46; Jo Ann Hackett, "Rehabilitating Hagar: Fragments of an Epic Pattern," in *Gender and Difference in Ancient Israel,* ed. Peggy L. Day (Philadelphia: Fortress, 1989), p. 24; and Susan Niditch, "Genesis," in *The Women's Bible Commentary,* ed. Carol A. Newsom and Sharon H. Ringe (Louisville: Westminster/John Knox, 1992), p. 17.

6. Trible, *Texts of Terror,* p. 9.

7. John W. Waters, "Who Was Hagar?" in *Stony the Road We Trod: African American Biblical Interpretation* (Minneapolis: Fortress, 1991), pp. 199-200; Renita J. Weems, "A Mistress, A Maid, and No Mercy: Hagar and Sarah," in *Just a Sister Away: A Womanist Vision of Women's Relationships in the Bible* (San Diego: LuraMedia, 1988), pp. 12-15; and Williams, *Sisters in the Wilderness,* pp. 19-21. For a Latina perspective, see Elsa Tamez, "The Woman Who Complicated the History of Salvation," in *New Eyes for Reading: Biblical and Theological Reflections by Women from the Third World,* ed. John S. Pobee and Bärbel von Wartenberg-Potter (Geneva: World Council of Churches, 1986), pp. 5-17.

8. Abraham's conduct was decried over a century ago by Elizabeth Cady Stanton;

see *The Original Feminist Attack on the Bible (The Woman's Bible)*, 2 vols. (1895-98; one-volume reprint; New York: Arno, 1974), 1:40. More recently, see Niditch, "Genesis," p. 18.

9. See the Introduction, above, p. 4.

10. Observations along these lines are recorded by Athalya Brenner, "Female Social Behaviour: Two Descriptive Patterns within the 'Birth of the Hero' Paradigm," in *A Feminist Companion to Genesis* (Sheffield: Sheffield Academic Press, 1993), pp. 220-21; Esther Fuchs, "A Jewish Feminist Reading of the Hagar Stories," p. 8 (an unpublished paper cited by Katheryn Pfisterer Darr in *Far More Precious than Jewels: Perspectives on Biblical Women* [Louisville: Westminster John Knox, 1991], p. 155); and J. Cheryl Exum, *Fragmented Women: Feminist (Sub)versions of Biblical Narratives* (Valley Forge: Trinity, 1993), pp. 134-36.

11. Darr's exclamation (in *Far More Precious than Jewels*, p. 139) may be taken as representative: "Should we then conclude that YHWH sanctions abuse? Where is the God of the exodus, who liberates people from their oppressors? Where is Hagar's redeemer?" See also Waters, "Who Was Hagar?" p. 200; Williams, *Sisters in the Wilderness*, p. 21; Fewell and Gunn, *Gender, Power, and Promise*, pp. 46, 51; Trible, *Texts of Terror*, p. 26; Stanton, *The Woman's Bible*, 1:40.

12. A more exhaustive survey of the history of the interpretation of Hagar through the Reformation can be found in chapter one of Thompson, *Writing the Wrongs*.

13. Philo, *On Mating with the Preliminary Studies*, 4-5, 31 (§§13, 24, 180; LCL 4:464-65, 470-71, 550-51); and *On the Cherubim* 2-3 (§§8-9; LCL 2:12-13).

14. Origen, *Homilies on Genesis* 6.3, 7.3-6, cf. 11.1-2 (FC 71:126, 130-35, 168-71). The desire to free the revered patriarch Abraham from the stigma of having been a polygamist was equally a factor in Philo's allegorizing of Hagar.

15. Didymus the Blind, *Sur la Genèse*, vol. 2, ed. Pierre Nautin with Louis Doutreleau (Sources Chrétiennes 244; Paris: Éditions du Cerf, 1978), pp. 204-32.

16. Ambrose, *De Abraham* 1.26-28, 1.65, 2.72-75 (PL 14:453-54, 467, 515-16).

17. Augustine, *The Correction of the Donatists* 2.11 (NPNF[1] 4:637); and *Tractate 11 on John*, §§12-15 (NPNF[1] 7:77-81). Hagar is one of several Old Testament types Augustine invoked to justify coercion of the Donatists; see Charles J. Scalise, "Exegetical Warrants for Religious Persecution: Augustine *vs.* The Donatists," *Review and Expositor* 93 (1996): 497-506.

18. Isidore, *Quæstiones in Vetus Testamentum* 17.1-6, on Gen. 21:9-17 (PL 83:248-49). Isidore's debt to Origen can be proved by his close reliance on an earlier treatise from Gregory of Elvira, which was itself probably influenced by a translation of Origen on Genesis made early in the fifth century by Rufinus. For fuller discussion, see Thompson, *Writing the Wrongs*, pp. 47-48.

19. Bede, *Adnotationes* on Gen. 16:13-14 (CCSL 118a:201; PL 91:159).

20. Raban Maur, *Comm. Gen.* §2.18 on Gen. 16:12-13 (PL 107:544-45).

21. *Midrash Rabbah: Genesis* 53.11 (2 vols.; third edition; London and New York: Soncino, 1983), 1:470.

22. Jerome, *Hebrew Questions on Genesis* 21:9 (Hayward ed., p. 53).

23. Chrysostom, *Hom. 46.1 on Gen.* 21:9-11 (FC 87:5); *Comm. Gal.* 4:29-30 (NPNF[1] 13:35).

24. Theodoret, *Quaestiones in Octateuchum* §72 (PG 80:179-182); Procopius, *Catena in Octateuchum* on Gen. 21:10 (PG 87/1:385-86). This is not to claim that either writer hesitated also to criticize Hagar or Ishmael; see Thompson, *Writing the Wrongs*, pp. 41-44.

25. Rabbi Nachmanides, as quoted in *The Soncino Chumash*, ed. A. Cohen (London: Soncino, 1947), p. 76. See also Ramban (Nachmanides), *Commentary on the Torah: Genesis*, trans. Charles B. Chavel (New York: Shilo, 1971), p. 213.

26. Cajetan, *Commentarii illustres . . . in Quinque Mosaicos libros* on Gen. 21:14 (Paris: Guillaume de Bossozel, 1539), p. 99.

27. Conrad Pellican, *Commentaria Bibliorum* on Gen. 21:11, 14 (5 vols.; Zurich: Christoph Froschauer, 1532-35), 1:26v, 27r.

28. Wolfgang Musculus, *In Mosis Genesim . . . Commentarii* on Gen. 21:14 (Basel: Johann Herwagen, 1554), pp. 515-16.

29. Peter Martyr Vermigli, *In Primvm Librvm Mosis . . . Commentarii* on Gen. 21:14 (Zurich: Froschauer, 1569), fol. 84r.

30. Luther, *Lectures on Genesis* 21:14 (WA 43:161, my translation; cf. LW 4:36); hereafter cited as *Comm. Gen.*

31. Luther, *Comm. Gen.* 21:15-16 (LW 4:40-41).

32. Details in *Writing the Wrongs*, pp. 60-69.

33. Huldreich Zwingli, *Farrago annotationum in Genesim* (hereafter cited as *Comm. Gen.*) on Gen. 16:3-13, 21:9-16 (ZSW 13:93-97, 133-35).

34. Pellican, *Comm. Gen.* 21:16 (1:27r).

35. Musculus, *Comm. Gen.* 21:14 (p. 517).

36. Trible uses the words that Jesus uttered from Psalm 22 as an epitaph for Jephthah's daughter, while Hagar's comes from Isa. 53:5; Trible, *Texts of Terror*, pp. 8, 92.

37. Luther, *Comm. Gen.* 16:6, 13-14 (LW 3:56, 74).

38. Luther, *Comm. Gen.* 21:15-16 (WA 43:168, my translation; cf. LW 4:46). In his comments on Gen. 21:14, Luther eventually names everyone in the household as weeping; see LW 4:37-40.

39. Urban II, *Oratio II in Concilio Claromontano Habitae De Expeditione Hierosolymitana* (PL 151:569), November 27, 1095.

40. For details, see John L. Thompson, "Calvin's Exegetical Legacy: His Reception and Transmission of Text and Tradition," in *The Legacy of John Calvin: Calvin Studies Society Papers 1999*, ed. David L. Foxgrover (Grand Rapids: Calvin Studies Society, 2000), pp. 31-56.

Notes to Chapter Two, "Sacrificing Jephthah's Daughter"

1. Jephthah's daughter has been of great interest to feminist biblical scholars. The questions that follow (and many others) are variously raised by Mieke Bal, *Death and*

Dissymmetry: The Politics of Coherence in the Book of Judges (Chicago: University of Chicago Press, 1988); J. Cheryl Exum, *Fragmented Women: Feminist (Sub)versions of Biblical Narratives* (Valley Forge: Trinity, 1993); Danna Nolan Fewell and David M. Gunn, *Gender, Power, and Promise: The Subject of the Bible's First Story* (Nashville: Abingdon, 1993); Esther Fuchs, "Marginalization, Ambiguity, Silencing: The Story of Jephthah's Daughter," *Journal of Feminist Studies in Religion* 5, no. 1 (1989): 35-45; Alice L. Laffey, *An Introduction to the Old Testament: A Feminist Perspective* (Philadelphia: Fortress, 1988); Ann Michelle Tapp, "An Ideology of Expendability: Virgin Daughter Sacrifice in Genesis 19.1-11, Judges 11.30-39 and 19.22-26," in *Anti-Covenant: Counter-Reading Women's Lives in the Hebrew Bible,* ed. Mieke Bal (Sheffield: Almond, 1989), pp. 154-74; Phyllis Trible, *Texts of Terror: Literary-Feminist Readings of Biblical Narratives* (Philadelphia: Fortress, 1984); Renita J. Weems, *Just a Sister Away: A Womanist Vision of Women's Relationships in the Bible* (San Diego: LuraMedia, 1988).

2. Origen, *Commentary on the Gospel of John* 6.36 (ANF 10:377-78).

3. Allusions to the daughter as a martyr of some sort are found in many writers, including the first-century writers Pseudo-Philo (*Biblical Antiquities* 39-40) and Josephus (*Antiquities* 5.7.10), and in the fourth, Ambrosiaster (*Quaestiones Veteris et Novi Testamenti* 43, PL 35:2239).

4. Ambrose, *De virginitate* 2.5-9 (PL 16:281-82), written about 378. Jephthah's daughter figures as an exemplar in many patristic and medieval treatises that commend consecrated virginity and the religious life.

5. Procopius of Gaza, *Commentarii in Judices* 11:30 (PG 87:1069).

6. Augustine, *Quæstiones in Heptateuchum* 7.49 (PL 34:791-824; CCSL 33:335-77).

7. See Chapter One, p. 20. About the same time, Chrysostom had also appealed to the workings of providence behind this cautionary tale, but without the typological overtones; see his *Homilies on the Statues* 14.3 (PG 49:147, NPNF[1] 9:434).

8. Peter Abelard, *Planctus virginum Israelis super filia Jephtæ Galaditæ*. Latin text in Wolfram von den Steinen, "Die Planctus Abaelards — Jephthas Tochter," *Mittellateinisches Jahrbuch* 4 (1967): 142-44; the 1838 edition is in PL 178:1819-20.

9. See Abelard, *Epistle* 7 (PL 178:245). Others who used Jephthah's daughter to inspire girls to take religious vows included Paschasius Radbertus and Raban Maur.

10. Abelard's views are both traditional and progressive; see Mary McLaughlin, "Abelard and the Dignity of Women," in *Pierre Abélard, Pierre le Vénérable* (Paris: Éditions du Centre national de la recherche scientifique, 1975), pp. 287-334.

11. Isidore of Seville, *Quæstiones in Vetus Testamentum* 7.1-3 (PL 83:388-89).

12. Debora Kuller Shuger, *The Renaissance Bible: Scholarship, Sacrifice, and Subjectivity* (Berkeley and Los Angeles: University of California, 1994), pp. 144, 148 n. 105.

13. Quodvultdeus, *Liber de promissionibus et prædictionibus Dei* 2.20.36-38 (CCSL 60:105-8, PL 51:789-90).

14. Denis the Carthusian, *Comm. Jud.* 11:36-40, in his *Opera Omnia* (42 vols.; Monstrolii, 1896-1913), 3:174.

15. Denis the Carthusian, *Comm. Jud.* 11 (*Opera* 3:178). Denis goes on to draw a

typology connecting the annual lament for Jephthah's daughter with Holy Week, when the church remembers and mourns the passion of Christ.

16. Trible's epitaphs paraphrased Isa. 53:5 ("Hagar, Egyptian Slave Woman: She was wounded for our transgressions; she was bruised for our iniquities") and Isa. 53:3 ("Tamar, Princess of Judah: A woman of sorrows and acquainted with grief"). See also Chapter One at n. 35 for a similar allusion drawn by Wolfgang Musculus.

17. Even the earliest accounts, beginning with Josephus and Pseudo-Philo, append some sort of censure to Jephthah's deed — even if only as a one-word gloss, as in the *Apostolic Constitutions*, where Jephthah's vow is modified by a single word: "rash" (§7.37, ANF 7:474-75).

18. Kimhi, *Commentary on Judges* 11:31, as translated by Frank Ephraim Talmage, *David Kimhi: The Man and the Commentaries* (Cambridge: Harvard University Press, 1975), p. 7. The argument continues to find occasional advocates even today; see David Marcus, *Jephthah and His Vow* (Lubbock: Texas Tech Press, 1986).

19. For Lyra's remarks (*c.* 1320s) on Jud. 11:39, see *Biblia Sacra cvm Glossis, Interlineari & Ordinaria, Nicolai Lyrani Postilla & Moralitatibus, Burgensis Additionibus, & Thoringi Replicis* (Lyons, 1545), 2:47v. Sebastian Münster summarized Kimhi's argument in his *Hebraica Biblia latina* (Basel, 1534-35).

20. Luther, *Praelectio in Librum Iudicium* (WA 4:574-75); and *Tischreden* §§354, 2753ab (WATr 1:148, 2:632-34).

21. Pellican's comments on Judges 11 date from 1533 and appear in his five-volume commentary on the Old Testament, *Commentaria Bibliorum* (Zürich, 1532-1535), 2:44v. Brenz's commentary on Judges appeared in 1535 and was reprinted in his *Opera* (Tübingen, 1576), 2:151.

22. Vermigli, *In Librvm Ivdicvm . . . Commentarii* (Zürich, 1561), pp. 137-41; translated as *Most fruitfull & learned Commentaries. . . .* (London, 1564), fol. 190-96.

23. Richard Rogers, *A Commentary upon the Whole Book of Judges* (London, 1615; facsimile reprint; Edinburgh: Banner of Truth, 1983), Sermon 68, pp. 582-88.

24. Wilbur Owen Sypherd, *Jephthah and His Daughter: A Study in Comparative Literature* (Newark: University of Delaware [Press], 1948).

25. For a fuller discussion of this phenomenon, see Joanne Carlson Brown and Carole R. Bohn, eds., *Christianity, Patriarchy, and Abuse: A Feminist Critique* (New York: Pilgrim Press, 1989).

Notes to Chapter Three, "Psalms and Curses"

1. See William L. Holladay, *The Psalms through Three Thousand Years: Prayerbook of a Cloud of Witnesses* (Minneapolis: Fortress, 1993), pp. 304-14.

2. The Consultation on Common Texts, *The Revised Common Lectionary* (Nashville: Abingdon, 1992).

3. Most commentaries offer introductions that address such matters, among

which see especially the historical survey by Holladay noted above, *Psalms through Three Thousand Years.*

4. In preparing this survey, I've focused on the laments and imprecations cited at the outset of this chapter, along with Psalms 22, 41, 55, 58, 109, and 140.

5. Origen, *On First Principles,* especially book 4.1-3. Note that allegory as an interpretative tool or strategy had been used earlier by other philosophically-sophisticated readers of the Old Testament, such as Philo of Alexandria in the first century, as well as by some readers of Homer and the Olympian myths.

6. These examples are furnished in part by Holladay, *Psalms through Three Thousand Years,* pp. 170-71; details of Psalm 137 are supplemented from PG 12:1660.

7. Athanasius, "Letter to Marcellinus on the Interpretation of the Psalms" §12, in *The Life of Anthony and the Letter to Marcellinus* (New York: Paulist, 1980), p. 111. See also Quasten, *Patrology* 3:37-38.

8. In *Life of Anthony* §6, Anthony cites Psalm 118:7 (similar to 69:13) against the Devil as one of the "enemies" overcome by "the Lord . . . my helper"; cf. §13, where Psalm 68:1-2 is used to banish demonic "enemies." Athanasius spiritualizes the Babylonian captors in Psalm 137 as the enthrallment of "foreign thoughts" ("Letter to Marcellinus" §25, p. 122). However, in his *Defense of His Flight* §20, he ties Pss. 54:7 and 92:11 to David's flight from Saul in order to justify his own flight from *his* enemies, the Arians; his conclusion (§27) cites Pss. 27:1-2 and 31:7-8 as further parallels to his own deliverance from these enemies of Christ (NPNF² 4:262, 265).

9. Jerome, *Homily* 35 on Psalm 109 (FC 48:267).

10. See Jerome, *Homily* 12 on Psalm 79 (FC 48:91-92); *Commentariolum* on Psalm 140:9 (CCSL 72:243); *Homily* 48 on Psalm 137 (FC 48:357-60). Jerome liked the image of bashing one's sins against Christ the rock; he repeats the allusion in his *Commentariolum* (CCSL 72:242.35) and in his famous treatise for Eustochium, Letter 22, composed by mid-384 (§6, NPNF² 6:24). Augustine may have known these works; his own exposition of this part of the psalm essentially follows Jerome.

11. Augustine, *On Christian Doctrine* 1.35.39-1.36.40.

12. Michael Cameron, "Enarrationes in Psalmos," in *Augustine through the Ages: An Encyclopedia,* ed. Allan D. Fitzgerald (Grand Rapids: Eerdmans, 1999), p. 292. A precedent may be found in Jerome's *Homily* 35 on Psalm 109 (FC 48:255).

13. I am indebted here to Michael Fiedrowicz's introduction to Maria Boulding's translation of Augustine's commentary; see esp. WSA III/15:43-65.

14. Thus all of Psalm 69 is spoken by Christ, but the lament in v. 26 about those "you have struck down" is Christ speaking in the name of the flesh he had assumed, that is, in the name of Adam and all of sinful humanity (WSA III/17:393).

15. Here, Augustine largely mirrors Origen's "head-body-members" schema. Any text that says something about Christ (the head) also applies, indirectly, to the church (his body) and to individual Christians as well (the members of the body).

16. For an example of Augustine's quick transition from David to Christ and the

church ("David's members"), see his opening remarks on Psalm 55 (WSA III/17:54). Psalm 51 is an exception to this generalization (WSA III/16:410-29).

17. One explicit digression on the Sermon on the Mount occurs in his comments on Psalm 79:10 (WSA III/18:137-38).

18. See his remarks on Psalm 140:6 (LFC 6:273), as well as Psalm 137, below; and the brief remarks of Fiedrowicz on Augustine's "enemies" (WSA III/15:34-35).

19. Augustine, *Sermon* on Psalm 137:9, §21 (PL 37:1773, cf. LFC 6:176).

20. For an example, see Augustine's comment on Psalm 69:6: "'Let it happen' is equivalent to 'Things cannot turn out otherwise than that this fate befall such people'" (WSA III/17:390). Likewise, Psalm 79:6 (WSA III/18:133).

21. "This it is to hate with a perfect hatred, that neither on account of the vices thou hate the men, nor on account of the men love the vices" (LFC 6:215).

22. Augustine, *Exposition* of Psalm 79:10 (WSA III/18:137); cf. Psalm 140:10 (LFC 6:231).

23. For Augustine, Jews figure among the enemies in Psalms 41:10-11, 69:25, and 137:7, among others (WSA III/16:237, 17:392; LFC 6:178). Donatists are even more common in this role; see Psalms 55:15 and 139:21 (WSA III/17:69, LFC 6:215). See also Paula Fredriksen, "*Excaecati Occulta Iustitia Dei:* Augustine on Jews and Judaism," *Journal of Early Christian Studies* 3 (1995): 299-324, who ascribes Augustine's ambiguity toward Judaism more to his Old Testament polemics than to encounters with contemporary Jews. For Augustine's use of Scripture against the Donatists, see Charles J. Scalise, "Exegetical Warrants for Religious Persecution: Augustine *vs.* the Donatists," *Review and Expositor* 93 (1996): 497 506.

24. See Robert C. Hill, Introduction to St. John Chrysostom, *Commentary on the Psalms* (2 vols.; Brookline, Mass.: Holy Cross Orthodox Press, 1998), 1:4. It is not known if he wrote on every psalm; comments survive on fifty-eight.

25. Chrysostom, *Commentary on Psalms* 109 (2:4-7).

26. Chrysostom, *Commentary on Psalms* 109 (2:2-3).

27. Chrysostom, *Commentary on Psalms* 139 (2:261); italics original.

28. Chrysostom, *Commentary on Psalms* 137 (2:244-45).

29. Theodoret of Cyrus, *Commentary on the Psalms* (FC 101-102), p. 41 and n. 10. Robert C. Hill, editor and translator, reports that Theodoret may have in mind the extremes represented by Apollinaris or Origen on one side, and Theodore of Mopsuestia on the other. For the dating of this work, see FC 101:3-4.

30. Theodoret, *Commentary on the Psalms* 137.6 (FC 102:324).

31. Theodoret, *Commentary on the Psalms* 28.3 (FC 101:179). A similar explanation is offered at Psalm 69:25, which looked to "the just verdict" not only against the Chaldeans but also, later, against the Jews themselves (§69.12, FC 101:400).

32. Theodoret, *Commentary on the Psalms* 55.9, 139.10 (FC 101:319, 102:334).

33. Theodoret, *Commentary on the Psalms* 109.1 (FC 102:200).

34. Thomas Aquinas, *Commentary on Psalms* 54:5. The Latin text is available at http://www.niagara.edu/aquinas/Psalm_53.html, with translation by Gregory Sadler.

35. For a complete listing, see Kurt Aland, *Hilfsbuch zum Lutherstudien* (Witten: Luther-Verlag, 1970), §§593-627.

36. For an account of the emergence of Lefèvre's view in its late medieval context and its relationship to the young Luther, see James Samuel Preus, *From Shadow to Promise: Old Testament Interpretation from Augustine to the Young Luther* (Cambridge, Mass.: Harvard University Press, Belknap Press, 1969), pp. 137-49.

37. Luther, Psalm 69:3, in "First Lectures on the Psalms" (WA 3:417-18, my translation; cf. LW 10:353).

38. Luther, Preface to Psalm 109 in "Four Psalms of Comfort" (LW 14:257-58).

39. For Calvin's alleged "Judaizing" exegesis, see David C. Steinmetz, "The Judaizing Calvin," in *Die Patristik in der Bibelexegese des 16. Jahrhunderts* (Wiesbaden: Harrassowitz, 1999), pp. 135-45; and David L. Puckett, *John Calvin's Exegesis of the Old Testament* (Louisville: Westminster John Knox, 1995), pp. 1-4, 52-81.

40. In my discussion of Calvin, I have been helped by the recent work of Paul Mbunga Mpindi, "Calvin's Hermeneutics of the Imprecations of the Psalms" (Ph.D. dissertation, Calvin Theological Seminary, 2003).

41. Calvin, *Commentary on Psalms* 79:6 (CTS 3:287).

42. Calvin, *Commentary on Psalms* 41:10 (CTS 2:123-24).

43. Calvin, *Commentary on Psalms* 137:7 (CTS 5:196).

44. Calvin, *Commentary on Psalms* 69:22 (CTS 3:67).

45. Calvin, *Commentary on Psalms* 79:10, 109:6 (CTS 3:292-93, 4:276).

46. Calvin, *Commentary on Psalms* 109:16 (CTS 4:283, altered).

47. Citing, in turn, C. S. Lewis, *Reflections on the Psalms* (New York: Harcourt, Brace, & World, 1958), p. 18; and Bernhard W. Anderson, *Out of the Depths: The Psalms Speak for Us Today* (Louisville: Westminster John Knox, 1999), p. 70.

48. Citing Holladay, *Psalms through Three Thousand Years,* p. 313; and James Luther Mays, *The Lord Reigns: A Theological Handbook to the Psalms* (Louisville: Westminster John Knox, 1994).

49. Patrick D. Miller, *They Cried to the Lord: The Form and Theology of Biblical Prayer* (Minneapolis: Fortress, 1994), pp. 302-3; Eugene H. Peterson, *Answering God: The Psalms as Tools for Prayer* (San Francisco: Harper & Row, 1989), p. 102.

50. Holladay, *Psalms through Three Thousand Years,* pp. 311-12.

51. Walter Brueggemann, "Psalm 109: Steadfast Love as Social Solidarity," in *The Psalms and the Life of Faith,* ed. Patrick D. Miller (Minneapolis: Fortress, 1995), pp. 268-82; cf. Brueggemann, *The Message of the Psalms: A Theological Commentary* (Minneapolis: Augsburg, 1984), pp. 85-86.

52. See Rosemary Radford Ruether, *Women-Church: Theology and Practice of Feminist Liturgical Communities* (San Francisco: Harper & Row, 1985), pp. 153-59; discussed also by Holladay, *Psalms through Three Thousand Years,* pp. 296-97. For Trible's epitaphs, see notes 36 and 16 in Chapters One and Two (respectively).

53. Lewis (*Reflections on the Psalms,* p. 136) essentially follows Origen here.

54. Anderson, *Out of the Depths,* pp. 74-75. Brevard S. Childs commends Calvin for

a similar approach; see "The Struggle for God's Righteousness in the Psalter," in *Christ in Our Place: The Humanity of God in Christ for the Reconciliation of the World* (Exeter: Paternoster, and Allison Park, Penn.: Pickwick, 1989), pp. 255-64.

55. Miller, *They Cried to the Lord*, p. 303; italics mine.

56. Holladay, *Psalms through Three Thousand Years*, p. 348.

57. Brueggemann, *Message of the Psalms*, pp. 20-23, 85-87; see also his essay on Psalm 109, cited in n. 51 above.

58. See W. Stanford Reid, "The Battle Hymns of the Lord: Calvinist Psalmody of the Sixteenth Century," in *Sixteenth Century Essays and Studies*, ed. Carl S. Meyer (St. Louis: Foundation for Reformation Research, 1971), pp. 36-54.

Notes to Chapter Four, "Patriarchs Behaving Badly"

1. These stories of the patriarchs are all found in the book of Genesis, as follows: Abraham and Isaac lie about their wives in 12:10-20, 20:1-18, and 26:6-11. Abraham rescues Lot in 14:11-16. Abraham's polygamy is described in 16:1-6; Jacob's, in 30:1-4. Lot endangers his daughters in 19:8 and commits incest in 19:30-38. Jacob deceives Isaac in 27:1-46 and manipulates Laban's flocks in 30:25-43. His sons slaughter the Shechemites in 34:1-31. Judah's incest with Tamar occurs in 38:8-26. Joseph deceives his brothers in 42:7 and 44:1-5. I offer a fuller treatment of these texts in "The Immoralities of the Patriarchs in the History of Exegesis: A Reassessment of Calvin's Position," *Calvin Theological Journal* 26 (1991): 9-46.

2. See Paul J. Hill, "Defending The Defenseless" (August 2003); online at http://www.armyofgod.com/PHill_ShortShot.html, accessed 9/5/2003.

3. These remarks in *The Woman's Bible* are attributed to Clara Bewick Colby and Lillie Devereux Blake; see *The Original Feminist Attack on the Bible* (2 vols. in 1; New York: Arno, 1972), 1:42-44.

4. Ambrose, *Joseph* 1.1 (FC 65:189).

5. Augustine's *On Lying* and *Against Lying* were written in 395 and 420. English translations can be found in NPNF[1] 3:457-77 and 481-500.

6. Zwingli, *Comm. Gen.* 12:13, 31:33 (ZSW 13:71, 205); Augustine, *Reply to Faustus* 22.33 (NPNF[1] 4:285); Chrysostom, *Hom. Gen.* 32.10, 45.7-13 (FC 82:262, 473-76); Lyra, *Comm. Gen.* 20:11 (fol. 61, 75r); Denis, *Comm. Gen.* 20:11 (1:279b).

7. Augustine, *Reply to Faustus* 22.38 (NPNF[1] 4:287).

8. Chrysostom probably took the argument from Josephus; see *Hom. Gen.* 32.5, 45.19, 51.15 (FC 82:257, 479; 87:63).

9. The excuse is attributed to Burgos (Lyra's "corrector") in Lyra, *Comm. Gen.* 12:13 (fol. 61v). Also see: Denis, *Comm. Gen.* 12:16 (1:211a); Pellican, *Comm. Gen.* 12:10-20 (fol. 16v-17r); Oecolampadius, *Comm. Gen.* 12:9-15 (fol. 132); Vermigli, *Comm. Gen.* 12:10, 13, 20 (fol. 49v-50v), 20:1, 8 (fol. 79v, 81r); Musculus, *Comm. Gen.* 12:10 (p. 308); Luther, *Comm. Gen.* 20:4 (LW 3:333).

10. Augustine, *Reply to Faustus* 22.33 (NPNF¹ 4:285); Lyra, *Comm. Gen.* 12:13, 20:7-11 (fol. 61, 75); Pellican, *Comm. Gen.* 20:3 (fol. 25v); Vermigli, *Comm. Gen.* 12:20 (fol. 50v-51r); Luther, *Comm. Gen.* 20:2 (LW 3:320); Musculus, *Comm. Gen.* 12:13 (p. 309); Calvin, *Comm. Gen.* 20:7 (CTS 1:525).

11. Chrysostom says the fear of death was more acute in the Old Testament, before Christ came; see *Hom. Gen.* 32.14, 45.6 (FC 82:266, 473). Pellican (*Comm. Gen.* 20:11, fol. 26r) and Vermigli (*Comm. Gen.* 12:20, fol. 50v-51r) concur.

12. So Augustine, as well as Lyra, Denis, and Vermigli — though the later writers also express serious reservations about this argument's weaknesses.

13. Luther, Musculus, and Oecolampadius all ameliorate Abraham's lie by registering his good intention.

14. Josephus's account in *Antiquities* 1.162, 2.201 (LCL pp. 80, 250) is cited with some favor in comments on Gen. 12:10-20 by Lyra (fol. 61r), Pellican (fol. 16v), and Oecolampadius (fol. 131r). The stereotype about Egyptian morals is contested by Denis (1:209b), Luther (LW 2:305), and Musculus (p. 308) — the latter two on exegetical grounds. The argument from Esther 2:12 is found in Jerome's *Hebrew Questions on Genesis* 12:15 (Hayward ed., p. 44). It was taken up by Augustine (*Quaestiones in Heptateuchum* 1.26, PL 34:555) and others (all *Comm. Gen.* 12:13-20), including Lyra (fol. 61r), Vermigli (fol. 51r), and Luther (LW 2:304). Denis (1:210b) and Musculus (p. 309) found the argument far from persuasive.

15. Musculus, *Comm. Gen.* 12:13, 20:2 (pp. 309, 489). Vermigli anticipated this axiom in his lectures on Genesis; see Prop. 1n on Gen. 25–27 (*Loci*, p. 1012).

16. Calvin, *Comm. Gen.* 12:11, 20:2 (CTS 1:360, 521-22).

17. Luther, *Comm. Gen.* 27:34-35 (LW 5:149).

18. Luther, *Comm. Gen.* 30:25-43 (LW 5:365, 371, 385).

19. Calvin, *Comm. Gen.* 30:30, 37 (CTS 2:152, 155).

20. Luther, *Comm. Gen.* 12:11-13 (LW 2:291-94).

21. Luther, *Comm. Gen.* 38:16-22 (LW 7:31). Lyra makes a similar statement about incest at *Comm. Gen.* 19:32 (fol. 74r).

22. Denis, of course, proceeds to argue that what God dispensed Abraham from was something other than adultery; see his *Comm. Gen.* 30:4 (1:338b).

23. For a few exceptions, see my "Immoralities of the Patriarchs," p. 15 n. 19.

24. For this argument, see the commentaries on Gen. 19:8 of Denis (1:269a), Cajetan (p. 92), Luther (LW 3:259), and Musculus (p. 461). The argument is disputed by Musculus, as well as by Calvin, who thinks Lot merely seized the first defense that came to mind and so erred (CTS 1:499-500).

25. Luther, *Comm. Gen.* 19:9 (LW 3:260).

26. Ambrose, *De Abraham* 1.6.52 (PL 14:462).

27. Augustine, *Against Lying* 9.21 (NPNF¹ 3:489, abridged).

28. For a discussion of feminist perspectives on this issue, see *Writing the Wrongs*, pp. 180-85, 216-21.

29. After Augustine, some sort of mental disturbance is imputed to Lot by Lyra, Denis, Luther, Zwingli, Vermigli, and Musculus — but not by Calvin.

30. Augustine, *Against Lying* 9.22 (NPNF¹ 3:490, FC 16:149-50).

31. Pellican actually blamed Lot for seeking worldly affluence and thus preferring to live among the worst sort of people; see *Comm. Gen.* 19:8 (fol. 24r).

32. Luther, *Comm. Gen.* 19:8 (WA 43:59, my translation; cf. LW 3:258).

33. Calvin, *Comm. Gen.* 19:8 (CTS 1:499-500).

34. One clever hypothesis was that Abraham simply assumed — from the fact that she gave Hagar to him (16:2) — that *Sarah* must have received such permission.

35. Augustine, *Reply to Faustus* 4.2 (NPNF¹ 4:162).

36. Chrysostom, *Hom. Gen.* 56.12 (FC 87:124); Ambrose, *De Abraham* 1.4.24 (PL 14:451). The argument is in Augustine (*City of God* 16.38) and Jerome (*Against Jovinian* 1.24, NPNF² 6:364). Peter Lombard's variation (*4 Sent.* 33.1) is cited by Denis (*Comm. Gen.* 30, 1:342a) and Vermigli (*Comm. Gen.* 29:27, fol. 121r).

37. The patriarchs were husbands and fathers "not for the sake of this world, but for the sake of Christ" (Augustine, *On the Good of Marriage* 26.35, NPNF¹ 3:413). For Luther, see *Comm. Gen.* 4:1, 16:1, 30:1-3 (LW 1:237, 3:42-46, 5:328-34).

38. Cajetan, *Comm. Gen.* 16:2, 31:19 (pp. 79, 127). See John Cairncross, *After Polygamy Was Made a Sin: The Social History of Christian Polygamy* (London: Routledge & Kegan Paul, 1974), pp. 58-59; and my essay, "Patriarchs, Polygamy, and Private Resistance: John Calvin and Others on Breaking God's Rules," *Sixteenth Century Journal* 25 (1994): 3-27.

39. Luther to Robert Barnes, 3 Sept. 1531 (LW 50:33).

40. Luther, *Comm. Gen.* 16:1, 29:28, 30:1 (LW 42:578-81; 43:640-42, 652).

41. Hastings Eells, *The Attitude of Martin Bucer Toward the Bigamy of Philip of Hesse* (New Haven: Yale University Press, 1924), pp. 116, 120-30, 230-31, 236.

42. Bucer drew on the example of David (Eells, *Attitude of Martin Bucer*, pp. 33-42, 125).

43. Bucer set out three criteria — prayer, advice, conscience — in his *Argumenta Buceri pro et contra*, written late in 1539; see Eells, *Attitude of Bucer*, p. 100.

44. Bullinger excused the polygamy of Abraham and Jacob by special dispensation, yet also said their plural wives were not from God but from human error — from Sarah's presumption and Laban's fraud (Eells, *Attitude of Bucer*, pp. 181, 213-17).

45. Vermigli, *Comm. Gen.* 29:27 (fol. 120v-21r).

46. Eells, *Attitude of Bucer*, p. 220.

47. Calvin, *Serm. Eph.* 5:31-33 (p. 609); also see *Serm. Gen.* 27:3-9 (pp. 236-37), *Serm. 122 on Deut.* 21:15 (pp. 749-50), *Comm. Mal.* 2:15 (CTS 5:557), and *Comm. Matt.* 19:4-5 (CNTC 2:244-45), among other texts.

48. Cajetan, Luther, and Bucer had held just the opposite. See Calvin, *Comm. Gen.* 2:24, 29:27 (CTS 1:136-37, 2:133) and *Comm. Mal.* 2:16 (CTS 5:559).

49. Calvin, *Serm. 106 on Deut.* 17:17 (p. 652b); cf. *Serm. Titus* 1:6 (p. 1067).

50. For Vermigli, see *Comm. Gen.* 14 (fol. 56v). Because his arguments mirror Cal-

vin's, his views will not be presented separately. Note, however, that it is hard to tell which of these two Reformers might have used the other; see my "Patriarchs, Polygamy, and Popular Resistance," p. 17 n. 45.

51. Zwingli, *Comm. Gen.* 14 (ZSW 13:86).

52. Luther, *Comm. Gen.* 14:15 (LW 2:375). No appeal to Genesis 14 survives in Müntzer's writings, though he surely did see himself in the mantle of the patriarchs, the judges (including Gideon and Samson), and other biblical heroes; see Letters 71, 72, 84, 88, and 89 in *The Collected Works of Thomas Müntzer,* ed. Peter Matheson (Edinburgh: T. & T. Clark, 1988), pp. 135-36, 151, 156-57.

53. Luther, *Comm. Gen.* 30:1 (LW 5:325, emphasis added).

54. In his comments on the patriarchal misdeeds in the book of Genesis (up to twenty instances), Calvin appeals to special dispensation only three times.

55. Calvin, *Comm. Gen.* 14:13 (CTS 1:383); the same excuse is applied to Moses.

56. Calvin draws a parallel from Abraham's war not only to Moses' slaying of the Egyptian but also to Israel's deliverance by Gideon, Jephthah, and Samson; see *Comm. Gen.* 14:13 (CTS 1:383) and *Serm. Gen.* 14:13-17 (pp. 8-10). "Wait for a Moses" represents common advice, given by Luther (to the peasants, in "Admonition to Peace," LW 46:35), by Zwingli (*Commentary on True and False Religion* 27, ZSW 3:880), and by Calvin (*Institutes* 4.20.29-30).

57. Calvin mentions this as a possibility in his *Institutes* (4.20.30) from the earliest edition through the last: "Sometimes [God] raises up open avengers from among his servants . . . to deliver his people." But the expectation remains problematic, especially in light of Calvin's dislike for enthusiasts and conspirators.

58. Beza, *Traité du droit des Magistrats sur leurs suiets,* cited by Roland H. Bainton, "The Immoralities of the Patriarchs according to the Exegesis of the Late Middle Ages and of the Reformation," *Harvard Theological Review* 23 (1930): 48 n. 40a. Beza's remark licensed private resistance only against usurpers, not "legitimate" tyrants; see Robert M. Kingdon, *Myths about the St. Bartholomew's Day Massacres, 1572-1576* (Cambridge: Harvard University Press, 1988), pp. 153-59, 165, 181.

59. For Luther, see Bainton, "Immoralities of the Patriarchs," p. 44. Calvin replied to demands for miracles in his Prefatory Address to Francis I in the 1536 *Institutes.*

60. For a more detailed account, see *Writing the Wrongs,* pp. 247-49.

61. See their comments at notes 21 and 22, above.

62. Calvin, *Comm. Exod.* 1:18 (CTS 1:35).

63. Luther, *Comm. Gen.* 37:9 (LW 6:329-36).

64. Calvin, *Comm. Gen.* 25:22 (CTS 2:43).

65. Such groups can easily be found on the Internet, as at www.polygamy.net.

66. Calvin, *Comm. Exod.* 1:18 (CTS 1:35, altered).

Notes to Chapter Five, "Gomer and Hosea"

1. "Jezreel," like the other names, is a wordplay. The name signals *judgment* in 1:4, where God promises to punish the house of Jehu for "the blood of Jezreel," the town where Jehu murdered Ahab and Jezebel (though the account in 2 Kings 9–10 faults Jehu not for his many murders but for neglecting the law of God). In Hosea 1:11 and 2:22, Jezreel indicates *blessing*, presumably playing on the suggestion of prosperity in the name's meaning of "God sows." See Carolyn J. Pressler, "Jezreel," *Anchor Bible Dictionary* (6 vols.; New York: Doubleday, 1992), 3:849.

2. T. Drorah Setel, "Prophets and Pornography: Female Sexual Imagery in Hosea," in *Feminist Interpretation of the Bible,* ed. Letty M. Russell (Philadelphia: Westminster, 1985), pp. 86-95.

3. Setel made many of these points, but the debate has been continued by others, including Athalya Brenner, "On Prophetic Propaganda and the Politics of 'Love': The Case of Jeremiah," and Fokkelien van Dijk-Hemmes, "The Metaphorization of Woman in Prophetic Speech: An Analysis of Ezekiel 23," to whom Robert P. Carroll responded in "Desire under the Terebinths: On Pornographic Representation in the Prophets"; all three essays are gathered in *A Feminist Companion to the Latter Prophets,* ed. Athalya Brenner (Sheffield: Sheffield Academic Press, 1995).

4. Renita J. Weems, *Battered Love: Marriage, Sex, and Violence in the Hebrew Prophets* (Minneapolis: Fortress, 1995), p. 8.

5. Carroll, "Desire under the Terebinths," p. 300.

6. Renita J. Weems, "Gomer: Victim of Violence or Victim of Metaphor?" *Semeia* 47 (1989): 87, 89-90.

7. Weems, *Battered Love,* pp. 111, 104.

8. Weems, *Battered Love,* p. 107.

9. Weems, *Battered Love,* p. 109.

10. J. Cheryl Exum, "Prophetic Pornography," in *Plotted, Shot, and Painted: Cultural Representations of Biblical Women* (Sheffield: Sheffield Academic Press, 1996), pp. 112-14; italics mine.

11. Naomi Graetz, "God Is to Israel as Husband Is to Wife: The Metaphoric Battering of Hosea's Wife," in *A Feminist Companion to the Latter Prophets,* pp. 141-42.

12. Gail A. Yee, "Hosea," in *The Women's Bible Commentary,* ed. Carol A. Newsom and Sharon H. Ringe (Louisville: Westminster John Knox, 1992), p. 200.

13. Yvonne Sherwood, *The Prostitute and the Prophet: Hosea's Marriage in Literary-Theoretical Perspective* (Sheffield: Sheffield Academic Press, 1996), pp. 298-99.

14. Carroll, "Desire under the Terebinths," pp. 277, 287.

15. Raymond C. Ortlund, Jr., *Whoredom: God's Unfaithful Wife in Biblical Theology* (Grand Rapids: Eerdmans, 1996), p. 10.

16. Ortlund, *Whoredom,* pp. 181-82.

17. For example, Brenner, "Prophetic Propaganda," p. 273; and van Dijk-Hemmes, "Metaphorization of Woman," p. 254.

18. As recognized in Ortland's book by occasional disclaimers and apologies for the crassness of language in the prophets, which he justifies as appropriate to the crime of religious infidelity (*Whoredom,* pp. 8, 102 n. 2, 125 n. 70; cf. 180 n. 1).

19. John L. Farthing, "Holy Harlotry: Jerome Zanchi and the Exegetical History of Gomer (Hosea 1–3)," in *Biblical Interpretation in the Era of the Reformation,* ed. Richard A. Muller and John L. Thompson (Grand Rapids: Eerdmans, 1996), esp. pp. 295-303; and Sherwood, *The Prostitute and the Prophet,* pp. 40-82.

20. Other storehouses of exegetical opinion, all in Latin, are the monumental seventeenth-century commentaries of Matthew Poole and Cornelius à Lapide.

21. Farthing's study follows Zanchi's fourfold analysis, but I have conflated two of those categories, following a hint in "Holy Harlotry," p. 301; see n. 28 below.

22. ANF has "actual works" for the Latin *operationibus,* which could be rendered more simply as "by actions" or "deeds"; Irenaeus, *Against Heresies* 4.20.12 (ANF 1:492, PG 7:1042).

23. Augustine, *Reply to Faustus* 22.80 (NPNF[1] 4:304), alluding to Matt. 21:31. A literal marriage is also implied in *On Christian Doctrine* 3.12.18 (NPNF[1] 2:562); while *On Baptism against the Donatists* 3.19.26 (NPNF[1] 4:444) reads Gomer's recidivism in Hosea 2:5 as a type of false Israelites and thus also of false Christians.

24. As both Zanchi and Farthing attest ("Holy Harlotry," p. 296). Jerome's second thoughts occur in his commentary on Hosea 1:2; the work is not translated, though the preface is summarized in NPNF[2] 6:501.

25. Cornelius à Lapide, *Commentaria in Scripturam Sacram* (20 vols.; Paris: Ludwig Vivès, 1854-70), 13:283b. Lapide's work dates before 1637, the year of his death.

26. Matthew Poole, *Synopsis Criticorum* (5 vols.; London, 1673), 3:1617. Note that his shorter, posthumous, English commentary does not choose between the literal and the parabolic view; see *A Commentary on the Whole Bible* (1685; 3 vol. reprint ed.; London: Banner of Truth, 1962), 2:850b.

27. Farthing, "Holy Harlotry," pp. 295-98. Zanchi further notes that the scandal of begetting children of a prostitute is resolved if Hosea actually adopted Gomer's *existing* children rather than fathering his own. Zanchi's commentary on Hosea is found in the fifth volume of his *Opera Theologica* (Geneva, 1605); here, see pp. 6-9. For a more densely detailed (unfortunately, Latin) account of this view's strengths and weaknesses, see Poole, *Synopsis Criticorum* 3:1616-18.

28. Although Zanchi distinguished between the visionary view and an allegorical view, I have conflated the two views, since there is no practical difference between a fundamentally allegorical vision and a divinely-inspired allegory.

29. Zanchi, *Comm. Hosea* 1:3 (*Opera* 5:8); the Latin text is excerpted in Farthing, "Holy Harlotry," p. 298 n. 28.

30. Translation is from *The Targum of the Minor Prophets,* trans. Kevin J. Cathcart and Robert P. Gordon (The Aramaic Bible 14; Wilmington, Del.: Michael Glazier, 1989), p. 35. Sherwood discusses how the Targum linked "[daughter of] Diblaim" to a Hebrew

root-word meaning *fig,* so as to dissolve Gomer's family-name into a wholly unrelated phrase, "leaves of a fig-tree" (*The Prostitute and the Prophet,* p. 42).

31. A. Lipshitz, *The Commentary of Rabbi Abraham Ibn Ezra on Hosea* (New York: Sepher-Hermon Press, 1988), p. 20; as quoted by Sherwood, *The Prostitute and the Prophet,* p. 48. Sherwood discusses all the named rabbinic sources in the preceding paragraph in somewhat more detail; see pp. 40-50.

32. Quoted in Farthing, "Holy Harlotry," pp. 301-2.

33. See Lapide, *Commentaria* 13:283a; Poole, *Synopsis Criticorum,* 3:1617; also John Downame, *Lectures vpon the foure first chapters of the prophecie of Hosea* (London, 1608), pp. 31-36; Jeremiah Burroughs, *An exposition of the prophesie of Hosea* (London, 1652), pp. 18-21; George Hutcheson, *A brief exposition on the XII. smal prophets . . . Hosea, Joel, & Amos* (London, 1654), p. 6.

34. Luther, *Comm. Hosea* 1:1 (WA 13:3, my translation; cf. LW 18:4).

35. Calvin, *Comm. Hosea* 1:2 (CTS-prophets 1:45).

36. As in Calvin's passing reference to the prophet's "household."

37. In these 1524 lectures, Luther does not return to the charade of Hosea and Gomer (at least in chapters 1-3). Strangely, his brief gloss on 3:1 reads, "The Lord is again offering him a genuine adulteress, but he does not lie with her" (LW 18:16).

38. "If he had married a wife such as is here described, he ought to have concealed himself for life rather than to undertake the Prophetic office"; Calvin, *Comm. Hosea* 1:2 (CTS-prophets 1:44).

39. Lapide (*Commentaria* 13:286) cites Ambrose of Milan as his primary source for this twofold allegory, with support from Tertullian, Augustine, Prosper, and Jerome.

40. I discuss these concepts in greater detail in *Writing the Wrongs,* pp. 243-49.

41. See Chapter One, pp. 26-28.

42. Lapide, *Commentaria* 13:285.

43. Downame, *Lectures vpon . . . Hosea,* pp. 31, 35.

44. Farthing, "Holy Harlotry," pp. 312, 304-8.

45. Calvin, *Comm. Hosea* 2:1-5 (CTS-prophets 1:85; emended, italics mine).

46. This application is not uncommon among precritical commentators. Examples drawn from the writings of Musculus, Luther, and Calvin can be found in Thompson, *John Calvin and the Daughters of Sarah* (Geneva: Droz, 1992), pp. 174-79.

47. For details, sources, and some related discussion, see *John Calvin and the Daughters of Sarah,* pp. 9-10; and Chapter Seven, below.

48. Notable evidence is cited by Steven E. Ozment, *When Fathers Ruled: Family Life in Reformation Europe* (Cambridge: Harvard University Press, 1983), pp. 50-55.

49. Natalie Zemon Davis, "City Women and Religious Change," in *Society and Culture in Early Modern France* (Stanford: Stanford University Press, 1975), p. 90.

50. Calvin, *Comm. Hosea* 3:1 (CTS-prophets 1:123).

51. Exum, "Prophetic Pornography," pp. 122-28.

52. Ortlund, *Whoredom,* pp. 181-85.

53. Yvonne Sherwood, "Boxing Gomer: Controlling the Deviant Woman in Hosea

1-3," in Brenner, ed., *Feminist Companion to the Latter Prophets,* p. 105. Sherwood also describes some later "romantic" rewrites of Gomer in *The Prostitute and the Prophet,* pp. 53-66.

54. So, for instance, the New Living Translation, the Contemporary English Version, and Today's New International Version.

Notes to Chapter Six, "Silent Prophetesses?"

1. Tertullian, "On the Apparel of Women," ANF 4:14-25. No one should read this often-excerpted statement without considering also what Tertullian says about men; see especially F. Forrester Church, "Sex and Salvation in Tertullian," *Harvard Theological Review* 68 (1975): 83-101.

2. Zwingli, "The Preaching Office" (SWZ 2:171); Bullinger, *Comm. Acts* 2:14-21, 21:7-9 (fol. 25, 260) and *Comm. 1 Cor.* 11:4-5 (p. 200); and Pellican, *Comm. 1 Cor.* 11:4-6 (pp. 239-40). For detailed discussion and documentation for this chapter, see Thompson, *John Calvin and the Daughters of Sarah* (Geneva: Droz, 1992), pp. 65-105 and 187-226.

3. Bullinger, *Comm. Acts* 21:7-9 (fol. 260).

4. Chrysostom, *Greet Priscilla and Aquila* 1.3; trans. Elizabeth A. Clark, *Women in the Early Church* (Wilmington, Del.: Michael Glazier, 1983), pp. 158-60.

5. Origen's remarks survive in a fragment of his commentary on 1 Corinthians. ACCS-NT 7:146 omits the lines that identify the fragment's polemical character; a fuller translation is found in Roger Gryson, *The Ministry of Women in the Early Church* (Collegeville, Minn.: Liturgical Press, 1976), pp. 28-29.

6. So, e.g., Pelagius, *Comm. 1 Cor.* 11:5-6, *Comm. 1 Tim.* 2:12 (pp. 188, 482).

7. Aquinas, *Comm. 1 Cor.* 11:4, 14:34 (Marietti ed., pp. 346, 402); *Summa Theologica,* III.supp. 39.1 *ad* 1.

8. Cajetan, *Comm. 1 Cor.* 11:3, 14:34 (pp. 122, 139).

9. Calvin, *Comm. Acts* 18:26, 21:9; *Comm. 1 Cor.* 11:5 (CNTC 7:145, 195; 9:231).

10. Vermigli's discussion of 1 Cor. 11:5 occurs in his consideration of the prophet Deborah, in his *Comm. Jud.* 4:4 (fol. 93). His conviction that 1 Cor. 14:34 does not "cancel" 11:5 (as Cajetan argued, above) was shared by Musculus, for whom Paul's injunction to silence "does not extinguish the Spirit by which inspired women prophesied by predicting the future." Musculus clearly has in mind various women mentioned in Acts; see his *Comm. 1 Cor.* 11:4, 14:34 (col. 383-84, 590).

11. Calvin, *Comm. 1 Tim.* 2:11 (CNTC 10:217).

12. Vermigli, *Comm. Jud.* 4:5 (fol. 93v).

13. Although it is difficult to correlate these views with the activities of specific sixteenth-century women, the known ministry of lay women was certainly a factor. See *John Calvin and the Daughters of Sarah,* pp. 54-62; and my essay, "Patriarchy and Prophetesses: Tradition and Innovation in Vermigli's Doctrine of Woman," in *Peter*

Martyr Vermigli and the European Reformations, ed. Frank A. James III (Leiden: Brill, 2004), pp. 139-58.

14. This thesis is argued by Theodore N. Thomas, *Women against Hitler: Christian Resistance in the Third Reich* (Westport, Conn.: Praeger, 1995).

15. Bullinger's exegesis is in his *Comm. 1 Cor.* 11:4-16 (pp. 199-202); his outburst against unveiled women occurs in *Der Christliche Ehestand,* available in English as *The Christian State of Matrimony* (STC 4053; London, 1575), fol. 60v.

16. Aquinas, *Comm. 1 Cor.* 11:6, 14, 16 (Marietti ed, pp. 347, 350); the editor refers the reader to Augustine's letter to Casulanus (Epistle 36, NPNF[1] 1:265).

17. Denis the Carthusian, *Comm. 1 Cor.* 11:13-14, 16 (p. 177).

18. Cajetan, *Comm. 1 Cor.* 11:6, 16-17 (pp. 122-23).

19. Gaigny, *Comm. 1 Cor.* 11:16 (fol. 54); Guilliaud, *Comm. 1 Cor.* 11:16 (fol. 122); Catharinus, *Comm. 1 Cor.* 11:16 (pp. 191-92).

20. Erasmus, *Paraphrase* of 1 Cor. 11:2, 16 (*Opera* 7:894, 896).

21. Luther, *Instructions for the Visitors of Parish Pastors* (LW 40:310); *Comm. 1 Tim.* 2:9-10 (LW 28:274-75); *Infiltrating and Clandestine Preachers* (LW 40:393).

22. Pellican, *Comm. 1 Cor.* 11:3-4 (pp. 239-40).

23. Vermigli, *Comm. 1 Cor.* 11:3 (fol. 284-85).

24. Vermigli, *Comm. 1 Cor.* 14:37-38 (fol. 395).

25. Musculus, *Comm. 1 Cor.* 11:3, 11:14-15, 14:40 (col. 376, 395-96, 601-2).

26. Calvin, *Comm. 1 Cor.* 11:14 (CNTC 9:235), emphasis added.

27. Calvin, *Comm. 1 Cor.* 11:5-6 (CNTC 9:231).

28. Calvin, *Comm. 1 Cor.* 11:10 (CNTC 9:233). Malachi 2:7 says, "the lips of a priest should guard knowledge, and people should seek instruction from his mouth, for he is the messenger [= 'angel'] of the LORD of hosts." This identification can be found at least as early as the fourth century, in Pelagius (*Comm. 1 Cor.* 11:10, p. 188) and Ambrosiaster (*Comm. 1 Cor.* 11:8-10, CSEL 81/2:122-23), among others.

29. Cf. Calvin, *Institutes* 4.10.31, with what Melanchthon argued in §28 of the Augsburg Confession, above.

30. Which happens to be the apt title of a fine study by Kari Elisabeth Børresen, *Subordination and Equivalence: The Nature and Role of Woman in Augustine and Thomas Aquinas* (Washington, D.C.: University Press of America, 1981).

31. Augustine also found other theological correspondences. For instance, if our minds are images of God, and God is a Trinity, then our minds might well bear a trinitarian imprint — say, in the mind's structure as memory, intellect, and volition. Augustine's trinitarian psychology generated great interest among commentators, but it doesn't bear directly on the present discussion.

32. An article by David G. Hunter explains Ambrosiaster's exegesis in terms of a fourth-century dispute over the influence that ascetic women had come to have in the Roman church. See "The Paradise of Patriarchy: Ambrosiaster on Woman as (Not) God's Image," *Journal of Theological Studies* n.s. 43 (1992): 447-69.

33. See Kari Elisabeth Børresen, "Imago Dei, privilège masculin? Interprétation

Augustinienne et Pseudo-Augustinienne de *Gen* 1,27 et *1 Cor* 11,7," *Augustinianum* 25 (1985): 213-34; and Ida Raming, *The Exclusion of Women from the Priesthood: Divine Law or Sex Discrimination? A Historical Investigation of the Juridical and Doctrinal Foundations of the* Code of Canon Law, *canon 968, §1* (Metuchen, N.J.: Scarecrow, 1976).

34. Augustine discusses the image of God in women in at least five different works. His fullest discussions are in *The Literal Meaning of Genesis* 3.22.34 and *The Trinity* 12.7.10-12. See also *City of God* 15.7 and *The Work of Monks* 32.40.

35. Augustine offers yet another reading of 1 Cor. 11:7 in *The Literal Meaning of Genesis* 11.42 (ACW 42:175), conjecturing that Paul could have been thinking of woman as created, that is, at a moment when she had not yet received (through her husband's tutelage) the knowledge of God in which God's image consists. This terse speculation doesn't conflict with what the sexes symbolize, though it does betray Augustine's feelings about woman's mental inferiority.

36. Denis, *Comm. 1 Cor.* 11:7, 11 (pp. 176-77).

37. Luther makes this distinction in his earlier lectures on Genesis (WA 42:51); see David Cairns, *The Image of God in Man* (London: SCM, 1953), p. 122.

38. Musculus, *Comm. 1 Cor.* 11:7 (col. 389). Musculus here cedes the image of God to women, evidently as a lesser dominion.

39. See Capito, *Hexemeron Dei Opus* (Strasbourg, 1539), fol. 287v-288r; and the comments on 1 Cor. 11:7 of Bullinger (p. 210), Catharinus (p. 190b), and Vermigli (fol. 286).

40. Calvin, *Comm. Gen.* 2:18 (CTS 1:129).

41. Calvin, *Comm. 1 Cor.* 11:7 (CNTC 9:232, altered).

42. Calvin, *Comm. 1 Cor.* 11:4 (CNTC 9:230, altered for precision).

43. Calvin, *Serm. Job* 3:3 (pp. 54-55).

Notes to Chapter Seven, "Divorce"

1. The contest over the ethics and effects of divorce is heated and the literature is vast. My remarks here draw on Constance Ahrons, *The Good Divorce: Keeping Your Family Together When Your Marriage Comes Apart* (New York: HarperCollins, 1994); Barbara Dafoe Whitehead, *The Divorce Culture* (New York: Alfred A. Knopf, 1997); and Judith S. Wallerstein, Julia M. Lewis, and Sandra Blakeslee, *The Unexpected Legacy of Divorce: A Twenty-Five Year Landmark Study* (New York: Hyperion, 2000).

2. For a sampling of the diversity of opinion even among evangelicals regarding divorce and remarriage, see H. Wayne House, ed., *Divorce and Remarriage: Four Christian Views* (Downers Grove, Ill.: InterVarsity Press, 1990).

3. Westminster Confession of Faith (1647) 24.5-6.

4. Westminster Confession of Faith 26.5-7; numbering and quotations follow the text adopted by the Presbyterian Church in the United States.

5. Mentioned in Matt. 5:31, developed in Matt. 19:3-9 and Mark 10:2-9.

6. Remarkably, while all the words of Jesus make it into the Revised Common

Lectionary (at least as presented by Mark and Matthew), the passages from Moses and Paul mostly do not.

7. A brief survey of these patristic sources may be found in David Instone-Brewer, *Divorce and Remarriage in the Bible: The Social and Literary Context* (Grand Rapids: Eerdmans, 2002), pp. 238-55. Longer excerpts are provided by David G. Hunter, ed., *Marriage in the Early Church* (Minneapolis: Augsburg Fortress, 1992). See also Roderick Phillips, *Putting Asunder: A History of Divorce in Western Society* (Cambridge: Cambridge University Press, 1988), pp. 15-30; and John Witte, Jr., *From Sacrament to Contract: Marriage, Religion, and Law in the Western Tradition* (Louisville: Westminster John Knox, 1997), pp. 19-22.

8. Athenagoras, *A Plea Regarding Christians* 33 (LCC 1:337). Also in ANF 2:146.

9. *Shepherd of Hermas*, Fourth Commandment §29 [IV.1.6]; ET from Bart D. Ehrman, *The Apostolic Fathers* (LCL 25), p. 246. Also in ANF 2:21.

10. Origen's exposition of the Sermon on the Mount will be taken up shortly.

11. Instone-Brewer offers representative texts from Jerome and Chrysostom; the passage from Romans 7 is decisive for Chrysostom. Tertullian's *earlier* writings allowed remarriage to widows and, perhaps, those separated from an adulterous spouse; see *Divorce and Remarriage*, pp. 252-53, 245-46.

12. Origen, *Comm. Matt.* 14.25 (ANF 10:511).

13. Origen, *Comm. Matt.* 14.18 (ANF 10:507).

14. Origen, *Comm. Matt.* 14.19 (ANF 10:507-8).

15. Origen, *Comm. Matt.* 14.23 (ANF 10:510).

16. Origen, *Comm. Matt.* 14.24 (ANF 10:511).

17. Instone-Brewer, *Divorce and Remarriage*, pp. 250-53.

18. Augustine, *Sermon on the Mount* 1.14.39, 1.16.48 (NPNF[1] 6:17, 21; FC 11:59, 70). In 420, Augustine maintained this restriction against the alternate reading of Pollentius, who reconciled Paul and Jesus by taking 1 Cor. 7:10-11, 39 as forbidding separated spouses to remarry *except* when the separation was precipitated by a partner's fornication — in which case the partner, as an adulterer, would be regarded as spiritually "dead." See *On Adulterous Marriages* 1.1.1, 2.2.2 (FC 27:62, 103; WSA I/9:142, 167).

19. Augustine, *Sermon on the Mount* 1.16.44 (my translation; cf. FC 11:67, NPNF[1] 6:20).

20. Augustine, *Retractations* 1.18.6 (FC 60:83, altered; Latin text in PL 32:616).

21. Augustine, *Sermon on the Mount* 1.16.49 (NPNF[1] 6:21, FC 11:70). He adds another complicated and inconclusive case in 1.16.50, drawn from recent events.

22. Augustine, *On the Good of Marriage* 21 [18] (WSA I/9:49; cf. NPNF[1] 3:408).

23. Augustine, *On Marriage and Concupiscence* 1.11 (NPNF[1] 5:268).

24. Augustine, *On the Good of Marriage* 32 [24] (NPNF[1] 3:412, WSA I/9:56). The marriage bond is also like the sacrament of baptism, which persists even if a person is excommunicated; see *On Adulterous Marriages* 2.4.5 (WSA I/9:168, FC 27:105).

25. Augustine, *On the Good of Marriage* 7 [8] (NPNF[1] 3:402, WSA I/9:39).

26. Augustine, *On Faith and Works* 19.35 (FC 27:266; cf. PL 40:221: "venialiter . . .

fallatur" and ACW 48:43). Instone-Brewer finds Augustine "nuanced and balanced" here (*Divorce and Remarriage in the Bible*, p. 255), but Gregory J. Lombardo locates Augustine's definitive position in a later work (see ACW 48:98 at n. 198).

27. My discussion in this section is indebted to Phillips, *Putting Asunder*, pp. 18-27.

28. Phillips, *Putting Asunder*, p. 24.

29. Phillips, *Putting Asunder*, p. 29.

30. Witte, *From Sacrament to Contract*, pp. 34-35.

31. *Erasmus' Annotations on the New Testament: Acts — Romans — I and II Corinthians: Facsimile of the Final Latin Text with All Earlier Variants*, ed. Anne Reeve and M. A. Screech (Leiden: Brill, 1990), pp. 467-81. Hereafter cited as *Ann. 1 Cor.*

32. Erasmus, *Ann. 1 Cor.* 7:39 (p. 467).

33. Erasmus, *Ann. 1 Cor.* 7:39 (p. 467), where Origen is credited as his source.

34. Erasmus, *Ann. 1 Cor.* 7:6, 25 (pp. 462, 464).

35. Erasmus, *Ann. 1 Cor.* 7:39 (p. 475).

36. Erasmus, *Ann. 1 Cor.* 7:39 (p. 479).

37. The role of equity in Erasmus's theology on precisely this point is underscored by the fine study of H. J. Selderhuis, *Marriage and Divorce in the Thought of Martin Bucer* (Kirksville, Mo.: Thomas Jefferson University Press, 1999), pp. 41-42.

38. Erasmus, *Ann. 1 Cor.* 7:39 (p. 481).

39. Translated by David F. Wright, in *Common Places of Martin Bucer* (Appleford, England: Sutton Courtenay Press, 1972), p. 419. I used the Latin text of Bucer's *In Sacra Quatuor Evangelia, Enarrationes* (Basel, 1536), p. 399; cited hereafter as *Comm. Matt.* 19. See also Selderhuis, *Marriage and Divorce*, p. 275.

40. Erasmus himself had wondered why we read the Sermon on the Mount so selectively, taking Jesus' words on divorce with full rigor, while we mitigate what he taught about swearing, anger, forgiving others, litigation, revenge, etc., writing them off as "counsels of perfection." See Erasmus, *Ann. 1 Cor.* 7:39 (p. 474). Bucer makes the same point on p. 398 of his *Comm. Matt.* 19 (*Common Places*, p. 419).

41. Bucer, *Comm. Matt.* 19 (p. 390); ET from *Common Places*, pp. 403-4.

42. Bucer, *Comm. Matt.* 19 (p. 390); ET from *Common Places*, p. 404.

43. Bucer, *Comm. Matt.* 19 (p. 395). For alternate translations of some of these terms, see *Common Places*, p. 413.

44. Bucer, *Comm. Matt.* 19 (pp. 392, 397); *Common Places*, pp. 406-7, 418. Bucer's specific recommendations are probably reflected in the legislation proposed under Edward VI (but never implemented), which would have allowed divorce for sustained cruelty and hostility but denied private separations, referring cases to judges. See *The Reformation of the Ecclesiastical Laws of England, 1552*, ed. James C. Spalding (Kirksville, Mo.: Sixteenth Century Journal Publishers, 1992), pp. 99-106.

45. Bucer, *Comm. Matt.* 19 (p. 398); ET from *Common Places*, p. 417.

46. Bucer, *Comm. Matt.* 19 (p. 398); ET from *Common Places*, pp. 417-18.

47. Bucer, *Comm. Matt.* 19 (p. 396); ET from *Common Places*, p. 415.

48. Bucer, *Comm. Matt.* 19 (p. 398); ET from *Common Places*, pp. 418-19.

49. Heinrich Bullinger, *In Priorem D. Pauli ad Corinthios Epistolam* (Zurich, 1534), p. 168. The work reappeared in the first of his two volumes on all the epistles, *In Omnes Apostolicas Epistolas, Divi Videlicet Pavli xiiii. et vii. Canonicas, Commentarii* (Zurich, 1537), from which my references are drawn, cited as *Comm. 1 Cor.*

50. Bullinger, *Comm. 1 Cor.* 7:12 (p. 169).

51. Bullinger, *Comm. 1 Cor.* 7:12 (p. 169).

52. Bullinger's distinction is hardly original; antecedents can be found in Lombard and earlier still in Ambrosiaster.

53. Bullinger has essentially dressed up and more or less systematized what Ambrosiaster and Lombard had much earlier conveyed in two words: "not the Lord" really means "not the Lord *proprio ore* — by his own mouth."

54. Cf. Bullinger, *Comm. 1 Cor.* 7:12, 40 (pp. 169, 177), with Ambrosiaster on the same verses (CSEL 81/2:74, 91); at the latter verse Ambrosiaster calls attention to Paul's "humble words." Lombard and Aquinas make similar comments.

55. That the Apostle has worked deductively is suggested in 1 Cor. 7:10, 25, where Paul's remarks are framed, in effect, as glosses or amplifications of Jesus' words in Matthew 19; see Bullinger, *Comm. 1 Cor.* 7:12, 25 (pp. 168, 173).

56. Bullinger easily could have obtained his notion of the rule of faith and love from Augustine or other church fathers; he clearly used it throughout his career. For an early instance, see Heinold Fast and John H. Yoder, "How to Deal with Anabaptists: An Unpublished Letter of Heinrich Bullinger," *Mennonite Quarterly Review* 33 (1959): 83-95. The second chapter of his Second Helvetic Confession (1566) offers this rule as part of a general apology for Reformed hermeneutics.

57. Bullinger, *Comm. Matt.* (Zurich, 1542), fol. 179v; quoted in V. Norskov Olsen, *The New Testament Logia on Divorce: A Study of Their Interpretation from Erasmus to Milton* (Tübingen: J. C. B. Mohr [Paul Siebeck], 1971), p. 71; punctuation altered.

58. Details in Olsen, *Logia on Divorce* (pp. 74-75), who cites a modern printing of *Der christliche Ehestand* (Zurich, 1854), pp. 137-41, and the Parker Society Translation (1850) of the *Decades*, 3:228.

59. Bullinger mentions poisoning in *Der Christliche Ehestand* §25 (*vergäben*, but the text is obscure in my fiche copy of the 1540 Zurich printing); for an ET, see *The christian state of matrimony* (STC 4053; London, 1575), fol. 94v. Erasmus mentions poisoning (*veneficium*) in *Ann. 1 Cor.* 7:39 (p. 468), citing Origen [*Comm. Matt.* 14.24].

60. Calvin, *Comm. 1 Cor.* 7:12 (CNTC 9:147).

61. Calvin, *Comm. 1 Cor.* 7:25 (CNTC 9:155-56).

62. Olsen argues that Calvin similarly harmonized Moses, so that when a husband dismissed his wife with a "writ of divorce," he was implicitly confessing his own infidelity. In other words, the divorce was justified by his adultery, just as Jesus would later teach. See Olsen, *Logia on Divorce*, p. 101, where he discusses Calvin's *Harmony of the Pentateuch* on Deut. 24:1-4 (CTS 3:94) and other texts.

63. Calvin, *Comm. 1 Cor.* 7:11 (CNTC 9:147). The grounds Calvin dismisses include abuse, abandonment, and (sexually) incapacitating illness.

64. Calvin's advice is similar in his *Comm. Matt.* 19:9: "A remedy is not to be sought outside God's word. I also add that they will never lack the gift of continency if they give themselves to be ruled by the Lord and follow what He commands. . . . Those who walk in his ways never lack the help of the Spirit. . . . Even if everything does not turn out as he hoped, yet the man who has done this has fulfilled his part in the matter; and if anything is lacking, it will be made good by God's help. To go beyond is simply to tempt God" (CNTC 2:246-47). Calvin also repudiates his contemporaries' argument that secular authorities can make rules that relax what the Bible teaches: "The magistrate who gives a man permission to divorce his wife is abusing his power"; see *Comm. Matt.* 19:6 (CNTC 2:245).

65. Olsen, *Logia on Divorce*, p. 99; citing CO 10:110-14.

66. Robert M. Kingdon, *Adultery and Divorce in Calvin's Geneva* (Cambridge: Harvard University Press, 1995), p. 4.

67. See the case of Jean Bietrix in Kingdon, *Adultery and Divorce*, p. 111.

68. See *Calvin's Ecclesiastical Advice*, ed. Mary Beaty and Benjamin W. Farley (Louisville: Westminster John Knox, 1991), pp. 131-33; cf. pp. 61, 148.

69. Calvin, *Harmony of the Pentateuch* on Deut. 24:1-4 (CTS 3:94).

70. Hubert Jedin, *A History of the Council of Trent*, vol. 2: *The First Sessions at Trent, 1545-47* (London: Thomas Nelson and Sons, 1961), p. 169.

71. Catharinus argues his opinion both in his commentary on the Pauline epistles and in his writings for the Council of Trent. See Ambrosius Catharinus Politus, *Comm. 1 Cor.* 7:10-11 (Venice, 1551), p. 172b; and *De matrimonio quaestiones*, in idem, *Enarrationes, Assertationes, Disputationes* (Rome, 1551-52; facsimile reprint, Ridgewood, N.J.: Gregg, 1964), third book, cols. 275-77, 291-92. For the declaration of Trent, see *The Canons and Decrees of the Council of Trent*, trans. H. J. Schroeder, O.P. (Rockford, Ill.: Tan Books, 1978), p. 182.

72. Catharinus, *Comm. 1 Cor.* 7:10-11 (pp. 172b-173a).

73. Kingdon's observation (*Adultery and Divorce*, p. 89) is especially poignant in the context of Genevan history, in that it describes one of Bucer's main arguments — but also a position Calvin wished to avoid, despite its practical inevitability.

Notes to Chapter Eight, "Wasn't Adam Deceived?"

1. For a chart of when various Christian churches and groups began to ordain women, see Mark Chaves, *Ordaining Women: Culture and Conflict in Religious Organizations* (Cambridge: Harvard University Press, 1997), pp. 16-17. Websites such as http://www.guide2womenleaders.com/Chronolgy_Ordination.htm (accessed September 13, 2005) keep such lists up to date, though often without documentation.

2. Details of the arguments for and against the Pauline authorship of the Pastoral Epistles can be found in most scholarly commentaries and New Testament introductions; see, for example, Raymond F. Collins, *1 & 2 Timothy and Titus: A Commentary* (Louisville: Westminster John Knox, 2002), pp. 1-14.

3. Linda L. Belleville takes this approach in *The IVP Women's Bible Commentary,* ed. Catherine Clark Kroeger and Mary J. Evans (Downers Grove, Ill.: InterVarsity Press, 2002), s.v. "1 Timothy," pp. 738, 741. More details are found in her essay, "Teaching and Usurping Authority: 1 Tim. 2:11-15," in *Discovering Biblical Equality: Complementarity without Hierarchy,* ed. Ronald W. Pierce and Rebecca Merrill Groothuis (Downers Grove, Ill.: InterVarsity Press, 2004), pp. 205-23.

4. On 1 Timothy, see (in addition to Belleville, previous note) Richard Clark Kroeger and Catherine Clark Kroeger, *I Suffer Not a Woman: Rethinking 1 Timothy 2:11-15 in Light of Ancient Evidence* (Grand Rapids: Baker, 1992). Also see Catherine Clark Kroeger, "1 Corinthians," in *IVP Women's Bible Commentary,* pp. 662-63.

5. Wayne Grudem, *Evangelical Feminism and Biblical Truth: An Analysis of More Than One Hundred Disputed Questions* (Sisters, Ore.: Multnomah, 2004).

6. Eve's actual absence from Genesis 1 is affirmed by Origen, Chrysostom, Denis the Carthusian, Pellican, Musculus, and Vermigli, among others. Many details of this chapter are discussed and documented at length in Thompson, *John Calvin and the Daughters of Sarah,* pp. 107-59; on the absence of Eve, see p. 112 n. 8.

7. Chrysostom, *Hom. 8.2, 13.3 on Gen.* 1:26, 2:7 (FC 74:107, 174); Erasmus, *Paraphrase* of 1 Cor. 11:8 (*Opera* 7:895); Catharinus, *Comm. 1 Tim.* 2:13 (p. 432b). As these references suggest, exegetes traditionally interlinked the argument from sequence in 1 Tim. 2:13 not only with Genesis 1–2 but also with 1 Cor. 11:8-9.

8. Luther, *Comm. 1 Tim.* 2:13 (LW 28:278); Musculus, *Comm. 1 Tim.* 2:13 (p. 391); Vermigli, *Comm. 1 Cor.* 11:8-10 (fol. 287r); Calvin, *Comm. 1 Tim.* 2:13 (CNTC 10:271-72). Luther notes God's reversal of primogeniture in his *Comm. Gen.* 4:2, 27:5-10, 37:9, 48:17, 49:3 (LW 1:243-45, 5:112, 6:337, 8:169, 8:207).

9. See *Comm. 1 Cor.* 11:3 in Musculus (col. 378) and Vermigli (fol. 283r).

10. Augustine, *The Literal Meaning of Genesis* 11.37.50 (ACW 42:171); Ambrosiaster, *Comm. 1 Cor.* 14:34, *Comm. Eph.* 5:22-24 (CSEL 81/2:163, 81/3:117); Denis, *Comm. Gen.* 3:16 (p. 104a); Cajetan, *Comm. Gen.* 3:16 (p. 33); Erasmus, *Paraphrase* of 1 Cor. 11:2-16 (*Opera* 7:895); Zwingli, *Comm. Gen.* 3:12 (ZSW 13:27); Bullinger, *Comm. 1 Tim.* 2:11-15 (p. 569); Bucer, *Comm. Eph.* 5:23 (fol. 98r); Vermigli, *Comm. Gen.* 3:16 (fol. 17r); Catharinus, *Comm. 1 Cor.* 11:10, *Comm. Eph.* 5:23, *Comm. 1 Tim.* 2:13 (pp. 191a, 340b, 433b); Calvin, *Comm. Gen.* 3:16 (CTS 1:172).

11. Aquinas, *Comm. 1 Cor.* 11:3 (1:345, §588); echoed by Lyra, *Comm. 1 Cor.* 11:3 (fol. 49r). Thomas's notorious use of Aristotelian gynecology has often been discussed. See (e.g.) Prudence Allen, *The Concept of Woman: The Aristotelian Revolution, 750 BC–AD 1250* (Grand Rapids: Eerdmans, 1997), pp. 392-99. On Aristotle's career in the sixteenth century, see Ian Maclean, *The Renaissance Notion of Woman: A Study in the Fortunes of Scholasticism and Medical Science in European Intellectual Life* (Cambridge: Cambridge University Press, 1980), pp. 28-46.

12. Protestant examples range from accounts of what it means for a woman to be the "weaker vessel" in 1 Peter 3:7 to sexist clichés about "womanish affections." See (e.g.) Melanchthon, *Comm. Gen.* 3:1 (MO 13:777); Luther, *Comm. Gen.* 1:26, 27; 3:1 (LW

1:66, 69, 151); Bullinger, *Comm. 1 Pet.* 3:3-7 (pp. 34-36); Musculus, *Comm. Gen.* 2:21, 3:1, 3:16 (pp. 76, 84, 109).

13. Chrysostom, *Hom. 17.8 on Gen.* 3:16 (FC 74:240-41).

14. Luther, *Comm. Gen.* 2:18 (LW 1:115).

15. Luther, *Comm. Gen.* 1:27 (LW 1:69). Mickey Leland Mattox has suggested that the later Luther was more inclined to emphasize Eve's original equality; see *"Defender of the Most Holy Matriarchs": Martin Luther's Interpretation of the Women of Genesis in the* Enarrationes in Genesin, *1535-45* (Leiden: Brill, 2003), p. 74. For a thorough sampling of Luther's complexity, see *Luther on Women: A Sourcebook,* ed. Susan C. Karant-Nunn and Merry E. Wiesner-Hanks (New York: Cambridge University Press, 2003).

16. Chrysostom, *Hom. 26 on 1 Cor.* 11:3 (NPNF[1] 12:150).

17. Ambrose, *Paradise* 12.54 (FC 42:333); Oecolampadius, *Comm. Gen.* 3:6 (fol. 46r).

18. So Augustine, *The Literal Meaning of Genesis* 8.17.36 (ACW 42:58); Denis, *Comm. Gen.* 2 (p. 83b); Vermigli, *Comm. Gen.* 2:18 (fol. 11v).

19. Musculus, *Comm. Gen.* 2:16-17, 3:1 (pp. 64, 90).

20. In Christian exegesis, the allegory is traceable to Ambrose, who surely took it from Philo. It recurs constantly — in Jerome, Lyra, Denis, Lefèvre, Erasmus, Zwingli, Oecolampadius, Vermigli, and Musculus — though most Reformers held it at arm's length. See Thompson, *John Calvin and the Daughters of Sarah,* pp. 74-75, 126-27.

21. The list is from Pellican, *Comm. Gen.* 3:3 (fol. 6r), but vice lists are common. See also Chrysostom, *Hom. 16.3 on Gen.* 3:4-5 (FC 74:212-13); Augustine, *The Literal Meaning of Genesis* 11.30.39 (ACW 42:162); Melanchthon, *Comm. Gen.* 3:1-3 (MO 13:777); Oecolampadius, *Comm. Gen.* 3:6, 14 (fol. 45v, 51v).

22. Musculus, *Comm. Gen.* 3:2 (p. 91); Ambrose, *Paradise* 6.33-34 (FC 42:311-13).

23. Augustine, *The Literal Meaning of Genesis* 11.42.59-60 (ACW 42:176). The same motive is imputed to Adam by Chrysostom, Lyra, Oecolampadius, Pellican, Musculus, Guilliaud, and Catharinus.

24. Denis, *Comm. Gen.* 3:19 (p. 106a). Luther and Oecolampadius also concluded that Eve was punished more severely.

25. Lefèvre's rather one-sided claim (*Comm. 1 Tim.* 2:9-15, fol. 203v) is perfectly matched by the one-sided assertion of Agrippa von Nettesheim. Probably more a skeptic than a Christian, Agrippa exonerated Eve on the grounds of her ignorance; see his 1509 treatise, *Declamation on the Nobility and Preeminence of the Female Sex,* ed. Albert Rabil Jr. (Chicago: University of Chicago Press, 1996), p. 63.

26. Catharinus, *Comm. 1 Tim.* 2:13 (p. 433b).

27. Musculus, *Comm. 1 Tim.* 2:14 (p. 392). In his *Comm. 1 Tim.* 2:13 (CNTC 10:217), Calvin raised a similar objection, arguing that while Adam deserved to forfeit his dominion over Eve, there are two reasons why he did not. First, some remnants of the divine blessing (here, Adam's superiority) survive the Fall; second, it is not right for woman to improve her station by sinning (since she was subject to man even before her sin).

28. Musculus, *Comm. 1 Tim.* 2:14 (p. 392).

29. Cajetan, *Comm. Gen.* 3:6, 16 (pp. 30, 33), *Comm. 1 Tim.* 2:14 (p. 296b); Erasmus, *Paraphrase* of 1 Tim. 2:14 (*Opera* 7:1042); Musculus, *Comm. Gen.* 3:6 (p. 85), cf. *Comm. 1 Tim.* 2:14 (p. 392); Denis, *Comm. Gen.* 3:6 (pp. 97a-98a); Pellican, *Comm. 1 Tim.* 2:13-14 (pp. 488-89).

30. Chrysostom, *Hom. 9 on 1 Tim.* 2:14 (NPNF[1] 13:435); Ambrose, *Paradise* 4.24 (FC 42:301); Ambrosiaster, *Comm. 1 Tim.* 2:14 (CSEL 81/3.264); Aquinas, *Comm. 1 Tim.* 2:14 (2:229, §83); Luther, *Comm. Gen.* 3:13 (LW 1:182).

31. Theodoret, *Comm. 1 Tim.* 2:14 (Hill ed.), 2:216. The wording suggests accommodation or condescension: πρὸς τὴν προκειμένην χρείαν (PG 82:804).

32. Calvin, *Comm. Gen.* 3:6 (CTS 1:152) and *Comm. 1 Tim.* 2:14 (CNTC 10:218).

33. Calvin, *Comm. 1 Tim.* 2:14 (CNTC 10:218).

34. Calvin, *Comm. Gen.* 3:6 (CTS 1:152).

35. For an account of Origen, Ephrem, Augustine, and Milton, and of how Romans 5 came to "trump" 1 Timothy in the early church, see "Is Eve the Problem?" in Gary A. Anderson, *The Genesis of Perfection: Adam and Eve in Jewish and Christian Imagination* (Louisville: Westminster John Knox, 2001), pp. 99-116.

36. Tertullian, *On the Apparel of Women* 1.1.1-2 (ANF 4:14).

37. The other texts may be found in Church, "Sex and Salvation in Tertullian," pp. 86-88, along with this warning: "While details of his invective cannot be attributed entirely to rhetorical invention, one must always keep in mind that in Tertullian a given problem, such as the fall, may be adapted freely to the requirements both of subject and of audience." On Tertullian's support for prophetesses in his own day, see Cecil M. Robeck Jr., *Prophecy in Carthage: Perpetua, Tertullian, and Cyprian* (Cleveland: Pilgrim, 1992), pp. 120-39.

38. Ambrosiaster, *Comm. 1 Tim.* 2:15 (CSEL 81/3:264); the "excerpt" that appears in ACCS-NT 9:167a is a loose summary of the passage, not a direct translation.

39. Pelagius, *Comm. 1 Tim.* 2:15 (Souter ed.), p. 483.5: filiorum dei generatio.

40. Pelagius, *Comm. 1 Tim.* 2:15 (Souter ed.), p. 483, where Ezek. 14:14-18 and 18:20 are cited as proof that parents cannot save their children, nor vice versa.

41. Ambrose, *Paradise* 10.47 (FC 42:326-27, abridged).

42. Augustine, *On the Trinity* 12.7.11 (NPNF[1] 3:159). For a revival of Augustine's view, see Kenneth L. Waters, Sr., "Saved through Childbearing: Virtues as Children in 1 Timothy 2:11-15," *Journal of Biblical Literature* 123 (2004): 703-35.

43. Gregory of Nyssa, *On Virginity* 13 (FC 58:48, NPNF[2] 5:359b).

44. The distinction between *commands* and *counsels of perfection* is traceable to various fathers, notably Jerome and Cassian, though the distinction is older still. Aquinas, obviously writing much later, grounds the counsel of poverty in Matt. 19:21, which begins, "If you would be perfect . . ."; the counsel of chastity he finds in Matt. 19:12; see *Summa Theologica* I-II q.108 a.4 *ad* 1. The distinction was vigorously contested by the Protestant Reformers.

45. See Chrysostom's homily on 1 Cor. 7:2, partially translated in *On Marriage and Family Life* (Crestwood, N.Y.: St. Vladimir's Seminary Press, 2003), pp. 81-88; his com-

ment on Gen. 1:28 appears on p. 85 (PG 51:213). For Augustine, see *On the Good of Marriage* 9 (NPNF¹ 3:403b); and *The Literal Meaning of Genesis* 9.3.5 (ACW 42:73). For extended discussion, see Jeremy Cohen, *"Be fertile and increase, fill the earth and master it": The Ancient and Medieval Career of a Biblical Text* (Ithaca: Cornell University Press, 1989).

46. These three Roman Catholic writers span the mid-fifteenth to mid-sixteenth centuries; their views are found in their respective commentaries on 1 Tim. 2:15: Denis, p. 418a; Cajetan, p. 296b; Catharinus, pp. 433b-34a.

47. Zwingli, *Comm. Gen.* 3:16 (ZSW 13:29): diluunt et expiant.

48. Brenz, *Comm. Gen.* 3:16 (p. 56).

49. Luther, *Comm. 1 Tim.* 2:15 (WA 26:48, my translation; cf. LW 28:279); note the traditional penitential terminology: *pena manet, culpa transiit.*

50. Calvin, *Serm. 1 Tim.* 2:15 (pp. 228-29). See also Calvin's *Comm. 1 Tim.* 2:15 (CNTC 10:219) and *Comm. Gen.* 3:19 (CTS 1:178).

51. Origen, *Catenae on 1 Corinthians,* Greek text in *Journal of Theological Studies* 10 (1909): 41-42. The translation in Roger Gryson, *The Ministry of Women in the Early Church* (Collegeville, Minn.: Liturgical Press, 1976), pp. 28-29, is to be preferred to ACCS-NT 7:146a. Gryson's longer excerpt demonstrates the anti-Montanist impulse and context of Origen's heated remarks about women and prophetesses.

52. Pelagius, *Comm. 1 Tim.* 2:12 (Souter ed.), p. 482.15-16: "Publice non permittit: nam filium uel fratrem debet docere priuatim."

53. Denis the Carthusian, *Comm. 1 Tim.* 2:11-12 (*Opera* 13:417b).

54. Women were allowed to teach in private or all-female gatherings by (to name a few) Aquinas and Lyra in the Middle Ages; by the sixteenth-century Catholics Cajetan, Gaigny, and Guilliaud; and by Luther, Musculus, and Calvin.

55. For a detailed discussion of Luther and Calvin, see Thompson, *Calvin and the Daughters of Sarah,* pp. 198-206.

56. Theodoret, *Comm. 1 Tim.* 2:11-12 (Hill ed.), 2:216, where "inspiration" translates προφητικῆς (prophecy) in PG 82:802.

57. Calvin, *Comm. Acts* 21:9 (CNTC 7:195). For others who took this approach, see Thompson, *John Calvin and the Daughters of Sarah,* pp. 190-93.

58. Aquinas, *Comm. 1 Cor.* 14:34 (1:402, §879), *Comm. 1 Tim.* 2:12 (2:229, §80). He adds that Deborah's authority was over temporal matters, not priestly; if she had exercised religious authority, Aquinas assumes it would have been delegated to her by some man — details omitted from *Summa Theologica,* III.supp. 39.1 *ad* 1-3.

59. Most details in Thompson, *John Calvin and the Daughters of Sarah,* pp. 180-84.

60. Rudolf Gwalter, *Homily 76 on 1 Cor.* 14:34-35 (Zurich, 1572), fol. 222r.

61. Jerome made the point with reference to Huldah in *Against Jovinian* 1.25 (NPNF² 6:364). Chrysostom said as much in his *Hom. 7.6 Matt.* (NPNF¹ 10:49).

62. Denis, *Comm. Jud.* 4:4 (p. 130a); Pellican, *Comm. Jud.* 4:22 (fol. 44r); Brenz, *Comm. Jud.* 4:5 (p. 56); Calvin, *Serm. 1 Tim.* 2:13-15 (p. 225).

63. For details on Vermigli, see my essay, "Patriarchy and Prophetesses," p. 154.

64. Luther, *Comm. 1 Tim.* 2:15 (LW 28:280).

65. Jerome, *Against Helvidius* 22 (NPNF² 6:345a). Most surveys of women in this period address "ascetic egalitarianism," as do many specialized works.

66. See Chapter Six, pp. 118-20 above.

67. Vermigli, *Comm. 1 Cor.* 14:37-38, fol. 394v-95r. For a similar discussion from *c.* 1375, see John Brevicoxa, "A Treatise on Faith, the Church, the Roman Pontiff, and the General Council," translated in *Forerunners of the Reformation,* ed. Heiko A. Oberman (Philadelphia: Fortress, 1981), pp. 69-74.

68. Vermigli, *Comm. 1 Cor.* 14:37-38, fol. 395v. Bucer's comments on Deborah ran along similar lines: for a man to preside is nature's usual order, which "we ought to follow . . . *when we can.*" See his *Comm. Jud.* 4:4, 9 (p. 485, emphasis added).

69. Calvin, *Comm. 1 Cor.* 14:37 (CNTC 9:309, cf. CO 49:534-35).

70. Calvin, *Comm. 1 Cor.* 14:34 (CNTC 9:306).

71. Calvin, *Institutes* 4.10.31. For further discussion, see Thompson, *John Calvin and the Daughters of Sarah,* pp. 219-24, as well as chapter six of that work on polity and adiaphora ("indifferent matters").

72. For example, *Discovering Biblical Equality: Complementarity without Hierarchy,* twenty-nine essays edited by Ronald W. Pierce and Rebecca Merrill Groothuis, was published in October 2004. *The Journal for Biblical Manhood and Womanhood* wholly devoted its Spring 2005 issue to fifteen essays of rebuttal.

73. Daniel Doriani, "A History of the Interpretation of 1 Timothy 2," in *Women in the Church: A Fresh Analysis of 1 Tim. 2:9-15,* ed. Andreas J. Köstenberger, Thomas R. Schreiner, and H. Scott Baldwin (Grand Rapids: Baker, 1995), pp. 213-67. Doriani's survey has much to commend it, and it is odd that the second edition of this book (2005) chose to omit his piece.

74. Luther, *On the Misuse of the Mass* (LW 36:151-52). His advice continues: "The person who wishes to preach needs to have a good voice . . . and other natural gifts. . . . Thus Paul forbids women to preach in the congregation where men are present who are skilled in speaking . . . because it is much more fitting and proper for a man to speak, [and] a man is also more skilled at it."

75. Including Lefèvre, Luther, Bucer, Vermigli, Calvin, Guilliaud, and Catharinus.

76. The stories of such women continue to be recovered; for example, see *Women Preachers and Prophets Through Two Millennia of Christianity,* ed. Beverly Mayne Kienzle and Pamela J. Walker (Berkeley: University of California Press, 1998).

77. Harold O. J. Brown, "The New Testament Against Itself: 1 Timothy 2:9-15 and the 'Breakthrough' of Galatians 3:28," in *Women in the Church,* p. 190.

78. As per Article 23 of the 1982 Chicago Statement on Biblical Hermeneutics.

Notes to Chapter Nine, "Reading Sex and Violence"

1. Summaries of feminist readings (and debates) for all of these characters can be found in Alice Ogden Bellis, *Helpmates, Harlots, Heroes: Women's Stories in the Hebrew*

Bible (Louisville: Westminster John Knox, 1994), pp. 87-90, 131-35, 149-53. Classic accounts of the Levite's wife and Tamar appear in Phyllis Trible, *Texts of Terror,* chapters 2 and 3. Other notable studies include the following. On Dinah: Naomi Graetz, "Dinah the Daughter," in *A Feminist Companion to Genesis,* pp. 306-17. On the Levite's wife: Mieke Bal, "A Body of Writing: Judges 19," in *A Feminist Companion to Judges,* pp. 208-30, and *Death and Dissymmetry: The Politics of Coherence in the Book of Judges* (Chicago: University of Chicago Press, 1988), pp. 80-93; Cheryl Exum, "Raped by the Pen," in *Fragmented Women,* pp. 170-201; Fewell and Gunn, *Gender, Power, and Promise,* pp. 80-87. On Bathsheba: Cheryl Exum, "Bathsheba: Plotted, Shot, and Painted," in *Plotted, Shot, and Painted: Cultural Representations of Biblical Women* (Sheffield: Sheffield Academic Press, 1996), pp. 19-53; Shulamit Valler, "King David and 'his' Women: Biblical Stories and Talmudic Discussions," in *A Feminist Companion to Samuel and Kings,* ed. Athalya Brenner (Sheffield: Sheffield Academic Press, 1996), pp. 129-42.

2. Cheryl Exum ("Bathsheba," pp. 25-26) calls attention to one commentator, writing as recently as 1988, who concluded from the brief description in 2 Sam. 11:2 — "he saw from the roof a woman bathing" — that Bathsheba was negligent and, "it cannot be doubted . . . provocative," probably deliberately so, and therefore blameworthy. Another commentator wonders "whether Bathsheba did not count on this possibility" of being seen while bathing.

3. *Midrash Rabbah: Genesis* 80.1-5 (2:735-38).

4. Jerome, Letter 22.25 to Eustochium (NPNF[2] 6:32). My account of Dinah in patristic and medieval exegesis has benefited from a fine essay by Joy A. Schroeder, "The Rape of Dinah: Luther's Interpretation of a Biblical Narrative," *Sixteenth Century Journal* 28 (1997): 775-91. Schroeder has expanded her account in *Dinah's Lament: The Biblical Legacy of Sexual Violence in Christian Interpretation* (Fortress, forthcoming). Robin Parry, *Old Testament Story and Christian Ethics: The Rape of Dinah as a Case Study* (Waynesboro, Ga.: Paternoster, 2004), came to my attention too late to be incorporated here.

5. Gregory the Great, *Pastoral Rule* 3.29 (NPNF[2] 12:60-61), abridged.

6. Bernard of Clairvaux, *On the Steps of Humility and Pride* 10.29 (*c.* 1124), in *Bernard of Clairvaux: Selected Works,* trans. G. R. Evans (Mahwah, N.J.: Paulist, 1987), p. 124. For an account of how a later writer adapted Bernard to frame a rule for anchoresses, see Schroeder, "Rape of Dinah," pp. 777-78.

7. Peter Abelard, *Planctus Dinae Filiae Jacob* (PL 178:1817): Vae mihi miserae | Per memet perditae!

8. Richard of St. Victor, *The Twelve Patriarchs* 45-60, trans. Grover A. Zinn (Mahwah, N.J.: Paulist, 1979), pp. 102-17.

9. All *Comm. Gen.* 34:1-2: Pellican (1:45r); Vermigli (fol. 139v); Luther (LW 6:192); Musculus (p. 700); Calvin (CTS 2:218).

10. Calvin, *Comm. Gen.* 34:1 (CTS 2:218).

11. Luther, *Comm. Gen.* 34:1-2 (LW 6:192). Calvin writes similarly. Luther may be rebutting Cajetan, his Catholic contemporary, who had little to say against Dinah and insisted that she *did* have an escort, "as was fitting" (*Comm. Gen.* 34:1, p. 135).

12. Zwingli, *Comm. Gen.* 34:1-2 (ZSW 13:217): ut demum ab eo persuasa, ab eo raperetur.

13. Calvin does not go as far along these lines as Zwingli, but he does commend aspects of Shechem's character; the rape was an aberration and a mark against him, but Calvin thinks Shechem really loved Dinah (*Comm. Gen.* 34:4, 8; CTS 2:219, 222). For discussion, see Michael Parsons, *Luther and Calvin on Old Testament Narratives: Reformation Thought and Narrative Text* (Lewiston, N.Y.: Mellen, 2004), p. 194. Musculus, on the other hand, calls attention to the lack of textual support for the view (surely Zwingli's!) that Dinah was in the habit of wandering among the local women and visiting with Shechem (*Comm. Gen.* 34:1, p. 699).

14. Zwingli, *Comm. Gen.* 34:14 (ZSW 13:218, italics mine).

15. Parsons deftly exposes the patriarchal perspective of both Luther and Calvin regarding Dinah (*Luther and Calvin on Old Testament Narratives*, pp. 185-204), but equally pertinent are the mitigating observations of Schroeder (next note).

16. Schroeder, "Rape of Dinah," pp. 781-82.

17. Luther, *Comm. Gen.* 34:1-2 (WA 44:142, my translation; cf. LW 6:191).

18. Luther, *Comm. Gen.* 34:3-5 (LW 6:195-96).

19. Luther, *Comm. Gen.* 34:1-2 (WA 44:142, my translation; cf. LW 6:192).

20. Schroeder ("Rape of Dinah," p. 790) calls attention to the *Ancrene Wisse,* but the suggestion is present already in Gregory the Great and Richard of St. Victor, as well as in Zwingli. Later in the sixteenth century, Johann Wolf can refer without hesitation to "Dinah's fornication" *(scortatione);* see *In Sacram Historiam Iosuae* (Zurich, 1592), fol. 49v.

21. Luther, *Comm. Gen.* 37:1 and 43:5 (LW 6:315, 7:310); I owe these references to Schroeder, "Rape of Dinah," p. 790.

22. For Dinah as the mother of Asenath, see Louis Ginzburg, *The Legends of the Jews* (7 vols., reprint; Philadelphia: Jewish Publication Society, 1967-69), 2:38, 5:336-37 nn. 96-97. *Midrash Rabbah: Genesis* 80.11 (2:744) has a different version.

23. We will have to pass over a lesser question raised by the various translations of Judges 19:1-2, namely, whether the woman was the Levite's wife or his concubine.

24. My account of the Levite's wife here draws on my more detailed study, "Four Expendable Women," in *Writing the Wrongs,* pp. 179-221.

25. Josephus, *Antiquities* 5.2.8 §§147-48 (Loeb ed., 5:68-69).

26. Ambrose, Epistles 5 and 6 to Syagrius (numbered as Epistles 32 and 33 in FC 26:152-71). Jerome's slight references are too brief to bother with here.

27. The briefer account in Sulpicius (*c.* 400) is not quite as "improved," but it still may reflect Josephus in the way it polishes the character and behavior of the Levite and his wife; see Sulpicius Severus, *Chronica* 1.29 (PL 20:113).

28. Details in Thompson, *Writing the Wrongs,* pp. 198-201.

29. Lyra, *Comm. Jud.* 19:2-3, 25 (2:53v-54r). Lyra goes on to offer a typological reading of the wife's horrible death as prefiguring the persecutions and tribulations inflicted upon the apostles and other early Christians. While Lyra did not approve of the

adultery of the Levite's wife, her earlier sin did not disqualify her from a noble figurative role in which her sufferings were taken seriously and with empathy.

30. See Chapter Four, pp. 74, 80-81.

31. See Lev. 20:20, 21:9, and Deut. 22:22-24.

32. Bucer, *Comm. Jud.* 19:29 (p. 520). For similar remarks, see the Judges commentaries of Brenz (p. 177) and Vermigli (fol. 248v).

33. Vermigli's protest against the double standard arises in an 11-page excursus from his comments on David's adultery with Bathsheba, in the course of which he acutely dismantles the usual case for women's greater sin and guilt in adultery, observing repeatedly that the case is built on human laws, not divine, and that the perspective of human laws is often skewed against women precisely because such laws were written by men rather than women. See his *Comm. 2 Sam.* 12:14 (fol. 241r-46v; ET in Vermigli's *Common Places*, pp. 482-95); and pp. 107, 158, above.

34. Precisely this conclusion is drawn by Louise Simons, but her references (to Joseph Hall and Richard Rogers) do not bear her out; see "'An Immortality Rather than a Life': Milton and the Concubine of Judges 19–21," in *Old Testament Women in Western Literature*, ed. Raymond-Jean Frontain and Jan Wojcik (Conway, Ark.: UCA Press, 1991), p. 145. For the seriousness with which the Reformers regarded adultery in both men and women, see Robert M. Kingdon's chapter, "Death for Adultery," in *Adultery and Divorce in Calvin's Geneva*, pp. 116-42.

35. I have culled these descriptors from Pellican and Vermigli, though the last phrases are applied to the men of Sodom in Calvin's *Comm. Gen.* 19:6 (CTS 1:499).

36. Vermigli, *Comm. Jud.* 19:21-30 (ET fol. 253r); Cajetan, *Comm. Jud.* 19:25 (2:67).

37. See Luther, *Comm. Gen.* 19:8 (LW 3:258); Calvin, *Comm. Gen.* 19:8 (CTS 1:499-500), and *Serm. 90 on Gen.* 19:6-9 (SC 11:1017-21); Musculus, *Comm. Gen.* 19:6-8 (p. 461); Vermigli, *Comm. Gen.* 19:9 (fol. 76r).

38. This question is discussed by Fewell and Gunn (*Gender, Power, and Promise*, p. 133), among others; see Thompson, *Writing the Wrongs*, pp. 180-81.

39. Ambrose's *Apologia prophetiae David* (PL 14:891-960) — which in some manuscripts is dedicated to Emperor Theodosius — may have been provoked by the misdeeds of contemporary rulers, such as the "spiritual adultery" of Valentinian II or the treachery of Maximus; see Quasten, *Patrology*, 4:162.

40. On the discomfort with David that the use of allegory here may mask, see Jan Wojcik, "Discriminations against David's Tragedy in Ancient Jewish and Christian Literature," in *The David Myth in Western Literature*, ed. Raymond-Jean Frontain and Jan Wojcik (West Lafayette, Ind.: Purdue University Press, 1980), pp. 31-35.

41. Augustine, *Reply to Faustus* 22.87 (NPNF[1] 4:308).

42. Josephus, *Antiquities* 7.7.1 (LCL 5:431); he says nothing about stoning David.

43. Peter Comestor, *Historia Scholastica* on 2 Samuel 11–12 (PL 198:1333).

44. Denis the Carthusian, *Comm. 2 Sam.* 11:2, 4, 26 (*Opera* 3:498-500).

45. Lyra, *Comm. 2 Sam.* 11 (2:108v). Lyra's account, along with Paul of Burgos's rebuttal, is summarized by Denis, *Comm. 2 Sam.* 11:26 (*Opera* 3:500).

46. See Calvin, *Serm. 2 Sam.* 11 (pp. 476-77, 479, 485, 511); Vermigli, *Comm. 2 Sam.* 11 (fol. 234r). Both writers repeat the traditional criticism of David for indulging his leisure — behavior especially inappropriate for a king at war.

47. Calvin, *Serm. 2 Sam.* 11 (p. 485).

48. Vermigli, *Comm. 2 Sam.* 11 (fol. 234r).

49. Calvin, *Serm. 2 Sam.* 11 (pp. 487-88); Vermigli, *Comm. 2 Sam.* 11 (fol. 234r).

50. Calvin, *Serm. 2 Sam.* 11 (pp. 515-17); Vermigli, *Comm. 2 Sam.* 11 (fol. 235v).

51. Calvin, *Serm. 2 Sam.* 12 (pp. 599-600); Vermigli, *Comm. 2 Sam.* 12 (fol. 248r).

52. The Greek version of v. 21 adds the explanation (adopted by the NRSV) that David did not punish Amnon because of his love for him as his firstborn.

53. Jerome, Letter 22.12 to Eustochium; Letter 147.9 rebukes the deacon Sabinianus for adultery, comparing him to Amnon (NPNF[2] 6:27, 294). A similar point is made by another ascetic, Fructuosus of Braga (excerpted in ACCS-OT 4:368).

54. This allegory derives from Raban Maur and is the longest of merely three comments on the story in the *Ordinary Gloss* (PL 113:573).

55. Peter Comestor, *Historia Scholastica* on 2 Samuel 13 (PL 198:1335); Josephus, *Antiquities* 7.8.1 (LCL 5:451). For Lyra, see *Comm. 2 Sam.* 13:13 (2:110r).

56. Denis the Carthusian, *Comm. 2 Sam.* 13:13 (*Opera* 3:512-13).

57. Lyra, *Comm. 2 Sam.* 13:13 (2:110v).

58. Denis the Carthusian, *Comm. 2 Sam.* 13:21 (*Opera* 3:514-15).

59. Denis the Carthusian, *Comm. 2 Sam.* 13:13 (*Opera* 3:514-15).

60. Calvin, *Serm. 2 Sam.* 13:1-14 (pp. 618, 622, 624). Calvin thinks Amnon was divinely constrained to say "my sister," to awaken him to his crime. "In fact it only resulted in hardening him, for the devil had such control of him that he did not know any more about kinship than a dumb animal" (p. 624).

61. Vermigli, *Comm. 2 Sam.* 13:15-21 (fol. 253r). Calvin and Vermigli thus recognized Amnon's rhetorical assault on Tamar and anticipated, at least in part, the feminist critiques of our own day. See, e.g., Trible's fine rhetorical analysis of Amnon's shifting designations for Tamar in *Texts of Terror*, pp. 40-42, 46, 48.

62. Calvin, *Serm. 2 Sam.* 13:1-14 (pp. 615-18).

63. Calvin, *Serm. 2 Sam.* 13:15-25 (pp. 640-41).

64. Vermigli, *Comm. 2 Sam.* 13:15-21 (fol. 253v).

65. Calvin, *Serm. 2 Sam.* 13:1-14 (pp. 626-27). One marvels at this presumption of ignorance, when Calvin began by praising David for instructing his household.

66. Calvin, *Serm. 2 Sam.* 13:15-25 (pp. 630, 633).

67. For the case of Antoine Calvin and Anne Le Fert, see Kingdon, *Adultery and Divorce in Calvin's Geneva*, pp. 71-97. Anne Le Fert had been accused of adultery once before, in 1548. In both cases, Calvin was clearly mortified, but he ably represented his brother before the Geneva Consistory.

68. Vermigli, *Comm. 2 Sam.* 13:6-14 (fol. 251v), italics and punctuation altered.

69. Vermigli, *Comm. 2 Sam.* 13:6-14 (fol. 251v). Vermigli was quite opposed to the notion that any human — whether David or the Pope — may relax divine laws, but he

does not excoriate Tamar for the suggestion, which he had earlier taken as insincere (i.e., a ruse) anyway. His broadening of the scope of excuses from what is allowed by Deut. 22:24 may be in rebuttal of Cajetan (*Comm. 2 Sam.* 13:21 [2:152]), who had ruled that Tamar was liable to death for not crying out.

70. Luther made the first point in 1523, in *Prefaces to the Old Testament* (WADB 8:18.12-13; cf. LW 35:239); cf. also *The Estate of Marriage,* 1522 (LW 45:23). The second point emerges from his 1525 *Lectures on Deuteronomy* 22 (WA 14:704, my translation; cf. LW 9:224).

71. Vermigli, *Comm. 2 Sam.* 13:15-21 (fol. 253r).

72. Elsewhere I have argued that Calvin is unique in his uncompromising propensity to indict even the patriarchs for their misdeeds. See Chapter Four, above; and my essay, "Patriarchs, Polygamy, and Popular Resistance."

73. For Calvin's stern advice to women in hard situations, see Charmarie Jenkins Blaisdell's essays, "Calvin's Letters to Women: The Courting of Ladies in High Places," *Sixteenth Century Journal* 13 (1982): 67-84; and "Calvin's and Loyola's Letters to Women," in *Calviniana: Ideas and Influence of Jean Calvin,* ed. Robert V. Schnucker (Kirksville, Mo.: Sixteenth Century Journal Publishers, 1988), pp. 235-53.

74. As Michael Parsons concludes in his essay, "Luther and Calvin on Rape: Is the Crime Lost in the Agenda?" *Evangelical Quarterly* 74 (2002): 123-42; revised as chapter ten in his book, *Luther and Calvin on Old Testament Narratives,* pp. 185-204.

Notes to the Conclusion, "On Cultivating the Habit of History"

1. Many have written on Calvin's exegesis; my own views are developed further in "Calvin as a Biblical Interpreter," in *The Cambridge Companion to John Calvin,* ed. Donald A. McKim (Cambridge: Cambridge University Press, 2004), pp. 58-73. In the conclusion to *Writing the Wrongs,* I have noted the continuity between the Reformers (such as Bullinger) and the church fathers (such as Origen and Augustine).

2. See W. Ian P. Hazlett, "Calvin's Latin Preface to His Proposed French Edition of Chrysostom's Homilies," in *Humanism and Reform: The Church in Europe, England, and Scotland,* ed. James Kirk (Oxford: Blackwell, 1991), p. 141.

3. Calvin's intense interaction with his predecessors is finely considered by A. N. S. Lane, *John Calvin: Student of the Church Fathers* (Grand Rapids: Baker, 1999).

4. Roger E. Olson's *The Story of Christian Theology: Twenty Centuries of Tradition and Reform* (Downers Grove, Ill.: InterVarsity Press, 1999) is lauded for its readability, though I admire William C. Placher, *A History of Christian Theology* (Philadelphia: Westminster, 1983) for clarity and conciseness. Surveys of the history of interpretation include Gerald Bray, *Biblical Interpretation: Past and Present* (Downers Grove, Ill.: InterVarsity Press, 1996); and Donald K. McKim, ed., *Historical Handbook of Major Biblical Interpreters* (Downers Grove, Ill.: InterVarsity Press, 1998).

Glossary of Biblical Commentators
and Other Writers or Writings

Abelard, Peter (1079-c. 1142)   Medieval philosopher, theologian, and poet, and by turns an abbot and lecturer in Paris. Denounced by Bernard of Clairvaux, he authored many and diverse works, including a controversial textbook, *Sic et Non*, in which he highlighted contradictions among the church fathers.

Agrippa von Nettesheim (1486-1535)   German humanist best known in his day for his interests in occultism and skepticism, he also authored an influential and controversial defense of the dignity of women.

Ambrose (c. 339-397)   Bishop of Milan and author of numerous works, including treatises on the Old Testament saints and a commentary on Luke.

Ambrosiaster (*fl.* 363-384)   Unidentified author of an influential Latin commentary on the epistles of Paul that was long ascribed to Ambrose.

Apostolic Constitutions (c. 350-380)   A collection of ecclesiastical regulations of Syrian origin, though based on various earlier documents.

Aquinas, Thomas (c. 1225-1274)   Dominican philosopher and theologian whose theological synthesis was influential not only in his own day but also at the Council of Trent in the sixteenth century; he continues to be esteemed in the Roman Catholic Church today. Best known for his *Summa Theologica*, he also commented on many New Testament writings.

Arias Montanus (1527-1598)   Spanish humanist, theologian, and Hebrew scholar who commented extensively on the Old Testament prophets.

Athanasius (*c.* 296-373)   Bishop of Alexandria and arch-defender of the Nicene Creed against Arianism. His most famous treatise is *On the Incarnation,* but he also commented on Genesis, Psalms, Ecclesiastes, and the Song of Solomon; only fragments of these works remain.

Athenagoras (later 2nd c.)   Greek Christian apologist who addressed his *Supplication for the Christians* to Emperor Marcus Aurelius sometime around 177.

Augsburg Confession (1530)   Lutheran confession of faith presented to Emperor Charles V in Augsburg. Its final form is credited largely to Melanchthon; it became part of the Lutheran *Book of Concord* in 1580.

Augustine (354-430)   Christian convert and Bishop of Hippo in North Africa, Augustine was a prolific writer and hugely influential on the course of Christianity in the Latin West through the Reformation and beyond. Though better known for writing theological treatises than exegetical works, he shaped later exegesis as well as theology and was widely quoted.

Basil of Caesarea (*c.* 330-379)   Also known as Basil the Great, one of the three Cappadocian Fathers and renowned defender of Nicene orthodoxy.

Bede, the Venerable (*c.* 673-735)   English monk, historian, and theologian, as well as author of more than twenty works on the Bible, often allegorical or typological in character and relying heavily on patristic sources.

Bernard of Clairvaux (1090-1153)   Cistercian abbot, monk, and mystic, influential in ecclesiastical matters in his day, and best known for his allegorical sermons on the Song of Solomon.

Brenz, Johannes (1499-1570)   Lutheran reformer in Schwäbisch-Hall and Württemberg, defender of Lutheran orthodoxy, and important theologian and commentator.

Brevicoxa, John (*fl.* 1367-1375)   French theologian and little-known colleague of Jean Gerson, Brevicoxa wrote on matters of papal *vs.* conciliar authority.

Bucer, Martin (1491-1551)   Former Dominican and one of the earliest reformers in Strasbourg, though he spent his last two years in Cambridge. Bucer was active as an ecclesiastical adviser and ecumenist, and wrote many influential commentaries, especially on the Gospels and Romans.

Bullinger, Heinrich (1504-1575)   Zwingli's associate and successor in Zurich, and a central figure in defining Reformed theological positions against both Lutherans and Anabaptists. He authored commentaries on many Old and New Testament books, as well as the Second Helvetic Confession and an influential book on Christian marriage.

Burroughs, Jeremiah (1600-1646)   English Congregationalist, moderate Puritan preacher, and participant in the Westminster Assembly, he authored an extensive commentary on Hosea and various other sermons and treatises.

Cajetan, Cardinal [Thomas de Vio] (1469-1534)   Dominican theologian and later an extensive biblical commentator, Cajetan was also a papal legate who attempted to elicit a recantation from Luther in 1518.

Calvin, John (1509-1564)   French-born reformer of Geneva; theologian, controversialist, and ecclesiastical statesman; prolific author of the influential *Institutes of the Christian Religion* and numerous sermons and biblical commentaries.

Capito, Wolfgang (*c.* 1478-1581)   Hebrew scholar who broke with Erasmus over the teachings of Luther, though more influenced by Bucer, with whom he guided the Strasbourg reform on an irenic course.

Catharinus, Ambrosius [Lancelot Politi] (1484-1553)   Dominican theologian, opponent of Luther, Cajetan, and Erasmus. He was influential at the first period of the Council of Trent and commented on the New Testament epistles.

Chrysostom, John (*c.* 347-407)   Bishop of Constantinople and outstanding orator who left sermon collections on several Old Testament books and much of the New Testament, and who favored practical and moral exegesis over allegory.

Clement of Alexandria (*c.* 150–*c.* 215)   Christian convert and teacher in Alexandria who defended the philosophical and theological respectability of Christianity against pagan philosophy and Gnosticism.

Cyril of Alexandria (d. 444)   Patriarch of Alexandria and fierce opponent of Nestorius in the Christological debates of the fifth century, he also authored numerous exegetical and homiletical works.

Denis the Carthusian (1402-1471)   Theologian and mystic, prolific homiletic writer, and compiler of an extensive commentary on the entire Bible.

Didymus the Blind (*c.* 313-398)   Director of the catechetical school of Alexandria, ally of Athanasius, devotee of Origen, and teacher of Jerome. His commentaries on Genesis, Job, and Zechariah were discovered only in 1941.

Diodore of Tarsus (d. *c.* 390)   Bishop of Tarsus, teacher of Theodore of Mopsuestia and John Chrysostom, and proponent of literal and historical exegesis in the Antiochene school. Few of his many exegetical works survive.

Downame, John (1571-1652)   Minister in the Church of England and author of various treatises and sermons, including a partial commentary on Hosea.

Ephrem the Syrian (*c.* 306-373)   Syrian poet and theologian whose extensive exegetical writings were composed largely in verse or as hymns.

Erasmus, Desiderius (*c.* 1467-1536)   Controversial Dutch humanist, satirist, scholar, and editor; noted for his numerous editions of the church fathers but above all for his text-critical Greek New Testament of 1516, which was followed by his *Annotations* and *Paraphrases.*

Gaigny, Jean de (d. 1549)   Conservative Roman Catholic theologian and opponent of Cajetan, as well as chancellor of the University of Paris from 1546, he also wrote commentaries on the entire New Testament.

Gratian (d. *c.* 1160)   The father of canon law, he collected a mass of patristic writings, conciliar documents, and papal decrees into his *Concordance of Discordant Canons,* a foundational source for church law.

Gregory the Great (*c.* 540-604)   Pope from 590 who authored an influential treatise on pastoral care. His best known exegetical work is his lengthy *Morals on the Book of Job,* which explains Job's literal, mystical, and moral meanings.

Gregory of Nazianzus (*c.* 330-390)   One of the three Cappadocian Fathers, a defender of Nicene orthodoxy and opponent of Apollinaris.

Gregory of Nyssa (*c.* 330-395)   One of the three Cappadocian Fathers, younger brother of Basil, a defender of Nicene orthodoxy, and notable for his Origenist and mystical interests.

Guilliaud, Claude (1493-1551)   Roman Catholic scholar and at one time librarian of the Sorbonne, his commentary on the New Testament epistles nonetheless drew on Bucer's commentary on Romans, which may explain why the first edition was censured by the Faculty of Theology at the University of Paris.

Gwalter, Rudolf (1519-1586)   Successor to Zwingli and Bullinger in leading the Protestant church in Zurich, he wrote Latin homilies on the minor prophets and on the entire New Testament except for Revelation.

Hugh of St. Victor (d. 1142)   Augustinian canon in Paris and wide-ranging scholar whose numerous commentaries attended to the literal and mystical meanings of Scripture.

268

Hutcheson, George (1615-1674)   Minister in the Church of Scotland who wrote popular commentaries on Job, the minor prophets, and the Gospel of John.

Ibn Ezra, Abraham (1089-1164)   Rabbinic exegete and poet who lived in Spain and North Africa and commented on all of the Old Testament except Samuel, Kings, Chronicles, Jeremiah, Ezekiel, Proverbs, Ezra and Nehemiah.

Irenaeus of Lyons (*c.* 130–*c.* 200)   Bishop of Lyons and opponent of Gnosticism. His major work, *Against All Heresies,* was also notable for his teachings about apostolic tradition and Christology.

Isidore of Seville (*c.* 560-636)   Bishop of Seville and encyclopedic author, famous especially for his *Etymologies.* Isidore's exegetical writings emphasized allegorical and typological readings of Scripture.

Jerome (*c.* 345-420)   Preeminent biblical scholar of his day, best known for translating most of the Bible into Latin (= the Vulgate or "common version"). He wrote commentaries on selected Bible books, including the prophets and a few of Paul's epistles, and he also composed a philological study, *Hebrew Questions on Genesis.*

Josephus, Flavius (*c.* 38-100)   Jewish soldier and historian whose *Antiquities of the Jews* commented on most of the narrative of the Old Testament; he was widely read by Christian commentators.

Jovinian (d. *c.* 405)   An unorthodox monk who argued against the superior merits of abstinence, fasting, and celibacy, and thus drew heated responses from Jerome and others.

Kimhi, David (*c.* 1160-1235)   Jewish grammarian and commentator, also known by acronym as Radak. He wrote on Genesis, Chronicles, the prophetic books, Psalms, and Proverbs, including some allegorical commentaries.

Lambert, François (1487-1530)   Franciscan convert to mostly Lutheran beliefs and author of numerous Bible commentaries, including a specialized study of prophecy in 1 Corinthians.

Lapide, Cornelius à (1567-1637)   Jesuit scholar and professor of exegesis at Louvain and Rome who composed learned and popular commentaries on all the books of the Bible except Job and the Psalms.

Lefèvre d'Étaples, Jacques [Faber Stapulensis] (*c.* 1469-1536)   Early humanist scholar and moderate Roman Catholic who wrote on Aristotle, theology, and mysticism, as well as on the Psalms and most of the New Testament.

Lombard, Peter (*c.* 1100-1160) Teacher in the Cathedral School in Paris, best known for his *Four Books of Sentences*, a systematic compendium of patristic teachings and the standard theological textbook even to Luther's day. He also composed commentaries on the Psalms and on the Pauline epistles.

Luther, Martin (1483-1546) Augustinian monk whose protest against indulgences is often credited as precipitating the Reformation. In addition to his influential treatises and confessional writings, Luther wrote many sermons and commentaries, the greatest of which is his ten-year series of lectures on Genesis.

Lyra, Nicholas (*c.* 1270-1379) Franciscan biblical scholar whose massive commentary on Scripture was notable for its interest in both the literal and moral meaning of the text and for its familiarity with Hebrew and rabbinic exegetical views. Often published together with the *Ordinary Gloss*.

Maimonides, Moses (1135-1204) Jewish philosopher and physician, also known by acronym as Rambam, whose *Guide to the Perplexed* attempted to reconcile Jewish tradition with Aristotelian philosophy.

Melanchthon, Philip (1497-1560) Professor of Greek and Luther's colleague at Wittenberg, he shaped Protestant views on systematic theology, rhetoric, and Aristotle and authored several New Testament commentaries.

Methodius of Olympus (d. *c.* 311) Bishop in Lycia, best known for his *Symposium* or *Banquet of the Ten Virgins*, a commendation of Christian virginity. His commentaries on Genesis and the Song of Solomon are lost.

Midrash Rabbah (5th c.) Midrash is a rabbinic term for the non-literal exegesis of Scripture, often comprised of a series of rabbis' moral or allegorical insights. The Midrash Rabbah or "Great" Midrash usually designates the midrashim on the Pentateuch; the midrash on Genesis ("Genesis Rabbah") was the earliest to be compiled.

Münster, Sebastian (1480-1553) Convert to Protestantism and teacher of Hebrew at the University of Basel from 1528. He published Hebrew dictionaries and grammars, and his translation of the Hebrew Old Testament into Latin was especially important for its detailed annotations drawing on rabbinic sources.

Müntzer, Thomas (*c.* 1489-1525) German radical reformer and mystic whose role as a leader in the Peasants' War of 1524-26 led to his execution. He left an assortment of writings, including his fiery *Sermon to the Princes* on Daniel 2.

Musculus, Wolfgang (1497-1563) Former Benedictine monk turned reformer, he preached in Augsburg from 1531, then taught in Berne from 1549, where he wrote many widely-admired biblical commentaries.

Nachmanides (1194-1270)   Jewish physician, poet, kabbalist, and exegete, also known by acronym as Ramban, who wrote on the Pentateuch, Job, and Daniel.

Oecolampadius, Johannes (1482-1531)   Swiss humanist scholar and reformer in Basel, he was once a colleague of Erasmus but became closely associated with Zwingli. He produced editions of patristic commentaries as well as his own commentaries on Genesis, Job, the Old Testament prophets, as well as much of the New Testament.

Ordinary Gloss (12th c.)   The standard medieval commentary on the Bible, composed largely of patristic and early medieval excerpts. It was compiled over the course of the twelfth century by many writers, including Gilbert the Universal and Anselm and Ralph of Laon.

Origen (*c.* 185–*c.* 254)   Speculative theologian and mystic of Alexandria. A prolific exegete, he wrote allegorical commentaries on most books of the Bible, but few survive.

Paul of Burgos (*c.* 1351-1435)   Christian convert and archbishop, former rabbi and talmudic scholar, best known for contesting the accounts of Jewish exegesis reported by Nicholas of Lyra. The "additions" of Burgos were often published as part of Lyra's *Postils*.

Pelagius (*fl. c.* 354-418)   Best known as the ascetic opponent of Augustine on questions of nature, grace, and human capacity, he was also the author of a Latin commentary on the Pauline epistles.

Pellican, Conrad (1478-1556)   Franciscan monk, associate of Erasmus, and the first Christian to publish a grammar of Hebrew, in 1501. He was influenced by Luther but accepted Zwingli's call to teach Old Testament in Zurich from 1526, where he published a commentary on the entire Bible.

Peter Comestor (d. *c.* 1178)   Chancellor of Notre Dame in Paris from 1168, best known for his *Scholastic History,* a mixture of commentary and biblical history with patristic and pagan citations.

Philo (d. 50)   Jewish philosopher and exegete of Alexandria whose allegorical readings of Old Testament history were influential on the development of Christian allegorical exegesis.

Poole, Matthew (*c.* 1624-1679)   Presbyterian controversialist and English biblical commentator, whose greatest work was his *Synopsis criticorum*, a massive condensation of critical biblical scholarship.

Procopius of Gaza (*c.* 475–*c.* 538)   Exegete and rhetorician who composed somewhat derivative commentaries on the Octateuch (Genesis-Ruth), as well as Samuel, Kings, Chronicles, Isaiah, and the Song of Solomon.

Pseudo-Philo (1st c.)   Author of the *Biblical Antiquities*, an imaginative retelling of Old Testament history from Adam to David, misattributed to Philo.

Quodvultdeus (d. *c.* 454)   Friend of Augustine and later Bishop of Carthage. Among his pastoral writings is his *Book of God's Promises*, essentially a typological history and biblical narrative written for catechumens.

Raban Maur (*c.* 780-856)   Abbot of Fulda and later Archbishop of Mainz, he wrote on theology and ecclesiastical law, composed textbooks on grammar and a handbook for clergy, and commented on nearly every book of the Bible.

Radbertus, Paschasius (*c.* 790–*c.* 860)   Abbot of Corbie, best known for his controversy with Ratramnus over the Eucharistic presence, but also a commentator on Lamentations and Matthew.

Rashi (1040-1105)   Acronym of Rabbi Shelomoh Yitshaqi, preeminent French commentator on the Talmud and on the entire Bible except Chronicles. He favored the "plain" meaning but often added mystical or homiletic insights.

Richard of St. Victor (d. 1173)   Prior of the Abbey of St. Victor in Paris from 1162, he wrote an important work on the Trinity as well as a number of exegetical works that emphasized allegory and spiritual readings.

Rogers, Richard (1551-1618)   Minister in the Church of England and Puritan author. His most extensive work of biblical scholarship was a series of sermons on Judges, which openly drew on the commentary of Vermigli.

Shepherd of Hermas (2nd c.)   Hermas is one of the Apostolic Fathers and is known only from this work, which presents itself as a series of visions, mandates, and similitudes. The work offers instruction in Christian behavior and addresses the possibility of penance for post-baptismal sin.

Sulpicius Severus (*c.* 360–*c.* 430)   Christian ascetic who wrote a biography of Martin of Tours and a *Chronicle* of Old Testament and early church history.

Targums (2nd c.)   Aramaic translations or paraphrases of the Bible. Targum Onkelos (on the Pentateuch) and "Rabbi Jonathan" (on the prophets) are regularly noted by sixteenth-century Christian commentators.

Tertullian (*c.* 160–*c.* 225)   Christian convert of North Africa whose moral rigor later drove him into Montanism. He authored numerous works of theology, apologetics, polemics, and Christian conduct.

Theodore of Mopsuestia (*c.* 350-428)   Antiochene theologian and bishop, pupil of Diodore of Tarsus, and biblical commentator noted especially for his literal and historical exegesis of the Old Testament.

Theodoret of Cyrus (*c.* 393–*c.* 460)   Bishop, apologist, theologian, and historian, as well as a commentator on most of the Old Testament in the tradition of the Antiochene school of exegesis.

Trent, Council of (1545-1547, 1551-1552, 1561-1563)   The Roman Catholic council that met in three periods in belated response to the Protestant Reformation. It reformed some practices but hardened many doctrines against Protestants, establishing Catholic positions for centuries thereafter.

Urban II (*c.* 1035-1099)   Pope from 1088, he initiated the First Crusade in 1095 in response to an appeal from the Greek emperor for help against the Seljuk Turks.

Vatable, François (*c.* 1493-1547)   Moderate Roman Catholic, assistant to Lefèvre d'Étaples, and professor of Hebrew in Paris. Robert Estienne's 1545 Bible incorporated some of Vatable's lecture notes on the Old Testament.

Vermigli, Peter Martyr (1499-1562)   Augustinian canon who converted to Protestantism and fled Italy in 1542. A prolific commentator, he lectured on theology in Strasbourg, Oxford, and Zurich alongside Bucer, Bullinger, and others.

Wolf, Johann (1521-1571)   Professor of theology in Zurich who wrote commentaries on many books of the Old Testament. He also completed the commentary on 2 Kings that Vermigli left unfinished at his death.

Zanchi, Girolamo (1516-1590)   Influenced by Vermigli, this Augustinian canon fled to Calvin's Geneva in 1552. He later taught theology in Strasbourg, Heidelberg, and Neustadt, and left an extensive set of writings, including his commentary on Hosea.

Zwingli, Huldreich (1484-1531)   Humanist scholar and pastor, and first reformer of Zurich. Known for his conflict with Luther and the early Anabaptists, he wrote pastoral and theological treatises as well as many works of exegesis.

A Finding Guide to English Translations
of Commentary Literature Written before 1600

The end-date for this catalogue of exegetical literature in English was chosen so as to keep the list manageable, at a cost of omitting many works of Puritan exegesis. (For various reasons, a few later works are, in fact, included.) While a truly comprehensive catalogue would need to list exegetical opinions found in unlikely places or expressed merely in passing, this list favors "concentrations" of exegetical comment, in that these works generally treat substantial passages or whole books of the Bible. Commentaries thus take pride of place, but collections of sermons on specific Bible books have been included wherever possible — recognizing, again, that it would take a huge amount of space to inventory sermons and sermon-texts one at a time. Translations found only in single copies (including dissertations and archival manuscripts) have been omitted. This guide is also available and periodically updated at http://purl.oclc.org/net/jlt/exegesis, a persistent URL where readers can find a supplement that continues the list to the year 1700, and a link to Jonathan Hall's listing of medieval exegetical works in translation that identifies individual sermons and shorter excerpts. Traditional commentators excerpted in the ACCS and *The Church's Bible* are not inventoried here, but readers should be aware of these and similar series.

Many exegetical writings carry obvious titles and are collected in standard series and sets; I have omitted titles of individual volumes in these series whenever I judged a volume's identity sufficiently evident. Ellipses sometimes replace superfluous title elements (". . . St. Paul's Epistle to the . . ."); page numbers are provided only where a work might be difficult to locate within a larger volume; sixteenth-century English books available in EEBO are identified only by STC numbers. Rabbinic commentaries are indicated by an asterisk. Many of these writers are little known even among historians, but the editions below often provide useful introductions. Otherwise, readers may wish to consult a dictionary of church history — or, of course, reliable Internet resources.

Pentateuch etc. (harmonies and works on multiple books)

Augustine. *Questions on the Heptateuch.* ET in WSA I/14 (projected).

*Bahya ben Asher ben Hlava (d. 1340). *Torah Commentary.* 7 vols. ET by E. Munk (Jerusalem and New York: Lambda, 1998).

Biblical Commentaries from the Canterbury School of Theodore and Hadrian. ET by B. Bischoff and M. Lapidge (Cambridge: Cambridge University Press, 1994).

Calvin, John. *Harmony of Exodus, Leviticus, Numbers, and Deuteronomy.* ET by C. W. Bingham in CTS.

[Pseudo-] Ephrem the Syrian. *The Armenian Commentary on Genesis attributed to Ephrem the Syrian* and *The Armenian Commentaries on Exodus-Deuteronomy attributed to Ephrem the Syrian.* ET by E. G. Mathews Jr. in CSCO 573 (1998) and CSCO 588 (2001).

*Horowitz, Isaiah (*c.* 1565-1630). *Shney luchot habrit = Shlah ha-kadosh: on the written Torah.* 3 vols. ET by E. Munk (Jerusalem and New York: Lambda, 1999).

*Ibn Ezra, Abraham. *Commentary on the Pentateuch.* 5 vols. ET by J. F. Shachter (Hoboken: Ktav, 1900); and by H. N. Strickman and A. M. Silver (New York: Menorah, 1988).

*Jacob ben Asher (*c.* 1269-*c.* 1340). *Tur on the Torah: Commentary on the Torah.* 4 vols. ET by E. Munk (New York: Lambda, 2005).

**Midrash Rabbah.* 10 vols. ET by H. Freedman et al. (third edition; London and New York: Soncino, 1983). [Midrash on Pentateuch, Lamentations, Ruth, Ecclesiastes, Esther, and Song of Songs.]

**Midrash Tanhuma.* 3 vols. ET by J. T. Townsend (Hoboken, N.J.: Ktav, 1989).

*Nachmanides (Ramban). *Commentary on the Torah.* 5 vols. ET by C. B. Chavel (New York: Shilo, 1971-76).

*Rashi. *Pentateuch with Targum Onkelos, Haphtaroth and Rashi's Commentary.*

5 vols. ET by M. Rosenbaum and A. M. Silbermann (1929; reprinted, Jerusalem: Silbermann Family, 5733 [1973]).

*Sforno, Obadiah ben Jacob (1475-1550). *Sforno: Commentary on the Torah.* 2 vols. ET by R. Pelcovitz (New York: Mesorah, 1987).

Theodoret of Cyrus. *Questions on the Octateuch.* ET by R. C. Hill in LEC (2006). [Covers Genesis through Ruth.]

Genesis

Ambrose. *Hexameron, Paradise, and Cain and Abel.* ET by J. J. Savage in FC 42 (1961). [Homilies on Genesis 1–4.]

———. *On Abraham.* ET by T. Tomkinson (Etna, Ca.: Center for Traditionalist Orthodox Studies, 2000).

———. *Seven Exegetical Works.* ET by M. P. McHugh in FC 65 (1972). [Homilies mostly on the patriarchs.]

Augustine. *Unfinished Literal Commentary on Genesis.* ET by E. Hill in WSA I/13 (2002): 103-51; and by R. J. Teske in FC 84 (1990): 143-88.

———. *On Genesis against the Manichees.* ET by R. J. Teske in FC 84(1990): 45-141; and by E. Hill in WSA I/13 (2002): 23-102.

———. *The Literal Meaning of Genesis.* ET by J. H. Taylor in ACW 41-42 (1982); by E. Hill in WSA I/13 (2002): 152-506.

Babington, Gervase. . . . *notes, vpon euery chapter of Genesis.* 1592 (STC 1086-88).

Basil of Caesarea. *Homilies on the Hexaemeron* [Genesis 1–11]. ET by B. Jackson in NPNF² 8; and by A. C. Way in FC 46 (1963): 3-150.

Bede. *On Genesis.* ET by C. Kendall (Liverpool: Liverpool University Press, in preparation).

Biblical Commentaries from the Canterbury School of Theodore and Hadrian. ET by B. Bischoff and M. Lapidge (Cambridge: Cambridge University Press, 1994).

Bonaventure. *Collations on the Six Days.* ET by J. de Vinck (Patterson, N.J.: St. Anthony Guild, 1969).

Calvin, John. *Commentary on Genesis.* ET by T. Tymme, 1578 (STC 4393); and by J. King in CTS.

———. *Sermons on Melchizedek, Abraham's justification, Abraham's sacrifice* [Gen. 14:13-24, 15:4-7, 21:33-22:14]. ET by T. Stocker, 1592 (STC 4440); reprinted (Audubon, N.J.: Old Paths, 1998).

———. *Sermons on election and reprobation . . . Jacob & Esau* [Genesis 25–27]. ET by J. Field, 1579 (STC 4457); reprinted (Audubon, N.J.: Old Paths, 1996).

Chrysostom, John. *Eight Sermons on Genesis.* ET by R. C. Hill (Brookline, Mass.: Holy Cross Orthodox Press, 2004).

———. *Homilies on Genesis.* ET by R. C. Hill in FC 74, 82, 87 (1986-92).

Didymus the Blind. *Commentary on Genesis.* ET by R. C. Hill in FC (forthcoming).

Ephrem the Syrian. *Commentary on Genesis.* ET by E. G. Mathews Jr. in FC 91 (1994): 59-213. Also see entry under Pentateuch, above.

———. *Hymns on Paradise.* ET by S. Brock (Crestwood, N.Y.: St. Vladimir's Seminary Press, 1997).

Gregory of Nyssa. *On the Making of Man.* ET by W. Moore and H. A. Wilson in NPNF² 5:387-427.

Hugh of St. Victor. *Noah's Ark* [Books 1 & 3]. ET by anon. in *Selected Spiritual Writings* (New York: Harper and Row, 1962).

Hunnis, William. *Hunnies recreations: conteining . . . discourses, intituled Adams Banishment: Christ his crib. The lost sheepe. The complaint of old age. . . . The creation or first weeke. The life and death of Ioseph.* 1595 (STC 13973).

Jerome. *Hebrew Questions on Genesis.* ET by C. T. R. Hayward (Oxford: Clarendon Press, 1995).

Luther, Martin. *Lectures on Genesis.* ET by G. V. Schick in LW 1-8. ET of Gen. 1–5 by H. P. Cole (Edinburgh: T. & T. Clark, 1858), revised to cover Gen. 1–8 by J. N. Lenker (Minneapolis: Lutherans in All Lands, 1904-10); abridged ET of Gen. 1–50 by J. T. Mueller (2 vols.; Grand Rapids: Zondervan, 1958).

*Midrash. See *Midrash Rabbah,* under Pentateuch (above). ET also by J. Neusner (3 vols.; Atlanta: Scholars Press, 1985).

Origen. *Homilies on Genesis.* ET by R. E. Heine in FC 71 (1982).

Overton, John. *Iacobs troublesome iourney to Bethel.* 1586 (STC 18924). [Gen. 33:1-4.]

Richard of St. Victor. *The Book of the Patriarchs, The Mystical Ark, Book Three of The Trinity.* ET by G. A. Zinn (Mahwah, N.J.: Paulist, 1979).

Robert Grosseteste. *On the Six Days of Creation.* ET by C. F. J. Martin (Oxford: Oxford University Press, 1996).

*Samuel ben Meir (Rashbam, *c.* 1080-1160). *Commentary on Genesis.* ET by M. I. Lockshin (Lewiston, N.Y.: Edwin Mellen, 1989).

Severian of Gabala. *Homilies on Creation and Fall.* ET by R. C. Hill (Downers Grove, Ill.: InterVarsity Press, forthcoming).

Vermigli, Peter Martyr. *Commentary on Genesis.* ET in PML¹ 12 (projected).

Victorinus of Pettau (d. 304). *On the Creation of the World.* ET by R. E. Wallis in ANF 7:341-43.

Exodus

Babington, Gervase. . . . *notes upon Exodus and Leuiticus.* 1604 (STC 1088.5).

———. . . . *exposition of the Commaundements.* 1583 (STC 1095).

Bede. *On the Tabernacle* [Exod. 24–30]. ET by A. G. Holder (Liverpool: Liverpool University Press, 1994).

Ephrem the Syrian. *Commentary on Exodus*. ET by J. P. Amar in FC 91 (1994): 217-65. Also see entry under Pentateuch, above.

Gregory of Nyssa. *Life of Moses*. ET by A. J. Malherbe and E. Ferguson (Mahwah, N.J.: Paulist, 1978).

Hooper, John. *A declaration of the ten holy co[m]maundementes*. 1549 (STC 13746); reprinted in PS 20.

Knewstubs, John. *Lectures . . . vpon the twentith chapter of Exodus*. 1577 (STC 15042).

Nicholas of Lyra. *Commentary on Exodus* [selections]. ET by C. Patton in *The Theological Interpretation of Scripture: Classic and Contemporary Readings*, ed. S. E. Fowl (Malden, Mass.: Blackwell, 1997), pp. 114-28.

Origen. *Homilies on Exodus*. ET by R. E. Heine in FC 71 (1982).

Philips, Dirk. *The Tabernacle of Moses* [1556]. ET by C. J. Dyck, W. E. Keeney, and A. J. Beachy in *The Writings of Dirk Philips, 1504-1568* (Scottdale, Penn.: Herald, 1992), pp. 264-92.

Leviticus

Babington, Gervase. . . . *notes upon Exodus and Leuiticus*. 1604 (STC 1088.5).

Origen. *Homilies on Leviticus: 1–16*. ET by G. W. Barkley in FC 83 (1990).

Thomas, Lewis. *The anatomy of tale-bearers* [Lev. 19:16]. 1600 (STC 24002).

Numbers

Bede. *On the Resting-Places* [Num. 33]. ET by A. G. Holder in *Bede: A Biblical Miscellany* (Liverpool: Liverpool University Press, 1999), pp. 27-34.

Deuteronomy

Calvin, John. *Sermons on Deuteronomy*. ET by A. Golding, 1581 (STC 4442, 4443a); facsimile reprint (Edinburgh: Banner of Truth, 1987).

———. *Sermons on the Ten Commandments* (Deut. 4:44–6:4). ET by J. Harman, 1579 (STC 4452-54); and by B. W. Farley (Grand Rapids: Baker, 1980).

Luther, Martin. *Lectures on Deuteronomy*. ET by R. R. Caemmerer Jr. in LW 9.

*Samuel ben Meir (*c.* 1080-1160). *Rashbam's Commentary on Deuteronomy*. ET by M. I. Lockshin (Providence, R.I.: Brown Judaic Studies, 2004).

Joshua

Calvin, John. *Commentary on Joshua.* ET by W. Fulke, 1578 (STC 4394); and by H. Beveridge in CTS.

Origen. *Homilies on Joshua.* ET by B. J. Bruce in FC 105 (2002).

Judges

E. R. *A Christian discourse vpon . . . Iudges* [16:16-17], *. . . The portreature of Dalila. The bridle of lust. The seale of secrets.* 1588 (STC 20571).

*Kimhi, David. *Commentary on the Book of Judges.* ET by M. Celniker (Toronto and Buffalo: Rabbi Dr. M. Celniker Book Committee, 1983).

Vermigli, Peter Martyr. *Most fruitfull & learned Commentaries* [on Judges]. ET by anon., 1564 (STC 24670); and in PML² (projected).

Ruth

Lavater, Ludwig. *The book of Ruth expounded in twenty eight sermons.* ET by E. Pagitt, 1586 (STC 15319).

Topsell, Edward. *The revvard of religion Deliuered in sundrie lectures vpon the booke of Ruth.* 1596 (STC 24127).

Various authors. *Commentaries on the Book of Ruth.* ET by L. Smith (Kalamazoo, Mich.: Medieval Institute Publications, 1996). [Selections from Isidore of Seville, the *Ordinary Gloss,* Peter Comestor, Hugh of St. Cher, Nicholas of Lyra.]

1 2 Samuel, 1-2 Kings, 1-2 Chronicles

Bede. *On the Temple.* ET by S. Connolly (Liverpool: Liverpool University Press, 1995). [1 Kings 5–7.]

————. *Thirty Questions on the Book of Kings.* ET by W. T. Foley in *Bede: A Biblical Miscellany* (Liverpool: Liverpool University Press, 1999), pp. 81-143.

Calvin, John. *Sermons on 2 Samuel* [1–13]. ET by D. Kelly (Edinburgh: Banner of Truth, 1992).

Chrysostom, John. *Old Testament Homilies 1: On Hannah, David and Saul.* ET by R. C. Hill (Brookline, Mass.: Holy Cross Orthodox Press, 2003).

Luther, Martin. *The Last Words of David* [2 Sam. 23:1-7]. ET by M. H. Bertram in LW 15.

Origen. *Homily on 1 Kings 28.* ET by J. C. Smith in FC 97 (1998): 319-33.

Theodoret of Cyrus. *Questions on Kingdoms and Chronicles.* ET by R. C. Hill in
LEC (forthcoming).

Vermigli, Peter Martyr. *Commentary on 1-2 Samuel and 1-2 Kings.* ET in PML²
(projected).

Ezra, Nehemiah, Esther

Bede. *On Ezra and Nehemiah.* ET by S. DeGregorio (Liverpool: Liverpool University Press, 2006).

Brenz, Johannes. *A right godly and learned discourse vpon the book of Ester.* ET by
J. Stockwood, 1584 (STC 3602).

Pilkington, James. *Treatise against the grosse sinne of oppression, taken out of . . . the
fift chapter of Nehemiah.* 1585 (STC 19929.5).

Job

Ambrose. *The Prayer of Job [and David].* ET by M. P. McHugh in FC 65 (1972): 329-
67.

Aquinas, Thomas. *The Literal Exposition on Job: A Scriptural Commentary Concerning Providence.* ET by A. Damico (Atlanta, Ga.: Scholars Press, 1989).

Augustine. *Notes on Job.* ET in WSA I/14 (projected).

Bèze, Théodore de. *Iob . . .* and *Ecclesiastes, or the preacher.* 1589 (STC 2020).

Calvin, John. *Sermons on Job.* ET by A. Golding, 1584 (STC 4445); facsimile reprint
(Edinburgh: Banner of Truth, 1993). Partial ET by L. Nixon (Grand Rapids:
Eerdmans, 1952).

Chrysostom, John. *Chrysostom on the Sages: Commentary on Job.* ET by R. C. Hill
(Brookline, Mass.: Holy Cross Orthodox Press, 2006).

Gregory the Great. *Morals on the Book of Job.* ET by anon. and J. Bliss in LFC 18, 21,
23, 31 (1844-50).

Holland, Henry. *Meditations on the 1. and 2. chapters of Iob.* 1596 (STC 13586).

Psalms

Aepinus (= Hoeck), Johann. *Exposition vpo[n] the. xv. Psalme.* ET by N. Lesse, 1548
(STC 166.5).

Ambrose. *The Prayer of [Job and] David.* ET by M. P. McHugh in FC 65 (1972): 368-
420. [Pss. 42–43, 73.]

―――. *Commentary . . . on Twelve Psalms.* ET by Í. M. Ní Riain (Dublin: Halcyon, 2000). [Pss. 1, 36–41, 44, 46, 48–49, 61.]

Aquinas, Thomas. *Commentary on the Psalms.* ET of Prologue and Psalm 45 by M. Rzeczkowski in *Thomas Aquinas, The Gifts of the Spirit: Selected Spiritual Writings* (Hyde Park, N.Y.: New City Press, 1995) pp. 95-133. ET of Aquinas on various Psalms is available online at http://www.niagara.edu/aquinas/

Athanasius. "Letter to Marcellinus on the Interpretation of the Psalms." ET R. C. Gregg in *The Life of Anthony and the Letter to Marcellinus* (New York: Paulist, 1980).

Augustine. *Expositions on the Book of Psalms.* ET by J. E. Tweed et al. in LFC 24, 25, 30, 32, 37, 39 (1847-57), abridged by A. C. Coxe in NPNF[1] 8; by S. Hebgin and F. Corrigan in ACW 29-30 [Pss. 1–37] (1960-61); and by M. Boulding in WSA III/15-20 (2000-04).

Basil of Caesarea. *Exegetic Homilies.* ET by A. C. Way in FC 46 (1963): 151-359. [Pss. 1, 7, 14, 28, 29, 32, 33, 44, 45, 48, 59, 61, and 114.]

Becon, Thomas. *David's Harp, full of Most Delectable Harmony,* 1542 (STC 1717); reprinted in *The Early Works of Thomas Beacon,* PS 2:262-303. [Ps. 116:10-19.]

Bèze, Théodore de. *The Psalmes of Dauid . . . explained by paraphrasis.* ET by A. Gilby, 1580 (STC 2033).

―――. *Christian meditations vpon eight Psalmes of the prophet Dauid.* ET by J. Stubbes, 1582 (STC 2004). [Penitential psalms.]

Bird, Samuel. *Lectures . . . vpon the 38. Psalme.* 1580 (STC 3088).

Blake, David. *An exposition vppon the thirtie two psalme.* 1600 (STC 3122).

Bucer, Martin. *The Psalter of David.* ET by G. Joye, 1530 (STC 2370); reprinted (Appleford, England: Sutton Courtenay, 1971).

Calvin, John. *Commentary on the Psalms.* ET by A. Golding, 1571 (STC 4395), revised by T. H. L. Parker (Edinburgh: James Clarke, 1965); and by J. Anderson in CTS.

―――. *Thre notable sermones, made . . . in Maye, the yere 1561 vpon Psalm. 46.* ET by W. Warde, 1562 (STC 4458).

―――. *Sermons on Psalm 119.* ET by T. Stocker, 1580 (STC 4460); reprinted (Audubon, N.J.: Old Paths, 1996).

Cassiodorus. *Explanation of the Psalms.* ET by P. G. Walsh in ACW 51-53 (1990-91).

Chandieu, Antoine de. *Meditations vppon the xxxii. Psalme.* ET by W. Watkinson, 1579 (STC 15256).

Chrysostom, John. *Commentary on the Psalms.* ET by R. C. Hill (Brookline, Mass: Holy Cross Orthodox Press, 1998).

―――. *Old Testament Homilies 3: On the Obscurity of the Old Testament, Homilies on the Psalms.* ET by R. C. Hill (Brookline, Mass.: Holy Cross Orthodox Press, 2003).

Diodore of Tarsus. *Commentary on Psalms 1–51*. ET by R. C. Hill in WGRW 9 (2005).

Erasmus, Desiderius. *Expositions of the Psalms*. ET of Pss. 1–4 by M. J. Heath in CWE 63 (1997); ET of Pss. 22, 28, 33, 85 by E. Kearns, C. White, and M. J. Heath in CWE 64 (2003). CWE 65 on Psalms is projected.

Fisher, John. *The seuen penytencyall psalmes* [Pss. 6, 31, 37, 50, 101, 129, 142]. 1508 (STC 10902). Modernized in *Exposition of the Seven Penitential Psalms* (San Francisco: Ignatius Press, 1998).

Gregory of Nyssa. *On the Inscriptions of the Psalms*. ET by C. McCambley (Brookline, Mass.: Hellenic College Press, 1990); and by R. E. Heine (Oxford: Clarendon, 1995).

————. "On the Sixth Psalm, Concerning the Octave." ET by R. McCambley, *Greek Orthodox Theological Review* 32, no. 1 (1987): 39-50.

Harrison, Robert. *A little treatise vppon the firste verse of the 122. Psalme*. 1583 (STC 12861).

Hemmingsen, Niels. *Exposition vpon the XXV. Psalme of David*. ET by R. R., 1580 (STC 13059.4).

Hilary of Poitiers. *Homilies on Psalms 1, 54, 131*. ET by H. F. Stewart in NPNF[2] 9:236-48.

Holland, Henry. *Spirituall preseruatiues against the pestilence . . . collected out of the 91 psalme*. 1593 (STC 13588).

Hooper, John. "Expositions of Psalms [23, 62, 73, 77]." 1580 (STC 13743, cf. 13752); reprinted in *Later Writings of Bishop Hooper*, PS 21:176-373.

Jerome. *Homilies*. ET by M. L. Ewald in FC 48, 57 (1964-66). [74 homilies on Pss.]

*Kimhi, David. *Commentary on the Psalms*. ET of Psalms 1–8 by A. W. Greenup (London: Palestine House, 1918); of Psalms 1–10, 15–17, 19, 22, 24 by R. G. Finch (London: SPCK; and New York: Macmillan, 1919); of Psalms 120–150 by J. Baker and E. W. Nicholson (Cambridge: Cambridge University Press, 1973).

Knox, John. *An exposition vppon the syxt psalme*. 1556 (STC 15074.6).

Luther, Martin. ET by H. J. A. Bouman of *First Lectures on the Psalms* in LW 10-11; by various translators of *Selected Psalms* in LW 12-14. There are other selections from Luther on the Psalms that date from the sixteenth century.

Mornay, Philippe de. *Meditations vpon Psal. 101*. ET by T. W[ilcox], 1599 (STC 18146).

Osiander, Andreas. *How and whither a Christen man ought to flye the horrible plage of the pestilence* [Ps. 91]. ET by M. Coverdale, 1537 (STC 18878).

Pigg, Oliver. *Sermons, vpon the 101. Psalme*. 1591 (STC 19916.7).

Rhegius, Urbanus. *The solace of Sion, and ioy of Ierusalem. Or consolation of Gods church in the latter age redeemed by the preaching of the Gospell vniuersallye* [Ps. 87]. ET by R. Robinson, 1587 (STC 20852).

Rainolds, John. *A Sermon upon Part of the Eighteenth Psalm*. 1586 (STC 20621.5).

Rashi. Rashi's Commentary on Psalms. ET by M. I. Gruber (Atlanta: Scholars Press, 1998; Leiden: Brill, 2003). [Commentary on Pss. 1–89.]

Richardson, Robert. *A briefe and compendious exposition vpon the Psalme* [130]. 1570 (STC 21021).

Rolle, Richard. "The English Psalter and Commentary." ET by R. Allen in *Richard Rolle: The English Writings* (New York: Paulist, 1988), pp. 9-64.

Savonarola, Girolamo. *Exposition . . . vpon ye .li. psalme, called Miserere mei Deus* [Ps. 51, with second meditation on Ps. 31]. ET by W. Marshall, 1534/38 (STC 21791; cf. 21789.3-98.5); and by J. P. Donnelly in *Prison Meditations on Psalms 51 and 31* (Milwaukee: Marquette University Press, 1994).

Savonarola, Girolamo. *An other meditatio[n] . . . vpon the lxxx Psalme of Dauid.* ET by anon. 1555 (STC 21799.2).

Simons, Menno. *Meditation on Psalm 25.* ET by L. Verduin in *The Complete Writings of Menno Simons, c. 1496-1561* (Scottdale, Penn.: Herald, 1992), pp. 65-86.

Strigel, Victorinus. *The harmony of King Dauids harp* [Exposition of Pss. 1–72]. 6 vols. ET by R. Robinson, 1582-98 (STC 23358-63).

Theodore of Mopsuestia. *Commentary on Psalms 1–81.* ET by R. C. Hill in WGRW 5 (2006).

Theodoret of Cyrus. *Commentary on the Psalms.* ET by R. C. Hill in FC 101-2 (2000-01).

Travers, Robert. *Exposition made vpon the CXI. psalme.* 1579 (STC 24180).

Wilcox, Thomas. *Works . . . containing an exposition vpon the whole booke of Davids Psalmes. . . .* 1586 (STC 25620; cf. 25625).

Wyatt, Thomas. *. . . the .vii. penytentiall psalmes.* 1549 (STC 2726).

Proverbs, Ecclesiastes

Bèze, Théodore de. *Iob . . .* and *Ecclesiastes, or the preacher.* 1589 (STC 2020).

Bonaventure. *Commentary on Ecclesiastes.* ET by C. Murray and R. J. Karris (St. Bonaventure, N.Y.: Franciscan Institute, 2005).

Chrysostom, John. *Chrysostom on the Sages: Commentary on Proverbs and Ecclesiastes.* ET by R. C. Hill (Brookline, Mass.: Holy Cross Orthodox Press, 2006).

Cope, Michael. *A Godly and Learned Exposition Vppon the Prouerbs of Solomon.* ET by M. Outred. 1580 (STC 5723).

Dionysius of Alexandria (d. 265). ET of comments on Ecclesiastes 1–3 by S. D. F. Salmond in ANF 6:111-14.

Gifford, George. *Eight sermons, vpon the first foure chapters, and part of the fift, of Ecclesiastes.* 1589 (STC 11853).

Gregory of Nyssa. *Commentary on Ecclesiastes.* ET by C. McCambley (Brookline,

Mass.: Hellenic College Press, 1990) and by S. G. Hall, *Homilies on Ecclesiastes* (Berlin: W. de Gruyter, 1993).

Gregory Thaumaturgus. *A Metaphrase of the Book of Ecclesiastes.* ET by S. D. F. Salmond in ANF 6:9-17; and by J. Jarick (Atlanta: Scholars Press, 1990).

Luther, Martin. *An Exposition of Ecclesiastes.* ET by anon., 1573 (STC 16979); and by J. Pelikan as *Notes on Ecclesiastes* in LW 15.

Wilcox, Thomas. *A short, yet sound commentarie; written on . . . the Prouerbes of Salomon.* 1589 (STC 25627; cf. 25620).

Song of Solomon

Andrewes, Bartimaeus. *Sermons, vpon the fifth chapiter of the Songs of Solomon.* 1583 (STC 585).

Bede. *On the Song of Songs and Other Spiritual Writings.* ET by A. Holder (New York: Paulist, in preparation).

Bernard of Clairvaux. *Sermons on the Song of Songs.* ET by K. Walsh and I. Edmonds (4 vols.; Kalamazoo, Mich.: Cistercian Publications, 1971-80).

Bèze, Théodore de. *Sermons vpon the three chapters of the canticle of canticles wherein are handled the chiefest points of religion controversed and debated betweene vs and the aduersarie at this day.* ET by J. Harmar, 1587 (STC 2025).

Brucioli, Antonio. *A Commentary upon the Canticle of Canticles.* ET by T. James, 1598 (STC 3928).

*Ezra ben Solomon of Verona (d. *c.* 1245). *Commentary on the Song of Songs and other Kabbalistic Commentaries.* ET by S. Brody (Kalamazoo, Mich.: Medieval Institute Publications, 1999).

Fenner, Dudley. *The song of songs . . . interpreted by a short commentarie.* 1587 (STC 2769).

Gifford, George. *Fifteene sermons, vpon the Song of Salomon.* 1598 (STC 11854).

Gilbert of Hoyland. *Sermons on the Song of Songs.* ET by L. C. Braceland (3 vols.; Kalamazoo, Mich.: Cistercian Publications, 1978-79).

Giles of Rome. *Commentary on the Song of Songs and Other Writings.* ET by J. E. Rotelle (Villanova, Penn.: Augustinian Press, 1998).

Gregory of Nyssa. *Commentary on the Song of Songs.* ET by C. McCambley (Brookline, Mass.: Hellenic College Press, 1987).

―――. *Homilies on the Song of Songs.* ET by R. A. Norris in WGRW (forthcoming).

*Ibn Ezra, Abraham. *Commentary on the Song of Songs.* ET by R. A. Block (Cincinnati: Hebrew Union College / Jewish Institute of Religion, 1982).

John of Ford. *Sermons on the Final Verses of the Song of Songs.* ET by W. M. Beckett (7 vols.; Kalamazoo, Mich.: Cistercian Publications, 1977-84).

Levi ben Gershom (1288-1344). Commentary on Song of Songs. ET by M. Kellner (New Haven: Yale University Press, 1998).

Luther, Martin. *Lectures on the Song of Solomon.* ET by I. Siggins in LW 15.

Midrash on the Song of Songs. See *Midrash Rabbah,* under Pentateuch (above). ET also by J. Neusner (2 vols.; Atlanta: Scholars Press, 1989).

Nicholas of Lyra. *The Postilla of Nicholas of Lyra on the Song of Songs.* ET by J. G. Kiecker (Milwaukee: Marquette University Press, 1998).

Moffett, Peter. *A Commentarie upon the booke of the Proverbes of Salomon.* 1592 (STC 18247); enlarged, 1596 (STC 18246).

Ordinary Gloss. ET by Mary Dove in *The Glossa Ordinaria on the Song of Songs* (Kalamazoo, Mich.: Medieval Institute Publications, 2004).

Origen. *The Song of Songs: Commentary and Homilies.* ET by R. P. Lawson in ACW 26 (1957).

Theodoret of Cyrus. *Commentary on the Song of Songs.* ET by R. C. Hill (Brisbane: Australian Catholic University, 2001).

Wilcox, Thomas. *The Booke of the Canticles, otherwise called Schelomons Song.* 1585 (STC 25622; cf. 25620).

William of St. Thierry. *Exposition on the Song of Songs.* ET by M. C. Hart (Kalamazoo, Mich.: Cistercian Publications, 1970).

Isaiah

Bede. *On What Isaiah Says* [Isa. 24:21-23]. ET by A. G. Holder in *Bede: A Biblical Miscellany* (Liverpool: Liverpool University Press, 1999), pp. 35-51.

Calvin, John. *Commentary on Isaiah.* ET by C. Cotton, 1609 (STC 4396); and by W. Pringle in CTS.

———. *Sermons . . . vpon the songe that Ezechias made after he had bene sicke and afflicted by the hand of God* [Isa. 38]. ET by A. Locke, 1560 (STC 4450); reprinted in *Mrs. Locke's Little Book* (London: Olive Tree, 1973).

———. *Sermons on Isaiah 53.* ET by L. Nixon, *The Gospel According to Isaiah* (Grand Rapids: Eerdmans, 1953); and by T. H. L. Parker, *Sermons on Isaiah's Prophecy of the Death and Passion of Christ* (London: James Clarke, 1956).

Carpenter, John. *The song of the beloued, concerning his vineyard* [Isa. 5:1-7]. 1599 (STC 4667).

Chrysostom, John. *Commentary on Isaiah 1–8.* ET by D. A Garrett in *An Analysis of the Hermeneutics of John Chrysostom's Commentary on Isaiah 1–8* (Lewiston, N.Y.: Edwin Mellen, 1992).

———. *Old Testament Homilies 2: On Isaiah and Jeremiah.* ET by R. C. Hill (Brookline, Mass.: Holy Cross Orthodox Press, 2003).

Cyril of Alexandria. *Commentary on Isaiah.* ET by R. C. Hill, in preparation.

*Ibn Ezra, Abraham. *Commentary on Isaiah.* ET by M. Friedländer (1873; reprinted, New York: P. Feldheim, 1968).

*Kimhi, David. *Commentary on Isaiah.* ET by L. Finkelstein (1926; reprinted, New York: AMS Press, 1966).

Luther, Martin. *Lectures on Isaiah.* ET by H. J. A. Bouman in LW 16-17.

Theodoret of Cyrus. *Commentary on Isaiah.* ET by R. C. Hill in WGRW (forthcoming).

*Various (10th century). *The Messiah in Isaiah 53: The Commentaries of Saadia Gaon, Salmon ben Yeruham, and Yefet ben Eli on Is. 52:13–53:12.* ET by J. Alobaidi (New York: Peter Lang, 1998).

Jeremiah, Lamentations

Calvin, John. *Commentary on Jeremiah and Lamentations.* ET of Jer. 1–5 by C. Cotton, 1620 (STC 4466); complete ET by J. Owen in CTS.

———. *Sermons on Jeremiah.* ET by B. Reynolds (Lewiston, N.Y.: Edwin Mellen, 1990).

Cottesford, Samuel. *A treatise against traitors* [on Jer. 40:13–41:4]. 1591 (STC 5840).

Gilbert the Universal. *Glossa Ordinaria in Lamentationes Ieremie Prophete: Prothemata et Liber I.* ET by A. Andrée (Stockholm: Almquist & Wiksell, 2005), pp. 162-287.

*Midrash on Lamentations. See *Midrash Rabbah,* under Pentateuch (above). ET also by J. Neusner (Atlanta: Scholars Press, 1989).

Origen. *Homilies on Jeremiah.* ET by J. C. Smith in FC 97 (1998).

Theodoret of Cyrus. *Commentary on Jeremiah, Lamentations, Baruch.* ET by R. C. Hill (Brookline, Mass.: Holy Cross Orthodox Press, 2006).

Tossanus, Daniel. *The lamentations and holy mourninges of the prophet Ieremiah.* ET by T. Stocker, 1587 (STC 2779.5).

Udall, John. *A commentarie vpon the Lamentations.* 1593 (STC 24494).

Vermigli, Peter Martyr. *Commentary on Lamentations.* ET by D. Shute in PML[1] 6.

Ezekiel, Daniel

Broughton, Hugh. *Daniel his Chaldie visions and his Ebrew: both translated . . . and expounded.* 1596 (STC 2785).

Calvin, John. *Commentary on Ezekiel 1–20.* ET by T. Meyers in CTS; and of Ezekiel 1–12 by D. L. Foxgrover and D. E. Martin (Grand Rapids: Eerdmans, 1994).

———. *Commentary on Daniel.* Abridged ET by A. Gilby, 1570 (STC 4397). ET by

T. Meyers in CTS; and of Daniel 1–6 by T. H. L. Parker (Grand Rapids: Eerd-mans, 1993).

Gregory the Great. *Homilies . . . on the Book of the Prophet Ezekiel.* ET by T. Gray (Etna, Calif.: Center for Traditionalist Orthodox Studies, 1990).

Hippolytus of Rome. ET of fragments on Daniel by S. D. F. Salmond in ANF 5:177-91.

*Japheth ben Ali, ha-Levi (10th century). *Angels and Fire: . . . Yefet ibn Ali Hallewi on Daniel and Nahum.* ET by D. S. Margoulith and H. Hirschfeld (Pleasanton, Calif.: Gan-Eiden Press, 2000); related edition (Troy, N.Y.: al-Qirqisani Center for the Promotion of Karaite Studies, 2003).

Jerome. *Commentary on Daniel.* ET by G. L. Archer (Grand Rapids: Baker, 1958); e-text at CCEL.

Joye, George. *The exposicion of Daniel the prophete gathered oute of Philip Melanchton, Iohan Ecolampadius, Chonrade Pellicane [and] out of Iohan Draconite.* 1545 (STC 14823).

*Sa'adia ben Joseph, Rabbi (882-942). *The book of Daniel.* ET by J. Alobaidi (New York: Peter Lang, 2006).

Smith, Henry. *The fall of King Nabuchadnezzar* [Dan. 4:28-30]. 1591 (STC 22662); and *The restitution of King Nabuchadnezzer* [Dan. 4:31-34]. 1591 (STC 22690).

Theodoret of Cyrus. *Commentary on Ezekiel.* ET by R. C. Hill (Brookline, Mass.: Holy Cross, forthcoming).

―――. *Commentary on Daniel.* ET by R. C. Hill in WGRW (forthcoming).

Minor Prophets

Abbot, George. *An exposition upon the prophet Ionah.* 1600 (STC 34.5).

Bede. *On Tobit and the Canticle of Habakkuk.* ET by S. Connolly (Portland, Ore.: Four Courts Press, 1997).

Brenz, Johannes. *Newes from Niniue to Englande, brought by the prophete Ionas.* ET by T. Tymme, 1570 (STC 3601).

Calvin, John. *Commentaries on the Minor Prophets.* ET by J. Owen in CTS. ET by N. Baxter of lectures on Jonah, 1578 (STC 4432-33).

―――. *Sermons on Micah.* ET by B. Reynolds (Lewiston: Edwin Mellen, 1990); and by B. W. Farley (Phillipsburg, N.J.: Presbyterian & Reformed, 2003).

Cyril of Alexandria. *Commentary on The Twelve Prophets.* ET by R. C. Hill in FC (2007), forthcoming.

Daneau, Lambert. *A fruitfull commentarie vpon the twelue small prophets.* ET by J. Stockwood, 1594 (STC 6227).

Denck, Hans. *Reflections on . . . Micah.* ET by E. J. Furcha in *Selected Writings of Hans Denck, 1500-1527* (Lewiston, N.Y.: Edwin Mellen, 1989), pp. 35-181.

Didymus the Blind. *Commentary on Zechariah.* ET by R. C. Hill in FC 111 (2006).

Gilby, Anthony. *A commentarye vpon the prophet Mycha.* 1551 (STC 11887).

―――. *A commentarye vpon the prophet Malaky.* 1553 (STC 11885.5).

Gwalther, Rudolf. *Certaine godlie homelies or sermons vpon the prophets Abdias and Ionas.* 1573 (STC 25010).

―――. *Sermons . . . vpon the prophet Zephaniah.* ET by M. Wilton, 1580 (STC 25014).

Gyrneus, Johann Jacob. *Haggeus the prophet.* ET by C. Fetherstone, 1586 (STC 2790).

Haimo of Auxerre (d. *c.* 875). *Commentary on the Book of Jonah.* ET by D. Everhart (Kalamazoo, Mich.: Medieval Institute Publications, 1993).

Hooper, John. *An oversighte and deliberacion uppon the holy prophet Jonas.* 1550 (STC 13763); reprinted in *Early Writings of John Hooper,* PS 20:431-558.

*Ibn Ezra, Abraham. *Commentary on Hosea.* ET by A. Lipshitz (New York: Sepher-Hermon Press, 1988).

*Japheth ben Ali, ha-Levi (10th century). *Angels and Fire: . . . Yefet ibn Ali Hallewi on Daniel and Nahum.* ET by D. S. Margoulith and H. Hirschfeld (Pleasanton, Cal.: Gan-Eiden Press, 2000); related edition (Troy, N.Y.: al-Qirqisani Center for the Promotion of Karaite Studies, 2003).

*Kimhi, David. *Commentary on Hosea.* ET by H. A. Cohen (New York: AMS Press, 1966).

―――. *Commentary upon the Prophecies of Zechariah.* ET by A. McCaul (London: James Duncan, 1837).

King, John. *Lectures vpon Ionas.* 1597 (STC 14976); reprinted (2 vols.; London: Grace Webster, 1845).

Luther, Martin. *Lectures on Jonah & Habakkuk.* ET by C. D. Froehlich in LW 19.

―――. *Lectures on Zechariah.* ET by R. J. Dinda in LW 20.

―――. *Lectures on Hosea, Joel, Amos, Obadiah, Micah, Nahum, Zephaniah, Haggai, & Malachi.* ET by R. J. Dinda in LW 18.

Pilkington, James. *Aggeus the prophete declared by a large commentary.* 1560 (STC 19926.7).

―――. *Aggeus and Abdias prophetes.* 1562 (STC 19927).

Rainolds, John. *A sermon vpon part of the prophesie of Obadiah.* 1584 (STC 20623).

―――. *The prophecie of Obadiah.* 1613 (STC 20619).

―――. *The Prophesie of Haggai.* 1649 (Wing R143).

Topsell, Edward. *An exposition on the prophet Ioel.* 1599 (STC 24131).

Tyndale, William. *The prophete Ionas.* 1531 (STC 2788).

Theodore of Mopsuestia. *Commentary on the Twelve Prophets.* ET by R. C. Hill in FC 108 (2004).

Theodoret of Cyrus. *Commentary on the Twelve Prophets.* ET by R. C. Hill (Brookline, Mass.: Holy Cross, forthcoming).

Gospels & Acts (harmonies and works on multiple books)

Aelred of Rievaulx. *The Liturgical Sermons: The First Clairvaux Collection, Advent — All Saints.* ET by T. Berkeley (Kalamazoo, Mich.: Cistercian Publications, 2001). [Sermons on Gospels.]

Anthony of Padua. *Sermones for the Easter Cycle.* ET by G. Marcil (St. Bonaventure, N.Y.: Franciscan Institute Publications, 1994).

Augustine. *The Harmony of the Gospels.* ET by S. D. F. Salmond in NPNF[1] 6.

———. *Sermons on Selected Lessons of the New Testament.* ET by R. G. MacMullen in LFC 16, 20 (1844-45); reprinted in NPNF[1] 6:245-406 (Matt.), 406-13 (Mark), 413-58 (Luke), 458-545 (John).

———. *Questions on the Gospels.* ET in WSA I/15 (projected).

Bede. *Homilies on the Gospels.* ET by L. T. Martin and D. Hurst (2 vols.; Kalamazoo, Mich.: Cistercian Publications, 1991).

Bernard of Clairvaux. *Sermons for the Summer Season.* ET by B. Kienzle and J. Jarzembowski (Kalamazoo, Mich.: Cistercian Publications, 1991).

Bonaventure. *Sunday Sermons.* ET by T. Johnson (St. Bonaventure, N.Y.: Franciscan Institute, 2007). [Sermons on assorted Gospel texts.]

Calvin, John. *Commentary on a Harmony of Matthew, Mark, and Luke.* ET by E. Pagit, 1584 (STC 2962-63); by W. Pringle in CTS; and by A. W. Morrison and T. H. L. Parker in CNTC 1-3.

Coverdale, Miles. *Fruitfull lessons, vpon the passion, buriall, resurrection, ascension, and of the sending of the holy Ghost: Gathered out of the foure Euangelists.* 1593 (STC 5891).

Erasmus, Desiderius. *Paraphrase of Erasmus vpon the Newe Testamente* [Gospels and Acts]. ET by N. Udall, 1548 (STC 2854.3); facsimile reprint (Delmar, N.Y.: Scholars' Facsimiles & Reprints, 1975).

Gregory the Great. *Forty Gospel Homilies.* ET by D. Hurst (Kalamazoo, Mich.: Cistercian Publications, 1990).

Guerric of Igny. *Liturgical Sermons.* ET by Monks at Mount St. Bernard Abbey (2 vols.; Kalamazoo, Mich.: Cistercian Publications, 1970).

Hemmingsen, Niels. *A postill, or exposition of the Gospels that are vsually red . . . vpon the Sundayes and feast dayes of saincts.* ET by A. Golding, 1569 (STC 13061).

Isaac of Stella. *Sermons on the Christian Year, I.* ET by H. McCaffery (Kalamazoo, Mich.: Cistercian Publications, 1979).

Luther, Martin. *Sermons of Martin Luther: The House Postils.* ET by E. F. A. Klug, variously reprinted (Grand Rapids: Baker, 1996, 2000). [3 vols., mostly on Gospels and Acts.]

———. *Sermons.* ET by J. W. Doberstein and J. G. Kunstmann in LW 51-52. [Sermons mostly from the Gospels.]

—————. *Sermons of Martin Luther.* ET by J. N. Lenker, 1904; variously reprinted (Grand Rapids: Baker, 1983, 1995, 2000). [Vols. 1-5 on Gospels.]

Peter Chrysologus (406-450). *Selected Sermons.* ET by G. E. Ganss in FC 17 (1953) and by W. B. Palardy in FC 109-10 (2004-5). [Gospels; a few on Rom. & Pss.]

Matthew

Aquinas, Thomas. "Lectures on St. Matthew" (excerpts). ET by S. Tugwell in *Albert and Thomas: Selected Writings* (New York: Paulist, 1988), pp. 445-75.

—————. *Commentary on Saint Matthew's Gospel, Ch. I-XII.* ET by F. R. Larcher (typescript at Dominican College Library, Washington, D.C., 1991).

Augustine. *Our Lord's Sermon on the Mount.* ET by W. Findlay, revised by D. S. Schaff, in NPNF[1] 6; by D. J. Kavanagh "with seventeen related sermons" in FC 11 (1951); by J. J. Epson in ACW 5 (1978); and in WSA I/16 (projected).

—————. *Seventeen Questions on Matthew.* ET in WSA I/15 (projected).

Bucer, Martin. *Commentary on Matthew.* ET by D. F. Wright in *Common Places of Martin Bucer* (Appleford, England: Sutton Courtenay, 1972). [Excerpts on Matt. 16:18-19 and 19:3-12 on pp. 235-51, 401-28.]

—————. *. . . exposition . . . vppon these wordes of S. Mathew: Woo be to the worlde bycause of offences. Math. xviii.* ET by anon., 1566 (STC 3964).

Catena aurea on Matthew [patristic excerpts collected by Thomas Aquinas]. ET by W. Whiston (2 vols., 1841-45), several reprints; e-text at CCEL.

Chrysostom, John. *Spiritual Gems from the Gospel of Matthew.* ET by R. C. Hill (Brookline, Mass.: Holy Cross Orthodox Press, 2004). [Excerpts from homilies.]

—————. *Homilies on . . . Matthew.* ET by G. Prevost in LFC 11, 15, 34 (1843-51), revised by M. B. Riddle in NPNF[1] 10.

Gilbert of Hoyland. *Treatises, Sermons and Epistles* [prologue, two sermons on Matt.]. ET by L. C. Braceland (Kalamazoo, Mich.: Cistercian Publications, 1981), pp. 127-81.

Gregory of Nyssa. *The Lord's Prayer, The Beatitudes.* ET by H. C. Graef in ACW 18 (1954).

Latimer, Hugh. *Certayn godly sermons, made vpon the Lords prayer.* 1562 (STC 15276). [27 sermons; 7 on Lord's Prayer.]

Luther, Martin. *The Sermon on the Mount* [sermons]. ET by J. Pelikan in LW 21.

Marlorat, Augustin, ed. *A catholike and ecclesiasticall exposition of the holy Gospell after S. Mathewe.* ET T. Tymme, 1570 (STC 17404). [Excerpts from two dozen Fathers and Reformers.]

Origen. *Commentary on . . . Matthew.* ET by J. Patrick in ANF 10.

Theophylact. *Explanation . . . of St. Matthew.* ET by C. Stade (House Springs, Mo.: Chrysostom Press, 1992).

Tyndale, William. *An exposicion vppon the v. vi. vii. chapters of Mathew.* 1533 (STC 24440).

Valerian of Cimiez (*fl.* 439-60). *Homilies.* ET by G. E. Ganss in FC 17 (1953): 291-440. [Eight homilies on Matt., with other isolated texts.]

W[ilmot], R[obert]. *Syrophaenissa or, the Cananitish womans conflicts in twelue seuerall tractats discouered.* 1601 (STC 25765).

Mark

Anonymous [Pseudo-Jerome, 7th century]. ET by Michael Cahill in *The First Commentary on Mark* (New York: Oxford, 1998).

Catena aurea on Mark [patristic excerpts collected by Thomas Aquinas]. ET by W. Whiston (2 vols., 1841-45), several reprints; e-text at CCEL.

Dionysius Exiguus (d. *c.* 540). *The exposition of Dionysius Syrus written above 900 years since on the evangelist St. Mark.* ET by D. Loftus, 1672 (Wing D1525).

Erasmus, Desiderius. *Paraphrase on Mark.* ET by E. Rummel in CWE 49 (1988).

Jerome. *Homilies.* ET by M. L. Ewald in FC 57 (1966). [10 homilies on Mark.]

Marlorat, Augustin. *A catholike and ecclesiasticall exposition of the holy gospell after S. Marke and Luke.* ET by T. Timme, 1583 (STC 17405). [Excerpts from eleven Reformers.]

Theophylact. *Explanation . . . of St. Mark.* ET by C. Stade (House Springs, Mo.: Chrysostom Press, 1993).

Luke

Ambrose. *Commentary . . . on the Gospel according to Saint Luke.* ET by Í. M. Ní Riain (Dublin: Halcyon Press, 2001).

Bernard of Clairvaux. *Homilies in Praise of the Blessed Virgin Mary.* ET by M.-B. Saïd (Kalamazoo, Mich.: Cistercian Publications, 1993).

Bernardine of Siena. *Sermon XXIV* [Luke 15:11-32]. ET by R. J. Karris in *Franciscan Studies* 62 (2006): 31-66.

Bonaventure. *Commentary on the Gospel of Luke.* ET by R. J. Karris (3 vols.; St. Bonaventure, N.Y.: Franciscan Institute, 2001-04).

Catena aurea on Luke [patristic excerpts collected by Thomas Aquinas]. ET by W. Whiston (2 vols., 1841-45), several reprints.

Cyril of Alexandria. *Commentary on . . . Luke.* ET by R. Payne Smith (2 vols., 1859), reprinted ([Astoria, N.Y.]: Studion, 1983).

Diego de Estella. *Commentary on Luke* [15:11-32]. ET by R. J. Karris in *Franciscan Studies* 61 (2003): 97-234.

Dionysius of Alexandria (d. 265). *The Works of Dionysius: Exegetical Fragments.* ET by S. D. F. Salmond in ANF 6:114-19. [Comment on Luke 22:42-48.]

Erasmus, Desiderius. *Paraphrase on Luke.* ET by J. E. Phillips in CWE [47]-48 (2003-).

Francis of Meyronnes. *Sermon 57 on the Parable of the Prodigal Son (Luke 15:11-32).* ET by R. J. Karris in *Franciscan Studies* 63 (2005): 131-58.

Hugh of St. Cher. *A Commentary on the Parable of the Prodigal Son.* ET by H. B. Feiss (Toronto: Peregrina, 1996).

Luther, Martin. *Commentary on the Magnificat.* ET by A. T. W. Steinhaeuser (Philadelphia: Muhlenberg, 1930); reprinted in LW 21.

Keltridge, John. *Exposition, . . . vpon . . . the. xi. of Luke.* 1578 (STC 14920).

Marlorat, Augustin. *A catholike and ecclesiasticall exposition of the holy gospell after S. Marke and Luke.* ET by T. Timme, 1583 (STC 17405). [Excerpts from eleven Reformers.]

Origen. *Homilies on Luke; Fragments on Luke.* ET by J. T. Lienhard in FC 94 (1996).

Theophylact. *Explanation . . . of St. Luke.* ET by C. Stade (House Springs, Mo.: Chrysostom Press, 1997).

John

Aquinas, Thomas. *Commentary on the Gospel of St. John.* ET by J. A. Weisheipl and F. R. Larcher (2 vols; Albany, N.Y.: Magi Books, 1980-88).

Augustine. *Lectures or Tractates on . . . John.* ET by H. Browne in LFC 26, 29 (1848-49); by J. Gibb & J. Innes in NPNF[1] 7; and by J. W. Rettig in FC 78, 79, 88, 90, 92 (1988-95).

Bonaventure. *Commentary on the Book of John.* ET by R. J. Karris (St. Bonaventure, N.Y.: Franciscan Institute Publications, 2006).

Brenz, Johannes. *A verye fruitful exposicion vpon the syxte chapter of Saynte Iohn.* ET by R. Shirrye, 1550 (STC 3603).

Calvin, John. *Commentary on John.* ET by C. Fetherstone, 1584 (STC 2962-63); by W. Pringle in CTS; and by T. H. L. Parker in CNTC 4-5.

Catena aurea on John [patristic excerpts collected by Thomas Aquinas]. ET by W. Whiston (2 vols., 1841-45), several reprints.

Chrysostom, John. *Homilies on . . . John.* ET by G. T. Stupart in LFC 28, 36 (1848-49), edited by P. Schaff in NPNF[1] 14; and by T. A. Goggin in FC 33, 41 (1957-59).

Cyril of Alexandria. *Commentary on . . . John.* ET by P. E. Pusey and T. Randell in LFC 43, 48 (1874-85); available at CCEL.

Erasmus, Desiderius. *Paraphrase on John.* ET by J. E. Phillips in CWE 46 (1991).

John Scotus Erigena. *The Voice of the Eagle: Homily on the Prologue to the Gospel of St. John.* ET by C. Bamford (Hudson, N.Y.: Lindisfarne, 1990).

Luther, Martin. *Sermons on the Gospel of St. John.* ET by M. H. Bertram in LW 22-24. [Covers John 1–4, 6–8, 14–16.]

Marlorat, Augustin, ed. *A catholike and ecclesiasticall exposition of the holy Gospell after S. Iohn.* ET by T. Timme, 1575 (STC 17406). [Excerpts from various Reformers.]

Theodore of Mopsuestia. *Commentary on the Gospel of John.* ET by G. Kalantzis (Strathfield, NSW, Australia: St. Pauls, 2004).

Theophylact. *Explanation . . . of St. John.* ET by C. Stade (House Springs, Mo.: Chrysostom Press, forthcoming).

Origen. *Commentary on the Gospel of John.* ET by A. Menzies in ANF 10; by A. E. Brook (Cambridge: Cambridge University Press, 1896); and by R. E. Heine in FC 80, 89 (1989-93).

Acts

Bede. *Commentary on the Acts of the Apostles.* ET by L. T. Martin (Kalamazoo, Mich.: Cistercian Publications, 1989).

Calvin, John. *Commentary on the Acts of the Apostles.* ET by C. Fetherstone, 1585 (STC 4398), revised by H. Beveridge in CTS; and by J. W. Fraser & W. J. G. McDonald in CNTC 6-7.

Chrysostom, John. *Homilies on the Acts of the Apostles.* ET by J. Walker, J. Sheppard, and H. Browne in LFC 33, 35 (1851), revised by G. B. Stevens in NPNF[1] 11.

Erasmus, Desiderius. *Paraphrase on the Acts of the Apostles.* ET by Robert D. Sider in CWE 50 (1995).

Epistles (works covering multiple epistles)

Ambrosiaster. *Commentary on the Pauline Epistles.* ET by D. G. Hunter, S. Cooper, and T. de Bruyn in WGRW (in preparation).

Augustine. *Sermons on Selected Lessons of the New Testament.* ET by R. G. MacMullen in LFC 20 (1845). [Lessons on Acts and Epistles; not in NPNF[1].]

Bede. *Excerpts from the Works of Saint Augustine on the Letters of the Blessed Apostle Paul.* ET by D. Hurst (Kalamazoo, Mich.: Cistercian Publications, 1999).

Chytraeus, David. *A postil or orderly disposing of certeine epistles vsually red . . . vppon the Sundayes and holydayes.* ET by A. Golding, 1570 (STC 5263).

Erasmus, Desiderius. *Paraphrase of Erasmus vpon the Newe Testament conteynyng the epistles of S. Paul, and other the Apostles.* ET by M. Coverdale, J. Olde, and E. Alen, 1549 (STC 2854).

Luther, Martin. *Sermons of Martin Luther.* ET by J. N. Lenker, 1904; variously reprinted (Grand Rapids: Baker, 1983, 1995, 2000). [Vols. 6-8 on Acts and Epistles.]

Theodore of Mopsuestia. *Commentaries on the Minor Epistles of Paul.* ET by R. Greer in WGRW (in preparation).

Theodoret of Cyrus. *Commentary on the Letters of St Paul.* ET by R. C. Hill (2 vols.; Brookline, Mass.: Holy Cross Orthodox Press, 2001).

Romans

Aquinas, Thomas. *Commentary on Romans.* ET by S. C. Boguslawaski, in preparation.

Augustine. *Propositions from the Epistle to the Romans* and *Unfinished Commentary on Romans.* ET by P. F. Landes in *Augustine on Romans* (Chico, Calif.: Scholars Press, 1982); and in WSA I/17 (projected).

Bucer, Martin. *Commentary on Romans.* ET by D. F. Wright in *Common Places of Martin Bucer* (Appleford, England: Sutton Courtenay, 1972). [Excerpts from preface and loci on Romans 5, 6, 8, 9 on pp. 95-105, 119-200, 285-311.]

Calvin, John. *Commentary on Romans.* ET by C. Rosdell, 1583 (STC 4399); by J. Owen in CTS; and by R. Mackenzie in CNTC 8.

Chaderton, Laurence. *A fruitfull sermon, vpon . . . Romanes* [12:3-8]. 1584 (STC 4926).

Chrysostom, John. *Homilies on . . . Romans.* ET by J. B. Morris & W. H. Simcox in LFC 7 (1841), revised by G. B. Stevens in NPNF[1] 11.

Colet, John. *An exposition of . . . Romans* [*c.* 1497]. ET by J. H. Lupton, 1874; reprinted (Ridgewood, N.J.: Gregg Press, 1965).

Erasmus, Desiderius. *Paraphrases on Romans and Galatians.* ET by J. B. Payne, A. Rabil Jr., and W. S. Smith Jr. in CWE 42 (1984).

————. *Annotations on Romans.* ET by J. B. Payne in CWE 56 (1994).

Hooper, John. *. . . annotations vpon the thirteenth chapter to the Romanes.* 1583 (STC 13756.5); reprinted in *Later Writings of Bishop Hooper,* PS 21:93-116.

Hugh of Saint-Victor (1096?-1141). *An exposition of certayne words of S. Paule, to the Romaynes.* ET by R. Curteys, 1577 (STC 13923).

Luther, Martin. *Commentary [Lectures] on Romans.* ET by J. T. Mueller (Grand Rapids: Zondervan, 1954); by W. Pauck in LCC 15; and by W. G. Tillmanns and J. A. O. Preus in LW 25.

Melanchthon, Philip. *Commentary on Romans.* ET by F. Kramer (St. Louis: Concordia, 1992).

Origen. *Commentary on . . . Romans.* ET by T. P. Scheck in FC 103-104 (2001-02).

Pelagius. *Commentary on . . . Romans.* ET by T. De Bruyn (Oxford: Oxford University Press, 2002).

Vermigli, Peter Martyr. *Most Learned and fruitfull Commentaries upon . . . Romanes.* ET by H. Billingsley, 1568 (STC 24672; e-text in EEBO); and in PML[1] 11 (projected).

Wilcox, Thomas. *Works . . . containing an exposition vpon . . . Romans* [8:18-23]. 1586 (STC 25620; cf. 25622, 25627).

William of St. Thierry. *Exposition on the Epistle to the Romans.* ET by J. B. Hasbrouk (Kalamazoo, Mich.: Cistercian Publications, 2000).

1-2 Corinthians

Aquinas, Thomas. *Commentary on Paul's First Epistle to the Corinthians.* ET by M. Rzeczkowski in *Thomas Aquinas, The Gifts of the Spirit: Selected Spiritual Writings* (Hyde Park, N.Y.: New City Press, 1995), pp. 21-78. [On 1 Cor. 12–13.]

Bird, Samuel. *Lectures . . . vpon the 8. and 9. chapters of the second Epistle to the Corinthians.* 1598 (STC 3087).

Calvin, John. *Commentary on 1-2 Corinthians.* ET by T. Tymme, 1577 (STC 4400); and by J. Pringle in CTS. ET of 1 Cor. by J. W. Fraser in CNTC 9; of 2 Cor. by T. A. Smail in CNTC 10.

———. *Sermons on 1 Corinthians.* ET by S. Skolnitsky of 1 Cor. 11:2-16 in *Men, Women and Order in the Church* (Dallas: Presbyterian Heritage, 1992).

Chrysostom, John. *Homilies on the Epistles . . . to the Corinthians.* ET of 1 Cor. by H. K. Cornish & J. Medley in LFC 4-5 (1839); of 2 Cor by J. Ashworth in LFC 27 (1848); revised ET of LFC by T. W. Chambers in NPNF[1] 12.

Colet, John. *Commentary on First Corinthians* (*c.* 1500). ET by J. H. Lupton, 1874; reprinted (Ridgewood, N.J.: Gregg, 1965); also by B. O'Kelly (Binghamton, N.Y.: Medieval and Renaissance Texts and Studies, 1985).

Erasmus, Desiderius. ET of *Annotations* on 1 Cor. 7:39 by N. Lesse in *The censure and iudgement of . . . Erasmus of Roterodam: whyther dyuorsemente betwene man and wyfe stondeth with the lawe of God,* 1550 (STC 10450).

Gregory of Nyssa. "A Treatise on First Corinthians 15:28." ET by R. McCambley, *Greek Orthodox Theological Review* 28 (1983): 1-25.

Luther, Martin. *Commentary on 1 Corinthians 7.* ET by W. Roy, 1529 (STC 10493); and by E. Sittler in LW 28.

———. *Commentary on 1 Corinthians 15.* ET by M. H. Bertram in LW 28.

Melanchthon, Philipp [*sic*]. *Annotations on the First Epistle to the Corinthians*. ET by J. P. Donnelly (Milwaukee: Marquette University Press, 1995).

Vermigli, Peter Martyr. *Commentary on 1 Corinthians*. ET in PML[1] 10 (projected).

Galatians

Aquinas, Thomas. *Commentary on . . . Galatians*. ET by F. R. Larcher (Albany, N.Y.: Magi Books, 1966).

Augustine. *Commentary on Galatians*. ET by E. Plumer (Oxford: Oxford University Press, 2003); and in WSA I/17 (projected).

Calvin, John. *Commentary on Galatians*. ET by R. Vaux, 1581 (STC 4401); by W. Pringle in CTS; and by T. H. L. Parker in CNTC 11.

———. *Sermons on Galatians*. ET by A. Golding, 1574 (STC 4449), reprinted (Audubon, N.J.: Old Paths, 1995).

Chrysostom, John. *Commentary on Galatians*. ET by anon. in LFC 6 (1840), revised by G. Alexander in NPNF[1] 13.

Erasmus, Desiderius. *Paraphrases on Romans and Galatians*. ET by J. B. Payne, A. Rabil Jr., and W. S. Smith Jr. in CWE 42 (1984).

Luther, Martin. *Commentary on Galatians*. ET by T. Vautrollier, 1575 (STC 16965-70), abridged by T. Gaebner (Grand Rapids: Zondervan, 1939), revised by P. S. Watson (London: J. Clarke, 1953). New ET of 1519 lectures by R. Jungkuntz in LW 27; of 1535 lectures by J. Pelikan in LW 26-27.

Perkins, William. *A Commentary on Galatians*. 1604 (STC 19680); reprinted (New York: Pilgrim, 1989).

Prime, John. *An exposition . . . upon Saint Paul to the Galathians*. 1587 (STC 20369).

Victorinus, Marius. *Commentary on Galatians*. ET by S. A. Cooper (Oxford: Oxford University Press, 2005).

Ephesians

Aquinas, Thomas. *Commentary on . . . Ephesians*. ET by M. L. Lamb (Albany, N.Y.: Magi Books, 1966).

Bucer, Martin. *Commentary on Ephesians*. ET by D. F. Wright in *Common Places of Martin Bucer* (Appleford, England: Sutton Courtenay, 1972). [Excerpts and loci on Ephesians 1 on pp. 107-18, 201-34.]

Calvin, John. *Commentary on Ephesians*. ET by William Pringle in CTS; and by T. H. L. Parker in CNTC 11.

———. *Sermons on Ephesians*. ET by A. Golding, 1577 (STC 4448); modernized edition (Edinburgh: Banner of Truth, 1973).

Chrysostom, John. *Homilies on Ephesians.* ET by anon., 1581 (STC 14632); and by
W. J. Copeland in LFC 6 (1840), revised by G. Alexander in NPNF[1] 13.

Hemmingsen, Niels. *The epistle . . . to the Ephesians.* ET by A. Fleming, 1580 (STC
13057.8).

Jerome. *The commentaries of Origen and Jerome on St. Paul's Epistle to the Ephesians.* ET by R. E. Heine (Oxford: Oxford University Press, 2002).

Origen. *The commentaries of Origen and Jerome on St. Paul's Epistle to the Ephesians.* ET by R. E. Heine (Oxford: Oxford University Press, 2002).

Ridley, Lancelot. *A commentary in Englyshe vpon . . . Ephesians.* 1540 (STC 21038.5).

Philippians

Aquinas, Thomas. *Commentary on Saint Paul's First Letter to the Thessalonians and
the Letter to the Philippians.* ET by F. R. Larcher and Michael Duffy (Albany,
N.Y.: Magi Books, 1969).

Calvin, John. *Commentary on Philippians.* ET by W. Becket, 1584 (STC 4402); by
J. Pringle in CTS; and by T. H. L. Parker in CNTC 11.

Chrysostom, John. *Homilies on Philippians.* ET by W. C. Cotton in LFC (1843), revised by J. A. Broadus in NPNF[1] 13.

Ridley, Lancelot. *An exposytion in Englyshe vpon . . . Philippia[n]s.* 1550 (STC
21040).

Colossians

Calvin, John. *Commentary on Colossians.* ET by R. Vaux, 1581 (STC 4403); by
J. Pringle in CTS; and by T. H. L. Parker in CNTC 11.

Chrysostom, John. *Homilies on Colossians.* ET by J. Ashworth in LFC (1843), revised by J. A. Broadus in NPNF[1] 13.

Melanchthon, Philip. *Paul's Letter to the Colossians.* ET by D. C. Parker (Sheffield:
Sheffield Academic Press, 1989).

Ridley, Lancelot. *An exposicion in Englishe vpon . . . Colossians.* 1548 (STC 21039).

1-2 Thessalonians

Aquinas, Thomas. *Commentary on Saint Paul's First Letter to the Thessalonians and
the Letter to the Philippians.* ET by F. R. Larcher and M. Duffy (Albany, N.Y.:
Magi Books, 1969).

Bullinger, Heinrich. *A commentary vpon the seconde epistle . . . of S Paul to the Thessalonia[n]s.* ET by R. H., 1538 (STC 4054).

Calvin, John. *Commentary on 1-2 Thessalonians.* ET by John Pringle in CTS; and by R. Mackenzie in CNTC 8.

Carlile, Christopher. *An interpretation vpon the second Epistle of S. Paul to the Thessalonians, the second chapter.* 1572 (STC 4655).

Chrysostom, John. *Homilies on Thessalonians.* ET by J. Tweed in LFC (1843), revised by J. A. Broadus in NPNF[1] 13.

Haimo of Auxerre. ET by K. L. Hughes in *Second Thessalonians: Two Early Medieval Apocalyptic Commentaries* (Kalamazoo, Mich.: Medieval Institute Publications, 2001), pp. 13-33.

Jewel, John. *An exposition vpon the two epistles . . . to the Thessalonians.* 1583 (STC 14603).

Theitland of Einsiedeln. ET by S. R. Cartwright in *Second Thessalonians: Two Early Medieval Apocalyptic Commentaries* (Kalamazoo, Mich.: Medieval Institute Publications, 2001), pp. 35-76.

Tymme, Thomas. *The figure of Antichrist with the tokens of the end of the world, . . . a Catholike and diuine exposition of the seconde epistle of Paul to the Thessalonians, collected out of the best and most approued diuines.* 1586 (STC 24417).

1-2 Timothy, Titus, Philemon

Aquinas, Thomas. *Exposition of Paul's Epistle to Philemon.* ET by R. McInerny in *Thomas Aquinas: Selected Writings* (New York: Penguin, 1998), pp. 812-21.

Calvin, John. *Commentary on 1-2 Timothy, Titus, and Philemon.* ET by W. Pringle in CTS; and by T. A. Smail in CNTC 10.

———. *Sermons on Timothy and Titus.* ET by L. Tomson, 1579 (STC 4441); facsimile reprint (Edinburgh: Banner of Truth, 1983).

Chrysostom, John. *Homilies on . . . 1-2 Timothy, Titus, and Philemon.* ET by J. Tweed in LFC 12 (1843), edited by P. Schaff in NPNF[1] 13.

Erasmus, Desiderius. *Paraphrases on the Epistles to Timothy, Titus, and Philemon, the Epistles of Peter and Jude, the Epistle of James, the Epistle of John, the Epistle to the Hebrews.* ET by J. J. Bateman in CWE 44 (1993).

Luther, Martin. *Lectures on 1 Timothy.* ET by R. J. Dinda in LW 28.

———. *Lectures on Titus & Philemon.* ET by J. Pelikan in LW 29.

Hebrews

Aquinas, Thomas. *Commentary on . . . Hebrews.* ET by C. Baer (South Bend, Ind.: St. Augustine's Press, 2005).

Bird, Samuel. *Lectures . . . upon the 11. chapter of . . . Hebrewes.* 1580 (STC 3088).

Calvin, John. *Commentary on Hebrews.* ET by C. Cotton, 1605 (STC 4405); by J. Owen in CTS; and by W. B. Johnston in CNTC 12.

Chrysostom, John. *Homilies on Hebrews.* ET by T. Keble & J. Barrow in LFC 44 (1877), revised by F. Gardiner in NPNF¹ 14.

Dering, Edward. *XXVII. lectures, or readings, vpon part of the epistle written to the Hebrues* [1:1-6:6]. 1572 (STC 6726); 1597 edition reprinted (Amsterdam: Theatrum Orbis Terrarum; New York: Da Capo Press, 1972).

Erasmus, Desiderius. *Paraphrases on the Epistles to Timothy, Titus, and Philemon, the Epistles of Peter and Jude, the Epistle of James, the Epistle of John, the Epistle to the Hebrews.* ET by J. J. Bateman in CWE 44 (1993).

Luther, Martin. *Lectures on Hebrews.* ET by James Atkinson in LCC 16:19-250; and by W. A. Hansen in LW 29.

Catholic Epistles: James, 1-2 Peter, 1-2-3 John, Jude

Augustine. *Homilies on the First Epistle of John.* ET by H. Browne in LFC 26, 29 (1848-49), revised by J. H. Myers in NPNF¹ 7; by J. W. Rettig in FC 92 (1995): 97-277; abridged ET by J. Burnaby in LCC 8 (1955): 251-348.

Bede. *Commentary on the Seven Catholic Epistles.* ET by D. Hurst (Kalamazoo, Mich.: Cistercian Publications, 1985).

Calvin, John. *Commentary on James and Jude.* ET by W. H., 1580 (STC 4404, Jude only); by J. Owen in CTS; and by A. W. Morrison in CNTC 3.

———. *Commentary on 1-2 Peter.* ET by J. Owen in CTS; and by W. B. Johnston in CNTC 12.

———. *Commentary on 1 John.* ET by W. H., 1580 (STC 4404); by J. Owen in CTS; and by T. H. L. Parker in CNTC 5.

Clement of Alexandria. *Comments on 1 Peter, Jude, 1-2 John* [fragments]. ET by W. Wilson in ANF 2:571-77.

Edgeworth, Roger. "An Exposition of the First Epistle of Saint Peter." In *Sermons . . . preached . . . by Maister Roger Edgeworth,* 1557 (STC 7482), fol. 98v-318r.

Erasmus, Desiderius. *Paraphrases on the Epistles to Timothy, Titus, and Philemon, the Epistles of Peter and Jude, the Epistle of James, the Epistle of John, the Epistle to the Hebrews.* ET by J. J. Bateman in CWE 44 (1993).

Gifford, George. *Sermon vpon the second chapter of Saint Iames.* 1582 (STC 11860).

———. *Tvvo sermons vpon 1. Peter 5. vers .8. and 9.* 1597 (STC 11871).

Hemmingsen, Niels. *A learned and fruitefull commentarie vpon the Epistle of Iames.* ET by W. G., 1577 (STC 13060).

Luther, Martin. *Commentary on 1-2 Peter & Jude.* ET by T. Newton, 1581 (STC 16978); by E. H. Gillet (New York: Anson D. F. Randolph, 1859); by J. N. Lenker (Minneapolis: Lutherans in All Lands, 1904); and by M. H. Bertram in LW 30.

————. *Lectures on 1 John.* ET by W. A. Hansen in LW 30.

Marlorat, Augustin. *A Catholike and ecclesiasticall exposition vppon . . . S. Iude..* ET by I. D., 1584 (STC 17406.5). [Excerpts from six Reformers.]

Morgan, John. *A short analysis of . . . S. Iames* [2:14-26]. 1588 (STC 18103).

Perkins, William. *The gouernement of the tongue* [James 3:1-12]. 1593 (STC 19688).

Pigg, Oliver. *Treatise vpon . . . the first Epistle of Saint Peter* [4:12-19]. 1582 (STC 19915).

Ridley, Lancelot. *An exposition in the epistell of Iude.* 1538 (STC 21042).

Trigge, Francis. *A touchstone, whereby may be easilie discerned, which is the true Catholike faith, . . . out of the Catholike Epistle of S. Iude.* 1599 (STC 24281).

Turnbull, Richard. *An exposition upon . . . Iames, . . . Iude, . . . [&] the fifteenth Psalme.* 1592 (STC 24339-41).

Tyndale, William. *The exposition of the fyrste, seconde, and thyrde canonical epistles of S. Jhon.* 1538 (STC 24444; cf. 24333).

Revelation

Bale, John. *The image of bothe churches after the moste wonderfull and heavenly revelation of Sainct John the Evangelist.* 1545 (STC 1296.5); reprinted in *Select Works of John Bale,* PS 1.

Bede. *On the Apocalypse.* ET by F. Wallis (Liverpool: Liverpool University Press, in preparation).

Brocardo, Iacopo. *The Reuelation of S. Ihon reueled or a paraphrase.* ET by J. Sanford, 1582 (STC 3810).

Bullinger, Heinrich. *A hundred sermons vpo[n] the Apocalips of Iesu Christe.* ET by J. Daus, 1561 (STC 4061-62).

Fulke, William. *Praelections vpon the . . . Reuelation of S. Iohn.* ET by G. Gyffard, 1573 (STC 11443).

Gifford, George. *Sermons vpon the whole booke of the Reuelation.* 1596 (STC 11866).

Geoffrey of Auxerre. *On the Apocalypse.* ET by J. Gibbons (Kalamazoo, Mich.: Cistercian Publications, 2000).

Junius, Franciscus. *Apocalypsis: A . . . commentarie vpon the reuelation of Saint Iohn.* ET by anon., 1592 (STC 2988).

Lyra, Nicholas. *Nicholas of Lyra's Apocalypse Commentary.* ET by P. D. W. Krey (Kalamazoo, Mich.: Medieval Institute Publications, 1997).

Marlorat, Augustin. *A catholike exposition vpon the Reuelation of Sainct Iohn.* ET by
A. Golding, 1574 (STC 17408). [Excerpts from sixteen Reformers.]

Napier, John. *A plaine discouery of the whole Reuelation of Saint Iohn.* 1593 (STC
18354).

Oecumenius. *Commentary on the Apocalypse.* ET by H. C. Hoskier (Ann Arbor:
University of Michigan Press, 1928); and by J. N. Suggit in FC 112 (2006).

Victorinus of Pettau (d. 304). *Commentary on the Apocalypse of the Blessed John.* ET
by R. E. Wallis in ANF 7:344-60.

Miscellaneous (fragmentary or eclectic collections)

Achard of St. Victor. *Works.* ET by H. B. Feiss (Kalamazoo, Mich.: Cistercian Publications, 2001). [Sermons on 2 Kings, Psalms, Proverbs, Isaiah, Sirach, Matthew.]

Augustine. *Sermons [1-50] on the Old Testament.* ET by E. Hill in WSA 3/1-2. *Sermons [51-183] on the New Testament.* ET by E. Hill in WSA 3/3-5. Various other
sermons in WSA 3/6-11.

Bede. *On Eight Questions.* ET by A. G. Holder in *Bede: A Biblical Miscellany* (Liverpool: Liverpool University Press, 1999), pp. 145-65. [Various texts.]

Bonaventure. *Sunday Sermons.* ET by T. J. Johnson (St. Bonaventure, N.Y.: Franciscan Institute Publications, 2007). [Sermons on various texts.]

Caesarius of Arles. *Sermons.* ET by M. M. Mueller in FC 31, 47, 66 (1956-73). [Ser-
mons on Old and New Testaments are found principally in FC 47.]

Calvin, John. *Sermons on the Saving Work of Christ.* ET by L. Nixon (Grand Rapids:
Baker, 1950). [Sermons on Gospels, Acts, and 2 Thessalonians.]

Cooper, Thomas. *A briefe exposition of such chapters of the olde testament as vsually
are redde in the church at common praier on the Sondayes set forth for the better
helpe and instruction of the vnlearned.* 1573 (STC 5684).

Early Medieval Theology. ET by G. E. McCracken in LCC 9 of commentary excerpts
from Gregory the Great (Job), Alcuin of York (Titus), Claudius of Turin
(Galatians), Rupert of Deutz (John); and sermons by Raban Maur, Ivo of
Chartres, and Agobard of Lyons.

Hippolytus of Rome (*c.* 170-*c.* 236). ET by S. D. F. Salmond of numerous exegetical
fragments from Old Testament and Gospels in ANF 5:163-203.

Savonarola, Girolamo. *Selected sermons.* ET by K. Eisenbichler in *A Guide to Righteous Living and Other Works* (Toronto: Centre for Reformation and Renaissance Studies, 2003). [Sermons on Exodus, Ruth, Psalms, Micah, Haggai.]

Bibliography

Listed here are all primary and secondary works mentioned in the text and notes, with the exception of works of exegesis prior to 1600 that are found in English, which may be found in the Finding Guide (above), sorted by canonical book.

Primary Sources

Abelard, Peter. *Epistolae.* PL 178:113-380.

―――. *Planctus Dinae Filiae Jacob.* PL 178:1817.

―――. *Planctus virginum Israelis super filia Jephtæ Galaditæ.* Latin text in Wolfram von den Steinen, "Die Planctus Abaelards — Jephthas Tochter," *Mittellateinisches Jahrbuch* 4 (1967): 142-44; the 1838 edition is in PL 178:1819-20.

Agrippa von Nettesheim. *Declamation on the Nobility and Preeminence of the Female Sex.* Ed. Albert Rabil, Jr. Chicago: University of Chicago Press, 1996.

Ambrose. *De Abraham.* PL 14:441-524.

―――. *Apologia prophetæ David.* PL 14:891-960.

―――. *Epistolae.* PL 16:913-1342. ET by Mary Melchior Beyenka in FC 26 (1954): 3-495.

―――. *De virginitate.* PL 16:279-316.

Ambrosiaster [Pseudo-Augustine]. *Quaestiones Veteris et Novi Testamenti.* PL 35:2213-2416.

————. *Ambrosiastri Qvi Dicitvr Commentarivs in Epistvlas Pavlinas.* Ed. Heinrich Joseph Vogels. CSEL 81/1-3 (1966-69).

Apostolic Constitutions. ET in ANF 7:391-505. Greek text in PG 1:555-1156.

Aquinas, Thomas. *Summa Theologiae.* 60 vols. London: Blackfriars, 1964.

————. *Super Epistolas S. Pauli Lectura.* 2 vols. Ed. P. Raphael Cai. Rome: Marietti, 1953.

Athanasius. *Defense of His Flight.* ET in NPNF² 4:255-65.

Athenagoras. *A Plea Regarding Christians.* ET in LCC 1:300-40.

Augustine. *On Adulterous Marriages.* ET in FC 27, WSA I/9.

————. *On Baptism against the Donatists.* ET in NPNF¹ 4:411-514. Latin text in PL 43:107-244.

————. *On Christian Doctrine.* ET in NPNF¹ 2:519-97. Latin text in CCSL 32 (1962):1-167 and PL 34:15-122.

————. *The City of God.* Tr. Henry Bettenson. New York: Penguin, 1972. Latin text in CCSL 47-48 and PL 41:13-804.

————. *The Correction of the Donatists.* ET in NPNF¹ 4:633-51. Latin text in PL 33:792-815.

————. *On Faith and Works.* ET in FC 27.

————. *On the Good of Marriage.* ET in NPNF¹ 3, FC 27, WSA I/9.

————. *Against Lying.* ET in NPNF¹ 3:481-500. Latin text in PL 40:517-48.

————. *On Lying.* ET in NPNF¹ 3:457-77. Latin text in PL 40:487-518.

————. *On Marriage and Concupiscence.* ET in NPNF¹ 5.

————. *Quæstionum in Heptateuchum, libri septem.* Ed. J. Fraipont and D. De Bruyne. CCSL 33 (1958):1-377. Text also in PL 34:547-824.

————. *Reply to Faustus.* ET in NPNF¹ 4:251-797. Latin text in PL 42:207-518.

————. *Retractations.* ET by M. I. Bogan in FC 60 (1968). Latin text in PL 32:583-656.

Bede. *Libri qvatvor in principivm Genesis vsqve ad nativitatem Isaac et eiectionem Ismahelis adnotationvm.* Ed. Charles W. Jones. CCSL 118A. 1967.

Bernard of Clairvaux. *Selected Works.* Trans. G. R. Evans. Mahwah, N.J.: Paulist, 1987.

Brenz, Johannes. *In Librum Iudicum et Ruth Commentarius.* Haganau: Peter Braubach, 1535. Also in *Opera* 2:87-286. Tübingen: George Gruppenbach, 1576.

Brevicoxa, John. "A Treatise on Faith, the Church, the Roman Pontiff, and the General Council." In *Forerunners of the Reformation,* ed. Heiko A. Oberman, pp. 69-74. Philadelphia: Fortress, 1981.

Bucer, Martin. *D. Martini Buceri in librum Iudicum Ennarationes.* In *Psalmorum libri quinque . . . a Martino Bucero enarrati,* pp. 473-522. Geneva: Robert Estienne, 1554.

————. *In Sacra Quatuor Evangelia, Enarrationes.* Basel, 1536.

Bullinger, Heinrich. *The Christian State of Matrimony.* London, 1575. STC 4053. ET of *Der Christlich Ehestand.* Zurich, 1540.

———. "How to Deal with Anabaptists: An Unpublished Letter of Heinrich Bullinger." Trans. Heinold Fast and John H. Yoder. *Mennonite Quarterly Review* 33 (1959): 83-95.

———. *In Omnes Apostolicas Epistolas, Divi Videlicet Pavli xiiii. et vii. Canonicas, Commentarii.* Zurich, 1537.

Burroughs, Jeremiah. *An exposition of the prophesie of Hosea.* London, 1652.

Cajetan, Cardinal (Thomas de Vio). *Commentarii illustres . . . in Quinque Mosaicos libros.* Paris: Guillelmum de Bossozel, 1539. [Includes Cajetan's *Comm. Gen.*]

———. *Opera Omnia qvotqvot in Sacrae Scripturae Expositionem Reperiuntur.* 5 vols. Lyons: Jean and Pierre Prost, 1639. [Includes all of his commentaries.]

Calvin, John. *Institutes of the Christian Religion.* Ed. John T. McNeill. Trans. Ford Lewis Battles. LCC 20-21. Philadelphia: Westminster, 1960.

———. *Calvin's Ecclesiastical Advice [Consilia].* Trans. Mary Beaty and Benjamin W. Farley. Louisville: Westminster John Knox, 1991.

Capito, Wolfgang. *Hexemeron Dei Opus.* Strasbourg, 1539.

[Catharinus.] Ambrosius Catharinus Politus. *Commentaria . . . in Omnes Divi Pauli et Alias Septem Canonicas Epistolas.* Venice, 1551.

———. *Enarrationes, Assertationes, Disputationes.* Rome, 1551-52. Facsimile reprint. Ridgewood, N.J.: Gregg, 1964.

Chrysostom, John. *Homilies on the Statues.* ET in NPNF 9:331-489. Greek text in PG 49:15-222.

———. *On Marriage and Family Life.* Crestwood, N.Y.: St. Vladimir's Seminary Press, 2003.

Denis the Carthusian. *Doctoris Ecstatici D. Dionysii Cartusiani Opera Omnia.* 42 vols. Monstrolii, 1896-1913.

Didymus the Blind. *Sur la Genèse.* Ed. Pierre Nautin with Louis Doutreleau. Sources Chrétiennes 244. Paris: Éditions du Cerf, 1978.

Downame, John. *Lectures vpon the foure first chapters of the prophecie of Hosea.* London, 1608. STC 7145.

Erasmus, Desiderius. *Erasmus' Annotations on the New Testament: Acts — Romans — I and II Corinthians: Facsimile of the Final Latin Text with All Earlier Variants.* Ed. Anne Reeve and M. A. Screech. Leiden: Brill, 1990.

———. *Opera Omnia.* 10 vols. Lyons, 1703-6. Reprint. Hildesheim: Georg Olms, 1961-62.

Gaigny, Jean de. *Divi Pauli apostoli epistolae brevissimis . . . scholiis per Io. Gagnaeium . . . illustratae.* Paris: Simon de Cloines and Galliot Du Pré, 1539.

Gregory the Great. *Pastoral Rule.* ET in NPNF² 12:1-72 and ACW 11.

Gregory of Nyssa. *On Virginity.* ET in NPNF² 5:343-71 and FC 58.

Guilliaud, Claude. *In omnes divi Pauli apostoli epistolas, collatio.* Paris: Jean de Roigny, 1552.

Gwalter, Rudolf. *In priorem . . . ad Corinthios epistolam homiliae.* Zurich, 1572.

Hutcheson, George. *A brief exposition on the XII. smal prophets . . . Hosea, Joel, & Amos.* London, 1654.

Irenaeus of Lyons. *Against Heresies.* ET in ANF 1:315-578. Original text in PG 7.

Isidore of Seville. *Questiones in Vetus Testamentum.* PL 83:207-442.

Jerome. *Against Helvidius.* ET in NPNF² 6:335-46.

————. *Against Jovinian.* ET in NPNF² 6:346-416. Latin text in PL 23:211-338.

Josephus, Flavius. *Jewish Antiquities.* Trans. H. St. J. Thackeray. LCL Josephus vol. 4 (1957). ET also in *The Works of Josephus.* Trans. William Whiston. Revised ed. Peabody, Mass.: Hendrickson, 1987.

Lapide, Cornelius à. *Commentaria in Scripturam Sacram.* 20 vols. Paris: Ludwig Vivès, 1854-70.

[Lefèvre d'Étaples, Jacques.] Faber Stapulensis, Jacobus. *S. Pauli epistolae XIV ex Vulgata, adiecta intelligentia ex graeca, cum commentariis.* Paris, 1512. Facsimile reprint. Stuttgart-Bad Cannstatt: Frommann-Holzboog, 1978.

Legends of the Jews. Ed. Louis Ginzburg. 7 vols. Reprint ed. Philadelphia: Jewish Publication Society, 1967-69.

Lombard, Peter. *Sententiae in IV Libris Distinctae.* 2 vols. Third edition. Rome: Colegii S. Bonaventurae Ad Claras Aquas, 1971, 1981.

Luther, Martin. *Praelectio in Librum Iudicium.* WA 4:527-86.

Lyra, Nicholas. *Biblia Sacra cvm Glossis, Interlineari & Ordinaria, Nicolai Lyrani Postilla & Moralitatibus, Burgensis Additionibus, & Thoringi Replicis.* 5 vols. Lyons: [Gaspard Trechsel], 1545.

Münster, Sebastian. *Hebraica Biblia latina planeque noua Sebast. Mvnsteri tralatione.* Basel: Michael Isengrin and Henricus Petri, 1534-35.

Müntzer, Thomas. *The Collected Works of Thomas Müntzer.* Ed. Peter Matheson. Edinburgh: T. & T. Clark, 1988.

Musculus, Wolfgang. *In Mosis Genesim . . . Commentarii.* Basel: Johann Herwagen, 1554.

Oecolampadius, Johannes. *Enarrationes in Genesim.* Basel, 1536.

Ordinary Gloss. Abbreviated Latin text in PL 113-114; also see Lyra (above).

Origen. *On First Principles.* Trans. G. W. Butterworth. Gloucester, Mass.: Peter Smith, 1973.

————. *Catenae on 1 Corinthians.* Greek text in *Journal of Theological Studies* 10 (1909): 41-42.

Pelagius. *Pelagius's Expositions of Thirteen Epistles of St. Paul: Text.* Ed. Alexander Souter. Texts and Studies IX.2. Cambridge: Cambridge University Press, 1926.

Pellican, Conrad. *Commentaria Bibliorum.* 5 vols. Zurich: Froschauer, 1532-35.

Peter Comestor. *Historia Scholastica.* PL 198:1053-1722.

Philo. *Philo.* 10 vols. Trans. F. H. Colson and G. H. Whitaker. LCL, 1949-62. ET also in *The Works of Philo.* Trans. C. D. Yonge. Revised ed. Peabody, Mass.: Hendrickson, 1993.

Poole, Matthew. *Synopsis criticorum.* 5 vols. London, 1669-76.

————. *A Commentary on the Whole Bible.* 1685. 3 vol. reprint. London: Banner of Truth, 1962.

Procopius of Gaza. *Catena in Octateuchum.* PG 87:21-1080.

Pseudo-Philo. *The Biblical Antiquities of Philo.* Trans. M. R. James. New York: Ktav, 1971.

Quodvultdeus. *Liber de promissionibus et prædictionibus Dei.* Ed. R. Braun. CCSL 60:1-223. 1976. Text also in PL 51:733-858.

Raban Maur. *Commentaria in Genesim.* PL 107:439-670.

The Reformation of the Ecclesiastical Laws of England, 1552. Ed. James C. Spalding. Kirksville, Mo.: Sixteenth Century Journal Publishers, 1992.

Rogers, Richard. *A Commentary upon the Whole Book of Judges.* London, 1615. Facsimile reprint. *A Commentary on Judges.* Edinburgh: Banner of Truth, 1983.

Shepherd of Hermas. Trans. Bart D. Ehrman. In LCL Apostolic Fathers vol. 2 (2003), pp. 161-473. ET also in ANF 2.

The Soncino Chumash. Ed. A. Cohen. London: Soncino, 1947.

Sulpicius Severus. *Chronica.* PL 20:95-160.

Targum of the Minor Prophets. Trans. Kevin J. Cathcart and Robert P. Gordon. The Aramaic Bible 14. Wilmington, Del.: Michael Glazier, 1989.

Tertullian. *On the Apparel of Women.* ET in ANF 4:14-25.

Theodoret of Cyrus. *Quaestiones in Octateuchum.* PL 80:75-528.

Trent, Council of. *The Canons and Decrees of the Council of Trent.* Trans. H. J. Schroeder. Rockford, Ill.: Tan Books, 1978.

Urban II, Pope. *Orationes in Concilio Claromontano Habitae: De Expeditione Hierosolymitana.* PL 151:565-82.

Vermigli, Peter Martyr. *In Primvm Librvm Mosis, Qui Vvlgo Genesis Dicitur Commentarii.* Zurich: Froschauer, 1569.

————. *In Librvm Ivdicvm . . . Commentarii.* Zurich: Froschauer, 1561.

————. *In duos Libros Samuelis Prophetae . . . Commentarii.* Zurich: Froschauer, 1564.

————. *Loci communes.* London: Thomas Vautrollerius, 1583. ET in *The Common Places of . . . Peter Martyr.* Ed. Anthonie Marten. London, 1583.

Wolf, Johann. *In Sacram Historiam Iosuae.* Zurich, 1592.

Zanchi, Girolamo. *Opera Theologica.* 5 vols. Geneva, 1613.

Zwingli, Huldreich. *Farrago annotationum in Genesim.* Latin text in ZSW 13:1-290.

————. *Commentary on True and False Religion.* Trans. Henry Preble. 1929. Reprint ed. Durham, N.C.: Labyrinth, 1981.

————. *The Preaching Office.* ET in SWZ 2:150-85.

Bibliography

Secondary Sources

Achtemeier, Elizabeth R. *Preaching Hard Texts of the Old Testament.* Peabody, Mass.: Hendrickson, 1998.

Ahrons, Constance. *The Good Divorce: Keeping Your Family Together When Your Marriage Comes Apart.* New York: HarperCollins, 1994.

Aland, Kurt. *Hilfsbuch zum Lutherstudien.* Witten: Luther-Verlag, 1970.

Allen, Prudence. *The Concept of Woman: The Aristotelian Revolution, 750 BC–AD 1250.* Grand Rapids: Eerdmans, 1997.

Anderson, Bernhard W. *Out of the Depths: The Psalms Speak for Us Today.* Louisville: Westminster John Knox, 1999.

Anderson, Gary A. *The Genesis of Perfection: Adam and Eve in Jewish and Christian Imagination.* Louisville: Westminster John Knox, 2001.

Bainton, Roland H. "The Immoralities of the Patriarchs according to the Exegesis of the Late Middle Ages and of the Reformation." *Harvard Theological Review* 23 (1930): 39-49.

Bal, Mieke. "A Body of Writing: Judges 19." In *A Feminist Companion to Judges,* ed. Athalya Brenner, pp. 208-30. Sheffield: Sheffield Academic Press, 1993.

―――. *Death and Dissymmetry: The Politics of Coherence in the Book of Judges.* Chicago: University of Chicago, 1988.

Belleville, Linda L. "1 Timothy." In *The IVP Women's Bible Commentary,* ed. Catherine Clark Kroeger and Mary J. Evans, pp. 738, 741. Downers Grove, Ill.: InterVarsity Press, 2002.

―――. "Teaching and Usurping Authority: 1 Tim. 2:11-15." In *Discovering Biblical Equality: Complementarity without Hierarchy,* ed. Ronald W. Pierce and Rebecca Merrill Groothuis, pp. 205-23. Downers Grove, Ill.: InterVarsity Press, 2004.

Bellis, Alice Ogden. *Helpmates, Harlots, and Heroes: Women's Stories in the Hebrew Bible.* Louisville: Westminster John Knox, 1994.

Blaisdell, Charmarie Jenkins. "Calvin's Letters to Women: The Courting of Ladies in High Places." *Sixteenth Century Journal* 13 (1982): 67-84.

―――. "Calvin's and Loyola's Letters to Women." In *Calviniana: Ideas and Influence of Jean Calvin,* ed. Robert V. Schnucker, pp. 235-53. Kirksville, Mo.: Sixteenth Century Journal Publishers, 1988.

Børresen, Kari Elisabeth. *Subordination and Equivalence: The Nature and Role of Woman in Augustine and Thomas Aquinas.* Washington, D.C.: University Press of America, 1981.

―――. "Imago Dei, privilège masculin? Interprétation Augustinienne et Pseudo-Augustinienne de *Gen* 1,27 et 1 *Cor* 11,7." *Augustinianum* 25 (1985): 213-34.

Bottigheimer, Ruth B. *The Bible for Children: From the Age of Gutenberg to the Present.* New Haven: Yale University Press, 1996.

Bray, Gerald. *Biblical Interpretation: Past and Present*. Downers Grove, Ill.: InterVarsity Press, 1996.

Brenner, Athalya. "Female Social Behaviour: Two Descriptive Patterns within the 'Birth of the Hero' Paradigm." In *A Feminist Companion to Genesis*, ed. idem, pp. 204-21. Sheffield: Sheffield Academic Press, 1993.

————. "On Prophetic Propaganda and the Politics of 'Love': The Case of Jeremiah." In *A Feminist Companion to the Latter Prophets*, ed. idem, pp. 256-74. Sheffield: Sheffield Academic Press, 1995.

Brown, Harold O. J. "The New Testament Against Itself: 1 Timothy 2:9-15 and the 'Breakthrough' of Galatians 3:28." In *Women in the Church: A Fresh Analysis of 1 Tim. 2:9-15*, ed. Andreas J. Köstenberger, Thomas R. Schreiner, and H. Scott Baldwin, pp. 197-208. Grand Rapids: Baker, 1995.

Brown, Joanne Carlson, and Carole R. Bohn, eds. *Christianity, Patriarchy, and Abuse: A Feminist Critique*. New York: Pilgrim Press, 1989.

Brueggemann, Walter. "Psalm 109: Steadfast Love as Social Solidarity." In *The Psalms and the Life of Faith*, ed. Patrick D. Miller, pp. 268-82. Minneapolis: Fortress, 1995.

————. *The Message of the Psalms: A Theological Commentary*. Minneapolis: Augsburg, 1984.

Cairncross, John. *After Polygamy Was Made a Sin: The Social History of Christian Polygamy*. London: Routledge & Kegan Paul, 1974.

Cairns, David. *The Image of God in Man*. London: SCM, 1953.

Cameron, Michael. "Enarrationes in Psalmos." In *Augustine through the Ages: An Encyclopedia*, ed. Allan D. Fitzgerald, pp. 290-96. Grand Rapids: Eerdmans, 1999.

Carroll, Robert P. "Desire under the Terebinths: On Pornographic Representation in the Prophets." In *A Feminist Companion to the Latter Prophets*, ed. Athalya Brenner, pp. 275-307. Sheffield: Sheffield Academic Press, 1995.

Chaves, Mark. *Ordaining Women: Culture and Conflict in Religious Organizations*. Cambridge: Harvard University Press, 1997.

Childs, Brevard S. "The Struggle for God's Righteousness in the Psalter." In *Christ in Our Place: The Humanity of God in Christ for the Reconciliation of the World*, ed. Trevor A. Hart and Daniel P. Thimell, pp. 255-64. Exeter: Paternoster, and Allison Park, Penn.: Pickwick, 1989.

Church, F. Forrester. "Sex and Salvation in Tertullian." *Harvard Theological Review* 68 (1975): 83-101.

Clark, Elizabeth A. *Women in the Early Church*. Wilmington, Del.: Michael Glazier, 1983.

Cohen, Jeremy. *"Be fertile and increase, fill the earth and master it": The Ancient and Medieval Career of a Biblical Text*. Ithaca: Cornell University Press, 1989.

Collins, Raymond F. *1 & 2 Timothy and Titus: A Commentary.* Louisville: Westminster John Knox, 2002.

Consultation on Common Texts. *The Revised Common Lectionary.* Nashville: Abingdon, 1992.

Darr, Katheryn Pfisterer. *Far More Precious than Jewels: Perspectives on Biblical Women.* Louisville: Westminster John Knox, 1991.

Davis, Natalie Zemon. "City Women and Religious Change." In Davis, *Society and Culture in Early Modern France,* pp. 65-95. Stanford: Stanford University Press, 1975.

Dijk-Hemmes, Fokkelien van. "The Metaphorization of Woman in Prophetic Speech: An Analysis of Ezekiel 23." In *A Feminist Companion to the Latter Prophets,* ed. Athalya Brenner, pp. 244-55. Sheffield: Sheffield Academic Press, 1995.

Doriani, Daniel. "A History of the Interpretation of 1 Timothy 2." In *Women in the Church: A Fresh Analysis of 1 Tim. 2:9-15,* ed. Andreas J. Köstenberger, Thomas R. Schreiner, and H. Scott Baldwin, pp. 213-67. Grand Rapids: Baker, 1995.

Eells, Hastings. *The Attitude of Martin Bucer Toward the Bigamy of Philip of Hesse.* New Haven: Yale University Press, 1924.

Exum, J. Cheryl. *Fragmented Women: Feminist (Sub)versions of Biblical Narratives.* Valley Forge: Trinity, 1993.

————. *Plotted, Shot, and Painted: Cultural Representations of Biblical Women.* Sheffield: Sheffield Academic Press, 1996.

Farthing, John L. "Holy Harlotry: Jerome Zanchi and the Exegetical History of Gomer (Hosea 1–3)." In *Biblical Interpretation in the Era of the Reformation,* ed. Richard A. Muller and John L. Thompson, pp. 292-312. Grand Rapids: Eerdmans, 1996.

Fewell, Danna Nolan, and David M. Gunn. *Gender, Power, and Promise: The Subject of the Bible's First Story.* Nashville: Abingdon, 1993.

Fiedrowicz, Michael. Introduction to Augustine, *Expositions of the Psalms.* WSA III/15:13-66.

Fredriksen, Paula. "*Excaecati Occulta Iustitia Dei:* Augustine on Jews and Judaism." *Journal of Early Christian Studies* 3 (1995): 299-324.

Fuchs, Esther. "Marginalization, Ambiguity, Silencing: The Story of Jephthah's Daughter." *Journal of Feminist Studies in Religion* 5 (1989): 35-45. Also in *A Feminist Companion to Judges,* ed. Athalya Brenner, pp. 116-30. Sheffield: Sheffield Academic Press, 1993.

Gordon, Cynthia. "Hagar: A Throw-Away Character among the Matriarchs?" *The Society of Biblical Literature Seminar Papers* 24 (1985): 271-77.

Graetz, Naomi. "Dinah the Daughter." In *A Feminist Companion to Genesis,* ed. Athalya Brenner, pp. 306-17. Sheffield: Sheffield Academic Press, 1993.

————. "God Is to Israel as Husband Is to Wife: The Metaphoric Battering of Hosea's Wife," in *A Feminist Companion to the Latter Prophets,* ed. Athalya Brenner, pp. 141-42. Sheffield: Sheffield Academic Press, 1995.

Grudem, Wayne. *Evangelical Feminism and Biblical Truth: An Analysis of More Than One Hundred Disputed Questions.* Sisters, Ore.: Multnomah, 2004.

Gryson, Roger. *The Ministry of Women in the Early Church.* Collegeville, Minn.: Liturgical Press, 1976.

Hackett, Jo Ann. "Rehabilitating Hagar: Fragments of an Epic Pattern." In *Gender and Difference in Ancient Israel,* ed. Peggy L. Day, pp. 12-27. Philadelphia: Fortress, 1989.

Hazlett, W. Ian P. "Calvin's Latin Preface to His Proposed French Edition of Chrysostom's Homilies." In *Humanism and Reform: The Church in Europe, England, and Scotland,* ed. James Kirk, pp. 129-50. Oxford: Blackwell, 1991.

Hill, Paul J. "Defending The Defenseless" (August 2003). Accessed 9/5/2003 at http://www.armyofgod.com/PHill_ShortShot.html

Holladay, William L. *The Psalms through Three Thousand Years: Prayerbook of a Cloud of Witnesses.* Minneapolis: Fortress, 1993.

House, H. Wayne, ed. *Divorce and Remarriage: Four Christian Views.* Downers Grove, Ill.: InterVarsity Press, 1990.

Hunter, David G. "The Paradise of Patriarchy: Ambrosiaster on Woman as (Not) God's Image." *Journal of Theological Studies* n.s. 43 (1992): 447-69.

————. *Marriage in the Early Church.* Minneapolis: Augsburg Fortress, 1992.

Instone-Brewer, David. *Divorce and Remarriage in the Bible: The Social and Literary Context.* Grand Rapids: Eerdmans, 2002.

Jeansonne, Sharon Pace. *The Women of Genesis: From Sarah to Potiphar's Wife.* Minneapolis: Fortress, 1990.

Jedin, Hubert. *A History of the Council of Trent,* vol. 2: *The First Sessions at Trent, 1545-47.* London: Thomas Nelson and Sons, 1961.

Karant-Nunn, Susan C., and Merry E. Wiesner-Hanks, eds. *Luther on Women: A Sourcebook.* New York: Cambridge University Press, 2003.

Kienzle, Beverly Mayne, and Pamela J. Walker, eds. *Women Preachers and Prophets Through Two Millennia of Christianity.* Berkeley: University of California Press, 1998.

Kingdon, Robert M. *Myths about the St. Bartholomew's Day Massacres, 1572-1576.* Cambridge: Harvard University Press, 1988.

————. *Adultery and Divorce in Calvin's Geneva.* Cambridge: Harvard University Press, 1995.

Kroeger, Richard Clark, and Catherine Clark Kroeger. *I Suffer Not a Woman: Rethinking 1 Timothy 2:11-15 in Light of Ancient Evidence.* Grand Rapids: Baker, 1992.

Kroeger, Catherine Clark. "1 Corinthians," in *IVP Women's Bible Commentary,* ed.

Bibliography

Catherine Clark Kroeger and Mary J. Evans, pp. 662-63. Downers Grove, Ill.: InterVarsity Press, 2002.

Laffey, Alice L. *An Introduction to the Old Testament: A Feminist Perspective.* Philadelphia: Fortress, 1988.

Lane, Anthony N. S. *John Calvin: Student of the Church Fathers.* Grand Rapids: Baker, 1999.

Lewis, C. S. *Reflections on the Psalms.* New York: Harcourt, Brace, & World, 1958.

Maclean, Ian. *The Renaissance Notion of Woman: A Study in the Fortunes of Scholasticism and Medical Science in European Intellectual Life.* Cambridge: Cambridge University Press, 1980.

Marcus, David. *Jephthah and His Vow.* Lubbock: Texas Tech Press, 1986.

Mattox, Mickey Leland. *"Defender of the Most Holy Matriarchs": Martin Luther's Interpretation of the Women of Genesis in the Enarrationes in Genesin, 1535-45.* Leiden: Brill, 2003.

Mays, James Luther. *The Lord Reigns: A Theological Handbook to the Psalms.* Louisville: Westminster John Knox, 1994.

McKim, Donald K., ed. *Historical Handbook of Major Biblical Interpreters.* Downers Grove, Ill.: InterVarsity Press, 1998.

McLaughlin, Mary. "Abelard and the Dignity of Women." In *Pierre Abélard, Pierre le Vénérable,* pp. 287-334. Paris: Éditions du Centre national de la recherche scientifique, 1975.

Miller, Patrick D. *They Cried to the Lord: The Form and Theology of Biblical Prayer.* Minneapolis: Fortress, 1994.

Mpindi, Paul Mbunga. "Calvin's Hermeneutics of the Imprecations of the Psalms." Ph.D. dissertation, Calvin Theological Seminary, 2003.

Niditch, Susan. "Genesis." In *The Women's Bible Commentary,* ed. Carol A. Newsom and Sharon H. Ringe, pp. 17-18. Louisville: Westminster John Knox, 1992.

Olsen, V. Norskov. *The New Testament Logia on Divorce: A Study of Their Interpretation from Erasmus to Milton.* Tübingen: J. C. B. Mohr [Paul Siebeck], 1971.

Olson, Roger E. *The Story of Christian Theology: Twenty Centuries of Tradition and Reform.* Downers Grove, Ill.: InterVarsity Press, 1999.

Ortlund, Raymond C., Jr. *Whoredom: God's Unfaithful Wife in Biblical Theology.* Grand Rapids: Eerdmans, 1996.

Ozment, Stephen. *When Fathers Ruled: Family Life in Reformation Europe.* Cambridge: Harvard University Press, 1983.

Parsons, Michael. "Luther and Calvin on Rape: Is the Crime Lost in the Agenda?" *Evangelical Quarterly* 74 (2002): 123-42.

———. *Luther and Calvin on Old Testament Narratives: Reformation Thought and Narrative Text.* Lewiston, N.Y.: Mellen, 2004.

Peterson, Eugene H. *Answering God: The Psalms as Tools for Prayer.* San Francisco: Harper & Row, 1989.

Phillips, Roderick. *Putting Asunder: A History of Divorce in Western Society.* Cambridge: Cambridge University Press, 1988.

Pierce, Ronald W., and Rebecca Merrill Groothuis, eds. *Discovering Biblical Equality: Complementarity without Hierarchy.* Downers Grove, Ill.: InterVarsity Press, 2004.

Placher, William C. *A History of Christian Theology.* Philadelphia: Westminster, 1983.

Pressler, Carolyn J. "Jezreel." In *The Anchor Bible Dictionary,* 6 vols., ed. David Noel Freedman, 3:849. New York: Doubleday, 1992.

Preus, James Samuel. *From Shadow to Promise: Old Testament Interpretation from Augustine to the Young Luther.* Cambridge, Mass.: Harvard University Press, Belknap Press, 1969.

Puckett, David L. *John Calvin's Exegesis of the Old Testament.* Louisville: Westminster John Knox, 1995.

Raming, Ida. *The Exclusion of Women from the Priesthood: Divine Law or Sex Discrimination? A Historical Investigation of the Juridical and Doctrinal Foundations of the* Code of Canon Law, *canon 968, §1.* Metuchen, N.J.: Scarecrow, 1976.

Reid, W. Stanford. "The Battle Hymns of the Lord: Calvinist Psalmody of the Sixteenth Century." In *Sixteenth Century Essays and Studies,* ed. Carl S. Meyer, pp. 36-54. St. Louis: Foundation for Reformation Research, 1971.

Robeck, Cecil M., Jr. *Prophecy in Carthage: Perpetua, Tertullian, and Cyprian.* Cleveland, Ohio: Pilgrim, 1992.

Ruether, Rosemary Radford. *Women-Church: Theology and Practice of Feminist Liturgical Communities.* San Francisco: Harper & Row, 1985.

Scalise, Charles J. "Exegetical Warrants for Religious Persecution: Augustine *vs.* The Donatists." *Review and Expositor* 93 (1996): 497-506.

Schroeder, Joy A. "The Rape of Dinah: Luther's Interpretation of a Biblical Narrative." *Sixteenth Century Journal* 28 (1997): 775-91.

Selderhuis, H. J. *Marriage and Divorce in the Thought of Martin Bucer.* Kirksville, Mo.: Thomas Jefferson University Press, 1999.

Setel, T. Drorah. "Prophets and Pornography: Female Sexual Imagery in Hosea." In *Feminist Interpretation of the Bible,* ed. Letty M. Russell, pp. 86-95. Philadelphia: Westminster, 1985.

Sherwood, Yvonne. *The Prostitute and the Prophet: Hosea's Marriage in Literary-Theoretical Perspective.* Sheffield: Sheffield Academic Press, 1996.

————. "Boxing Gomer: Controlling the Deviant Woman in Hosea 1–3," in *A Feminist Companion to the Latter Prophets,* ed. Athalya Brenner, pp. 101-25. Sheffield: Sheffield Academic Press, 1995.

Shuger, Debora Kuller. *The Renaissance Bible: Scholarship, Sacrifice, and Subjectivity*. Berkeley and Los Angeles: University of California Press, 1994.

Simons, Louise. "'An Immortality Rather than a Life': Milton and the Concubine of Judges 19–21." In *Old Testament Women in Western Literature*, ed. Raymond-Jean Frontain and Jan Wojcik, pp. 144-73. Conway, Ark.: UCA Press, 1991.

Stanton, Elizabeth Cady. *The Women's Bible*. 2 vols. New York: European Publishing Co., 1895, 1898. Reprinted in one volume as *The Original Feminist Attack on the Bible*. New York: Arno Press, 1974.

Steinmetz, David C. "The Judaizing Calvin." In *Die Patristik in der Bibelexegese des 16. Jahrhunderts*, ed. idem, pp. 135-45. Wiesbaden: Harrassowitz, 1999.

Sypherd, Wilbur Owen. *Jephthah and His Daughter: A Study in Comparative Literature*. Newark, Del.: University of Delaware [Press], 1948.

Talmage, Frank Ephraim. *David Kimhi: The Man and the Commentaries*. Cambridge: Harvard University Press, 1975.

Tamez, Elsa. "The Woman Who Complicated the History of Salvation." In *New Eyes for Reading: Biblical and Theological Reflections by Women from the Third World*, ed. John S. Pobee and Bärbel von Wartenberg-Potter, pp. 5-17. Geneva: World Council of Churches, 1986.

Tapp, Ann Michelle. "An Ideology of Expendability: Virgin Daughter Sacrifice in Genesis 19.1-11, Judges 11.30-39 and 19.22-26." In *Anti-Covenant: Counter-Reading Women's Lives in the Hebrew Bible*, ed. Mieke Bal, pp. 154-74. Sheffield: Almond Press, 1989.

Taylor, Barbara Brown. "Hard Words." In *The Christian Century* 118, no. 14 (May 2, 2001), 24.

Thompson, John L. "Calvin as a Biblical Interpreter." In *The Cambridge Companion to John Calvin*, ed. Donald A. McKim, pp. 58-73. Cambridge: Cambridge University Press, 2004.

———. "Calvin's Exegetical Legacy: His Reception and Transmission of Text and Tradition." In *The Legacy of John Calvin: Calvin Studies Society Papers 1999*, ed. David L. Foxgrover, pp. 31-56. Grand Rapids: Calvin Studies Society, 2000.

———. "The Immoralities of the Patriarchs in the History of Exegesis: A Reassessment of Calvin's Position." *Calvin Theological Journal* 26 (1991): 9-46.

———. *John Calvin and the Daughters of Sarah: Women in Regular and Exceptional Roles in the Exegesis of Calvin, His Predecessors, and His Contemporaries*. Geneva: Droz, 1992.

———. "Patriarchs, Polygamy, and Private Resistance: John Calvin and Others on Breaking God's Rules." *Sixteenth Century Journal* 25 (1994): 3-27.

———. "Patriarchy and Prophetesses: Tradition and Innovation in Vermigli's Doctrine of Woman." In *Peter Martyr Vermigli and the European Reformations*, ed. Frank A. James III, pp. 139-58. Leiden: Brill, 2004.

———. *Writing the Wrongs: Women of the Old Testament among Biblical Commen-*

tators from Philo through the Reformation. New York: Oxford University Press, 2001.

Thomas, Theodore N. *Women against Hitler: Christian Resistance in the Third Reich.* Westport, Conn.: Praeger, 1995.

Trible, Phyllis. *Texts of Terror: Literary-Feminist Readings of Biblical Narratives.* Philadelphia: Fortress, 1984.

Valler, Shulamit. "King David and 'His' Women: Biblical Stories and Talmudic Discussions." In *A Feminist Companion to Samuel and Kings,* ed. Athalya Brenner, pp. 129-42. Sheffield: Sheffield Academic Press, 1996.

Wallerstein, Judith S., Julia M. Lewis, and Sandra Blakeslee. *The Unexpected Legacy of Divorce: A Twenty-Five Year Landmark Study.* New York: Hyperion, 2000.

Waters, John W. "Who Was Hagar?" In *Stony the Road We Trod: African American Biblical Interpretation,* ed. Cain Hope Felder, pp. 187-205. Minneapolis: Fortress, 1991.

Waters, Kenneth L., Sr. "Saved through Childbearing: Virtues as Children in 1 Timothy 2:11-15." *Journal of Biblical Literature* 123 (2004): 703-35.

Weems, Renita J. *Just a Sister Away: A Womanist Vision of Women's Relationships in the Bible.* San Diego: LuraMedia, 1988.

———. "Gomer: Victim of Violence or Victim of Metaphor?" *Semeia* 47 (1989): 87-104.

———. *Battered Love: Marriage, Sex, and Violence in the Hebrew Prophets.* Minneapolis: Fortress, 1995.

Whitehead, Barbara Dafoe. *The Divorce Culture.* New York: Alfred A. Knopf, 1997.

Williams, Delores S. *Sisters in the Wilderness: The Challenge of Womanist God-Talk.* Maryknoll, N.Y.: Orbis, 1993.

Witte, John, Jr. *From Sacrament to Contract: Marriage, Religion, and Law in the Western Tradition.* Louisville: Westminster John Knox, 1997.

Wojcik, Jan. "Discriminations against David's Tragedy in Ancient Jewish and Christian Literature." In *The David Myth in Western Literature,* ed. Raymond-Jean Frontain and Jan Wojcik, pp. 12-35. West Lafayette, Ind.: Purdue University Press, 1980.

Yee, Gail A. "Hosea." In *The Women's Bible Commentary,* ed. Carol A. Newsom and Sharon H. Ringe, pp. 195-202. Louisville: Westminster John Knox, 1992.

Index of Subjects and Names

McLaughlin, Mary, 236

Melanchthon, Philip, 122, 123, 125, 249, 255, 256

Messianic expectation, 85, 174

Messianic psalms, 42, 53, 56, 59, 61

Methodius of Olympus, 38

Midrash Rabbah, 23, 188, 193, 234, 260, 261

Miller, Patrick D., 67, 240, 241

Ministry of women, 131, 161, 162, 178, 179, 248, 258

Misogyny, 4, 108, 172

Monasticism, 39, 40, 46, 122, 147, 175

Moral sense (of scripture), 2, 8, 9, 16, 22, 24, 26, 39, 43, 54-57, 61, 67, 76, 187, 188, 204, 211

Mortal sin, 148, 195

Moses, 25, 84, 87-88, 137-60, 191, 196, 244, 250, 253

Mpindi, Paul Mbunga, 240

Mujerista, 3, 232

Münster, Sebastian, 43, 44, 84, 90, 237

Muntzer, Thomas, 87, 89, 90, 244

Musculus, Wolfgang, 25, 27, 28, 76-78, 87, 123, 124, 129, 165, 166, 168-71, 190, 197, 235, 241-43, 247-50, 255-58, 260-62

Nachmanides, 24, 235

Nathan, 185, 198-99, 203

Nature, natural law, 81, 90, 113, 114, 120-22, 124-26, 133, 165, 167, 183, 206, 207, 259

Necessity, 79, 85, 89, 131, 149, 150, 152

Niditch, Susan, 233, 234

Oecolampadius, Johannes, 76, 101, 241, 242, 256

Offensive texts, 7, 54, 222

Olsen, V. Norskov, 253, 254

Ordaining women, 117, 120, 145, 147, 161, 162, 254

Ordinary Gloss, 22, 189, 194, 195, 199, 263

Origen, 2, 3, 18-21, 36, 37, 54-57, 70, 75,

101, 105, 117, 141-44, 177, 234, 238-40, 251-53, 257, 258

Original righteousness, 127

Ortlund, Raymond C., Jr., 108, 110, 245, 247

Ozment, Stephen, 247

Parry, Robin, 260

Parsons, Michael, 261, 264

Paul, 3, 13-14, 18-22, 29, 31, 53, 71, 74-75, 83, 94, 99, 104, 107, 113-84, 223, 248-53, 259

Pauline privilege, 139, 153, 156

Pelagius, 173, 177, 248, 249, 257, 258

Pellican, Conrad, 25, 27, 44, 76, 81, 87, 116, 122, 123, 171, 178, 196, 197, 235, 241-43, 248, 249, 255-58

Peter Comestor, 80, 200, 204, 205, 262, 263

Peterson, Eugene H., 240

Pharaoh, 6-7, 71-72, 75, 77

Philip's daughters, 134, 178

Phillips, Roderick, 251, 252

Philo, 18-20, 233, 234, 236-38, 256

Piety, as a virtue, 27, 37, 65, 125, 149, 150, 212

Polity, as subordinate to doctrine, 10, 124, 130, 133-35, 180, 182, 183, 259

Polygamy, 6, 13, 16, 18, 20, 39, 54, 72, 73, 75, 82-87, 90, 105, 110, 174, 243, 244

Poole, Matthew, 100, 101, 246, 247

Pornographic, scripture as, 96, 97, 108, 245

Precritical exegesis, defined, 233

Pressler, Carolyn J., 245

Preus, James Samuel, 240

Pride, 169, 189

Primogeniture, 165, 255

Priscilla, 117-18

Procopius of Gaza, 23, 26, 37, 38, 235, 236

Prophecy, 55, 58, 61, 68, 102, 116-18, 131, 134, 177, 180, 182, 258

Index of Scripture References